John Lawes

Experimental inquiry into the composition of some of the animals fed and slaughtered as human food

John Lawes

Experimental inquiry into the composition of some of the animals fed and slaughtered as human food

ISBN/EAN: 9783337201456

Printed in Europe, USA, Canada, Australia, Japan

Cover: Foto ©Andreas Hilbeck / pixelio.de

More available books at **www.hansebooks.com**

EXPERIMENTAL INQUIRY

INTO

THE COMPOSITION

OF SOME OF

THE ANIMALS FED AND SLAUGHTERED AS HUMAN FOOD.

BY

JOHN BENNET LAWES, F.R.S., F.C.S.,

AND

JOSEPH HENRY GILBERT, Ph.D., F.C.S.

From the PHILOSOPHICAL TRANSACTIONS.—Part II. 1859.

LONDON:

PRINTED BY TAYLOR AND FRANCIS, RED LION COURT, FLEET STREET.

1860.

EXPERIMENTAL INQUIRY

INTO

THE COMPOSITION

OF SOME OF

THE ANIMALS FED AND SLAUGHTERED AS HUMAN FOOD.

BY

JOHN BENNET LAWES, F.R.S., F.C.S.,

AND

JOSEPH HENRY GILBERT, Ph.D., F.C.S.

From the PHILOSOPHICAL TRANSACTIONS.—Part II. 1859.

LONDON:

PRINTED BY TAYLOR AND FRANCIS, RED LION COURT, FLEET STREET.

1860.

[493]

XXV. *Experimental Inquiry into the Composition of some of the Animals Fed and Slaughtered as Human Food.* By J. B. LAWES, *F.R.S., F.C.S.,* and J. H. GILBERT, *Ph.D., F.C.S.*

Received June 17,—Read June 17, 1858.

CONTENTS.

SECTION I.—STATEMENT OF THE OBJECTS, AND GENERAL PLAN, OF THE INVESTIGATION.

A KNOWLEDGE of the quantitative relation of the organs or parts, and of the ultimate
and proximate composition, of animal bodies, is of great interest in many points of view.
More or less accurate conceptions on these subjects, are essential to the Chemical

Physiologist, in determining the relations of the system, to the matters ingested as food ; nor is such knowledge an unimportant element in studying the changes which the latter undergo, and the offices they subserve, in their passage through the body. Especially, is a knowledge of the general composition of the animals slaughtered as human food, of great importance in the application of Chemistry and Physiology to Dietetics. This, indeed, is a branch of applied physiology, so to speak, which, owing in great part to the attention drawn to it by the labours of BOUSSINGAULT, MULDER, and LIEBIG, from fifteen to twenty years ago, may be said to have entered upon a new era about that period. It is, moreover, daily gaining ground, both with the Physician and the Economist. To the Farmer, too, who is engaged in producing animal food for the consumption of the community at large, it is very desirable to know something of the chemical relations of the substance so produced and sold, to the constituents expended in producing it. In other words, he should possess some data for determining—what is the probable proportion of the consumed food, or of its several constituents, which he recovers in the form of *meat* ?—how much he may calculate as *manure* ?—and how much as *expenditure* or *loss* by the feeding process?

It is obvious, that these comprehensive factors involved in the great question of animal nutrition, may be sought, individually, or collectively, and in various ways. For valuable contributions on special points, we are indebted to DULONG and DESPRETZ, to ALLEN and PEPYS, to DUMAS and MILNE-EDWARDS, to ANDRAL and GAVARRET, to REGNAULT and REISET, to COATHUPE, SCHARLING, VIERORDT, MARCHAND, BECQUEREL, LECANU, CHOSSAT, BISCHOFF, PERSOZ, and others. For the study of the subject in its more collective form, we are indebted, more particularly, to LINING, to DALTON, to BOUSSINGAULT, to LIEBIG, to PLAYFAIR, R. D. THOMSON, PAYEN, VALENTIN, SIMON, BIDDER and SCHMIDT, BARRAL, and LEHMANN. So far as the animals of the farm are concerned, the labours of BOUSSINGAULT, E. WOLFF, RITTHAUSEN, and HENNEBERG, stand prominent for persevering experimental research ; whilst to LIEBIG we owe much for the stimulus given, and the discussion incited, by his generalizations on various branches of animal chemistry. To LEHMANN again, independently of his own original researches, we are indebted for a systematic review of the labours of others ; and we are glad to have the sanction of one who has ably executed the task herein implied, to the importance, under the existing conditions of our knowledge, of the *statistical* method of inquiry. Thus, he says—

" As long as zoo-chemistry and the theory of the juices continue to occupy their present subordinate position, the only method by which the foundation necessary to an exact investigation can be obtained is that which we may term the statistical. LIEBIG, BOUSSINGAULT, and VALENTIN have indeed, with a more correct view of what was required, attempted to compare the final effects of the whole with the material substrata supplied to the organism. We cannot, it is true, arrive at any conclusion regarding the working of the process itself by a mere juxtaposition and quantitative comparison of the ingesta and excreta of the animal organism, any more than we can judge of the causes and course of diseases by the number of fatal cases recorded ; but such experiments furnish us with certain general results which serve as guides to further investigations*."

The statistical method itself, may, however, be very variously carried out. It may be sought to determine the several separate factors coincidently upon one and the same animal, placed under given conditions. Or, they may be investigated, either one by one, or coincidently, upon a large number of animals, so as to exclude, as far as possible, the influence of special circumstances, or of individual peculiarities. We have found it necessary to have recourse to each of these modes of operation.

Our more immediate branch of the subject on the present occasion—that of *Animal Composition*—obviously constitutes but an item in a general inquiry into the chemical statistics of animal nutrition. Such an inquiry, looking at it from an *agricultural* point of view, we have considered as involving the following distinct objects of research :—

1st. The amount of food, or its several constituents, consumed *in relation to a given weight of animal within a given time.*

2nd. The relation of the *gross increase in live-weight*, to the amount of food, or its constituents, consumed.

3rd. The comparative development of the different *organs*, or *parts*, of fattening animals ;—their final *ultimate* and *proximate composition* ;—and the probable composition of their *gross increase of live-weight*, during the feeding process.

4th. The composition of the *solid* and *liquid excrements*—that is, the *manure*—in relation to that of the food consumed.

5th. The *loss* or *expenditure* of constituents, by respiration, and by the cutaneous exhalations—that is, in the mere sustenance of the living meat and manure-making machine.

The general plan of experimenting adopted may be briefly described as follows :—

Some hundreds of animals, Oxen, Sheep, and Pigs, were supplied, for many weeks consecutively, with given quantities of food of known composition. The weights of the animals themselves were also taken, both at the beginning and at the end of the experiments. The data were thus provided for ascertaining the amounts of food, or of certain of its constituents, which were consumed in relation to a *given weight of animal within a given time*, or which were required to yield a given amount of *gross increase in live-weight*. Most of the results relating to these first two branches of the main inquiry, have been published in detail elsewhere† ; and we shall have to adduce only a condensed summary of them, when we come to apply the more special results of the present Paper.

To ascertain the *relations*, and the *tendency of development*, of the *different parts of the system*, the weights of the organs, and parts—also of several hundred animals—

* Cavendish Society's translation of LEHMANN's Physiological Chemistry, vol. i. p. 14.

† Journal of the Royal Agricultural Society of England, vol. x. part 1 ; vol. xii. part 2 ; vol. xiii. part 1 ; vol. xiv. part 2 ; vol. xvi. part 1. Report of the British Association for the Advancement of Science, for 1852 ; ibid. for 1854.

were determined. It is one of the objects of the present Paper to treat of the *summaries* of the results so obtained; and the details will be given for reference in the Appendix.

To determine the *ultimate composition*, and in a sense the *proximate composition* also, of Oxen, Sheep, and Pigs, and to acquire the data in such manner that they might serve to estimate the probable composition of their *increase* whilst fattening, was a labour obviously too great to be undertaken with a large number of such animals. A few individuals only, of each of the above descriptions of animal, but in different conditions of maturity, were therefore selected for the purpose. It is to the *methods*, and to the *results*, of the analysis of the animals so selected, and to the application of the data thus arrived at, that we shall have chiefly to address ourselves on the present occasion.

Ten animals were submitted to analysis. Those taken were—

1. A Fat Calf;—of the Durham breed; 9 or 10 weeks old; taken from the dam feeding upon grass; killed September 12, 1849.
2. A Half-fat Ox;—Aberdeen breed; about 4 years old; had been fed on fattening food, but had grown rather than fattened; killed November 14, 1849.
3. A moderately Fat Ox;—Aberdeen breed; about 4 years old; fed on fattening food; killed October 30, 1849.
4. A Fat Lamb;—Hampshire Down; about 6 months old; killed August 17, 1849.
5. A Store* Sheep;—Hampshire Down; about a year old; killed February 28, 1850.
6. A Half-fat old Sheep;—Hampshire Down Ewe; 3¼ years old; killed May 3, 1849.
7. A Fat Sheep;—Hampshire Down; 1¼ year old; killed May 7, 1849.
8. A very Fat Sheep;—Hampshire Down; 1¾ year old; killed December 13, 1848.
9. A Store* Pig; killed May 12, 1850.
10. A Fat Pig; same litter as last; fed on fattening food for 10 weeks; killed July 18, 1850.

The still remaining points of the main inquiry are:—first, as to the composition of the *solid* and *liquid excreta*, in regard to which we have collected much experimental data, which must form the subject of a separate Report:—and, secondly, as to the proportion of the food-constituents *expended* or *lost* by the respiratory and other processes. The latter amount is obviously the complementary quantity making up the constituents consumed, those assimilated being estimated, and those voided in the solid and liquid form determined experimentally, and the sum deducted from the whole amount of the solid and liquid ingesta.

After this brief outline of the scope of the main inquiry, of which the subject of the present Paper constitutes but a branch, it will be sufficiently understood, that it was chiefly with a view to the agricultural bearings of the results, and to their connexion with collateral investigations, that the researches now to be recorded were planned and executed. So enormous, indeed, has been the labour necessarily expended in so determining the ultimate composition of several animals as to serve the special purposes pro-

* The term "store" is applied to animals not yet put upon fattening food.

minently in view, that it was found quite out of the question to comprehend in the inquiry much that otherwise would have been desirable. Attempts were in fact made, to associate with ourselves a Veterinary Physiologist, but the undertaking was found to be impracticable. Still, it is hoped, that the analytical labour of several years devoted to such a subject, though it may lack the special direction of either the Physician or the Physiologist, may yet supply important facts to both. We have, then, only faithfully to record the manner and circumstances of attaining our results, leaving it to others to determine, to what they are, and to what they are not, applicable, beyond that to which we ourselves apply them.

SECTION II.—METHODS OF EXPERIMENTING, ANALYSIS, ETC.

The following is an outline of the plan adopted, in determining the actual, and proportional weights, of the organs and parts of the numerous animals operated upon with that view, and in determining the composition of the ten animals which were further analysed.

1st. *Determination of the Original or Fresh-weights of the Entire Bodies, and of the Internal Organs, and other separated Parts, of Calves, Oxen, Lambs, Sheep, and Pigs.*

After being fasted eighteen to twenty-four hours, the weight of the animal was taken, immediately before being killed. This weight, is that which is afterwards spoken of as the "*Fasted-weight*," or the "*Fasted Live-weight*." It is in relation to this *Fasted Live-weight*, that the *percentages* of the organs, or parts, or of the several constituents of the animals, are calculated.

The animal being killed, and the blood then flowing carefully collected and weighed, the different organs and parts were separated by the butcher in his ordinary way; but with more than usual care, and with particular attention to uniformity in the manipulations. The weight of each part was taken as rapidly as possible after separation, in order that the amount of loss to be attributed to evaporation might be reduced to the minimum. The weights so taken, constitute the *Actual Fresh-weights*; and when these are calculated to the *Fasted Live-weight* as 100, they are called the *Percentage Fresh-weights*. In the Tables, however, for the sake of convenience, the different parts are classified, in the butcher's way, into "*Carcass*," and "*Offal*."

In Calves and Oxen, Lambs and Sheep, the "Offal" includes the head, the feet, and the skin, as well as the whole of the internal organs or parts, excepting the kidneys, and the fat in which they are embedded. The "Carcass," in the case of these animals, comprises, therefore, the whole of the skeleton (excluding the head and feet), with the whole of the muscles, membranes, vessels, and fat, attaching to it; also the kidneys, and the fat surrounding them. The so-called "Offal" of the *Pig*, however, does not include either the head, the feet, or the skin. In its case these parts are weighed with the Carcass; and its Offal consists, therefore, only of the internal organs and parts, excluding the kidneys and kidney-fat. Such a classification of the parts of the animals, into *Carcass* and *Offal*, is, of course, to a certain extent, arbitrary. But, whilst its adoption will not interfere with the study of the results in their more physiological or scientific bearings, it will much facilitate the perception of their practical and economic application.

Fresh-weights, as here described, both actual and percentage, have been determined in the cases of 18 Calves, Heifers, and Bullocks, 249 Sheep, and 59 Pigs. Attention will be called to a summary of these results further on in the course of our Paper; and the details will be given for reference in the Appendix (Tables XV.—LXIV. pp. 594—677).

So much for the separation, the determination, and the calculation, of the weights of the *fresh* matters. We have next to describe the further treatment of the fresh matters themselves, in the case of the ten animals submitted to further analysis.

2nd. *Determination of the Water, and Crude Dry Substance, in the Animals Analysed.*

Half of the Carcass, and the whole of every separated organ or part comprised in the Offal, were in each case operated upon. The half-carcass was separated into—

(*a*) Flesh and fat:
(*b*) Bones:
(*c*) Kidney and kidney-fat.

After being cut up, as required, these Carcass parts separately, and each of the separate internal organs or parts constituting the Offal, were put into a large water-bath, and were arranged in it in such a manner, that the fat which melted from any one, or any number of the parts, could be collected and weighed separately at pleasure, in vessels placed under them for that purpose. After being kept in the bath at a temperature of 212° FAHR., for several days, those parts which still retained a large quantity of fat were tied up in a dried and weighed canvass-cloth, and squeezed in a screw-press. The further fat so obtained, was added to that obtained from the same parts by melting only. The whole of the separated fat, after a little further exposure to the heat of the water-bath, was then weighed; and this, together with the amount retained by the press and cloth, which were weighed both before and after the operation, constitutes the weight of the *melted and expressed fat*, as given in the Tables. The remaining *crude dry substance*, generally, still retained a considerable amount of fat. But, excluding the bones, which had to be first otherwise broken, all these dried parts were now in such a state as to allow of being ground through a steel mill, made for the purpose, into a coarse but manageable powder. This, then, is the *crude dry substance*, excluding melted and expressed fat.

3rd. *Treatment of the Crude Dry Substance.*

Accurately calculated and weighed *proportional* parts of the whole of the respective *crude dry matters* were taken as follows:—

(*a*) For the determination of the *Ash* of each separated part.

(*b*) For a mixed sample of *entire Carcass Parts*, for analysis as such.

(*c*) For a mixed sample of *entire Offal Parts.*

(*d*) For a mixed sample of the *Entire Animal;*—that is, including both Carcass and Offal parts (but of course excluding the melted and expressed fat).

The remaining portion of the *crude dry substance* of each separated part is preserved as such.

4th. *Determination of the Mineral Matter, or Ash.*

The proportional part of each separate *crude dry substance* weighed out for *ash*, was burnt in a platinum dish, 10 inches long and 5 inches wide, placed in a cast-iron muffle heated by coke. The weight of the ash of each separate part being taken, *proportional* parts of the respective ashes were weighed out, and mixtures made, as follows *:—

(*a*) Of the ashes of all *Carcass* parts.

(*b*) Of the ashes of all *Offal* parts.

(*c*) Of the ashes of *all* parts; that is, of the *Entire Animal.*

The remaining ash of each separate part is preserved as such.

5th. *Determination of the Fat not separated by melting and expression, and which still remained therefore in the separate, and proportionally mixed samples, of the crude dry substance.*

This remaining Fat was determined by extraction with ether. A portion, amounting generally to about 4 or 5 grammes, of the *crude dry substance*, was weighed in a small porcelain capsule, and the hygroscopic water determined by drying in a water-bath at 212°. The re-dried substance was then transferred into a small flask, and the capsule rinsed into it with ether. More ether being added, and the flask lightly closed, the mixture was digested for some time, and then thrown upon a weighed filter. The filter and its contents were first washed with the ethereal rinsings of the flask, and finally with pure ether, until the filtrate no longer stained bibulous paper. The ethereal filtrate, containing the dissolved fatty matter, was collected in a small balanced flask, the ether distilled off over a water-bath, and the flask with its fatty contents, after being fully dried at 212°, was re-weighed. The filter, containing the matters insoluble in ether, was

---

* The statement of the method of preparing the ashes of the *collective* parts given in the text, applies to those of all the animals operated upon, excepting the two pigs. Of these, the collective carcass, the collective offal, and the entire animal ashes, were made by burning, at one process, carefully made mixtures of the proportional parts of the respective crude dry matters.

also dried and re-weighed. The hygroscopic water, the fat, and the matters insoluble in ether, were thus all estimated upon the same weighed quantity of crude dry substance. A very good control was therefore obtained of the accuracy of the fat determinations. Moreover, two or more analyses were always made of each specimen. The results of these Fat determinations will be found tabulated in detail in the Appendix (Table XIII. p. 592).

6th. *Determination of the Nitrogen.*

The *nitrogen* was determined by burning with soda-lime, and collecting and weighing as the double chloride of platinum and ammonium, in the usual way. The crude dry matters in which the nitrogen was determined, were, for the most part, as under *:—

(a) Mixed Carcass parts, without bones.
(b) Mixed Carcass Bones.
(c) Mixed Offal parts, including bones, if any.
(d) Hair or Wool.
(e) Mixed parts of the Entire Animal, excluding hair or wool.

It will be obvious, that, owing to the heterogeneous character of these mixed specimens, very great care was requisite, both in the preparation of the mixtures themselves, and in taking the weighed quantities for analysis. Duplicate nitrogen determinations were always made, and the individual results are given in the Appendix (Table XIV. p. 593).

7th. *Constituents of the Ash determined.*

The substances determined under this head were—

(a) Phosphoric acid.
(b) Potash and Soda.
(c) Lime and Magnesia.
(d) Matter insoluble in acid.

As the results of the analyses of the animal-ashes must form the subject of a separate Paper, the description of the methods adopted need not be given here.

The experimental results obtained by the methods above described are given for reference, in full detail, in the Appendix. The discussion, *seriatim*, of the voluminous data thus provided, would tend rather to embarrass than to facilitate the perception of

* The exceptions were the cases of the two Pigs. In these, the sample of *mixed carcass parts*, upon which the nitrogen was determined, *included* all the bones, excepting those of the head and feet; a separate mixed sample was made of the head and feet, including both soft and bony parts, excepting the tongue and brains, which latter went with the *mixed offal parts* in the samples prepared for nitrogen determinations. The mixed samples of the *offal* parts of the Pigs did not therefore contain bone, as did those in the cases of the other animals.

the main and more prominent facts and conclusions, which the investigation, as a whole, is calculated to establish. We shall seek, therefore, to bring these to view by reference to a series of *Summary Tables* only. The first point to be illustrated, is the *percentage composition of the ten animals actually analysed.* This is shown in Tables I. to VII. inclusive; in which we have recorded the percentages—of *mineral matter,* of *fat,* of *nitrogen* or *nitrogenous compounds,* of *total dry substance,* and of *water*—in certain classified parts, and in the entire fasted live-weight, of each of the ten animals.

SECTION III —THE MINERAL MATTER—IN CERTAIN SEPARATED PARTS, AND IN THE ENTIRE BODIES, OF 10 ANIMALS ANALYSED.

In Table I. is given the percentage of *mineral matter* in the fresh carcass, in the fresh total offal parts, and in the fasted live-weight, of each of the ten animals; there is at the same time shown, the distribution of the mineral matter in certain classified parts of these collective weights. But, as some of the points of general interest can be more easily studied by reference to the results given in a still more summary form, they are so arranged in Table II. In this second Table, the only subdivision of the carcass, the offal, and the entire animal, respectively, is into *—

(a) Flesh, membrane, &c., or soft parts:
(b) Bones:
(c) Hair or wool (if any).

It has already been explained, that in all the animals, except Pigs, the so-called "*carcass,*" which comprises the most important edible portions, is generally understood to include the whole of the frame (excepting the head and feet) with the flesh and fat adhering to it, and, in addition, the kidneys, and the fat in which they are imbedded. Thus, the head and feet, the skin, and the whole of the internal organs or parts, except the kidneys, constitute the "*offal.*" In Pigs, on the contrary, the head, feet, and skin are weighed with the Carcass. For the sake of the better comparison of the composition of pigs with that of other animals, the constituents of their head and feet are, in our Tables, included with those of the offal parts; but for reference, so far as the mineral matter is concerned, the percentages for the pigs are given, at the foot of Table I., on the assumption that the head and feet, as in usual practice, are included with the carcass.

---

* For the *actual amount* of mineral matter, or ash, due to each organ or part, as separated in the original dissection of the animals, see Tables I. to X. inclusive in the Appendix (pp. 580—589); and for the *percentage amount* in the separate parts, see Appendix, Table XII. (p. 591).

TABLE I.—Percentages of Mineral Matter in Ten Animals.

1st. In Fresh Carcass.—2nd. In Fresh Offal (equal Sum of Parts excluding Contents of Stomachs and Intestines)—3rd. In Entire Animal (Fasted Live-weight—including therefore Contents of Stomachs and Intestines).

Description of animal.	Percentages in fresh Carcass				Percentages in fresh Offal										Percentages in fasted live-weight of Entire Animal															
	From flesh, membranes, brawn, &c.	From kidney and kidney fat membranes.	From bones.	From total carcass parts.	From blood.	From thoracic viscera; lungs and windpipe, heart and aorta, thymus gland, &c.	From abdominal viscera, &c.; stomachs, intestines, spleen, liver, bladder, pancreas, throat glands, diaphragm, membranes, &c.	From head-flesh, brains, and tongue.	Tail, tail-flesh.	Head.	Legs and feet.	From skin or pelt.	From hair or wool.	From total offal parts.	From flesh, membranes, brawn, &c.	From kidney and kidney fat membranes.	From bones.	From total carcass parts.	From blood.	From thoracic viscera; lungs and windpipe, heart and aorta, thymus gland, &c.	From abdominal viscera, &c.; stomachs, intestines, spleen, liver, bladder, pancreas, throat glands, diaphragm, membranes, &c.	From head, flesh, brains, and tongue.	From tail-flesh.	Tail.	Head.	Legs and feet.	From skin or pelt.	From hair or wool.	From total offal parts.	From total parts.
Fat calf	0·771	0·004	3·707	4·492	0·193	0·299	0·074	0·008	0·026	1·387	1·249	0·170	0·014	3·415	0·479	0·002	2·301	2·782	0·068	0·089	0·022		0·001	0·008	0·413	0·372	0·051	0·004	1·018	3·900
Half-fat ox	0·795	0·009	4·760	5·564	0·157	0·052	0·246	0·064	0·043	1·964	1·274	0·191	0·036	4·061	0·515	0·006	3·089	3·603	0·011	0·014	0·065	0·067	0·001	0·011	0·314	0·334	0·060	0·009	1·061	4·664
Fat ox	0·597	0·010	3·953	4·560	0·190	0·254	0·063	0·071	0·035	1·554	1·177	0·175	0·021	3·401	0·395	0·007	2·617	3·019	0·032	0·067	0·017		0·001	0·009	0·412	0·312	0·046	0·005	0·901	3·920
Fat lamb	0·473	0·004	3·145	3·622	0·116	0·275	0·071			1·203	0·263	0·276	0·244	2·448	0·283	0·005	1·888	2·173	0·036	0·096	0·022				0·275	0·482	0·068	0·076	0·763	3·936
Store sheep	1·246	0·008	3·106	4·369	0·093	0·054	0·189	0·056		0·917	0·240	0·242	0·401	2·187	0·664	0·004	1·657	2·325	0·036	0·021	0·070	0·022			0·351	0·099	0·093	0·154	0·839	3·164
Half-fat old sheep	0·631	0·002	3·501	4·134	0·103	0·247	0·051			1·462	0·185	0·164	0·392	2·716	0·338	0·001	1·875	2·214	0·084			0·018			0·516	0·099	0·055	0·184	0·959	3·173
Fat sheep	0·464	0·012	2·973	3·449	0·075	0·247	0·063			0·976	0·307	0·311	0·568	2·334	0·266	0·007	1·789	2·063	0·097	0·089		0·018			0·349	0·074	0·076	0·197	0·839	2·811
Extra fat sheep	0·255	0·079	2·447	2·772	0·116	0·175				0·961	0·214	0·232	1·942	3·641	0·161	0·041	1·543	1·746	0·037	0·055					0·305	0·068	0·074	0·616	1·155	2·903
Store pig*	0·636	0·010	1·925	2·572	0·133	0·467	0·306	0·150	0·007	1·766	0·600	0·022	3·073	0·425	0·007	1·279	1·706	0·046	0·021	0·096	0·047		0·002	0·352	0·198	0·007	0·961	3·669		
Fat pig*	0·369	0·009	1·190	1·586	0·208	0·066	0·278	0·134	0·007	1·591	0·667	0·025	2·970	0·304	0·007	0·951	1·062	0·041	0·012	0·055	0·027		0·001	0·314	0·132	0·005	0·587	1·649		
Means	0·614	0·014	3·065	3·692	0·133	0·347	0·071			1·378	0·406	0·378		3·023	0·373	0·009	1·880	2·262	0·039	0·103				0·018	0·410	0·172	0·126	0·907	3·169	
Store pig†	0·605			2·283	0·218	0·495	0·049							0·831	0·458	0·007	2·021	2·486	0·048	0·021	0·066	0·011			0·352	0·198	0·060	0·007	1·183	3·669
Fat pig‡	0·275	0·008	1·568	1·851	0·317	0·435	0·028							0·900	0·297	0·007	1·298	1·532	0·041	0·012	0·055	0·004			0·314	0·132	0·005	0·117	1·649	

* For comparison with the other animals, the ashes of the head and feet of the pigs are here included in the offal.
† Here the ashes of the head and feet of the pigs are included with the carcase, they generally being sold with it, and not with the offal, as in the case of the other animals.
‡ These ashes, especially those of the extra-fat sheep, are too high, owing to adventitious matter retained by the wool. The statements of ash from total offal parts will, of course, be too high, from the same cause.

3 U 2

TABLE II.—Summary of Percentages of MINERAL MATTER in Ten Animals.

1st. In Fresh Carcass.—2nd. In Fresh Offal (equal Sum of Parts excluding Contents of Stomachs and Intestine).—3rd. In Entire Animal (Fasted Live-weight—including therefore Contents of Stomachs and Intestines).

Description of animal.	Percentages in fresh Carcass.			Percentages in fresh Offal.				Percentages in fasted live-weight of Entire Animal.							Final Summary. Per cent. in Entire Animal.		
	From flesh, membrane, &c.	From bones.	From total carcass.	From flesh, membrane, &c.	From bones.	From hair or wool.	From total offal.	From Carcass parts. From flesh, membrane, &c.	From bones.	From Offal parts. From flesh, membrane, &c.	From bones.	From hair or wool.	From total soft parts.	From total bones.	From carcass parts.	From offal parts.	From all parts.
Fat calf	0·775	3·707	4·482	0·739	2·662	0·014	3·415	0·481	2·301	0·221	0·793	0·004	0·706	3·094	2·782	1·018	3·800
Half-fat ox	0·804	4·760	5·564	0·734	3·281	0·036	4·051	0·521	3·082	0·193	0·859	0·009	0·723	3·941	3·603	1·061	4·664
Fat ox	0·607	3·953	4·560	0·614	2·766	0·021	3·401	0·402	2·617	0·163	0·733	0·005	0·570	3·350	3·019	0·901	3·920
Fat lamb	0·477	3·155	3·632	0·738	1·466	0·244*	2·448	0·985	1·888	0·230	0·457	0·075*	0·591	2·345	2·173	0·763	2·936
Store sheep	1·254	3·106	4·360	0·629	1·157	0·401*	2·187	0·658	1·657	0·242	0·443	0·164*	1·064	2·100	2·325	0·839	3·164
Half-fat old sheep	0·633	3·501	4·134	0·647	1·647	0·522*	2·716	0·339	1·875	0·193	0·582	0·184*	0·716	2·457	2·214	0·959	3·173
Fat sheep	0·476	2·973	3·449	0·686	1·183	0·556*	2·424	0·273	1·709	0·209	0·423	0·197*	0·679	2·132	1·982	0·829	2·811
Extra fat sheep	0·325	2·447	2·772	0·524	1·175	1·942*	3·641	0·205	1·543	0·166	0·373	0·616*	0·987	1·916	1·748	1·155	2·903
Store pig	0·646	1·925	2·572*	0·678	2·373	0·022	3·073	0·499	1·279	0·212	0·742	0·007	0·648	2·021	1·708	0·961	2·669
Fat pig	0·278	1·120	1·398	0·680	2·265	0·025	2·970	0·211	0·851	0·135	0·447	0·005	0·351	1·298	1·062	0·587	1·649
Means of all	0·627	3·065	3·692	0·647	1·998	0·378	3·023	0·382	1·880	0·196	0·585	0·126	0·704	2·465	2·262	0·907	3·169
Means of the 8, excluding store sheep and store pig	0·647	3·202	3·749	0·645	2·056	0·420	3·121	0·340	1·983	0·189	0·583	0·137	0·656	2·567	2·323	0·909	3·232
Means of the 6, excluding the store and half-fat animals	0·490	2·892	3·382	0·647	1·919	0·467	3·033	0·310	1·818	0·187	0·538	0·161	0·647	2·356	2·128	0·876	3·003

* These ashes, especially those of the extra-fat sheep, are too high, owing to adventitious matter retained by the wool. The statements of ash from the total offal parts, will, of course, be too high, from the same cause.

Looking first to the percentage of mineral matter, obtained by incineration, in the so-called Carcass, it is seen, as was to be expected, that the *bones* yielded by far the larger portion of it. The total *soft parts*, indeed, in most cases, provided only about one-fifth to one-seventh as much mineral matter as the solid framework of bones. The proportion of the whole mineral matter which was obtained from the soft parts, was, as well with bullocks, sheep, and pigs, the less the more matured the animal—that is, the fatter; and it was much the greater in the lean condition. Thus, in the *store* or *lean* sheep, and also in the *store* pig, the soft parts of the Carcass yielded somewhat more than a third as much ash as the bones. On the other hand, in the *fattest* sheep there was less than one-seventh, and in the *fat* pig only a fourth as much mineral matter derivable from the soft parts as from the bones. That is to say, it is with the *nitrogenous matters* of the soft parts, that the constituents yielding ash on incineration are shown to be associated. In what chemical relation the several ash-constituents stand to these nitrogenous matters, it is not within the scope of the present inquiry to determine. But, it is probable, that at any rate some of them (for example, the sulphuric, and perhaps the phosphoric acid also) are, in a greater or less degree, products of the incineration. This remark may apply to the ashes of other parts also. To what extent there may be a loss of certain mineral constituents, when, as is usually the case, it is sought to collect the whole by the process of incineration, depends in part on the mineral composition of the substance, but also on the conduct of the incineration itself. The ashes here in question were, however, prepared with great care, and at as low a temperature as possible, so as at least to avoid all unnecessary source of loss. It seemed desirable to call attention to these points, that in assuming, as is usually done, that the total mineral matter of animal and vegetable products is represented by the amount of ash they leave on burning, no more of exactitude should be attributed to the assumption than is really due.

To proceed: in Table II. the total ash of the Offal parts is divided into—that of the soft parts exclusive of hair or wool, that of the bones, and that of the hair or wool. On the amount of ash indicated in the hair or wool, no great stress must be laid; for, as will be easily understood, it was almost impossible to free these parts from adventitious dirt, which would leave a considerable incombustible residue. As in the Carcass, so in the Offal (which included the head, feet, and tail), by far the larger proportion of the ash was due to the bones. The portion of the total percentage of ash in the Offal due to the soft parts, is generally as great as in the Carcass. A part is doubtless attributable to debris of the food not entirely removed by washing from the alimentary cavities and passages. The blood too yielded a not inconsiderable quantity; and this portion may be looked upon as not belonging to the fixed substance of the body, or to those portions of the Offal which are, as the rule, appropriated as human food. The blood of the Pig is, however, frequently appropriated to this purpose. After making some allowance on these heads, there is still, at least in the fattened animals, about as high a percentage of mineral matter in the collective soft parts of the Offal, as in those of the Carcass. It will be seen further on, how good an index is the percentage of mineral matter, to the amount of the fixed nitrogenous compounds of the total body, or its parts.

In the third main Division of Table II., the amounts of ash yielded by the same collective parts of the Carcass and of the Offal, are calculated to 100 *of the entire animal* (fasted live-weight), instead of to 100 of the Carcass, or of the Offal respectively.   From this arrangement of the results we learn, that, on the average, the ash yielded by the total soft parts of the body, amounted to considerably less than 1 per cent. of its entire or live-weight.   That yielded by the bones, on the other hand, amounted always to more than 1, generally to more than 2, and in some cases to from 3 to 4 per cent. of the whole body.   Thus, the bones of the Pigs yielded ash amounting to 2 per cent. and under, of the weight of the animal; those of the Sheep to from 2 to 2½ per cent.; and those of the Calf and Bullocks to, from 3 to nearly 4 per cent., of the live-weight.

It is worthy of remark, that in the fat Pig the ash due to the soft or more edible portions of the Carcass, amounted to only 0·211 per cent. of the whole weight of the animal; the ash from the soft Carcass parts, of the three fatter Sheep to, from 0·205 to 0·339 of the live-weight; and that from the same parts in the fat Bullock to only 0·402 per cent. of its whole weight.   Again, the per cent. in the entire animal of ash due to bones, is 3·35 per cent. in the fat Bullock, against 3·94 per cent. in the half-fat one.   There is among the Sheep, in like manner (if we exclude the half-fat one), a diminution in the entire animal in the amount of ash from bones, from 2·10 per cent. in the store animal, to 1·916 per cent. in the very fat one.   In the Pig, the proportion in the entire animal of bony structure, as indicated by the amount of ash of bone yielded, declines still more markedly as the animal fattens.   Thus, the ash of the total bones of the store Pig amounted to 2·021 per cent. of the entire animal, and that from the total bones of the fat Pig to only 1·298 per cent. of its live-weight.

Turning now to the last division, or "Final Summary," of Table II., the decline in the percentage of mineral matter in the *entire animal*, as it fattens, is very clearly brought to view.   This decline is indicated not only in the amount of ash derived from all parts of the body collectively, but in that from both total Carcass, and total Offal parts, taken separately.   The exception is the case of the Offal parts of the fattest Sheep; but the large amount of ash in this instance was due to the great quantity of adventitious matter not removed by washing from the wool.   Calling attention to the actual figures in some of the other cases, it is seen, that, whilst the half-fat Bullock yielded, from all parts, 4·664 per cent. of mineral matter or ash, the fatter Bullock gave only 3·92 per cent.   Again, the whole body of the store Sheep yielded 3·164 per cent. of ash, and that of the fat Sheep only 2·811 per cent.   And lastly, whilst the whole of the store Pig gave 2·669 per cent. of mineral matter or ash, that of the fat one gave only 1·649 per cent.

From the results as to *mineral matter* as a whole, it would appear, that during the fattening process, neither the accumulation of mineral matter in the bony structure, nor that in the soft parts, takes place commensurately with the increase of some other constituents of the body. It will presently be seen which are the constituents that accumulate most rapidly under that process.

SECTION IV.—THE FAT—IN CERTAIN SEPARATED PARTS, AND IN THE ENTIRE BODIES, OF 10 ANIMALS ANALYSED.

When speaking on the subject of method, it was explained, that a large portion of the Fat of the animals analysed, was obtained from their different parts by *melting and expression*, the remainder being determined by *extraction with ether*. In the melting and expression manipulations, the parts were generally classed as under:—

        (*a*) Kidneys, with the fat surrounding them:
        (*b*) Other carcass parts, including bones:
        (*c*) Head, and miscellaneous offal parts:
        (*d*) Heart with its accompanying fat:
        (*e*) Caul or omentum fat:
        (*f*) Mesenteric or intestinal fat.

The determinations of Fat *by ether* were made upon the dry residues after the melting and expression, which, for the purpose, were mixed or classified to represent—

        (*a*) Total carcass parts, including bone:
        (*b*) Head, and other offal parts, including bone:
        (*c*) Hair or wool.

Separate Fat determinations, by ether, were also made upon a mixture representing *the whole carcass and offal parts together*, excluding only hair or wool, and of course the previously melted and expressed fat. The actual results of the melting and expression experiments will be found in Tables I. to X. inclusive, in the Appendix. The ether determinations are given in Table XIII. of the Appendix. From the data thus provided, have been calculated the percentages of *melted* and *expressed*, of *ether-extracted*, or of *total* Fat (and its distribution), in the Carcass, in the Offal, and in the Entire Fasted Live-weight, of the several animals. These particulars are given in a somewhat detailed form in Table III., and in a more summary one in Table IV., which now follow.

TABLE III.—Percentages of Fat (by Melting, by Expression, and by Extraction with Ether), in Ten Animals.

1st. In Fresh Carcase.—2nd. In Fresh Offal (equal Sum of Parts excluding Contents of Stomachs and Intestines).—3rd. In Entire Animal (Fasted Live-weight, including therefore Contents of Stomachs and Intestines).

Description of animal	Fresh Carcase: melt & expr. from around kidneys	Fresh Carcase: melt & expr. from other carcass parts	Fresh Carcase: by ether, from mixed carcass parts	Fresh Carcase: from total carcase parts, by melting, expression, and ether	Fresh Offal: melt & expr. from misc. head	Fresh Offal: melt & expr. from caul or omentum	Fresh Offal: melt & expr. from caul or heart	Fresh Offal: melt & expr. mesenteric or intestinal	Fresh Offal: ether, from wool	Fresh Offal: ether, from head and feet	Fresh Offal: ether, from other offal parts	Fresh Offal: from total offal parts, by melting, expression, and ether	Entire Animal – Carcass: melt & expr. from around kidneys	Entire Animal – Carcass: melt & expr. from other carcass parts	Entire Animal – Carcass: by ether, from mixed carcass parts	Entire Animal – Carcass: from total carcase parts, by melting, expression, and ether	Entire Animal – Offal: melt & expr. from misc. head	Entire Animal – Offal: melt & expr. from caul or heart	Entire Animal – Offal: melt & expr. from caul or omentum/intestinal	Entire Animal – Offal: melt & expr. mesenteric or intestinal	Entire Animal – Offal: ether, from wool	Entire Animal – Offal: ether, from head and feet	Entire Animal – Offal: ether, from other offal parts	Entire Animal – Offal: from total offal parts, by melting, expression, and ether	From Total Parts, by melting, expression, and ether
Fat calf	2·57	10·0	4·00	16·4	3·39			7·11		3·86		14·6	1·59	6·2	2·48	10·3	1·07			2·12		1·15		4·34	14·6
Half-fat ox	3·07	13·0	7·51	23·6	1·88	0·88	4·63	4·66		3·62		15·7	1·99	7·8	4·96	14·6	0·49	0·93	1·91	1·22		0·96		4·11	19·7
Fat ox	5·44	24·5	4·87	34·8	3·87	1·49	7·93	8·79		3·98		26·3	3·60	16·2	3·23	23·1	1·08	0·45	2·10	2·33		1·05		6·96	30·0
Fat lamb	6·21	25·6	5·08	36·9	1·04			13·96	0·66	4·58		30·1	3·71	15·3	3·01	22·1	0·33			4·32	0·21	1·43		6·99	28·0
Store sheep	1·69	17·6	4·54	23·8	2·87	0·43	5·14	3·08	0·92	3·66		16·1	0·90	9·4	2·43	12·7	1·10	0·17	1·97	1·18	0·35	1·40		6·17	18·4
Half-fat old sheep	3·60	20·3	7·38	31·3	1·59	1·11	6·51	5·69	0·79	2·78		18·5		10·9	3·90	16·7	0·56	0·49	2·30	2·91	0·28	0·98		6·52	23·2
Fat sheep	8·38	38·8	3·90	51·1	2·55	13·19	6·57		1·17	2·95		26·4	4·81	19·4	1·84	26·1	0·91	4·71		2·34	0·42	1·05		9·43	35·5
Extra fat sheep		49·7	5·38	55·1	3·19	19·50	7·41		1·04	3·40		34·5		31·34	3·39	34·7	0·99	6·19		2·35	0·33	1·08		10·94	45·7
Store pig	1·67	23·5	2·91	28·1	9·60	2·12				*1·56	1·69	15·0	3·28	13·2	2·60	18·7	3·00	0·67				*0·49	0·53	4·69	23·4
Fat pig	4·32	42·4	2·78	49·6	1·84	8·35				*2·00	1·54	29·8		33·2	2·11	37·6	0·96	1·64				*0·40	0·31	4·50	42·1
Means		29·6	4·86	34·4					0·92	3·67		21·0	1·87	15·0	2·96	21·7	1·79				0·32	1·08		6·39	28·1

* In practice, the head and feet of the Pig generally go with the Carcass; but here they are classed with the Offal parts, for the sake of comparison with the other animals.

TABLE IV.—Summary of Percentages of TOTAL FAT (by Melting, Expression, and Ether) in Ten Animals.

1st. In Fresh Carcass.—2nd. In Fresh Offal (equal Sum of Parts excluding Contents of Stomachs and Intestines).—3rd. In Entire Animal (Fasted Live-weight—including therefore Contents of Stomachs and Intestines).

[The mean percentage of Fat from Total Parts in the Entire Animal is given—1st, by addition of the amounts in the separate items; 2nd, with the ether-determinations made direct on a mixture of Entire Animal crude-dry-matters (except wool, with the amount in wool added).]

Description of animal.	Percentages in fresh Carcass.	Percentages in fresh Offal (excluding contents of stomachs and intestines).	Percentages in fasted live-weight of Entire Animal.		From Total Parts.	
			From Carcass parts.	From Offal parts.	By addition of items.	By ether determinations direct on mixture of entire animal dry matter (except wool) and wool fat added.
Fat calf	16·6	14·6	10·3	4·34	14·6	14·8
Half-fat ox	22·6	15·7	14·6	4·12	18·7	19·1
Fat ox	34·8	26·3	23·1	6·96	30·0	30·1
Fat lamb	36·9	20·1	22·1	6·28	28·3	28·5
Store sheep	23·8	16·1	12·7	6·18	18·9	18·7
Half-fat old sheep	31·3	18·5	16·7	6·52	23·2	23·5
Fat sheep	45·4	26·4	26·1	9·43	35·5	35·6
Extra fat sheep	55·1	34·5	34·7	10·94	45·7	45·8
Store pig	28·1	15·0	18·7	4·68	23·3	23·3
Fat pig	49·6	22·8	37·6	4·30	42·1	42·2
Means of all	34·4	21·0	21·7	6·40	28·0	28·2
Means of the 8, excluding store sheep and store pig	36·5	22·3	23·2	6·64	29·8	29·9
Means of the 6, excluding the store and half-fat animals ...	39·7	24·1	25·6	7·08	32·7	32·8

Taking first the percentage of Fat in the fresh Carcass yielded by melting and expression, it is seen, that the amount around the kidneys increases very considerably as the animal fattens. In fact, practically, the judgment of the butcher on first disembowelling an animal is perhaps more influenced by the fatness of the kidneys than by any other single point. The figures show (Table III.), that, whilst the Carcass of the half-fat Ox afforded 3·07 per cent. of fat, by melting and expression, from around the kidneys, that of the fatter, but only moderately fat Ox, gave 5·44 per cent. of such fat. Of the Sheep, the Carcass of the store animal gave only 1·69 per cent. of melted and expressed kidney fat; that of the half-fat old one 3·60 per cent.; and that of the moderately fat one 8·38 per cent. Again, the percentage of melted and expressed kidney fat in the Carcass of the store Pig was 1·67, against 4·32 per cent. in that of a Pig in every respect similar, excepting that, from the time the former was slaughtered, it was fed on fattening food during a period of ten weeks. It must be remembered, that these amounts of fat obtained by melting and expression are exclusive of a not immaterial quantity afterwards extracted by ether, from the *mixed* Carcass parts, in which the kidneys and kidney-fat expressed residue were included.

The increase in the proportion of *Fat* in the other Carcass parts, during the period in which the animal is currently said to be *fattening*, is, as indicated by the amount obtainable from them by melting and expression, equally striking. But time and space will be saved, if we illustrate this accumulation by special reference to only the *total* amount of fat from *all* Carcass parts, whether obtained by melting, expression, or ether. Referring the reader, then, to the first three columns in Table III., to see how the total amount of Carcass fat is made up, we will proceed to draw our illustrations as to the total amount itself, from the fourth column of the same Table—or, as there repeated without the detail, in column 1 of Table IV. It is seen, that the Carcass of the half-fat Ox contained 22·6 per cent., that of the store Sheep 23·8, and that of the store Pig 28·1 per cent. of pure fat*. The Carcass of even a *fat* Calf, on the other hand, gave only 16·6 per cent. of total fat; which, however, is quite consistent with the current notion, that veal is leaner than any other of our ordinary meats. Of the Carcasses better representing the average condition of butcher's meat of good quality, that of the moderately fat Ox yielded 34·8 per cent. of pure fat; that of the fat Lamb 36·9; that of a moderately fat Sheep 45·4; that of a very fat Sheep 55·1; and that of an only moderately fattened Pig 49·6 per cent.

It is thus seen, that the *animal food*, of reputed high quality, as sold by the butcher, and to which such a *highly nitrogenous* character is generally attributed, will probably consist of *fat* to the extent of from one-third, to one-half, or even more, of the total fresh-weight of the Carcasses. To this point we shall have to recur, when taking a review of the *collective composition* of the animals; and also when we come to the application of the results, and to a consideration of the general conclusions to be drawn from them. But it may be here remarked in passing, in reference to the percentages of Fat above enumerated, that they would have been even somewhat higher in the condition of the Carcasses as weighed out by the butcher; for, in the Tables, the percentages are calculated in relation to the weight of the fresh carcass taken as soon as possible after the animal was killed; but between this condition and that in which the meat is generally sold to the consumer, there may be a loss in weight of even several per cent. by the evaporation of water.

From the want of a strict uniformity in classifying the several parts of the Offal in the different animals, for the determination of the Fat they contained, a detailed comparison of its amount in the corresponding parts in the different animals is not so practicable as might be wished. But, since only a small proportion of the fat from the Offal parts is consumed as human food, such a comparison is of the less importance in a prac-

---

* The fat obtained by *melting* and *expression* contained but very immaterial amounts of foreign substance; whilst, independently of other considerations, the composition of the final residue afforded confirmation of the fact, that the *ether determinations* very closely indicated the complementary amounts of the originally existing fat.

tical point of view. Still, there are here some points worthy of notice, as indicating the accumulation of Fat internally as the animal matures.

The percentage in the total Offal parts of fat obtained by melting and expression from the caul or omentum, was, in the half-fat Ox, 4·63, and in the moderately fat Ox, 7·93. In the Offal of the store Sheep the percentage of melted and expressed fat from the same source was 5·14, and in that of the very fat Sheep it was 19·5. Another item of fat, which is a considerable index to the fattening character and maturity of an animal—but which, with frequently a portion of the omentum fat also, is generally employed for tallow, and therefore not as food—is the mesenteric or intestinal fat. This also is seen to increase as the animals fatten; though those breeds which have the greater tendency to fatten on the outer frame or Carcass, have the less aptitude to do so around the internal organs. To go to the figures, it is seen, that the intestinal fat of the half-fat Ox amounted to 4·66 per cent. of the total Offal parts, and that of the fatter Ox to nearly double, or 8·79 per cent. The intestinal fat of the store Sheep amounted to 3·08, that of the half-fat Sheep to 5·69, that of the fat Sheep to 6·57, and that of the very fat Sheep to 7·41 per cent. of the collective Offal parts. The Offal of the store Pig again, yielded only 2·12 per cent. of its weight of melted fat from the intestinal regions (including the so-called caul-fat), and that of the fat Pig 8·35 per cent. It need hardly be remarked, that it is only in a practical or economic point of view, that any comparisons can be drawn between animals differing so essentially in their characters and habits, as the Pig and the Ruminant. But, whilst speaking of the amounts of fat deposited around the internal organs in the two cases, it may not be out of place to call to mind how much more concentrated, so far as digestible matter is concerned, is the food of the Pig than that of the bulky-feeding Ruminant, and that, in conformity with this, the alimentary cavities and passages constitute, collectively, a much less proportion of the bulk and weight of the animal in the former, than in the latter.

It is seen that nearly 1 per cent. of the collective Offal parts of the Sheep is fatty matter contained in the wool.

Of *total fat* obtainable by melting, expression, and ether, the collective Offal parts yielded only from one-half to two-thirds as high a percentage as the collective Carcass or more universally edible parts. Even in the Offal, however, the fat, in the cases of the fattened animals (excluding the calf and lamb), amounted to about one-fourth of the total Offal, as, for example, in the fat Bullock, the fat Sheep, and the fat Pig, and to more than one-third in the case of the very fat Sheep. Of the probable proportions of the fat of the *carcass* and of the *offal*, respectively, which are, on the average, consumed as human food, and of the relation of this consumed fat to the nitrogenous substance taken with it, we shall have to speak further on.

Let us now turn from the percentages of Fat in the collective Carcass, or collective Offal parts, respectively, to the amounts derived from the same sources, calculated in relation to the *entire* or *fasted live-weight* of the animals taken as 100. Looking to the percentages as so calculated, and which are given in the more detailed form in Table III., it is obvious that the *relation* of the figures, comparing one animal with another, in

3 x 2

regard to the fat of any corresponding part or parts, will be nearly the same as in the comparisons already drawn, wherein the percentages were given in relation to the total Carcass, or total Offal parts, separately. The actual figures are of course less when taking the larger weight—that of the Entire Animal—as the divisor in the calculation; but the relation of the figures representing any given part or set of parts of one animal compared with another, will only differ from that in the forms of calculation already considered, in so far as the proportion, in the Entire Live-weight, of the contents of stomachs and intestines (included in the live-weight) is different in the different animals. Some space may be saved, therefore, by leaving to the reader the study of the further details in Table III., and proceeding to call attention to the more summary view of the percentages of fat in the Entire Animals, as given in columns 3, 4, 5, and 6, of Table IV.

In column 3 of Table IV., the percentages in the Entire or Fasted Live-weight of the animals, of fat due to total Carcass parts, are given; and in column 4, those yielded by the total Offal parts. Taking the average of the ten animals, more than three-fourths of their total fat belonged to their Carcass, or more valuable edible parts. The proportion of the whole fat due to the Carcass parts is seen to be generally greater the "riper," or more matured, the animal. The proportion of the whole fat, due to carcass and offal respectively, is about the same in both the half-fat and the moderately fat Ox. In the Sheep, however, the proportion of the whole fat due to carcass is much greater in all the more mature animals than in the one in the store condition. In the latter, there was only about twice as much of the total fat coming from the carcass as from the offal; whereas, taking the average of the four fatter animals—the fat Lamb, the half-fat Sheep, the fat Sheep, and the very fat Sheep—there was three times as much of the total fat due to the carcass as to the offal parts. In even the *store* Pig there was four times as much of the total fat of the body, in the Carcass, as in the Offal parts; and in the fat Pig there were from eight to nine times as much fat from the Carcass as from the Offal parts. The general conclusion would seem to be then, that, perhaps on the average, three-fourths or more of the total fat of a slaughtered animal, in good condition, will belong to the *carcass parts*—that is to say, to those parts which may be reckoned as almost entirely devoted, in some form or other, as human food.

It has been already seen in Table III., and the column illustrating the fact is repeated in Table IV., that the percentage of fat in the collective Carcass parts of the fattened animals amounted to from one-third to one-half, or even more, of the total weight of the Carcass. We will now consider what was the proportion of the *whole animal* at the time of its being slaughtered, which was nearly, if not quite, *pure fat*.

In the fifth column of Table IV., the percentage of total fat in the Fasted Live-weight of the several animals has been calculated by the addition of the respective items recorded in Table III. In the sixth and last column of Table IV., are given the percentages of total fat in the Live-weight of the ten animals, obtained, for the purposes of control, by another method. In this check column No. 6, the amount of fat obtained by melting and expression is calculated by the addition of the amounts thus obtained from the several parts, as in the other case; but, the fat remaining in the different expressed parts, is now obtained by ether determinations made on proportionally mixed samples of *all* the parts of the animal, Carcass and Offal together, the wool only excepted; the fat in the wool itself being extracted separately, and its amount taken into the calculation. A glance at the two columns (5 and 6) will show that there is never half, and in only one or two cases, one-fourth of 1 per cent. of variation between the results obtained by the two different methods.

The striking fact appears, that, of the *whole body* (fasted live-weight), 45¾ per cent. of the very fat Sheep, and 42 per cent. of the moderately fat Pig, were *dry fatty matter.* Of the moderately fat Sheep 35½ per cent., of the moderately fat Bullock 30 per cent., and of the fat Lamb 28½ per cent. were dry fat. The half-fat old Sheep contained 23¼, and the half-fat Bullock 18¾ per cent. of fat. The *store* Sheep even contained 18¾, and the *store* Pig 23¼ per cent. Of the Calf, on the other hand, the entire body, though professedly fat, yielded only 14¾ per cent. of its weight of dry fatty substance.

It may, perhaps, from these data be concluded, that fattened Oxen of good quality, will, on the average, consist of *fat*, to the amount of nearly one-third of their whole weight; moderately fattened Sheep, to rather more; and moderately fattened Pigs, to more still; whilst, probably, fat Bacon-Pigs will frequently contain fat to the amount of one-half of their whole live-weight.

Section V.—THE NITROGEN—IN CERTAIN SEPARATED PARTS, AND IN THE ENTIRE BODIES, OF 10 ANIMALS ANALYSED.

It has been shown, how large is the proportion of the whole body, of some of the animals of most importance as human food, which is *fatty matter*. It has been further seen, that the proportion of fat in the collective Carcass parts, that is those which are the more exclusively appropriated to food purposes, is still greater than in the whole body. The next point of interest is as to the proportion, in the whole body or certain collective parts, of *nitrogen* and the thence calculated amount of protein or other nitrogenous compounds, a class of constituents, the comparative predominance of which is generally supposed so prominently to characterize our *animal food.*

The *nitrogen* was determined upon mixed samples of the crude dry matters remaining after the removal of fat by melting and expression, as follow:—

(a) Of all soft parts of the carcass:
(b) Of carcass bones:
(c) Of offal, soft parts and bones together (excluding hair or wool):
(d) Of all parts, carcass and offal together (excluding hair or wool).

It was also determined upon the hair or wool separately. The exceptions to the above arrangement were, that, in the cases of the Pigs, the mixed sample of Carcass included both soft parts and bones, that of the Offal was without bones, and a separate mixture was made of the head and feet, soft parts and bones together.

The actual experimental determinations of nitrogen, in the expressed nitrogenous residues, mixed as above described, are given in Table XIV. in the Appendix. The calculated *mean* results are given in a detailed form in Table V., and in a summary one in Table VI., which now follow.

TABLE V.—Mean Percentages of NITROGEN in Ten Animals.

1st. In Fresh Carcass.—2nd. In Fresh Offal (equal Sum of Parts excluding Contents of Stomachs and Intestines).—3rd. In Entire Animal (Fasted Live-weight, including therefore Contents of Stomachs and Intestines).

Description of animal.	Fresh Carcass — From fleshy and membranous parts.	Fresh Carcass — From bones.	Fresh Carcass — From total carcass parts.	Fresh Offal — From hair or wool.	Fresh Offal — From head and feet.	Fresh Offal — From other offal parts.	Fresh Offal — From total offal parts.	Entire Animal, Carcass parts — From fleshy and membranous parts.	Entire Animal, Carcass parts — From bones.	Entire Animal, Carcass parts — From total carcass parts.	Entire Animal, Offal parts — From hair or wool.	Entire Animal, Offal parts — From head and feet (excluding tongue and brains).	Entire Animal, Offal parts — From other offal parts.	Entire Animal, Offal parts — From total offal parts.	From Total Parts.
Fat calf	2·121	0·487	2·608	0·142	2·670		2·812	1·316	0·302	1·618	0·042	0·796		0·838	2·456
Half-fat ox	2·331	0·462	2·793	0·242	3·194		3·436	1·509	0·299	1·808	0·063	0·837		0·900	2·708
Fat ox	1·919	0·432	2·351	0·216	2·656		2·872	1·271	0·286	1·557	0·057	0·704		0·761	2·318
Fat lamb	1·371	0·341	1·712	1·099	1·923		3·022	0·820	0·204	1·024	0·343	0·600		0·943	1·967
Store sheep	1·896	0·454	2·350	1·193	1·727		2·920	1·012	0·242	1·254	0·457	0·662		1·119	2·373
Half-fat old sheep	1·925	0·364	2·289	1·344	1·584		2·928	1·031	0·195	1·226	0·475	0·559		1·034	2·260
Fat sheep	1·467	0·324	1·791	1·129	1·480		2·609	0·843	0·186	1·029	0·403	0·528		0·931	1·960
Extra fat sheep	1·136	0·261	1·397	1·220	1·554		2·774	0·716	0·164	0·880	0·387	0·493		0·880	1·760
Store pig*			2·319		0·757*	1·415	2·172			1·541		0·237*	0·442	0·679	2·220
Fat pig*			1·712		0·800*	1·513	2·313			1·300		0·158*	0·299	0·457	1·757
Means of all			2·132	0·659	2·127		2·786			1·324	0·223	0·631		0·854	2·178
Means of the 8, excluding store sheep and store pig			2·082	0·674	2·172		2·846			1·305	0·221	0·622		0·843	2·148
Means of the 6, excluding the store and half-fat animals			1·928	0·634	2·099		2·734			1·235	0·205	0·596		0·802	2·036

* For comparison with the other animals, the nitrogen of the *head* and *feet* of the pig is here included in the Offal; but in practice these parts generally go with the Carcass.

TABLE VI.—Summary of Mean Percentages of NITROGEN in Ten Animals.

1st. In Fresh Carcass.—2nd. In Fresh Offal (equal Sum of Parts excluding Contents of Stomachs and Intestines).—3rd. In Entire Animal (Fasted Live-weight, including therefore Contents of Stomachs and Intestines).

[The mean percentage of Nitrogen from Total Parts in the Entire Animal is given—1st, by addition of the amounts in the separate items—2nd, by direct determination on the mixture of all crude dry parts (except wool, the amount in wool being added by calculation)—3rd, by calculation, deducting fat and mineral matter from total dry, and dividing by 6·3= an average per cent. of nitrogen, of 15·873, in the nitrogenous substance.]

| Description of animal. | Per cent. in fresh Carcass. | Per cent. in fresh Offal (excluding contents of stomachs and intestines). | Per cent. in Entire Animal (fasted live-weight). | | From Total Parts. | | |
			From carcass parts.	From offal parts.	1. By addition.	2. By direct determinations on hair or wool separately, and on a mixture of all other parts collectively.	3. By deducting fat and mineral matter, from total dry, and dividing by 6·3.
Fat calf	2·608	2·812	1·618	0·838	2·456	2·471	2·421
Half-fat ox	2·793	3·436	1·808	0·900	2·708	2·781	2·635
Fat ox	2·351	2·872	1·557	0·761	2 318	2·333	2·304
Fat lamb	1·712	3·022	1·024	0·943	1·967	1·974	1·949
Store sheep	2·350	2·920	1·254	1·119	2·373	2·380	2·353
Half-fat old sheep	2·289	2·928	1·226	1·034	2·260	{2·267 / 2·282*}	2·226
Fat sheep	1·791	2·609	1·029	0·931	1·960	{1·947 / 2·035*}	1·941
Extra fat sheep	1·397	2·774	0·880	0·880	1·760	{1·814 / 1·747*}	1·736
Store pig	2·319	2·172	1·541	0·679	2·220	2·196	2·180
Fat pig	1·712	2·313	1·300	0·457	1·757	1·773	1·725
Means of all	2·132	2·786	1·324	0·854	2·178	2·194	2·147
Means of the 8, excluding store sheep and store pig	2·082	2·845	1·305	0·834	2·148	2·170	2·117
Means of the 6, excluding the store and half-fat animals	1·928	2·733	1·235	0·802	2·036	2·052	2·013

These Tables of the percentages of actual *nitrogen* (V. and VI.), will enable us conveniently to compare the relative nitrogenous percentage of one animal, or its several parts, with that of another, and also, the duplicate results obtained by different methods of experimentation, or calculation, as the case may be. The amounts of *nitrogenous compounds* which the amounts of the nitrogen itself are supposed to represent, will be better considered further on, when we shall have before us, side by side, and at one view, the percentages in the ten animals or their collective parts, of the several *classes of constituents* of which the whole is made up, namely—mineral matter, dry nitrogenous compound, fatty matter, and the total dry substance and the complementary water.

* In these cases, two sets of determinations were made, at different times.

When speaking of the *mineral matter*, it was found that there was four or five times as much in the total bones, as in the total soft parts of the Carcasses. A reference to Table V. shows, that the amount of *nitrogen* was, on the other hand, four or five times as great in the soft parts of the Carcasses, as in the hard or bony parts. Still it would result, that, whenever no nutriment was reclaimed from the bones, one-fifth or one-sixth of the total nitrogenous substance of the Carcasses would be lost to human food.

Comparing first the percentage of nitrogen in the different *carcasses*, it is seen greatly to decrease with the progress of the animal from the store to the fat condition. It will be seen further on, that the fattening or maturing is accompanied by a considerable diminution in the percentage of *water* in the body. The dry matter accumulated consists, however, in a much greater proportion of fatty substance, than of nitrogenous compound. Indeed, it would seem probable that, necessarily, the larger the amount of the nitrogenous compounds, the larger the amount of water required for their proper hydration, for the purposes they subserve in the system.

To go to the figures, Table V. shows, that whilst the entire *carcass* of the half-fat Ox contained 2·793 per cent. of nitrogen, that of the moderately fat Ox contained about one-sixth less, or 2·351 per cent. Of the Sheep, the carcass of the store animal contained 2·350 per cent., that of the half-fat one 2·289 per cent., that of the fat one 1·791 per cent., and that of the very fat one only 1·397 per cent. of nitrogen. Again, whilst the carcass of the store Pig contained 2·319 per cent. of nitrogen, that of the moderately fatted one contained only 1·712 per cent. Lastly, the carcass of the fat Calf, which yielded a less proportion of fat than that of any of the other animals, contained of nitrogen on the other hand, a higher percentage than that of any but the half-fat Ox, namely, 2·608 per cent. This, again, is perfectly consistent with the reputed relatively lean character of veal.

Turning to the percentage of nitrogen in the collective *offal* parts (exclusive of contents of stomachs and intestines), it is seen at a glance, to be in every instance excepting that of the store Pig, higher than in the collective Carcass. In the Lamb, and in the four Sheep, however, more than one-third of the nitrogen of the offal is contained in the wool. Deducting this, the percentage of nitrogen in their collective other Offal parts would be less than in their collective Carcass parts.

In the right-hand portion of Table V., the amounts of nitrogen in the respective parts are calculated so as to show their percentage in the *total* or *fasted live-weight* of the animals, instead of in the Carcass or the Offal taken separately. Particular attention need only be called, however, to the more summary view of the percentage of nitrogen in the *entire animal*, as given in Table VI. The third column of this Table shows that amount of the total percentage of nitrogen in the Entire Animal which is contributed by the Carcass parts, and the fourth column that due to the total Offal parts. The last three columns of the Table give the percentage of nitrogen in the Entire Animals due to all parts together, both Carcass and Offal; but determined or calculated by three different methods. Before considering the actual composition of the animals, in regard to nitrogen, as shown in these three concluding columns, it will be interesting to consider the degree of agreement in the percentages obtained by the three different methods referred to.

In the first of the three concluding columns (Table VI.), headed "*By Addition*," the figures there recorded are obtained by the addition of the percentages afforded by the separate items or parts, the details of which are given in Table V.   The percentages so obtained, are, in fact, the result of duplicate nitrogen determinations made on each of *four* separate parts or mixed samples, for each animal.   The next column, headed—" By direct determinations on hair or wool separately, and on a mixture of all other parts collectively"—is obtained, as the description indicates, by duplicate determinations on *two* series of parts only.   The last column, on the other hand, is obtained entirely by *calculation*, as a check upon the percentages of nitrogen made by direct experimental determination.   The method of calculation is as follows:—From the percentage of the crude dry substance, remaining after the removal of most of the fat by melting and expression, the fat afterwards extracted by ether is deducted.   From the result so obtained, is next deducted the amount of the mineral matter.   The remainder—the water, the fat, and the mineral matter, being thus all excluded—consists, of course, of nitrogenous compounds of some kind or other.   With the view of founding an estimate as to the probable amount of nitrogen contained in the mixed nitrogenous matter of entire animal bodies, upon a basis of something like specific and detailed facts, we have in vain endeavoured to find sufficient published data for estimating the probable relative proportions in the body of albumen, fibrin, (*quasi*) gelatin, or chondrin, &c.   In the absence of any appropriate data on this subject, we have assumed, of necessity somewhat arbitrarily, 6·3 as probably the nearest round number applicable as a divisor of the crude nitrogenous substance of the animal bodies in question, to reduce it to nitrogen.   This number, 6·3, supposes an average percentage of nitrogen in the mixed nitrogenous compounds, of 15·873.   This is slightly higher than in either albumen or fibrin; considerably higher than in chondrin; but on the other hand, considerably lower than in gelatin *.   It is probably, therefore, as good a figure as could be taken under the circumstances, as some confirmation of nitrogen determinations made upon such heterogeneous matters, and of the propriety of their application to the objects we have in view.

If we are to assume, that the direct nitrogen determinations are nearer the truth than the calculated estimates, it would appear that the collective nitrogenous compounds of the whole body, in the cases in question, had a rather higher percentage of nitrogen than that represented by our number 6·3—namely, 15·873.   For, although the discrepancy in the percentages of nitrogen obtained by the different methods is invariably within the range of the second decimal place, the percentage indicated by the method of calculation merely, is in every instance somewhat lower than that by the direct expe-

---

* M. BOUSSINGAULT formerly adopted 15·0 per cent. of nitrogen (=6·666), in his calculations of nitrogenous *vegetable* compounds from the amounts of nitrogen; but he has more recently adopted 16·0 per cent. of nitrogen (=6·25).

rimental determinations. It would be easy to suggest several sources of probable inaccuracy, in thus assuming a percentage of nitrogen in the collective nitrogenous compounds of the body determined as a whole by the deduction of the amounts of other matters. For instance; it may be a question—how far the mineral matters determined by incineration, and deducted by calculation, contain the oxidated sulphur and phosphorus of the nitrogenous compounds themselves?—what were the relative proportions of the different nitrogenous compounds in the collective mixture of all of them?—and so on. Any consideration, of the interference with strict accuracy, of such sources of error, is, with our present main objects, immaterial.

Looking to the figures obtained by the three different methods, we are free to confess, that the correspondence between them is such as we had scarcely hoped to attain. We accept it as a proof of success in a difficult and extremely laborious undertaking, such as gives us more confidence in our final results, and in the conclusions derived from them, than at the commencement we had at all anticipated. It will be easily understood, that, although the difficulty of getting, for analysis, perfectly proportional and uniform mixtures, of such heterogeneous matters as those in question, must be very great, yet, that success on this point will depend only upon the amount of care and labour devoted to it. Feeling that so much depended upon these, we were, particularly in the preparation of the samples, not sparing in their exercise.

So far as the nitrogen determinations themselves are concerned, we are very glad to have this opportunity of stating, that they were, for the most part, made by Mr. F. A. MANNING. The degree of credit due to Mr. MANNING for this labour, will be best ascertained by an examination of the duplicate determinations given in Table XIV. in the Appendix, and of the coincidence of the final results, by the different methods, as given in Table VI. now under consideration. In this examination the extremely heterogeneous character of the substances operated upon should not be forgotten.

It has already been remarked, that the difference between the percentage of nitrogen indicated for the Entire Animals, obtained on the one hand by direct determinations, and on the other by calculation merely, was, pretty uniformly, within the limits of the second decimal place; and further, that the calculated percentage was invariably somewhat lower than the experimental ones. Comparing with each other the two differently obtained experimental results, the difference between them is always within the same limit. In the majority of cases, the difference, even in the second decimal place, amounts to very few units. The actual figures, in these three columns, may then be taken as pretty closely indicating the real percentages of nitrogen in the Entire Bodies operated upon. They furnish, therefore, a concise view of the differences in this respect, between the different animals, according to their description or condition.

It is remarkable, that, of the beef-yielding animals, the whole body of the half-fat Ox contained scarcely $2\frac{3}{4}$ per cent. of nitrogen, and that of the moderately fat one only about $2\frac{1}{3}$ per cent. The fat Calf contained a rather larger proportion of nitrogen than the fat Ox; namely, nearly $2\frac{1}{2}$ per cent.

The entire body of the fat Lamb contained less than 2 per cent. of nitrogen.   The store Sheep contained less than 2·4 per cent. of nitrogen; the half-fat old Sheep 2¼ per cent.; the moderately fat Sheep not quite 2 per cent.; and the very fat Sheep scarcely more than 1¾ per cent.

The store Pig contained about 2½ per cent. of nitrogen; and the moderately fat one, only about 1¾ per cent.

The striking fact of there being so small a percentage of nitrogen in the bodies of the animals which we feed to supply our meat-diet, is one of great interest and importance. On the one hand, as will be fully illustrated further on, the proportion of the nitrogen consumed in the fattening food, which remains stored up in the animal, and is sent to market as meat, is extremely small; and on the other, as already alluded to, a considerable proportion of the nitrogen which really is retained by the animals is not appropriated as human food; whilst, of that which is so appropriated, a considerable portion will exist in the form of gelatin and chondrin-yielding matters, the value of which as food is, to say the least, questioned.

Before leaving the Tables showing the percentage of *nitrogen* in the different animals and their several parts, attention may be recalled to the illustrations of the latter point, afforded in the lines of *mean percentages*, given at the foot of Table VI.   It has already been noticed, that the collective Offal parts of the animals contained a higher percentage of nitrogen than the collective Carcass parts.   But it is seen, that the actual amount in the *entire body*, of nitrogen accumulated in the Carcass parts, is still about three-fifths of the whole.   It was shown, that about one-fifth of this is due to the bones.   It results, that there is left, in round numbers, only about *half* of the entire nitrogen of the body associated with the *soft edible parts of the carcass*.   As to the proportion of the two-fifths of the total nitrogen in the body contained in the Offal parts, which will probably, on the average, be consumed as human food, some observations will be made further on.

Section VI.—SUMMARY OF THE COMPOSITION OF THE TEN ANIMALS ANALYSED:—
Mineral Matter, Dry Nitrogenous Compounds, Fat, Total Dry Substance, and Water.

Having considered the percentages of mineral matter, of fat, and of nitrogen, *individually*, in the different animals and their respective parts, it will be well now to take a summary view of their *collective* composition as deducible from the data thus provided. In Table VII., therefore, which now follows, are given side by side, at one view, the percentages in the Carcass, in the Offal, and in the Entire Animal respectively, of—

    1st.   Mineral matter (ash):

    2nd.   Total dry nitrogenous compounds (by deduction of other constituents):

    3rd.   Total fat (by melting, expression, and extraction by ether):

    4th.   Total dry substance (sum of the mineral, nitrogenous, and fat):

    5th.   Water (the complementary quantity to the total dry):

And, in the Entire Animal, the percentage of the whole due to contents of Stomachs and Intestines is also given.

TABLE VII.—Summary of the Composition of the Ten Animals;—showing the Percentages of Mineral Matter, Dry Nitrogenous Compounds, Fat, Total Dry Substance, and Water.

1st. In Fresh Carcass.—2nd. In Fresh Offal (equal Sum of Parts excluding Contents of Stomachs and Intestines).—3rd. In Entire Animal (Fasted Live-weight, including therefore the weight of Contents of Stomachs and intestines).

Description of animal	Per cent. in Carcass.					Per cent. in Offal (sum of parts excluding contents of stomachs and intestines).					Per cent. in Entire Animal (fasted live-weight).					
	Mineral matter.	Dry nitrogenous compounds.	Fat.	Total dry substance.	Water.	Mineral matter.	Dry nitrogenous compounds.	Fat.	Total dry substance.	Water.	Mineral matter.	Dry nitrogenous compounds.	Fat.	Total dry substance.	Contents of stomachs and intestines (in moist state).	Water.
Fat calf	4·48	16·6	16·6	37·7	62·3	3·41	17·1	14·6	35·1	64·9	3·80	15·2	14·8	33·8	3·17	63·0
Half-fat ox	5·56	17·8	22·6	46·0	54·0	4·05	20·6	15·7	40·4	59·6	4·66	16·6	19·1	40·3	8·19	51·5
Fat ox	4·56	15·0	24·8	44·4	45·6	3·40	17·5	26·3	47·2	52·8	3·92	14·6	30·1	48·5	5·98	45·5
Fat lamb	3·53	10·9	36·9	51·4	48·6	2·45	18·9	20·1	41·6	58·5	2·94	12·3	28·5	43·7	8·54	47·8
Store sheep	4·36	14·6	23·8	42·7	57·3	2·19	18·0	16·1	36·3	63·7	3·16	14·8	18·7	36·7	6·00	57·3
Half-fat old sheep	4·13	14·9	31·3	50·3	49·7	2·72	17·7	18·5	38·9	61·1	3·17	14·0	23·5	40·7	9·05	50·2
Fat sheep	3·45	11·6	45·4	60·3	39·7	2·32	16·1	26·4	44·8	55·2	2·81	12·2	35·6	50·6	6·02	43·4
Extra fat sheep	2·77	9·1	55·1	67·0	33·0	3·64	16·8	34·5	54·9	45·1	2·90	10·9	45·8	59·6	5·18	35·2
Store pig	2·57	14·0	28·1	44·7	55·3	3·07	14·0	15·0	32·1	67·9	2·67	13·7	23·3	39·7	5·22	55·1
Fat pig	1·40	10·5	49·5	61·4	38·6	2·97	14·8	22·8	40·6	59·4	1·65	10·9	42·2	54·7	3·97	41·3
Means of all	3·69	13·5	34·4	51·6	48·4	3·02	17·2	21·0	41·2	58·8	3·17	13·5	28·2	44·9	6·13	49·0
Means of 8; namely, of the half-fat, fat, and very fat animals	3·75	13·3	36·5	53·6	46·4	3·12	17·4	22·4	42·9	57·1	3·23	13·3	29·9	46·4	6·26	47·3
Means of 6; namely, of the fat, and very fat animals	3·38	12·3	39·7	55·4	44·6	3·03	16·9	24·1	44·0	56·0	3·00	12·7	32·8	48·5	5·48	46·0

Looking more particularly to the first Division in the Table (VII.), which shows the collective composition of the *carcasses*, and comparing one animal with another, there is seen to be a general disposition to a rise or fall in the percentage of mineral matter, with the rise or fall in that of the nitrogenous compounds.   In fact, all the results tend to show a prominent connexion between the amount of the mineral matters, and that of the nitrogenous constituents of the body.

Next comparing the relative proportions of *fat*, and of *nitrogenous compounds*, in the different Carcasses, it is seen, that, in every instance excepting that of the Calf (in which case the percentages of nitrogenous substance and of fat were equal), there was considerably more of dry fat than of dry nitrogenous compounds.   In the Carcass even of the *store* or *lean* Sheep, there was more than one and a half time as much fat as nitrogenous substance.   In that of the *store* or *lean* Pig there was twice as much.   In the Carcass of the half-fat Ox, there was one-fourth more fat than nitrogenous matter; and in that of the half-fat Sheep there was more than twice as much.   Of the fatter animals, the Carcass of the fat Ox contained twice and one-third as much dry fat as nitrogenous substance; that of the fat Sheep four times, and that of the very fat Sheep even six times as much.   Lastly, in the Carcass of the moderately fat Pig, there was nearly five times as much fatty matter as nitrogenous compounds.

From these results, it may perhaps be safely inferred, that in Carcasses of *beef* of reputed good condition, there will be seldom less than twice as much, and frequently nearly three times as much dry fat as dry nitrogenous substance.   In the Carcasses of *sheep* we should conclude, that the fat would generally amount to more than three, and frequently to four or even more times as much as the nitrogenous matter.   Finally, it may be estimated that in the Carcasses of *pigs killed for fresh pork*, there will be seldom as little as four times as much fat as nitrogenous compounds; whilst, in those *fed for curing*, the fat will generally be in a higher proportion still.

The *fat* of the bones bears but a small proportion to that of the whole Carcass.   As has been seen, however, perhaps one-fifth of the whole *nitrogen* of the Carcasses will be contained in the bones, and not included therefore in the more currently edible portions.   It results, that, provided the whole of the fat of the soft parts of the Carcass be consumed as human food, its proportion to the amount of the consumed nitrogenous substances will, on the average of such consumption, be still greater than the actual composition of entire Carcasses would indicate.

The question here arises, what proportion of the fat of our slaughtered animals is probably, on the average, actually consumed as human food in one form or another? We have instituted numerous inquiries on this point; and we cannot do better than quote the opinion given by an experimenter and writer of great observation and experience in such matters.   Mr. JOHN EWART, of Newcastle, writes in answer to our inquiry for his opinion as follows:—

" As to beasts.   The *opening* or the thick vein of fat that is presented and protrudes from the internal cavity on the first opening of the carcass, and also the *crook of the reed* or the fat on the *reticulum* or second stomach is reserved for suet, whilst the mesentery or web of fat which holds the intestines is sent to the tallow-melter.   The proportion of the internal fat spoken of as reserved for suet may amount to about one-fourth of the whole of the loose or offal fat yielded by the beast; but the demand for suet not being at all times equal to the quantity reserved for such in addition to the real suet or the fat on the inside of the loins and covering the kidneys, a portion of the loose fat reserved for suet is sometimes added to the tallow, by which the quantity of offal fat of beasts used as human food will be reduced to one-fifth, or twenty per cent. of its entire quantity, and which must be understood as in addition to the whole of the carcass fat.   Before dismissing this portion of the subject, I may remark, that the suet in the victualling of shipping always consists of loose or offal fat, some being taken for that purpose even when entire carcasses are purchased.

"In sheep, although a portion of loose fat is generally reserved for suet, yet there being a portion of the carcass fat, when redundant—which is very frequently the case—sent to the tallow-melter, the whole of the carcass fat, but without any addition of offal fat, will represent, very nearly, the quantity used as human food from this description of stock.

"I am fully aware that the disposition of the fat yielded by the kinds of stock already spoken of is not uniformly alike, and exactly that stated above in all localities, but I do not think that the variation is such as to affect the statement as an average for England.   In Ireland and Scotland the consumption of flesh is insignificant, when compared to that in England.

"The whole of the fat of both calves and lambs is eaten, or at least used—sometimes also with the addition of sheep's offal fat—in the process of cooking their flesh.

"The mesentery in swine is very small, and that of small animals slaughtered for fresh pork is entirely used in the process of cooking their edible offals, such as the liver, &c.   Hog's lard is the melted *leaf* or the layer of fat which accumulates in and lines the internal cavity in this description of stock, together with the melted mesentery of large animals slaughtered for being cured.   The principal uses of hog's lard are as a substitute for butter by the pastry-cooks and others, and in adulterating that article by unprincipled dealers.   Another use of the fat of swine in the form of lard is in the preparation of ointments by apothecaries, and in that of pomatum—particularly in the kind sold as bear's grease—by the perfumers."

With these statements, our information, derived from other sources, leads us to concur. It would appear, then, that as an average, we may assume:—that the whole of the Carcass fat, and about one-fifth of the Offal fat, of beasts, will be consumed as human food; that, of Sheep, an amount equal to the whole of their Carcass fat, but without reckoning any from their Offal parts, will be so consumed;—and that, of the Pig, an amount equal to the whole of its Carcass fat, which is in greater proportion than in the other animals, and probably a part of its Offal fat also, will be consumed as food.   So far then as *carcasses* are concerned, the conclusion would seem to be fully borne out, that the proportion of the consumed fat to the consumed nitrogenous substance, will, on the average, be greater than that indicated by the relation of the total fat to the total nitrogenous matter in the Carcasses of fattened animals.

Still confining attention for the present to the composition of the *carcasses*, the Table (VII.) shows, that, whilst the percentages of both mineral matter and nitrogenous substance decrease, as the animals mature, that of the fat, on the other hand, very considerably increases. Indeed, the increase in the percentage of fat is much more than equivalent to the collective decrease in that of the other solid matters: that is to say, as the animal matures, the percentage in its Carcass, of *total dry substance* (and especially of fat), much increases. There is then, of course, a corresponding diminution in the proportion of the water. Thus, in the Carcasses of the leaner animals, there were from 54 to 62 per cent. of water; namely, 62¼ per cent. in that of the Calf; 57⅓ per cent. in that of the store Sheep; 55⅛ per cent. in that of the store Pig; and 54 per cent. in that of the half-fat Ox. The Carcasses of all the other animals contained less than 50 per cent., and those of the fattest less than 40 per cent. of water. That of the moderately fattened Ox contained 45½ per cent.; that of the fat Lamb 48¾ per cent.; that of the half-fat Sheep 49¾ per cent.; that of the fat Sheep 39¾; and that of the very fat Sheep scarcely one-third of its weight, or 33 per cent. only, of water. Lastly, in the Carcass of the moderately fattened Pig, there were 38½ per cent. of water. It may be remarked, that these particular Carcasses, in the condition in which they would have been sold by the butcher, would perhaps have contained 1 to 2 per cent. less water than is indicated in the Table. For, between the condition in which these Carcasses were weighed, namely, as soon as possible after killing, and that in which the meat is usually sold to the consumer, it would probably have lost 1 or 2 per cent. of water by evaporation. On the other hand, as the bones contain a higher percentage of dry matter than the collective soft parts, the percentage in these edible soft parts will be somewhat lower than in the entire Carcass including bones. The actual fresh and dry weights of the bones of the different animals analysed will be found in Tables I. to X., in the Appendix; and the percentages of dry matter in the bones in Table XI., also in the Appendix. It may be here observed, however, that the proportion of bone was much less in the Sheep than in the Oxen, and much less in the Pigs than in the Sheep. It was, too, in all cases less, the fatter the animal. The percentage of dry matter in the bone increased, however, as the animal matured; and it was higher in that of the Oxen than in that of the Sheep; and higher in that of the Sheep than in that of the Pigs. For example: the percentage of bone in the Carcass of the fat Ox was 11·8, in that of the fat Sheep 8·9, and in that of the fat Pig 4·6. The percentage of dry matter in the Carcass bones of the fat Ox and fat Sheep was from 73 to 74, and in those of the fat Pig only 61·7. From the large proportion of bone, and the high percentage of dry matter in the bone, of the Carcass of the fat Ox, the percentage of dry matter in the soft parts would be about 2½ lower than in the entire Carcass with bones. In the same way, the percentage of dry matter in the soft Carcass parts of the fat Sheep would be 59·1, instead of 60·35, as in the entire

Carcass. In the fat Pig, however, owing to the much smaller proportion of the bone, and the percentage of dry matter in the bone being so nearly the same as that in the total Carcass, the percentage of dry substance in the soft parts will not differ materially from that in the whole Carcass.

From the whole of the data adduced on the point, it may perhaps be safely concluded, that the average of Carcass *beef*, in well-fattened condition, will contain 50 per cent., or rather more of dry substance; that the average of properly fattened *mutton* will contain rather more dry matter than beef, say, 55 to 60 per cent.; that the Carcasses of Pigs killed for *fresh pork* will be rather drier than those of mutton; whilst the sides of Pigs killed for *curing* will, no doubt, be drier still. *Lamb* carcasses would seem to contain a smaller proportion of total dry substance than either moderately fattened beef, mutton, or pork. Their proportion of bone is also comparatively high. Lastly, *veal* appears to be the most watery of all. The Carcass of the Calf experimented upon, though the animal was considered to be well-fattened, contained only $37\frac{3}{4}$ per cent. of dry substance; its proportion of bone was also higher than in any of the other cases.

Turning to the second division of Table VII., which shows the composition of the *collective offal parts* (excluding contents of stomachs and intestines), the figures do not show such a uniform tendency to a diminution in the percentage of mineral matter coincidently with that of the nitrogenous substance, as was observed in the case of the Carcasses. But, as already referred to, the percentage of mineral matter in the *collective* Offal parts (and it is this which is here under notice), does not represent only the mineral matter properly associated with the other constituents of the parts, but includes a quantity of adventitious matter adhering to the pelt, hair, or wool, of the animals.

It is seen that the percentage of dry nitrogenous substance is, in every case, greater, and that of the fat very much less, in the collective Offal, than in the collective Carcass parts. In Oxen and Sheep, the pelt, hair or wool, hoofs, and for the most part stomachs and intestines, as well as some other nitrogenous parts of the Offal, will not be consumed as human food. The parts that will as a rule, or at least frequently be so consumed, are the head flesh with tongue and brains, the heart, the liver, the pancreas, the spleen, the diaphragm, and sometimes the lungs. Calculation leads us to estimate that the nitrogenous substance of these parts will in these animals (beasts and sheep) amount to about one-sixth of the whole nitrogenous matter of their collective Offals. This portion of edible nitrogenous substance from the Offal parts must, therefore, be added to the amount estimated as eaten from the Carcass, when considering the proportion of the whole nitrogen of the slaughtered animals which is appropriated as human food. Calculation further shows, however, that in the cases of Oxen and Sheep, the whole of the nitrogenous matter reclaimed as food from the Offal parts will fall short of the amount contained in the bones of the Carcass. So nearly, however, will these quantities balance one another (especially if a portion of the gelatine from the carcass bones be considered as eaten), that the total nitrogen of the Carcass parts, excluding any from the Offal, may perhaps be taken as little exceeding the average proportion of the whole nitrogen of the bodies of these animals which will be consumed as human food. In the case of Pigs, a larger proportion of the total nitrogenous parts of the Offal will be consumed; an amount indeed more than equivalent to that in the bones of the Carcass, supposed to be not consumed. It results in fact upon the whole, that there would appear to be a larger proportion of the total nitrogen of the body of the Pig consumed, than of that of the other animals. But, as has been seen in the Pig, the percentage in the body of that total nitrogen is less, and the percentage of the fat greater than in the other cases. The Offal parts enumerated as eaten, are of themselves associated with very little fat; so that, such food, which is chiefly used by the poorer classes, would be highly nitrogenous, if not combined with extraneous fatty matter. In cooking, it is generally so combined. Moreover, the classes which consume the most of the internal organs of slaughtered animals, are also those which consume the larger proportion of Pig-meat, in which the proportion of the fat to nitrogenous substances is higher than in any other description.

It is observable, that with their larger percentage of nitrogenous substance and less percentage of fat, the collective Offal parts have invariably a less percentage of total dry substance, and therefore a larger proportion of water, than the collective Carcass parts.

The next point to consider is the collective composition of the *entire animal*, as it stands at the time of being slaughtered. The information on this head will be found in the third and last division of Table VII.

The marked diminution in the percentage of *mineral matter* as the animal fattens, which was observed in reference to the composition of the Carcasses, is clearly illustrated in that of the Entire Animals, notwithstanding the inclusion here of the Offal ash, in which was contained the incombustible impurity of the hair or wool.

We should judge from the figures, that from $3\frac{1}{2}$ to 4 per cent. (according to breed and condition) of the standing fasted weight of a fattened Ox will be mineral matter. The proportion in Sheep appears to be less. Excluding the adventitious matter of the wool, it would probably be often as little as $2\frac{1}{2}$ and seldom more than 3 per cent. of the fasted weight. In Pigs, the proportion of mineral matter is still less. We should gather, that in a well-fattened animal of good breed, it would amount to only $1\frac{1}{2}$ per cent., or even less, of its standing fasted live-weight. In a young unfattened Pig, there were 2·67 per cent. of mineral matter; but in an animal of a worse breed, or in a leaner condition still, we should judge that there might be 3 per cent. As an average estimate of the mineral matter in *store* animals, sold off or brought on the farm, we should be disposed to adopt $4\frac{1}{2}$ to 5 per cent. of their live-weight for Bullocks, 3 to $3\frac{1}{2}$ per cent. for Sheep, and $2\frac{1}{2}$ to 3 per cent. for Pigs. As an average estimate for the mineral matter in *fattened* animals so far as the data at command enable us to form an opinion, we should take $3\frac{1}{2}$ to 4 per cent. of their live-weight for Calves and Bullocks, $2\frac{1}{2}$ to $2\frac{3}{4}$ per cent. for Sheep and Lambs, and $1\frac{1}{4}$ to $1\frac{3}{4}$ per cent. for Pigs.

Of total *nitrogenous compounds*, as well as total mineral matter, the beef-yielding animals contain in parallel conditions, rather more than Sheep, and Sheep rather more than Pigs. Of the standing fasted live-weight of the moderately fat Ox, there were, including bones, pelt, and internal organs, &c., only 14½ per cent. of dry nitrogenous compounds. The fat Sheep contained only 12¼ per cent.; the very fat one not quite 11 per cent.; and the moderately fattened Pig about the same, namely, 10·9 per cent. The store animals contained from 2 to 3 per cent. more total dry nitrogenous substance than the moderately fat ones.

Of the standing live-weight of the animals, the *fat* obviously constitutes the most prominent item in the dry or solid matter. In the half-fat Ox there was nearly as much fat as nitrogenous substance and mineral matter put together; in the store Sheep there was more of fat than other solid matter; in the half-fat Sheep the proportion of fat to other matters was larger still; and in the store Pig it was larger than in the half-fat Sheep.

In the fat Calf alone was the total fat less than the total nitrogenous substance of the body. Of the other animals fit for the butcher, the fat Ox and fat Lamb consisted of fat to the amount of about 30 per cent. of their live-weight, which was nearly twice as much as the total amount of the remaining solid matters, and more than twice as much as the total nitrogenous substance only. The fat Sheep contained 35½ per cent. of fat, or nearly three times as much as of nitrogenous substance. The very fat Sheep yielded 45¾ per cent. of fat, and less than one-fourth as much of nitrogenous substance. Lastly, the fat Pig, with 42¼ per cent. of its entire body consisting of fat, had just about one-fourth as much, or 10·9 per cent., of dry nitrogenous substance. Taking the mean composition of the six animals assumed to be fit for the butcher—namely, the fat Calf, the fat Ox, the fat Lamb, the fat Sheep, the very fat Sheep, and the fat Pig—we have in round numbers, 3 per cent. of mineral matter, 12½ per cent. of nitrogenous compounds (dry), and 33 per cent. of fat, in their fasted live-weight. The proportion to one another, and the proportion to the whole amount of each contained in the different descriptions of animal, in which the *fat*, and the *nitrogenous substance*, respectively, will probably be consumed as human food, has already been considered in some detail in the proper place. To these points reference will again be made, when calling attention at the end of our Paper to the application of the experimental results as a whole, and to the general conclusions to be drawn from them.

All the experimental evidence which has been adduced conspires to show, that the so-called "*fattening*" of animals for the butcher, is properly so designated. Even the so-called "*store*" or "*lean*" animals are seen to contain as much, or more, of dry fatty substance, than of dry nitrogenous compounds. After the feeding or fattening process, the percentage of the collective dry substance of the body was considerably increased; whilst fatty matter had accumulated in much larger proportion than the nitrogenous compounds. It is obvious, therefore, that in the *increase itself* of the fattening animal, the proportion of fat to the nitrogenous substance of growth, must be *greater* than in the total or standing live-weight of the animal. In other words, the composition of the *increase* in weight of a fattening animal, must show a less percentage of nitrogenous substance, and a higher one both of fat and total dry substance, than that of the whole body of the slaughtered animal.   With the decrease in the proportion of bone, moreover, as well as the small accumulation of soft nitrogenous parts, we should also expect the percentage of mineral matter in the *increase* to be very small.

SECTION VII.—ESTIMATED COMPOSITION OF THE INCREASE IN WEIGHT OF FATTENING ANIMALS.

The first and most obvious application of the data provided in the preceding sections, is, to employ them as a means of estimating the composition of the *increase in weight* of an animal whilst passing from one given point of progress to another—as distinguished from the actual composition of the entire body, or its several parts, as furnished by analysis at any one fixed period.   So far as the analysed fat Pig is concerned, the result of such a calculation has been already given elsewhere*.   It will be interesting, however, to extend the application to numbers of such animals, and also to the equally, or even more important animals of the farm—Oxen and Sheep.

It is obvious, that provided we know the exact composition of an animal when it weighs any given weight, say 100 lbs.—and again, when, after fattening, it has reached another weight, say 150 lbs.—nothing would be easier than to calculate the actual and the percentage composition of the 50 lbs. that has been gained.   By deducting the amount of the respective constituents in the 100 lbs. weight, from the amount of the same in the 150 lbs., we should at once ascertain the *actual* amount of each in the 50 lbs. of *increase*.   The calculation of the *percentage* composition of the *increase* would then of course be a very simple matter.   The practical difficulty obviously rests on the fact, that we cannot know the exact composition of a fattened animal at the time it was put upon fattening food, or when it had reached any given previous weight.

In the case of the store and fat Pigs which were analysed, the two animals selected for experiment were of the same breed and age—indeed of the same litter; of very nearly equal weights; and, so far as competent judges could decide, as nearly as possible alike in all other particulars.   One of these animals was killed at once in the *store* condition, and its composition determined.   Of the other, the exact increase in weight from this store or lean to the fat condition, as well as the amount and the composition of the food it consumed in gaining it, is known; as also is its composition in the *fattened* state.   The application of the data in the manner above supposed, is likely therefore to lead to a pretty trustworthy estimate of the composition of the increase of this particular fattening Pig.

Unfortunately, equally parallel data are not available for calculating the composition of the increase of the other fattened animals analysed.   This is the more to be regretted, since, from the results of the Pigs it would appear, that data of this kind, if obtained under duly considered circumstances, are much more directly applicable to the determination of the composition of increase, than we had pre-supposed would be the case.   In illustration of the inapplicability of the data provided in regard to the other descriptions

* Report of the British Association for the Advancement of Science for 1852.

of animal, to determine the composition of the *increase* from one condition to another—supposing this to be represented by the difference in weight between the animal which was analysed in the lean, and that which was analysed in the fat condition—it may be observed, that owing to the larger frame, and growing rather than fattening character, of the half-fat Ox analysed, compared with the fatter one, it approached so nearly the actual weight of the latter, as to indicate (if the difference in weight were alone taken as the measure) a very small amount of actual increase; whilst the difference in the composition of the two animals was very considerable. In fact, in the case supposed, the so-calculated *total or gross increase* would be less than the estimated gain in *dry substance of increase alone*: that is to say, it would appear that there had been an actual displacement of water, and replacement of it by a corresponding amount of dry substance. It may be said that the displacement of water, and the replacement of it by fat, in the fattening animal, or in other words a greater increase in *dry substance* than in the *gross live-weight*, is not impossible. The consideration of the results relating to the Pigs, as well as the tendency of observation, comparing animals of this description with others, would, however, militate against such an assumption. For similar reasons to those alluded to in regard to the two Bullocks, the difference in weight between the Sheep analysed in the respective conditions of fatness, cannot be taken as representing the amount of gross increase in weight in passing from the one standard condition to the other. Instead, therefore, of taking the live-weights of the individual animals actually analysed, as the data upon which to calculate the composition of the increase from one condition to another, it will be more appropriate to adopt the known live-weights of considerable numbers of animals, taken first in a store or lean, and afterwards in a fatter condition.

So·far as *oxen* are concerned, we take for our illustrations the best experiments on record with which we are acquainted, that show, so far as can be judged, a progression comparable with that implied in the change from the condition of the "half-fat" to that of the "fat Ox" analysed.

In regard to *sheep*, we take the data supplied by published experiments of our own[*]. In some of these, considerable numbers of animals of different breeds were fed upon similar food; whilst in others, animals otherwise comparable were fed upon different foods.

Lastly, the compositions of the store and of the fat *pig* analysed, have, respectively, been applied to the weights store, and the weights fat, of numbers of pigs fed experimentally—the amounts of whose gross increase in live-weight, together with the particulars of the constituents consumed in food to produce it, have already been published elsewhere[†]. For the sake of comparison, by the side of the estimates of the compo-

[*] Journal of the Royal Agricultural Society of England, vol. x. part 1; vol. xii. part 2; vol. xiii. part 1; and vol. xvi. part 1.

[†] Journal of the Royal Agricultural Society of England, vol. xiv. part 2; Reports of the British Association for the Advancement of Science, for 1852 and 1854.

sition of the increase of fattening Pigs so obtained, is adduced that indicated by the direct application of the analytical results to determine the composition of the increase from the store to the fat condition, in the case of the two Pigs actually analysed, which provide the data for application to the other cases.

Table VIII. shows the estimated *percentage composition of the increase* of fattening *oxen.*

Table IX. shows the estimated *percentage composition of the increase* of fattening *sheep.*

Table X. shows the estimated *percentage composition of the increase* of fattening *pigs.*

In each case the *original* and *final* weights, and the *increase* in weight, of the animals are given. The composition to be applied to each in the calculation is also stated. There is always added some description of the food consumed. When at command, as in the case of most of the Sheep, and all the Pigs, the amount of certain constituents of the food which were consumed to produce a given amount of increase, are also given, by the side of the estimated composition of that increase.

TABLE VIII.—Showing the Estimated Percentage Composition of the Increase in Weight of fattening BULLOCKS and HEIFERS.

Note.—*Original* Weight, taken at the Composition of the "Half-fat Ox," analysed.
Final Weight, taken at the Composition of the "Fat Ox," analysed.

General particulars of the experiments.									Calculated percentages in *Increase.*			
Authority.	Descrip- tion of animal.	Num- ber of ani- mals.	Duration of expe- riment.	Description of fattening food.	Actual weights (fresh) in lbs.			In- crease upon 100 ori- ginal weight.	Mine- ral matter (ash).	Nitro- genous com- pounds (dry).	Fat.	Total dry sub- stance.
					Ori- ginal.	Final.	In- crease.					
			wks. days.									
Mr. TEMPLETON* ...	Heifers.	12	18 6	{ Swedish turnips, hay, and oat straw. }	12124	15274	3150	26·0	1·05	6·51	72·5	80·0
Hon. Capt. GREY† ...	Bullocks.	50	23½ 0	{ Oilcake, bean-meal, and turnips. }	54796	71470	16674	30·4	1·47	7·68	66·3	75·4
Hon. Capt. GREY† ...	Bullocks.	36	26½ 0	{ Oilcake, bean-meal, and turnips. }	41188	54530	13342	32·4	1·62	8·10	64·1	73·8
Average for the 98 animals									1·47	7·69	66·2	75·4

* Journal of the Royal Agricultural Society of England, vol. xvi. pp. 163–9.
† Gardeners' Chronicle and Agricultural Gazette, pp. 715 and 732 (1852).

TABLE IX.—Showing the Calculated Percentage Composition

Breed.	Number of animals.	Duration.	Description of fattening food. Given in limited quantities.	Given ad libitum.	Actual weights (fresh) in lbs. Original.	Final.	Increase.
Class I.†—*Original* weight taken at the composition of the "store sheep" analysed.							
		wks. days					
Cotswolds	46	19 5	Oilcake and clover hay	Swedish turnips.	5511	8439¾	2928¾
Leicesters	40	20 0	Oilcake and clover hay	Swedish turnips.	4053	5835½	1782½
Cross-bred wethers	40	20 0	Oilcake and clover hay	Swedish turnips.	3804	5584	1780
Cross-bred ewes	40	20 0	Oilcake and clover hay	Swedish turnips.	3650	5350	1700
Hants downs	40	26 0	Oilcake and clover hay	Swedish turnips.	4538	7322¼	2784¼
Sussex downs	40	26 0	Oilcake and clover hay	Swedish turnips.	3520	5629	2109
Class II.—*Original* weight taken at the composition of the "fat sheep" analysed.							
Cotswolds	6	34 6	Oilcake and clover hay	Grass, turnips, &c. in the field.	1037	1472	435
Leicesters	7	34 4	Oilcake and clover hay		948	1367	419
Cross-bred wethers	8	34 4	Oilcake and clover hay		1041	1490	449
Cross-bred ewes	8	34 4	Oilcake and clover hay		1006	1457	451
Hants downs	8	31 5	Oilcake and clover hay		1411	1897	486
Sussex downs	8	31 5	Oilcake and clover hay		1045	1428	383
Class III. (Series 1‡).—*Original* weight taken at the mean composition of the "store" and the							
Hants downs	5	13 6	Oilcake	Swedish turnips.	558	688 ·	130
Hants downs	5	13 6	Oats	Swedish turnips.	548	689 7/10	141 7/10
Hants downs	5	11 6	Clover chaff	Swedish turnips.	558 6/10	714	155 6/10
Class IV. (Series 2‡).—*Original* weight taken at the mean composition of the "store" and the							
Hants downs	5	19 1	Oilcake	Clover chaff	607	759 6/10	152 6/10
Hants downs	5	19 1	Linseed	Clover chaff	607	750	143
Hants downs	5	19 1	Barley	Clover chaff	602	741	139
Hants downs	5	19 1	Malt	Clover chaff	602	723	121
Class V. (Series 4‡).—*Original* weight taken at the composition of the "store sheep" plus Final weight taken at the composi-							
Hants downs	4	10 0	Barley (ground)	Mangolds	519	600	81
Hants downs	5	10 0	Malt (ground) and malt dust	Mangolds	653	758	105
Hants downs	4	10 0	Barley (ground) and steeped	Mangolds	536	637 7/10	101 6/10
Hants downs	4	10 0	Malt (ground and steeped) and malt dust	Mangolds	560	638	78
Hants downs	5	10 0	Malt (ground) and malt dust	Mangolds	666	774	108

* The amounts of "*mineral matter*" are too high, owing to the adventitious matters retained by the

† Journal of the Royal Agricultural Society of England, vol. xii. part 2; vol. xiii. part 1; and vol. xvi.

of the *Increase in Weight* of fattening SHEEP.

Non-nitrogenous substance, to 1 nitrogenous substance, in food.	Increase upon 100 original weight.	Per cent. carcass in fasted live-weight.	Consumed to produce 100 *Increase* in live-weight.				Calculated Composition of 100 *Increase* in live-weight.			
			Mineral matter (ash).	Nitrogenous compounds (dry).	Non-nitrogenous substance.	Total dry substance.	Mineral matter (ash*).	Nitrogenous compounds (dry).	Non-nitrogenous substance (fat).	Total dry substance.
Final weight taken at the composition of the "fat sheep" analysed.										
3·51	53·1	59·6	53·7	166	582	802	2·14	7·34	67·5	77·0
3·31	44·0	57·2	63·7	187	619	870	2·01	6·34	74·2	82·5
3·31	46·8	58·0	63·6	186	616	866	2·06	6·70	71·8	80·6
3·30	46·6	58·6	63·1	185	610	858	2·05	6·67	72·0	80·7
3·28	51·4	59·5	65·6	187	613	866	2·23	8·01	63·2	' 73·5
3·26	59·9	58·9	67·2	190	620	877	2·22	7·90	63·9	74·0
					Means		2·12	7·16	68·2	78·0
Final weight taken at the composition of the "extra fat sheep" analysed.										
......	39·5	64·1	......	......	......	......	3·13	7·86	70·0	81·0
......	41·0	64·6	......	......	......	......	3·13	8·02	68·7	79·9
......	40·2	64·8	......	......	......	......	3·09	7·95	69·3	80·4
......	42·1	64·3	......	......	......	......	3·10	8·07	68·5	79·6
......	33·2	63·2	......	......	......	......	3·17	7·18	75·3	85·6
......	34·0	63·2	......	......	......	......	3·13	7·41	73·5	84·1
					Means		3·12	7·75	70·9	81·8
"fat sheep" analysed. *Final* weight taken at the composition of the "fat sheep" analysed.										
3·89	23·3	56·6	48·1	167	650	865	2·00	6·69	72·0	80·7
6·71	25·8	56·5	37·0	102	684	823	2·12	7·21	68·5	77·8
7·21	27·8	53·3	55·0	102	736	893	2·19	7·59	66·1	75·7
					Means		2·10	7·16	68·8	78·1
"fat sheep" analysed. *Final* weight taken at the composition of the "fat sheep" analysed.										
3·44	25·1	56·6	124	321	1103	1548	2·10	7·08	69·4	78·5
3·96	23·6	57·5	116	289	1144	1549	2·10	6·71	71·6	80·3
5·40	23·1	58·5	115	235	1269	1619	2·01	6·62	72·4	81·0
5·48	20·1	59·2	130	266	1458	1854	1·90	5·78	77·8	85·4
					Means		2·03	6·55	72·8	81·3
two-thirds of the difference between the "store" and "fat sheep" analysed. tion of the "fat sheep" analysed.										
6·20	15·6	58·3	55·3	118	732	905	2·10	6·67	71·8	80·6
6·10	16·1	57·9	52·0	111	677	840	2·10	6·86	70·7	79·7
6·03	18·9	57·1	58·3	121	730	909	2·17	7·68	65·4	75·3
6·04	13·9	56·6	65·0	136	822	1023	1·92	5·90	76·1	84·2
6·11	16·2	55·9	58·9	127	776	962	2·04	6·94	70·5	79·4
					Means		2·07	6·81	70·9	79·8
					General means of all		2·34	7·13	70·4	79·9

wool; the numbers for "Class II." will be the most excessive from this cause.

part 1.   ‡ Journal of the Royal Agricultural Society of England, vol. x. part 1.

TABLE X.—Showing the Calculated Percentage Com-

Note.—In all cases, *Original* Weight taken at the Composition of the " Store Pig "

			General particulars of the experiments.					
Pens.	No. of animals.	Duration.	Description of fattening food.		Actual weights (fresh), in lbs.			Total non-nitrogenous substance, to 1 nitrogenous substance, in food.
			Given in limited quantity.	Given *ad libitum.*	Original.	Final.	Increase.	
						The " Store " and " Fat		
1	1	wks. dys. 10 0	.... None	.... Bran one part, bean and lentil meal two parts, and barley meal three parts..........................	 103	 191	 88	...... 3·57
						Series 1. (For further particulars, see Journal of the		
1	3		None	Bean and lentil meal......	440	743	303	1·99
2	3		Indian meal	Bean and lentil meal......	422	758	336	2·43
4	3		Indian meal and bran...	Bean and lentil meal......	427	679	252	2·91
5	3	8 0	None	Indian meal	431	652	221	6·61
6	3		Bean and lentil meal ...	Indian meal	445	743	298	4·65
7	3		Bran	Indian meal	415	724	309	5·69
8	3		Bean and lentil meal, and bran	Indian meal	432	779	347	4·26
12	3		None	Bean and lentil meal, Indian meal and bran, each *ad libitum*	429	685	256	3·28
	24			Means	3441	5763	2322	3·48
						Series 2. (For further particulars, see Journal of the		
1	3		None	Bean and lentil meal......	433	628	195	2·17
2	3		Barley meal...............	Bean and lentil meal......	446	730	284	2·72
3	3		Bran........................	Bean and lentil meal......	405	647	242	2·29
4	3		Barley meal and bran...	Bean and lentil meal......	431	671	240	3·04
5	3	8 0	None	Barley meal·	448	739	291	6·02
6	3		Bean and lentil meal ...	Barley meal	428	679	251	3·87
7	3		Bran	Barley meal	426	703	277	5·71
8	3		Bean and lentil meal, and bran	Barley meal	419	606	187	3·71
9 and 10	6		None......................	Mixture of one part bran, two parts barley meal, and three parts bean and lentil meal	841	1377	536	3·10
11 and 12	6		None......................	Mixture of one part bran, two parts bean and lentil meal, and three parts barley meal........	827	1444	617	3·66
	36			Means	5104	8224	3120	3·37
						Series 3. (For further particulars, see Journal of the		
1	4	8 0	Dried cod-fish............	Bran and Indian meal (equal parts)	632	955	323	3·13
2	4		Dried cod-fish............	Indian meal	647	1036	389	3·80
	8			Means	1279	1991	712	3·37
						Series 4. (For further particulars, see Report of the British		
1	3		Lentil meal and bran ...	Sugar	286	533	247	4·06
2	3	10 0	Lentil meal and bran ...	Starch	285	533	248	4·06
3	3		Lentil meal and bran ...	Sugar and starch	281	555	272	4·71
4	3		None......................	Lentils, bran, sugar, starch, each *ad libitum*	292	604	312	3·90
	12			Means	1144	2223	1079	4·17
				General means ...	......	......	......	......

* These figures are somewhat corrected from those given in the Report of the British Association for the as follows :—Mineral matter 0·43, nitrogen 1·33 (equal about 8·38

position of the *Increase in Weight* of Fattening Pigs.

analysed. *Final* Weight taken at the Composition of the "Fat Pig" analysed.

Increase upon 100 original weight.	Per cent. carcass in fasted live-weight.	Consumed to produce 100 Increase in live-weight.					Calculated Composition of 100 Increase in live-weight.			
		Mineral matter (ash).	Nitrogenous compounds (dry).	Total non-nitrogenous substance (including fat).	Fatty matter.	Total dry substance.	Mineral matter (ash).	Nitrogenous compounds (dry).	Non-nitrogenous substance (fat).	Total dry substance.

Pig " actually analysed.

| | 75·7 | | | | | | | | | |
| 85·4 | 82·8 | 19·9 | 100 | 358 | 15·6 | 478 | 0·53* | 7·76* | 63·1* | 71·4* |

Royal Agricultural Society of England, vol. xiv. part 2.)

68·9	81·9	24·1	138	275	11·2	437	0·16	6·73	69·6	76·5
79·6	83·0	19·2	114	278	13·8	412	0·36	7·29	65·9	73·6
59·0	82·2	24·2	120	351	20·5	496	−0·07	6·03	74·2	80·1
51·3	85·4	17·3	57	378	26·3	452	−0·36	5·29	79·0	84·0
67·0	84·4	10·2	72	337	21·7	420	0·10	6·61	70·4	77·1
74·5	83·7	11·0	58	333	22·5	401	0·26	7·02	67·5	74·9
80·3	83·5	13·8	73	309	21·4	396	0·37	7·32	65·7	73·4
59·7	83·9	17·7	107	350	20·4	474	−0·04	6·05	73·9	79·8
67·5	83·5	17·0	93	323	19·5	433	0·09	6·54	70·8	77·4

Royal Agricultural Society of England, vol. xiv. part 2.)

45·0	......	20·8	146	317	10·5	484	−0·66	4·56	84·1	88·0
63·7	......	21·3	137	374	12·5	533	0·03	6·37	71·9	78·3
59·7	......	25·4	152	348	13·5	525	−0·04	6·07	73·8	79·8
55·7	......	22·1	125	378	14·8	525	−0·17	5·71	76·1	81·7
64·9	......	12·2	64	385	12·4	461	0·07	6·46	71·2	77·8
58·6	......	15·0	91	352	12·0	459	−0·08	5·98	74·4	80·3
65·0	......	14·7	66	378	14·1	460	0·07	6·46	71·3	77·8
44·6	......	14·8	100	372	14·6	491	−0·64	4·49	84·4	88·2
63·7	......	21·0	113	351	14·5	486	0·06	6·38	71·8	78·3
74·6	......	17·4	87	320	13·1	425	0·27	7·05	67·4	74·8
61·1	......	18·7	105	354	13·3	478	−0·10	5·95	74·6	80·5

Royal Agricultural Society of England, vol. xiv. part 2.)

51·1	84·6	34·9	104	326	25·1	464	−0·37	5·26	79·1	84·1
60·1	87·3	19·7	75	287	20·9	382	−0·03	6·12	73·6	79·7
55·7	86·0	26·6	90	303	22·8	419	−0·21	5·69	76·3	81·8

Association for the Advancement of Science for 1854.)

86·4	83·1	15·8	81	330	......	427	0·48	7·53	64·1	72·1
87·0	80·1	15·2	81	329	......	425	0·48	7·58	63·9	72·0
96·8	81·7	14·5	74	351	......	439	0·58	7·98	62·0	70·6
106·8	80·8	14·7	82	320	......	417	0·70	8·17	59·9	68·8
94·3	81·4	15·0	80	332	......	427	0·56	7·81	62·5	70·9
......	......	......	......	......	......	......	0·06	6·44	71·5	78·0

Advancement of Science for 1852, where the composition of the increase of this analysed "fat pig" is given nitrogenous compounds), 63·4 fat, and 71·8 total dry substance.

It is obvious, that the correctness of the indications of these Tables will entirely depend upon the appropriateness of the composition of the animals actually analysed in different conditions of maturity, to represent that of the animals (in their respective conditions), to which the direct analytical data are to be applied. The results must, therefore, be only looked upon as approximations; though, so far as we believe, the data now supplied constitute the most reliable basis for estimates of this kind at present at command. Indeed, in corroboration of the probable general correctness of the indications, it may be remarked, that, as fattened animals are seen to contain a much larger proportion of dry substance than leaner ones, and as their dry substance contains a larger proportion of fat, and less of nitrogenous and mineral matters, it is clear, that the *increase itself* must contain a higher percentage of total dry substance and of fatty matter, and less of nitrogenous and mineral matters, than the entire body of the fattened animal. The estimates of the composition of *increase* recorded in the Tables agree in fact very well with what we might anticipate; and they are, with some slight qualifications, in the main consistent with the *direct* results arrived at, as to the composition of the increase of the individual fattened *pig*. It should be remarked that the compositions of the animals analysed, which form the basis of these estimates of the composition of increase, are given (see Table VII.) on the *fasted* live-weight, so as to eliminate as far as possible the influence of the variable amount of contents of stomachs and intestines. The *percentages* thus calculated to the *fasted live-weight*, are, however, for the purposes of the Tables now under consideration, applied to the original and final weights of animals, in the *un*fasted condition. The tendency of the correction due on this head, would be slightly to *reduce* our estimated percentages of *fat*, and of *total dry matter*, and slightly to *raise* those for the *nitrogenous* and *mineral matters*.

With regard to *oxen*, it was difficult to find the record of experiments, in which the animals had been fed over a period of time sufficiently long to represent a change in condition equal to that assumed between the Bullock taken as "half-fat," and that analysed as "fat." As is seen, in Table VIII., the calculation has, in all, been made for ninety-eight animals; twelve of which were fed for nearly nineteen weeks; fifty for $23\frac{3}{4}$ weeks, and thirty-six for $26\frac{3}{4}$ weeks. It is probable that the estimate is the most nearly correct for the thirty-six animals, whose period under experiment was the longest, and whose proportion of increase upon 100 of their original weight was the highest. The mean of all the ninety-eight animals gives for the *composition of the increase* 75·4 per cent. of total dry substance, of which 66·2 was fat, 7·67 dry nitrogenous compounds, and 1·47 mineral matter. These figures may, perhaps, be taken as pretty nearly representing the average composition of the increase over the concluding period of half a year or more, of animals well fed on fattening food, and brought at last to a fair condition of maturity and fatness. In passing a judgment as to the probable direction of their error, we should say, that the fat and total dry matter are more likely to be given somewhat too high, and the nitrogenous matter somewhat too low.

For *sheep*, the composition of the increase has been calculated for 348 animals, in lots of never less than four, and in some cases forty or more.   These animals were all carefully selected for the purposes of experiment; their weights were accurately taken at the different periods; and, in most cases, the amount and the composition of the food they consumed were determined.   The compositions applied in the calculations to the *original* and *final* weights respectively, of the different lots, are adopted, or deduced, from those of the Sheep actually analysed, according to the reputed condition of the animals at the commencement and the conclusion of the feeding experiments.   In Class I. (see Table IX.), large numbers of animals were fed for a considerable period of time, from a fair "*store*," to a fair "*fat*" condition.   Accordingly, the composition of the "store Sheep" analysed, is applied to the original weights, and that of the "fat Sheep" to their final weights.   In Class II. the animals were fed from the "*fat*" to a "*very fat*" condition.   In these cases, therefore, the original weights are calculated at the composition of the "fat Sheep," and the final weights at that of the "extra-fat Sheep."   In Classes III. and IV. the animals were taken in a partially fattened condition, and fed to that of moderate fatness.   The per cent. of *carcass in fasted live-weight* as given in the Table, shows pretty well the comparative *final* condition of the different lots; and this was obviously not very widely different, in Classes I., III., IV., and V.   In Class III., however, the period of the feeding experiment was comparatively short; and in Class IV., though the period was longer, the food was not so well adapted; so that, in both these cases, the proportion of *increase to the original weight* is seen to average only about half as much as in Class I.   Owing to the circumstances here enumerated, the composition of the *original* weights of the Sheep of Classes III. and IV. is taken at the *mean* between that of the "store," and that of the "fat Sheep," analysed; and that of their final weights at the composition of the "fat Sheep" itself.   From considerations of a similar nature, in Class V. the original weights are taken at a composition between that of the "store" and that of the "fat Sheep"—but supposed to be *two-thirds*, instead of only one-half, advanced towards the fatter state.   The final weights are, as in most of the cases, taken at the composition of the "fat Sheep" analysed.

It will not, of course, for a moment be supposed, that the differences indicated in Table IX., between the composition of the increase of the animals of *different breeds*, or those fed on *different foods*, are really to be attributed to the variations in those conditions as there described.   It is enough to claim, that the results, as a whole, give us the best indication of the probable composition of the increase of fattening Sheep, at present at command.

To go to the figures (see Table IX.), the increase of fattening *Sheep* appeared to contain from 2 to 3 per cent. of *mineral matter*.   Either of these estimates is, however, undoubtedly too high.   The error is due to the amount of adventitious mineral matter in the ash of the wool, as before referred to, which happened to be the greater in that of the fatter animals.   It was still thought better to record the numbers in the Table as calculation gave them, as it would thus be seen (with the explanation given) *below* what amounts the truth must really fall.   In fact, excluding altogether from the calculations the ash of the wool, the percentage of mineral matter in the increase would appear to be certainly under 2, and sometimes under $1\frac{1}{2}$ per cent., for the cases of the fattening Sheep given in the Table.

The average estimated percentage of *nitrogenous compounds* in the increase of the fattening Bullocks, is 7·69; that for the fattening Sheep is, as would be expected, somewhat less, namely, 7·13. The average estimated percentage of *fat* in the increase of the Oxen is 66·2; whilst that in the Sheep is 70·4. The *direction* of the difference is, here again, that which would be anticipated. Finally, the estimated percentage of *total dry substance* in the increase of the Oxen, was 75·4; and that for the Sheep, was 79·9. Granting that the estimates for the composition of the increase of the Sheep, like those for that of the Oxen, are more probably too high than too low, still there can be little doubt, that, under at all comparable conditions, the increase of the fattening Sheep would contain a somewhat less proportion of nitrogenous matter, and a somewhat larger one of both fat and total dry substance, than that of Oxen.   On the other hand, common observation would lead to the supposition, that the increase of the fattening Pig would be less nitrogenous, and contain both more fat and more total dry substance, than that of the Sheep.

In Table X. are given the calculated estimates of the composition of the *increase* of about eighty fattening Pigs—divided into lots of three, four, or six animals each.   The composition of the increase of the analysed "fat Pig" (given at the top of the Table for the sake of comparison with the other estimates), shows 0·53* per cent. of mineral matter, 7·76 per cent. of nitrogenous compounds, 63·1 per cent. of fat, and in all, 71·4 per cent. of total dry substance.   Against these numbers, which undoubtedly represent the truth very closely for the particular case in question, the average of all the other estimates in the Table gives 0·06 per cent. of mineral matter, 6·44 per cent. of nitrogenous compounds, 71·5 per cent. of fat, and 78·0 per cent. of total dry substance. We have then, in the average of the estimated composition of the increase of these numerous fattening Pigs, rather less mineral matter and nitrogenous compounds, and several per cent. more fat and total dry substance, than in that of the single analysed "fat Pig."   Most of the animals, the composition of whose increase is thus estimated, were, however, in a somewhat further advanced condition, both at the commencement and the conclusion of the experiment, than the single analysed "fat Pig."   Some evidence of this is to be found in the relation of the "original" weights, and of the *percentages of carcass in fasted live-weight*, as recorded in the Table.   It would therefore in all probability be really the case, that in the average of the instances brought under the calculation, the *increase* would contain a less proportion of both mineral and nitrogenous matter, and a larger one of both fat and total dry substance, than that of the single

---

* These figures are somewhat corrected from those given in the Report of the British Association for the Advancement of Science for 1852, where the composition of the increase of this analysed "fat pig" is given as follows:—mineral matter 0·43, nitrogen 1·33 (equal about 8·38 nitrogenous compounds), 63·4 fat, and 71·8 total dry substance.

analysed Pig. With regard to the amount of mineral matter in the increase, attention should be called to the fact, that, according to the figures in the Table, it was always very small; whilst, in many cases, there was *apparently* no increase whatever, but even a loss of mineral matter during the fattening process. From the general character and habits of the animal, and its known tendency to fatten rather than to grow, we should indeed anticipate that the bony frame-work, which is the chief storehouse of mineral matter, would develop proportionally much less in the fattening Pig, than in either fattening Sheep or Oxen. Still, it would be hardly safe to assume, upon the evidence of the analysis of two animals alone, that there would frequently be an actual reduction of the total mineral matter of the body, during the fattening period. The alternative is to suppose, that the analysed fattened Pig was of rather lighter frame, than should have been, for strict comparison with the analysed leaner one.

The following is a Summary of these numerous estimates of *the composition of the increase of fattening oxen, sheep, and pigs*:—

TABLE XI.—Summary of the Estimated Composition of the *Increase* of fattening Oxen, Sheep, and Pigs.

Cases.	Calculated composition of 100 *Increase* whilst fattening.			
	Mineral matter.	Nitrogenous compounds (dry).	Fat.	Total dry substance.
Average for 98 Oxen	1·47	7·69	66·2	75·4
Average for 348 Sheep......................	2·34*	7·13	70·4	79·9
Average for 80 Pigs	0·06	6·44	71·5	78·0
The analysed fat Pig......................	0·53	7·76	63·1	71·4
Mean............	1·10	7·26	67·8	76·2

It would appear, that we may probably estimate the *increase* in weight of *liberally fed Oxen*, over six months or more of the final fattening period, to contain from 70 to 75 per cent. of its weight of total dry substance. Of this, by far the larger proportion, say 60 to 65 parts, will be fat; 7 to 8 parts will be nitrogenous substance; and 1 to 1¼ part mineral matter.

On the same plan of calculation, the final *increase* of *well-fed Sheep*, fattening during several months, will probably consist of 75 per cent., or more, of total dry substance; of which 65 to 70 parts will be fat; 7 to 8 parts nitrogenous compounds; and (making allowance for the error in the ash of the wool) perhaps about 1½ part of mineral matter.

The *increase* of *Pigs fed for fresh pork*, during the final two or three months on fattening food, may be taken at about 70 to 75 per cent. total dry substance, 63 to 68 per cent. of fat, 6 to 8 per cent. nitrogenous substance, and considerably less than 1 per

* Probably from 0·5 to 1·0 per cent. too high; owing to the amount of adventitious matters in the wool of the sheep analysed—particularly the fatter ones.

cent. of mineral matter. The increase over the last few months of high feeding, of *Pigs fed for curing*, will however contain *higher* percentages of both fat and total dry substance, and lower ones of both nitrogenous compounds and mineral matter, than that of the more moderately fattened animal.

From the whole of the evidence the striking fact appears, that about three-fourths of the gross increase in live-weight of animals "feeding" for the butcher, will be dry or solid matter of some kind. About two-thirds of the gross increase will be pure fat. Only about 7 or 8 per cent. of the gross increase, and scarcely more than one-tenth of its total dry substance, will be nitrogenous compounds. Lastly, such increase may frequently contain less than 1, and seldom more than 1½ per cent. of mineral matter.

Section VIII.—RELATION OF THE CONSTITUENTS STORED UP IN THE INCREASE, TO THOSE CONSUMED IN THE FOOD, BY FATTENING ANIMALS.

1. *Amounts of Mineral Matter, Nitrogenous Compounds, Non-nitrogenous substance, and Total Dry Substance, stored up in Increase, for 100 of each, consumed in Food.*

Having now arrived at approximate estimates of the *composition of the increase* accumulated by certain animals, during the final fattening period, it will be interesting to consider the probable *relation of the constituents so stored up in the increase, to those consumed in the food which produced it*. In the cases of most of the Sheep, and of all the Pigs, to which Tables IX. and X. respectively refer, the amounts of certain of the most important constituents of the food, which were consumed to produce a given weight of the increase whose composition is there estimated, had previously been determined, and are, for the sake of reference, recorded in the Tables, by the side of the estimated composition of the increase itself which was due to their consumption: that is to say, by the side of the estimated amounts of mineral matter, of nitrogenous compounds, of non-nitrogenous organic substance, and of total dry substance, respectively, contained in 100 lbs. of the increase in live-weight, there is recorded in the Tables, the amount of each of these consumed in the production of that 100 lbs. of increase. We have thus the easy means of estimating the proportion of each of these classes of constituents stored up in the increase, for 100 parts of the same consumed in the fattening food. The results of such a calculation are given in Table XII. for the different lots of Sheep, and in Table XIII. for the different lots of Pigs.

TABLE XII.—Showing the Estimated Proportion of certain constituents stored up in the *Increase of Weight* of Fattening SHEEP, for 100 of each, consumed in food.

	General particulars of the experiments.					Amount of each class of constituents stored up in increase for 100 of the same consumed in food.		
Breed.	Number of animals.	Dura- tion.	Description of fattening food.		Mineral matter (ash)*.	Nitro- genous com- pounds (dry).	Non-ni- trogenous sub- stance.	Total dry sub- stance.
			Given in limited quantity.	Given *ad libitum*.				
Class I. (For data, see Class I. Table IX.)								
Cotswolds	46	wks. days. 19 5	Oilcake and clover hay	Swedish turnips	3·98	4·43	11·6	9·60
Leicesters	40	20 0	Oilcake and clover hay	Swedish turnips	3·15	3·39	12·0	9·48
Cross-bred wethers	40	20 0	Oilcake and clover hay	Swedish turnips	3·24	3·60	11·6	9·31
Cross-bred ewes......	40	20 0	Oilcake and clover hay	Swedish turnips	3·25	3·60	11·8	9·40
Hants downs	40	26 0	Oilcake and clover hay	Swedish turnips	3·40	4·28	10·3	8·49
Sussex downs.........	40	26 0	Oilcake and clover hay	Swedish turnips	3·30	4·16	10·3	8·44
				Means	3·39	3·91	11·3	9·12
Class III. (For data, see Class III. Table IX.)								
Hants downs	5	13 6	Oilcake	Swedish turnips	4·18	4·01	11·1	9·33
Hants downs	5	13 6	Oats...............................	Swedish turnips	5·73	7·07	10·0	9·45
Hants downs	5	13 6	Clover chaff.....................	Swedish turnips	3·98	7·44	9·0	8·49
				Means	4·62	6·17	10·0	9·09
Class IV. (For data, see Class IV. Table IX.)								
Hants downs	5	19 1	Oilcake	Clover chaff......	1·69	2·20	6·3	5·07
Hants downs	5	19 1	Linseed	Clover chaff......	1·81	2·32	6·2	5·19
Hants downs	5	19 1	Barley	Clover chaff......	1·75	2·82	5·7	5·00
Hants downs	5	19 1	Malt................................	Clover chaff......	1·46	2·17	5·3	4·61
				Means	1·68	2·38	5·9	4·97
Class V. (For data, see Class V. Table IX.)								
Hants downs	4	10 0	Barley (ground)	Mangolds.........	3·80	5·65	9·8	8·91
Hants downs	5	10 0	Malt (ground) and malt dust....	Mangolds.........	4·04	6·18	10·4	9·49
Hants downs	4	10 0	Barley (ground and *steeped*) ...	Mangolds.........	3·72	6·35	8·9	8·28
Hants downs	4	10 0	{ Malt (ground and *steeped*) and malt dust .... }	Mangolds.........	2·95	4·34	9·3	8·23
Hants downs	5	10 0	Malt (ground) and malt dust....	Mangolds.........	3·46	5·46	9·1	8·25
				Means	3·59	5·60	9·5	8·63
				General means...	3·27	4·41	9·4	8·06

* The amounts of "*mineral matter*" are too high, owing to the adventitious matters retained by the wool.

TABLE XIII.—Showing the Estimated Proportion of certain constituents stored up in the *Increase of Weight* of Fattening PIGS, for 100 of each, consumed in food.

Pens.	Number of animals.	Duration.	Description of fattening food.		Mineral matter (ash).	Nitrogenous compounds (dry).	Non-nitrogenous substance.	Total dry substance.	Fat.
			Given in limited quantities.	Given *ad libitum*.					
			The "Fat Pig" analysed.						
	1	wks.days 10 0	None	Bran one part, bean and lentil meal two parts, and barley meal three parts	2·66	7·76	17·6	14·9	405
			Series 1* (For data, see Series 1. Table X.).						
1	3		None	Bean and lentil meal	0·68	4·86	25·3	17·5	621
2	3		Indian meal	Bean and lentil meal	1·86	6·39	23·7	17·9	477
4	3		Indian meal and bran	Bean and lentil meal	-0·33	5·02	21·1	16·1	362
5	3		None	Indian meal	-2·09	9·28	20·9	18·6	300
6	3	8 0	Bean and lentil meal	Indian meal	0·99	9·18	20·9	18·4	324
7	3		Bran	Indian meal	2·35	12·10	20·3	18·7	300
8	3		Bean and lentil meal, and bran	Indian meal	2·71	10·03	21·3	18·5	307
12	3		None	Bean and lentil meal, Indian meal and bran, each *ad libitum*	-0·22	5·65	21·1	16·8	362
				Means	0·74	7·82	21·6	17·8	382
			Series 2* (For data, see Series 2. Table X.).						
1	3		None	Bean and lentil meal	-3·90	3·12	26·5	18·2	801
2	3		Barley meal	Bean and lentil meal	0·16	4·65	19·2	14·7	575
3	3		Bran	Bean and lentil meal	-0·16	3·99	21·2	15·2	547
4	3		Barley meal and bran	Bean and lentil meal	-0·75	4·57	20·1	15·6	514
5	3	8 0	None	Barley meal	0·56	10·09	18·5	16·9	574
6	3		Bean and lentil meal	Barley meal	-0·53	6·57	21·1	17·5	620
7	3		Bran	Barley meal	0·49	9·79	18·9	16·9	506
8	3		Bean and lentil meal, and bran	Barley meal	-4·33	4·49	22·7	18·0	578
9 and 10	3		None	Mixture of one part bran, two parts barley meal, and three parts bean and lentil meal	0·27	5·85	20·4	16·1	495
11 and 12	3		None	Mixture of one part bran, two parts bean and lentil meal, and three parts barley meal	1·58	8·10	21·1	17·6	515
				Means	-0·59	6·10	21·0	16·7	572
			Series 3* (For data, see Series 3. Table X.).						
1	4	8 0	Dried cod-fish	Bran and Indian meal (equal parts)	-1·06	5·06	24·3	18·1	315
2	4		Dried cod-fish	Indian meal	-0·26	8·16	25·6	20·9	352
				Means	-0·66	6·61	24·9	19·5	333
			Series 4† (For data, see Series 4. Table X.).						
1	3		Lentil meal and bran	Sugar	3·07	9·30	19·4	16·9	
2	3		Lentil meal and bran	Starch	3·18	9·36	19·4	16·9	
3	3	10 0	Lentil meal and bran	Sugar and starch	4·06	10·78	17·7	16·1	
4	3		None	Lentils, bran, sugar, starch, each *ad libitum*	4·80	9·98	18·7	16·5	
				Means	3·78	9·85	18·8	16·6	
				General means	0·58	7·34	21·2	17·3	472

* Journal of the Royal Agricultural Society of England, vol. xiv. part 2.
† Report of the British Association for the Advancement of Science for 1854.

It will be observed, by reference to the columns in Tables IX. and X. respectively, which show the proportion of the total *non-nitrogenous* to the total *nitrogenous* constituents of the food, that it was in some cases nearly double as much as in others. It might be urged, therefore, that it was quite irrelevant to apply one and the same composition to the final weights of animals fattened on foods differing so widely in this respect. It is not denied, that, other things being equal, a highly nitrogenous food may give some tendency to a greater proportion of increase in frame and flesh; but all observation would lead to the conclusion, that, at least with animals fattening under ordinary conditions, this would happen but in a very limited degree; in fact, by no means in anything like a numerical proportion to the increased relation of the nitrogenous to the non-nitrogenous constituents of the food. It has been found, indeed, that as our current fattening food-stuffs go, the increase in weight is more in proportion to the amount of digestible *non-nitrogenous*, or *total dry organic substance*, than to that of the nitrogenous compounds consumed. And, although with a high proportion of available *non*-nitrogenous matter in the food there is a somewhat less tendency to increase in frame, and a greater one to fatten, yet animals which have been fed on very highly nitrogenous food, though as a rule they have appeared to grow somewhat more, have nevertheless frequently been extremely fat. Upon the whole then it is concluded, that the relation of the nitrogenous matter to the fat, in the *increase* of the fattening animal, is by no means increased in the degree which might be expected, by a considerable increase in the proportion of the nitrogenous to the non-nitrogenous compounds in the food. The proportion of the nitrogenous matters in the increase is, there is little doubt, much more affected by the age and habits of the animal than by the proportion (if not below a certain limit) of the nitrogenous constituents in the food. From these considerations, and owing to the comparatively small proportion of the several constituents of the food actually stored up and retained in the increase, any error arising from adopting the same composition for the final weights of animals fattened on very various foods, will be immaterial in forming general and average estimates of the proportion of the constituents stored up in the increase, to those consumed in the food. With these explanations then, and calling attention to the reservations which they obviously imply, we adopt as they stand, for the basis of our calculations, the records of constituents actually consumed, and the estimates of the composition of the increase produced as given in Tables IX. and X. respectively, and proceed at once to consider the indications so obtained.

From Table XII. it is seen, that taking the average of the numerous experiments with Sheep, rather more than 3 per cent. of the *total mineral matter* consumed in the fattening food would appear to be retained in the increase. Assuming the due correction made for the extraneous mineral matter in the wool of the fat animals analysed, the average of the cases in question would show rather less than 3 per cent. of the mineral matter consumed, to be stored up in the increase. In Class IV. dry food alone was given, and such as contained a large proportion of mineral matter to digestible organic substance. In this case, therefore, the *proportion* of the consumed mineral matter which appears to be

4 B

stored up in increase, is relatively very small—namely, only 1·68 per cent. The other Classes, however, in which there was a limited proportion of dry food, and the remainder consisted of succulent roots, much more nearly represent the usual conditions of the food of fattening Sheep. Upon the whole, it may be concluded, as an average estimate for Sheep fattening for the butcher on good mixed diet of dry and succulent food, that they will certainly not carry off more, and perhaps frequently less, than 3 per cent. of the consumed mineral matter. Were it not indeed that Sheep are now generally fattened when still young and growing, the proportion of the mineral matter consumed which would be retained during the so-called fattening period, would probably be extremely small. In fact, it can hardly be greater, on the average, than above supposed, taking the whole period of existence of the animal. But it is obvious, that the proportion will depend much more on the character of the food, as to the quantitative relation of its mineral matter to its available organic substance, than upon any other circumstance. At any rate, the proportion of the mineral matter consumed by either store or fattened animals, which is sent off the farm in their bodies, is comparatively small; and from the percentage indicated in the *live-weight* of the animals in the different conditions, as given in Table VII., the annual exhaustion of the farm from the sale of known weights of animals is a matter of easy calculation.

Table XII. shows the estimated proportion of the total *nitrogenous compounds* retained in the increase of the fattening Sheep, to have been, on the average, less than 5 per cent. of that consumed in the food. Assuming a liberal mixed diet of succulent roots and dry food, it is probable that when the latter consists chiefly of pulse, oilcake, or other highly nitrogenous matter, the proportion of the nitrogen consumed which will be carried off in the increase of animal, will be less than 5, and perhaps even less than 4 per cent. On the other hand, when the dry food consists to any great extent of cereal grain or other food containing a comparatively low percentage of nitrogen, it is probable that more than 5 per cent. of the total nitrogen consumed will be carried off in increase. It will be observed, that on either supposition, the proportion of nitrogen expired, perspired, or voided, will be considerably more than 90 per cent., whilst it may be more than 95 per cent., of the total nitrogen consumed by the fattening Sheep.

It appears that for 100 parts of *non*-nitrogenous substance consumed in food, there were on the average (excluding Class IV.) about 10 stored up in the fattening sheep, in the form of *fat itself*.

For 100 of *total dry substance* of the food, about 8 or 9 of dry substance would appear to be stored up in the increase of the animal. It will be remembered, that in the dry substance of the food of the Sheep, there is, compared with that of the Pig, a considerably larger amount of indigestible woody fibre. There is, therefore, a larger proportion of the consumed food necessarily at once effete.

Table XIII., which relates to the *Pigs*, would show that there is probably fully twice as much dry substance stored up for 100 consumed, as in the case of Sheep. The average of *all* the estimates shows 17·3 per cent. of the consumed dry substance stored up in the increase, against about 15 per cent. in the case of the *individual analysed fat pig*. As just stated, there were, in the case of the Sheep, only about 9 parts of dry substance stored up in increase, for 100 total dry substance consumed.

For 100 of *non*-nitrogenous constituents of food, the Pigs would seem to have stored up 20 or more of *fat*, whilst the Sheep yielded only half that amount.

Of *nitrogenous* compounds again, it would appear, according to the estimates, that there was on the average about one and a half time as much of the whole consumed stored up in the increase, as in the case of Sheep. The *average* of the estimates for the Pigs, shows 7·34 per cent. of the consumed nitrogen stored up, against 7·6 per cent. in the case of the *analysed fat pig*. The greater the proportion of pulse in the fattening food of the Pig, the smaller will be the *proportion* of the whole nitrogen consumed, which will be stored up in the increase. And on the other hand, the larger the proportion of cereal, with its comparatively small percentage of nitrogen, the larger will be the *proportion* of the whole carried off in the increase in weight of the animals. The evidence at command would lead to the belief, however, that there is almost uniformly less than 10 per cent., and sometimes perhaps as little as 5 per cent. of the nitrogen of the food of the *fattening pig* carried off in its increase.

It has already been pointed out, how small, in all probability, was the percentage of *mineral matter* in the increase of the rapidly fattening Pig. Reasons were given for supposing, however, that our estimates might show it to be lower than really was the case. There is little use therefore in examining at all closely results which are based upon those doubtful estimates. Moreover as the mineral matter in the food varies very much indeed in its proportion to those constituents which prominently rule the amount and character of the increase, the proportion of the mineral matter consumed by the fattening Pig, as well as the fattening Sheep, which will be stored up in the increase, will be much more variable than that of the other constituents. It is sufficient to say, that in the case of fattening Pigs at least, the proportion of the consumed mineral matter which will not be reclaimed in the manure is almost immaterial.

Finally, in regard to the results of Table XIII., it appears that for every 100 parts of *fatty matter* in the food there were probably, on the average (depending on the character of the food), 400 to 500 parts of *fat* stored up in the increase of the animal. It is obvious, therefore, that there was a *formation* of fat in the animal body, from some other constituent or constituents of the food. To this point we shall recur presently.

2. *Amounts of Mineral Matter, Nitrogenous Compounds, Fat, and Total Dry Substance stored up in Increase, and of matter expired, perspired, or voided, for 100 of Collective Dry Substance consumed in Food.*

Having by means of Tables XII. and XIII. shown the probable proportion of each of certain constituents of the food of fattening Sheep and Pigs, which will be stored up in the increase of the fattening animals for 100 of the same consumed in the food, it will be well to follow up the illustration by showing, on the same basis of calculation, how much of the several constituents would be stored up in the increase *for 100 of the collective dry substance of the foods consumed*; and lastly, how much of the whole would be *expired, perspired,* or *voided.* These particulars are shown in Table XIV. for the different sets of Sheep, and in Table XV. for the different sets of Pigs.

TABLE XIV.—Showing the Final Distribution of the Constituents of the Food consumed by fattening SHEEP.

Breed.	Number of animals.	Duration.	Description of fattening food. Given in limited quantity.	Given *ad libitum.*	Mineral matter (ash*).	Nitrogenous compounds (dry).	Non-nitrogenous substance (fat).	Total dry Increase.	Expired, perspired, or voided.
			Class I. (For data, see Class I. Table IX.)						
Cotswolds	46	wks. days. 19 5	Oilcake and clover hay	Swedish turnips	0·26	0·02	8·41	9·00	90·40
Leicesters	40	20 0	Oilcake and clover hay	Swedish turnips	0·23	0·73	8·53	9·48	90·52
Cross-bred wethers......	40	20 0	Oilcake and clover hay	Swedish turnips	0·24	0·77	8·29	9·31	90·63
Cross-bred ewes......	40	20 0	Oilcake and clover hay	Swedish turnips	0·24	0·78	8·39	9·41	90·59
Hants downs.........	40	26 0	Oilcake and clover hay	Swedish turnips	0·26	0·93	7·30	8·49	91·51
Sussex downs.........	40	26 0	Oilcake and clover hay	Swedish turnips	0·25	0·90	7·29	8·44	91·56
			Means		0·25	0·84	8·03	9·12	90·88
			Class III. (For data, see Class III. Table IX.)						
Hants downs	5	13 6	Oilcake	Swedish turnips	0·23	0·77	8·32	9·31	90·69
Hants downs	5	13 6	Oats	Swedish turnips	0·25	0·88	8·32	9·45	90·55
Hants downs	5	13 6	Clover chaff	Swedish turnips	0·24	0·85	7·40	8·49	91·51
			Means		0·24	0·83	8·01	9·08	90·92
			Class IV. (For data, see Class IV. Table IX.)						
Hants downs	5	19 1	Oilcake	Clover chaff......	0·13	0·46	4·48	5·07	94·93
Hants downs	5	19 1	Linseed	Clover chaff......	0·14	0·43	4·62	5·19	94·81
Hants downs	5	19 1	Barley	Clover chaff......	0·12	0·41	4·47	5·00	95·00
Hants downs	5	19 1	Malt............................	Clover chaff......	0·10	0·31	4·20	4·61	95·39
			Means		0·12	0·40	4·44	4·97	95·03
			Class V. (For data, see Class V. Table IX.)						
Hants downs	4	10 0	Barley (ground)	Mangolds........	0·24	0·74	7·93	8·91	91·09
Hants downs	5	10 0	Malt (ground) and malt dust....	Mangolds	0·25	0·62	8·42	9·49	90·51
Hants downs	4	10 0	Barley (ground and *steeped*) ..	Mangolds........	0·24	0·84	7·20	8·28	91·72
Hants downs	4	10 0	{ Malt (ground and *steeped*) } and malt dust	Mangolds........	0·19	0·58	7·45	8·23	91·77
Hants downs	5	10 0	Malt (ground) and malt dust.........	Mangolds........	0·21	0·72	7·33	8·25	91·75
			Means		0·23	0·74	7·66	8·63	91·37
			General means..............		0·21	0·72	7·13	8·06	91·94

* The estimated amounts of mineral matter are too high, owing to the adventitious matter retained by the wool.

TABLE XV.—Showing the Final Distribution of the Constituents of the Food consumed by fattening PIGS.

Pens.	Number of animals.	Duration.	Description of fattening food. Given in limited quantity.	Given ad libitum.	Mineral matter (ash).	Nitrogenous compounds (dry).	Non-nitrogenous substance (fat).	Total dry Increase.	Expired, per-spired, or voided.
The "Fat Pig" analysed.									
1	1	wks.days 10 0	None	Bran one part, bean and lentil meal two parts, and barley meal three parts	0·11	1·62	13·20	14·94	85·06
Series 1 (For data, see Series 1. Table X.).									
1	3		None	Bean and lentil meal	0·04	1·54	15·93	17·51	82·49
2	3		Indian meal	Bean and lentil meal	0·09	1·77	16·00	17·86	82·14
4	3		Indian meal and bran	Bean and lentil meal	−0·01	1·21	14·95	16·15	83·85
5	3	8 0	None	Indian meal	−0·08	1·17	17·48	18·38	81·42
6	3		Bean and lentil meal	Indian meal	0·02	1·57	16·76	18·35	81·65
7	3		Bran	Indian meal	0·07	1·75	16·83	18·68	81·32
8	3		Bean and lentil meal, and bran	Indian meal	0·09	1·85	16·59	18·53	81·47
12	3		None	Bean and lentil meal, indian meal and bran, each ad libitum	−0·01	1·27	15·59	16·84	83·16
				Means	0·03	1·51	16·27	17·81	82·19
Series 2 (For data, see Series 2. Table X.).									
1	3		None	Bean and lentil meal	−0·13	0·94	17·37	18·18	81·82
2	3		Barley meal	Bean and lentil meal	0·01	1·19	13·49	14·69	85·31
3	3		Bran	Bean and lentil meal	−0·01	1·15	14·06	15·20	84·80
4	3		Barley meal and bran	Bean and lentil meal	−0·03	1·09	14·50	15·56	84·44
5	3	8 0	None	Barley meal	0·02	1·40	15·45	16·87	83·13
6	3		Bean and lentil meal	Barley meal	−0·02	1·30	16·21	17·49	82·51
7	3		Bran	Barley meal	0·01	1·40	15·50	16·91	83·09
8	3		Bean and lentil meal, and bran	Barley meal	−0·13	0·91	17·18	17·96	82·04
9 and 10	6		None	Mixture, one part bran, two parts barley meal, and three parts bean and lentil meal	0·01	1·31	14·77	16·11	83·89
11 and 12	6		None	Mixture, one part bran, two parts bean and lentil meal, and three parts barley meal	0·06	1·66	15·88	17·60	82·40
				Means	−0·02	1·23	15·44	16·66	83·34
Series 3 (For data, see Series 3. Table X.).									
1	4	8 0	Dried cod-fish	Bran and Indian meal (equal parts)	−0·08	1·13	17·05	18·12	81·88
2	4		Dried cod-fish	Indian meal	−0·01	1·60	19·27	20·86	79·14
				Means	−0·04	1·36	18·16	19·49	80·51
Series 4 (For data, see Series 4. Table X.).									
1	3		Lentil meal and bran	Sugar	0·11	1·76	15·01	16·88	83·12
2	3		Lentil meal and bran	Starch	0·11	1·78	15·04	16·94	83·06
3	3	10 0	Lentil meal and bran	Sugar and starch	0·13	1·82	14·13	16·08	83·92
4	3		None	Lentils, bran, sugar, starch, each ad libitum	0·19	1·96	14·36	16·50	83·50
				Means	0·13	1·83	14·03	16·00	83·40
				General means	0·02	1·44	15·81	17·27	82·73

As already explained, in the cases to which these and the preceding Tables relating to Increase refer, the amounts and composition of the foods consumed to produce a given amount of increase, were determined by actual experiment; and the composition of the increase so produced, is deduced from that of the animals that were analysed. Thus, in Table IX. for the Sheep, and in Table X. for the Pigs, are given the experimentally determined amounts of dry substance, &c., consumed to produce 100 lbs. of increase in live-weight, and the estimated amounts of certain constituents in that 100 lbs. of increase. It is obvious, therefore, that we have an easy means of calculating the amount of the respective constituents stored up in increase, for 100 of dry matter consumed. The sum of these makes up *the total dry matter in increase for* 100 *dry matter in food*; and the difference between this dry matter in increase and that in food represents the amount *expired, perspired, or voided*. With these observations, the mode of construction of Tables XIV. and XV. will be sufficiently intelligible.

It was seen (in Table XII.), that in the Sheep there was probably an average of about 9 parts dry substance fixed as increase for 100 consumed in food. Table XIV. shows (taking the cases in which the food was of the most usual description) that about 8 parts out of the 9 of dry increase were non-nitrogenous substance—that is *fat*. It results then, that for 100 of dry substance in food, there would be little more than 1 part fixed in increase in other forms than fat;—that is, as nitrogenous and mineral matters put together. According to the Table there were only, in Class I., 0·84, in Class III. 0·83, and in Class V. 0·74 part of nitrogenous substance retained in the increase of the animals for 100 of collective dry substance in their food. The corresponding amounts of mineral matter fixed were, on the same basis of calculation, for Class I. 0·25, for Class III. 0·24, and for Class V. 0·23. But if due allowance were made for the excess in the estimate of the mineral matters in the increase, as before noticed, the average amount of them stored up for 100 of dry food consumed, would, in the cases in question, be about 0·2.

Taking the average of the cases in which the Sheep were fed upon food of a nature fairly representing that of the animals liberally fed for the butcher, it is assumed then, that for 100 parts of dry matter of such food, only about 9 parts were stored up as increase. There remained, therefore, 91 parts *expired, perspired, or voided*. In the food of Sheep (and of oxen also), the proportion of so-called "woody fibre" is very much greater than in that of Pigs. With the former, therefore, there will be a larger proportion of indigestible matter voided than with the latter; and, as will presently be seen, with the larger proportion of digestible or assimilable matter in the food of the fattening Pig, there is at the same time a less proportion of the consumed dry substance expired, perspired, or voided.

At the head of the other results in Table XV. are given the amounts of the main classes of constituents stored up in increase for 100 of collective dry matter in food in the case of the *analysed* "fat Pig." From the circumstances under which the data were obtained in this particular instance, it may be assumed that the figures exceedingly closely represent the actual facts. The indication is that, for 100 of dry matter of food consumed by this single fattening Pig, there were produced 14·94 parts of dry substance of increase.   Of these 14·94 parts of total dry increase, 13·2 were fat, 1·62 nitrogenous compounds, and 0·11 mineral matter.   Against these numbers we have, taking *the average of all the other estimates* (twenty-four in number, and comprising 80 animals), 17·27 total dry increase for 100 of dry food; of which 15·81 are estimated as fat, 1·44 nitrogenous substance, and an insignificant amount of mineral matter. It is admitted that the estimates in Table XIV. relating to the Sheep, show a higher proportion of mineral to other constituents, stored up, than was probably the fact.   On the other hand, the estimates of assimilated mineral matter in the case of the Pigs are probably in error in the other direction.   It is true, that Pigs, though young, if put upon highly fattening food will grow comparatively little in frame, whilst Sheep, fed as they now generally are at a comparatively early age, will develop more of hard bony structure.   It would be expected, therefore, that the proportion of mineral matter in the increase of fattening Sheep would be greater than that in fattening Pigs.   Indeed, Table VII. shows the percentage of mineral matter, in the total carcasses, to be more than twice as much in the fattened Sheep analysed, as in the fat Pig.   In the case of both Sheep and Oxen moreover, there seems to be a striking parallelism in the proportion of the mineral to the nitrogenous matters of growth; whilst with the Pig, not only is the actual amount of mineral matter much less, but its proportion to the nitrogenous matters seems to decrease as the animals fatten.   Thus, looking to the composition of the *carcasses* alone, in which there would be no error in the mineral matter as when the hair or wool with its extraneous dirt is brought into the calculation, it is found that the amount of mineral matter to 1 of nitrogenous substance, was—in the lean Ox 0·31, in the fat Ox 0·30, in the store Sheep 0·30, in the fat Sheep 0·30, and in the very fat Sheep 0·30.   On the other hand, in the carcass of the store Pig, the proportion of mineral matter to 1 of nitrogenous substance was 0·183, and in that of the fat Pig it was less still, or 0·133. From these considerations it is obvious, that the amount of mineral matter in the *increase* of the fattening Pig, will be much less both in proportion to the total increase itself, and to the coincidently accumulated nitrogenous compounds, than in that of the Sheep.   The distinctions which the Tables relating to the composition of increase show, between the two descriptions of animal in this respect, are then, without doubt, correct in the main ;— that is to say, at least in their *direction*, though probably *not* in the *degree* which the actual figures indicate.   It is pretty certain that the estimates of mineral matter in the increase of the Sheep are somewhat too high; and unless it be admitted as probable, that Pigs rapidly increasing in weight under the fattening process, may sometimes not only not fix any mineral matter whatever, but even lose some of that already fixed, it must be concluded, that the Pig killed and analysed as fat, had too small a proportion of bony structure to be strictly comparable with the one analysed in the leaner state.

It will be obvious, from the very nature of the subject, that these estimates of the composition of *increase*, must only be taken as applicable for any general purposes, after due regard to the various qualifying circumstances which have been pointed out.

It will be remembered, that in the average of the cases in which the Sheep had been fed upon a liberal mixed diet of dry food and succulent roots—admittedly favourable conditions for their increase—they gave only about 9 per cent. of dry increase, for 100 dry substance of food. The average of the 24 lots of Pigs (80 animals), shows on the other hand, nearly double as much, or 17·27 parts of dry increase, for 100 of dry food consumed. The yield of fat, and of nitrogenous compounds, of which these 17·27 parts are chiefly made up, is of course higher in a corresponding degree. When it is borne in mind, however, that the natural fattening food of the Pig consists chiefly of ripened seeds containing little indigestible woody fibre, or immatured vegetable products, and that that of the Sheep contains a large proportion of woody fibre, and also much of the less highly elaborated vegetable compounds, it will not appear surprising, that 100 parts of the dry substance of the food of the Pig should yield so much more of dry animal increase, than 100 parts of that of the Sheep. It results, of course, that of the fattening food of the Pig, a less proportion of the dry substance than of that of Sheep, will be *expired, perspired*, or *voided*. In the case of the Sheep, it was assumed, as the average of the cases wherein the food was of the most favourable kind, that about 91 per cent. of the dry substance consumed were in some form expired, perspired, or voided. In the case of the single analysed Pig, only 85 parts were expired, perspired, or voided, for 100 of dry matter consumed in food. And, taking the average of the twenty-four lots comprising the eighty animals, calculation shows only 82·7 parts of collective dry substance expired, perspired, or voided, for 100 consumed in the food.

In speaking of the proportion of dry substance stored up in increase, for a given amount consumed in food, it will not for a moment be assumed, that it is herein implied that the relation of the ultimate elements is the same in the dry matter assimilated and fixed, and in that given off in the various forms from the system. The very various amounts, respectively of mineral matter, of nitrogenous compounds, and of non-nitrogenous substance (fat), stored up for 100 of each consumed (as shown in Tables XII. and XIII.), give some means of judging how different must be the ultimate composition of the gross dry matter fixed in the body, from that of the matters of the food eliminated from it. It is not within the scope and object of the present Paper, to give any further indication of the composition of the matters collectively given off from the body in relation to those taken as food, than is implied in the figures in the Tables just referred to, which show the amounts of certain constituents stored up for a given amount consumed—the complementary quantity being of course that which is expired, perspired, or voided. Still less is it to our present purpose, to show the proportion of the different constituents of the matters collectively given out from the body, which will be respectively exhaled by the lungs, perspired by the skin, or voided in the liquid or the solid form. There is, however, one point in connection with the difference between the ultimate composition of the dry substance of increase, and that of the compounds of the food which produced it, which may be here appropriately illustrated; this is, the relation of the *fat in the increase*, to the *fat and other matters in the food*, which yielded it.

3. *Relation of the Fat stored up in the Increase, to the ready-formed Fat, and other Constituents, consumed in the Food ; &c.*

The amount of *fat* in the food of the different lots of Sheep which have served in the foregoing illustrations, was not determined, so that the relation of that estimated as stored up in increase, to that *ready-formed* in the food, cannot be shown in their case.

In the majority of the experiments with the Pigs, the amount of *ready-formed fat* in the food was determined. The amount stored up in the increase, has also been legitimately deduced from experimental evidence. The results show, as already noticed, that there were on the average, between 400 and 500 parts of Fat stored up in the increase, for 100 of Fatty matter consumed in food. In the case of the analysed fat Pig, there were 405 parts of Fat stored up for 100 consumed. The result in this instance was obtained in as direct a manner as the nature of the question will admit of, and it may be taken as representing the truth very closely. The average of the other experiments shows 472 parts of Fat in increase, for 100 ready-formed in food. Nor is there much reason to doubt the general accuracy of this latter indication. Upon the whole, it is obvious, that a large proportion of the Fat of the fattening animal is *produced* from *other constituents than Fat* in the food. Attention has elsewhere been called to the evidence of this, afforded in the instance of the analysed fat Pig[*]. It was shown that in its case rather more than three-fourths of the Fat of the increase gained on the fattening food, must have been formed in the body *from other constituents*; and it was pointed out, that if the *produced* Fat were due to the *Starch* of the food, it would require about $2\frac{1}{4}$ parts of that substance, to yield 1 part of Fat. On this supposition, it is obvious, that a much larger proportion of the non-nitrogenous constituents of the food, will directly contribute to the non-nitrogenous substance of the increase (fat), than is represented by the total amount of the Fat itself, stored up. It is equally obvious, that the proportion of the total dry substance of the food consumed, which has (if we may draw such a distinction) directly contributed to the dry matter of increase, including the produced Fat, will be much greater than that indicated by the total amount of the dry substance of the increase. The proportion which is expired, perspired, or voided, without having, in the sense implied, directly contributed to increase, will, of course, in a complementary degree, be less than the total amount represented as expired, perspired, or voided.

To illustrate, numerically, the points above alluded to, there are shown, in Table XVI., for the analysed fat Pig, and for most of the sets of Pigs before under consideration—the amount of Fat stored up in the increase for 100 of dry matter of food consumed; the proportion of Fat already formed in the food; the amount that must have been *produced* from other compounds; the amount of Starch that would be required if the produced Fat were formed from it; the proportion of the total dry matter consumed, which would be thus required directly to contribute to the fixed increase; and lastly, the proportion that would be expired, perspired, or voided, without thus directly contributing to the fixed increase.

[*] Report of the British Association for the Advancement of Science for 1852.

TABLE XVI.—Showing—the Amount of Fat stored up in the Increase of Fattening Pigs, for 100 of Dry Matter of Food consumed; the Proportion of Fat already formed in the Food; the Amount of Fat that must have been *produced* from other Compounds; the Amount of Starch that would be required if the produced Fat were formed from it; the Proportion of Total Dry Matter consumed, which would thus be required directly to contribute to the fixed Increase, &c.

General particulars of the experiment.						**100 dry matter of food gave—**						**Summary.**		
Pens.	No. of animals.	Duration.	Description of fattening food. Given in limited quantity.	Given *ad libitum*.		Total dry increase.	Total fat in increase.	Fat already formed in the food.	Fat produced from starch, &c.	Starch required for the produced fat.	Ready-formed fat, and starch in the food, contributing to the total fat in increase.	Nitrogenous and mineral matter, fixed in the increase.	Total dry matter of food fixed or contributing to the fixed increase.	Expired, perspired, or voided, without directly contributing to the fixed increase.
		wks / dys												
1	10	10 / 0	Bean one part, bean and lentil meal two parts, and barley meal three parts...	None		14·94	13·20	3·26	9·94	24·85	28·11	1·73	29·84	70·16
				The "Fat Pig" analysed.										
			Series 1 (For data, see Series 1, Table X., XIII., and XV.).											
1	3		None	Bean and lentil meal		17·51	15·93	2·89	13·04	32·60	35·49	1·58	37·07	69·93
2	3		Indian meal	Bean and lentil meal		17·86	16·00	3·66	12·34	30·85	34·51	1·86	36·37	63·63
4	3		Indian meal and bran	Bean and lentil meal		16·15	14·95	4·59	10·36	25·90	30·49	1·20	31·69	69·31
5	3	8 / 0	None	Indian meal		18·55	17·43	6·15	11·28	28·32	34·47	1·09	35·56	64·44
6	3		Indian meal	Indian meal		16·76	16·76	5·43	11·33	28·33	33·75	1·59	35·34	64·66
7	3		Bran	Indian meal		16·68	16·88	6·31	10·53	26·30	32·61	1·98	34·43	65·57
8	3		Bean and lentil meal	Indian meal		16·53	16·59	5·64	10·95	27·37	33·01	1·94	34·95	65·05
12	3		Bean and lentil meal, Indian meal and bran, each *ad libitum*.			16·84	15·59	4·65	10·94	27·35	33·00	1·26	33·26	66·74
			Means			17·81	16·97	4·99	11·35	28·39	33·29	1·54	34·83	65·17
			Series 2 (For data, see Series 2, Tables X., XIII., and XV.).											
1	3		None	Bean and lentil meal		18·18	17·37	2·40	14·97	37·49	39·83	0·81	40·63	59·37
2	3		Barley meal	Bean and lentil meal		14·69	13·49	2·55	10·94	27·35	29·90	1·20	31·10	68·90
3	3		Bran	Bean and lentil meal		15·20	14·06	2·85	11·21	28·02	30·87	1·14	32·01	67·99
4	3		Barley meal and bran	Bean and lentil meal		15·56	14·50	3·08	11·42	28·55	31·63	1·06	32·69	67·31
5	3	8 / 0	None	Barley meal		16·87	15·45	2·83	13·02	31·55	34·38	1·42	35·80	64·20
6	3		Bean and lentil meal	Barley meal		17·49	16·21	2·91	13·40	33·50	36·31	1·28	37·59	62·41
7	3		Bran	Barley meal		16·91	15·60	3·27	12·23	30·57	33·84	1·41	35·25	64·75
8	3		Bean and lentil meal, and bran	Barley meal		17·96	17·18	3·16	14·02	35·05	38·21	0·78	38·99	61·01
9 and 10	6		Mixture of one part bran, two parts barley meal, and three parts bean and lentil meal	None		16·11	14·77	2·99	11·78	29·45	32·44	1·32	33·76	66·24
11 and 12	6		Mixture of one part bran, two parts bean and lentil meal, and three parts barley meal	None		17·60	15·88	3·08	12·80	32·00	35·08	1·72	36·80	63·20
			Means			16·66	15·44	2·90	12·54	31·35	34·25	1·21	35·46	64·54
			Series 3 (For data, see Series 3, Tables X., XIII., and XV.).											
1	4	8 / 0	Dried cod-fish	Bean and Indian meal (equal parts)		19·12	17·05	5·40	11·65	29·12	34·52	1·05	35·57	64·43
2	4		Dried cod-fish	Indian meal		20·86	19·27	5·48	13·79	34·47	39·95	1·59	41·54	58·46
			Mean			19·49	18·16	5·44	12·72	31·79	37·23	1·32	38·55	61·45
			General means			17·40	16·04	2·96	13·08	30·30	34·16	1·36	35·52	64·48

Both practical and chemical considerations seem to indicate that Fat may be *produced* in the animal body, by the transformation within it of *nitrogenous* compounds. But it seems probable, that at least the main source of the produced Fat will be the *non-nitrogenous* constituents of the food. Of these, particularly in the fattening food of Pigs, the most prominent item is *starch*. It seemed desirable, therefore, to adopt this substance as the basis of the illustration of the probable amount of the constituents involved in the formation of the *produced* Fat, in the experiments in question.

The question arises, how much Starch will be required for the production of a given amount of Fat? At present but little is known as to the relative proportions in which the different Fats exist in different animals. Nor are chemists agreed as to the formulæ to be given to the several natural animal Fats. It would only be a doubtful refinement, therefore, to adopt for our purpose the exact rational formula given for any one of the more important fatty bodies, and from it to calculate, in equivalents, the amount of Starch required to produce an equivalent of the Fat, and also the number of equivalents of the collateral products. It is better to adopt an average *percentage* composition merely; and for want of more exact data, we take the mean of the three most important animal fats—namely, tri-stearine, tri-margarine, and tri-oleine. This gives, in round numbers, 77 per cent. of carbon, 12 per cent. of hydrogen, and 11 per cent. of oxygen for the *crude mixed fats*. It may be mentioned, however, that tri-oleine is stated to be in larger proportion to the other fats in Pigs, than in either Sheep or Oxen. Assuming the oxygen which is eliminated in the *formation* of Fat from Starch, to go off with a portion of its hydrogen in the form of water, and the remainder with carbon in the form of carbonic acid, it would require as a *minimum*, 2·45 parts by weight of Starch to contribute to the formation of one part by weight of the mixed Fats + the collaterally formed water and carbonic acid. If the stearine predominated, this mode of calculation would show the amount of Starch required to be rather higher, and if the oleine, rather lower than 2·45 for 1 of the Fat. As the above number is the *lowest* amount of Starch which would, in the manner supposed, yield 1 part of the mixed Fats of the percentage composition above assumed, we may adopt the convenient round number 2·5 as the amount of Starch probably on the average required for the formation of 1 part of the mixed Fats of the body, when these have their source in that substance. This number then (2·5), is that by which we multiply, for the purposes of the Table, the amount of the estimated Fat in the increase of the Pigs, over and above the *ready-formed fat* they consumed in their food, to ascertain the amount of the dry substance in the food (if in the form of starch), required for the production of that amount of Fat which could not have been directly derived from the food as such, and must therefore have been *formed* within the body of the animal. Whilst adopting the mode of calculation here described, as usefully, and sufficiently closely, illustrating the point in question, it may be remarked in passing, that when Fat is formed from the *nitrogenous* compounds in the body, a *less* amount of dry substance of the food would then be required for the formation of a given amount of Fat, than when it is produced from Starch. On the other hand, if *Sugar* were the source of the Fat, a rather *larger* quantity than of Starch would be required. Of the *pectine* bodies, again, which enter so largely into the roots which frequently constitute a large proportion of the fattening food of sheep and oxen, the quantity required would, on the same mode of calculation, be still more than of Sugar.

On a former occasion, it was shown, that according to the mode of estimation here supposed, the 15 parts of *dry solid increase* yielded during the fattening process by the analysed fat Pig for 100 parts of dry matter of food consumed, would have required for its formation about 30 parts of the *dry substance of the food consumed*. The actual figures relating to this single animal are given in Table XVI., at the head of the respective columns which refer to the numerous lots of Pigs, the Fat in whose food was determined by analysis, and that in their increase estimated.

For 100 dry matter in food, the dry matter in the increase of the analysed fat Pig was 14·94, and that taking the average of all the other cases in which the Fat in the food was determined was 17·40. Of these amounts of total dry substance assimilated, 13·2 in the case of the single fat Pig, and 16·04 in the average of the other lots, are estimated as *Fat*.

Of the 13·2 parts of Fat stored up in the increase of the single animal, 3·26 only (provided the whole supplied had been taken up) could have been derived from the Fat in the food. At least 9·94 parts must, therefore, have been formed in the body of the animal from some other constituent or constituents. If the constituent in question were primarily *Starch*, it would, on our basis of calculation, require 24·8 parts of dry Starch for the formation of the 9·94 parts of *produced Fat*. Of ready-formed Fat in the food, and Starch, thus contributing to the formation of Fat, taken together, there would therefore be 28·11 parts out of 100 of dry matter of food consumed, directly engaged in the storing up in the body, of the 13·2 parts of Fat. If we add to this, the 1·73 part of nitrogenous and mineral matters at the same time fixed in the increase, we have 29·84 parts out of the 100 of dry matter of food consumed, directly contributing, in the sense supposed, to the production of the 14·94 parts only, of dry increase. In the particular sense here implied, therefore, there would be only 70·16 parts of the 100 of dry matter of the food expired, perspired, or voided, without thus directly contributing to increase; instead of 85·06 parts, which is the difference between the 100 of dry matter in food, and the 14·94 only, of dry substance actually stored up.

Following the same line of illustration for the average result of all the other experiments cited, it appears that for 16·04 parts of Fat stored up in increase, for 100 of dry matter of food consumed, only 3·96 parts could have been derived from *ready-formed fatty matter supplied in the food*. At least 12·08 parts must, therefore, have been *formed from other substances*. If from Starch, it would require, at the rate of 2·5 parts Starch for 1 of Fat, 30·2 parts of that substance for the formation of the 12·08 parts of the *produced fat*. The ready-formed Fat, and the Starch, together thus contributing to the 16·04 parts of Fat in the increase, would amount to 34·16 parts of the 100 of dry food consumed. There were, further, 1·36 part of nitrogenous and mineral matters assimilated. In all therefore, 35·52 parts out of 100 of gross dry matter of food, contributed in this comparatively direct manner, to the formation of the 17·4 parts of gross dry increase.

In the case of the single animal, therefore, the indication is, that, owing to the large proportion of the stored-up Fat which must have been actually formed within the body, it would require, if the source of the produced Fat were Starch, 29·84 parts of dry substance out of every 100 consumed in food, to minister in this direct manner to the production of only 14·94 parts of dry animal increase. Owing to the same circumstance it is, that, on the average of the other instances, 35·52 parts out of 100 of dry substance consumed may, in the same manner, be estimated as directly engaged in the storing up of only 17·4 parts of dry increase. It is worthy of remark, that in thus assuming *Starch* to have been the source of the produced Fat, and in adopting its numerical equivalent for that purpose as above described, the resulting figures, in both cases, show almost exactly twice as much of dry substance in the food as directly contributing to the formation of increase, as there was of dry substance in the increase which was produced. In the case of Pigs fed on good food, it would appear that about one-third of the whole dry substance consumed may be so devoted. About two-thirds, therefore, will, if at all, only in a less direct manner, contribute to the production of increase. A large proportion will serve, more or less directly, for respiration only, or for the supply of material for the transformations constantly going on in the body independently of any increase in weight. And, besides the matters voided as indigestible, and necessarily effete, a larger or smaller quantity, according to the excess of the food, will pass off unused and comparatively unchanged.

As before stated, as the particular foods upon which the experimental *sheep* were fed had not their amounts of Fat determined, similar estimates cannot be made in regard to them as to the *pigs*. From a general knowledge, however, of the character of the fattening food of both Oxen and Sheep, considered in relation to the amount of increase it yields, and to the probable composition of that increase, there cannot be any doubt that in their case, as well as that of Pigs, a large amount of Fat will frequently be *formed* in the body from other constituents of the food. But the food of Oxen and Sheep, compared with that of the Pig, contains a large proportion of indigestible woody fibre ; and it has been seen, that in the case of Sheep, there was only about half as much dry increase produced for 100 of dry matter of food consumed, as in the case of Pigs. The proportion of *Fat* in the dry increase of the highly fed Sheep, for 100 of dry matter of food consumed, is also only half as great as in the case of the Pig. Its food, moreover, is frequently much more oleaginous. It would appear, then, that on the average, there will not only be less Fat *formed* by the Sheep for a given amount of dry matter consumed, but there will be a far less proportion of the consumed dry matter of its food appropriated in the direct production, so to speak, of the total dry increase. On the other hand, as before remarked, in the food of Oxen and Sheep, there will be a less proportion of Starch, and a larger one of Pectine bodies, than in that of Pigs. And so far as Pectine, rather than Starch, may serve for the formation of Fat, the amount of the dry substance of the food required directly to contribute to the increase, will be somewhat the greater.

From the whole of the foregoing considerations bearing upon the relation of the constituents of increase to those of the food consumed to produce it, it appears, that a large proportion of the *Fat*, of which the increase of the so-called fattening animals so largely consists, may be *formed in the body from other compounds of the food.* Of the *nitrogenous* compounds, on the other hand, it is probable that frequently as little, and even less than 5 per cent. of the whole consumed, will be found finally stored up in the increase of the animal. Of the *mineral* matter of the food, a less proportion still than of the nitrogenous compounds, will, especially in the case of Pigs, be thus retained in the increase.

It is not the province of the present Paper, nor are the facts applicable to such a purpose, to consider the chemical and physiological changes undergone, or the offices subserved, by the—say 95 per cent. of the consumed nitrogenous compounds in their passage through the system. But, it may be remarked, that from the form in which a large proportion of them leaves the body, it is to be concluded that they must have entered into its fluids, if not its solid structures, and therein been subjected to oxidation and transformation. That this must serve some essential purpose, even in the processes of fattening animals subject to little muscular movement, there cannot be a doubt[*]. It is indeed certain, that if the animals are to store up as much as they can do of matters not containing nitrogen, a very large amount of nitrogen must pass through the body, compared with that which is finally retained in the increase. That this apparently excessive supply of nitrogenous compounds, independently of any mere influence on the activity of the functions or processes of the body, may itself yield up the elements for the formation of *Fat*, is highly probable.

Since it is found that by far the larger proportion of the solid increase of so-called fattening animals is really *Fat* itself—since it is probable that at least a great part of the Fat formed in the body is normally derived from Starch and other *non*-nitrogenous constituents of the food,—and since the current fattening foods contain so very much more of nitrogen than is eventually retained in the increase—it cannot be surprising, that the tendency of the results of all careful feeding experiments should be to show, that the limit of applicability of the estimate of the comparative value of foods, according to their *percentage of nitrogenous compounds*, is in practice very easily reached. Practically, indeed, the amount of increase is much more frequently dependent on the proportion in the food, of the digestible and assimilable *non*-nitrogenous compounds, than

---

[*] We have found in the case of Pigs, that by far the larger portion of the nitrogen consumed in the fattening food, passed off in the form of *Urea*. This was the case with animals kept almost entirely without movement; and it was equally so, whether the food contained the proportion of nitrogenous to non-nitrogenous constituents, as in the Cereal grains; or the much higher amount and proportion of the former, as in Leguminous seeds.

on that of the *nitrogenous* ones. In fact, when we reflect upon what we already know of the relations of the constituents of the animal body to those taken into it as food—thanks more particularly to MULDER, to BOUSSINGAULT, and to LIEBIG—and when we further consider the facts now adduced as to the *Composition of Increase*, it would seem little else than a truism to say, that as our fattening food-stuffs go, their comparative values, *as such**, are not determinable by their percentage of nitrogenous compounds. In the absence of sufficient direct evidence, such as we have endeavoured to supply, as to the probable composition of the increase of animals feeding for the butcher, an opposite opinion has generally been maintained. A consideration of the essentialness of the nitrogenous compounds of food, for the formation of the most important animal structures, has doubtless had much to do with determining the view in question; and it would seem, that keeping this point very prominently in view, it has been assumed, without the requisite experimental data, that these essential nitrogenous compounds were generally relatively deficient in our current foods. It would be more nearly true to say, that the digestible and assimilable *non*-nitrogenous constituents are generally in defect relatively to the digestible and assimilable nitrogenous compounds in our foods.

The comparative values of food-stuffs are, however, not to be unconditionally determined by their percentage of either of these equally important classes of constituents. It has, it is true, been frequently maintained, that a certain relation of the one class of constituents to the other, varying according to circumstances, is essential in a truly rational diet. But the practical bearings of the principle, seem to have been lost sight of by some of those who have the most prominently insisted upon it in its abstract form, as soon as they came to estimate, according to analysis, the comparative values of different foods.

The records of the numerous ultimate analyses of foods which have been hitherto made, are nevertheless of high value and interest in a statistical point of view. But now possessing them, as the basis of certain general estimates, the next desideratum is —to examine more closely into the nature and condition of the proximate compounds of food-stuffs—to distinguish those which are digestible and assimilable, from those which are not so—to determine the comparative values of the comparable or mutually replaceable portions (both intrinsically and according to the varying exigencies of the system)—and above all, to fix our standards of comparative value with more of reference to direct experimental evidence on the point, and to existing knowledge of the composition of animal bodies, than has been hitherto usual or even possible.

---

* As, however, the *manure* from highly nitrogenous foods is the most valuable, it frequently becomes, in this point of view, the interest of the farmer—provided the character be in other respects equal—to purchase and use those having the higher amounts of nitrogen.

SECTION IX.—AVERAGE ACTUAL WEIGHTS, AND AVERAGE PERCENTAGE PROPOR-
TIONS IN THE ENTIRE BODIES, OF THE INDIVIDUAL ORGANS AND OTHER
SEPARATED PARTS, OF ANIMALS OF DIFFERENT DESCRIPTIONS, AND IN
DIFFERENT CONDITIONS OF GROWTH AND FATNESS.

Hitherto, we have endeavoured to illustrate, by means of a large amount of labo-
riously accumulated experimental data, the actual and comparative gross composition of
certain collective portions, and of the entire bodies, of animals of different descriptions,
and in different stages of growth and fatness.   By the aid of the information so derived,
we have sought to estimate the probable composition of the *Increase* of the animals
whilst fattening, and to show the relation of certain important constituents of the
increase, to those in the food consumed.   The results arrived at, under these heads,
comprise the most important which the inquiry can furnish, so far as its application to
Agriculture and Dietetics is concerned.   It seems desirable, however, at least to provide
some materials for the study of the question of the feeding of animals, from a somewhat
more Physiological point of view.   The data acquired with this view, relate to the *actual
weights*, and the *proportion in the entire body*, of the individual organs, and certain
more arbitrarily separated parts.   In the selection of subjects in which to determine
these points, it was sought—both to take a sufficient number, to secure pretty fair
average results for the different descriptions of animal—and, as far as possible, to provide the means of tracing *the tendency of the relative development* of the different parts,
as the animals grew and fattened.

In all, between 300 and 400 animals—Bullocks, Sheep, and Pigs—have been operated
upon.   The plan was, to determine the *live-weights* of the animals just before being
slaughtered; and as soon as possible afterwards (so as to lessen the error arising from
evaporation), the weights of their *carcasses*, of *each of the internal organs*, and of
some other separated parts.   The results for each of the individual animals—both the
actual weights, and the calculated percentages in the entire body—are given for reference in Tables XV. to LXIV. inclusive, in the Appendix.   Of these, Tables XVII.,
XVIII., XIX., XX., XXI. and XXII., which now follow, are Summaries; and in
them the results will be found in sufficient detail to bring to view the few main points,
to which alone, special attention will be directed.

In Table XVII. are given the *mean actual weights*, and in Table XX. the *mean percentages* in the entire body, of the different organs and parts of 2 Calves, 2 Heifers,
and 14 Bullocks.   Among these, are included the calf and the 2 bullocks selected
and killed for analysis.   The remainder were slaughtered for ordinary purposes; and
were taken without any special selection, so as to afford fair average results.   The data
relating to these animals are not particularly calculated (as those referring to the Sheep
will be found to be) to illustrate the comparative characters at different stages of growth
and fatness.   By the side of the mean, or average results, however, are given those
(both actual and percentage), for the individual Calf, the " Half-fat Bullock," and the
" Fat Bullock," which were selected for analysis.

In Tables XVIII. and XXI. are arranged, respectively, the *mean actual weights*, and the *mean percentages* in the entire animal, of the individual organs, &c., of 249 Sheep, divided into 5 Classes, according to age, condition of maturity and fatness, and mode of feeding.   Thus, there are given, the average results of:—

> 5 Sheep, each of a different Breed, which were killed in the *store* condition, in order to provide a standard with which to compare the others;
>
> 100 Sheep, comprising a number from six different Breeds, all fed upon good fattening food, and under cover, during a period of five or six months, commencing at the age and stage of progress at which the 5 *store* or standard animals above mentioned were taken;
>
> 45 Sheep, from the same six Breeds as the last, but fed from the point at which they were slaughtered, for about six or seven months longer (though not under cover), until more than ordinarily fat, or in the condition of so-called " Christmas mutton;"
>
> 78 Sheep, all of one Breed, but divided into a number of lots, each with a different kind of diet, but fed to a medium degree of fatness;
>
> 21 Sheep, from several different Breeds, all fed and slaughtered as "Christmas mutton."
>
> By the side of the columns showing the *mean results* for each of these 5 different Classes of Sheep, and for the whole 249 animals, respectively, are also given the results for the Fat Lamb, and for each of the 4 individual Sheep which were selected and killed in different conditions, for the purposes of analysis.

Table XIX. gives the *means* of the *actual weights*, and Table XXII. of the *percentages*, of the organs and parts of 59 Pigs; allotted into 7 Classes, distinguished one from another chiefly by the different character of the *food*, and the consequent and observed varying degree of growth and maturity.   The separate results for each of the 2 animals selected and slaughtered for analysis are also given.

Lastly, in Table XXIII. are brought together, at one view, the general averages (both actual and percentage), for each of the *three descriptions of animal*; that is to say, the means, side by side, respectively of 16 Heifers and Bullocks, 249 Sheep, and 59 Pigs.

TABLE XVII.—Showing the Mean *Actual* Weights (lbs. and ozs.), of the different Organs and Parts, of CALVES, HEIFERS, and BULLOCKS.

Description of parts.	Means of all slaughtered.				The animals selected for further analysis.		
	2 Fat Calves.	2 Fat Heifers.	14 Fat Bullocks.	Means of 16 Heifers and Bullocks.	Fat Calf.	Half-fat Ox.	Fat Ox.
	lbs. ozs.	lbs. ozs.	lbs. ozs.	lbs. ozs.	lbs. ozs.	lbs. ozs.	lbs. ozs.
Stomachs	3 6·5	32 0	36 6·7	35 13·9	2 13·1	32 1	36 6
Contents of stomachs	6 0·5	70 12	97 4·7	93 15·8	5 10·2	88 0	77 3·8
Caul fat	2 9·2	23 4	23 2·7	23 2·9	2 7·6	16 9·5	33 12·5
Small intestines and contents	5 5·5	15 4	17 13	16 13·6	6 3	26 6	14 10·5
Large intestines and contents	3 4	12 2	13 4·6	13 2·3	2 14·5		6 4
Intestinal fat	2 14	26 3	26 5·8	26 5·4	4 3·1	19 11·5	36 14
Heart and aorta	1 7·7	4 0	5 14·4	5 10·6	1 7·5	5 13·5	7 6
Heart fat	0 3·5	1 14	3 6·9	3 3·8	0 6·8	2 6·8	6 3
Lungs and windpipe	3 4·8	6 6·6	9 10·1	9 3·6	3 5·7	7 12·8	8 14·5
Blood	11 12·5	30 12	47 15·2	45 12·8	13 8·8	54 5	52 11·8
Liver	4 2·8	12 15	15 1·6	14 13·3	4 3·6	15 11	17 10
Gall-bladder and contents	0 2	0 10·8	1 0·5	0 15·7	with bladder	1 0	0 13
Pancreas ("sweetbread")	} 1 11	0 13	1 0·11	1 1	1 12·9	1 0	0 15·5
Thymus gland ("heartbread")		0 9·2	0 11	0 10·7		0 10·8	0 10·5
Glands about the throat ("throatbread")	0 13	0 5·7	0 5·5	0 5·5		0 6·2	0 6·5
Milt or spleen		4	1 15·3	1 13·9	0 12	2 2·2	2 4
Bladder	} 0 6	0 8	0 9·2	0 9·1	0 7·2	0 5	1 10·7
Penis			0 7·5	0 12		0 6·5	0 14
Brains			0 12·1			0 14·2	3 7·5
Tongue	13 9·5	21 7	32 0·6	30 10·7	11 7·3	7 7·5	39 15·5
Head	17 6·2	65 14	87 4·3	84 9·5	17 12·5	31 8·5	80 3·7
Hide	5 7·5	14 10	20 13	20 0·6	4 6	79 15·4	22 7·8
Feet and hoofs	2 5·2	0 12·8	1 1·3	1 1·9	0 5·3	20 2	1 7·5
Tail	1 1·5	4 9·6	5 3·2	5 2	1 1·6	1 12·4	7 9
Diaphragm ("skirts")		4 6	3 14·3	3 15·3		5 11·5	
Miscellaneous trimmings						1 7	
Total "offal" parts	85 4·9	351 6·5	452 13·3	439 13·9	85 4·7	423 10·3	460 13·3
Carcass	156 10·8	474 10	710 3·1	680 12	160 9	797 11	939 6
Loss by evaporation, error in weighing, &c. ...	8 12·3	27 13·5*	19 1·1	20 7·2	12 14·3	10 10·7	18 12·7
Live-weight after fasting	250 12	853 14	1182 1·5	1141 1·1	258 12	1232 0	1419 0

(Left margin group labels: "offal." and "Separate parts of the 'offal.'")

* This amount includes the Womb of the Heifers, one of which was with Calf.

TABLE XVIII.—Showing the Mean *Actual* Weights (lbs. and ozs.), of the different Organs and Parts of SHEEP.

Description of parts.	Graduationary Series.			Miscellaneous.			The animals selected for further analysis.				
	5 sheep of different breeds, killed in store condition, for a standard of comparison.	100 sheep of different breeds, moderately fattened. about 1¼ year old.	45 sheep of different breeds, excessively fattened. about 1¼ year old.	78 Hampshire down sheep, moderately fattened, on different foods. 1¼ to 1¼ year old.	21 sheep of various breeds, and modes of feeding, of more than average fatness. about 1¼ year old.	Means of 249 sheep, of different breeds, conditions of fatness, age, &c.	Fat Lamb.	Store Sheep.	Half-fat Sheep.	Fat Sheep.	Very fat Sheep.
	lbs. ozs.	lbs. ozs.	lbs. ozs.	lbs. ozs.	lbs. ozs.	lbs. ozs.	lbs. ozs.	lbs. ozs.	lbs. ozs.	lbs. ozs.	lbs. ozs.
Original weight	...	102 7	124 11·4	115 1	96 11·4	109 13·5					260 8
Final weight unfasted	99 0	152 5·8	202 7·5	144 13·1	129 15·2	160 4·9				127 2·5	252 8
Fasted live-weight	93 0·8	145 5·3	192 0·3	141 6·7	170 12·2	153 10·2	84 6·5	97 10	105 1		
Stomachs	2 11·5	3 9·9	4 1·9	3 13·5	3 11·2	3 12·3	1 8·6	3 3·8	2 13·7	3 2·5	4 2·3
Contents of stomachs	6 2·5	6 8·5	6 14·8	9 9·9	6 2·7	7 0·4	5 2·1	4 13·8	7 9·4	7 15·5	10 8·0
Caul fat	2 11·9	6 1·3	9 10·5	6 9·7	9 1·1	7 1·8	3 4	3 3·7	3 1·5	6 9	17 0
Small intestines and contents	2 2·6	2 12·4	2 4·1	2 4·7	3 4·2	2 7·6	4 1·7	3 11·1	3 3·2	3 1	2 9
Large intestines and contents	2 11·5	2 12	2 0·9	3 2·3	2 15·9	3 15·2		1 11·2	2 15·5	3 5·4	3 7
Intestinal fat	1 2·6	2 7·8	4 3·6	3 2·4	4 5·6	3 2·2	1 10·8	1 9·4	2 5·5	3 9·5	7 6
Heart and aorta	0 7·1	0 9·3	0 11	0 11·4	0 11·1	0 10·4	0 5·4	0 8·3	0 7·4	0 8·7	0 13
Heart fat	0 4·9	0 4·8	0 9·5	0 9·6	0 11·3	0 7·8	0 4·6	0 3·9	0 8	0 5	0 9·5
Lungs and windpipe	1 1·5	1 8·2	1 9·5	1 9·4	1 9	1 8·3	1 0·8	1 6·9	1 14	1 0·5	1 14
Blood	4 7·3	6 0·2	7 2·5	6 9·4	8 8·8	6 1·6	2 14·3	5 1·2	1 1·2	4 8·8	10 4
Liver	1 8·1	2 8·2	2 8·8	2 0·6	2 5·3	2 5·4	1 2·8	1 10·5	1 11·3	1 14·8	2 10
Gall-bladder and contents	0 1·	0 1·4	0 1·4	0 1·5	0 1·3	0 1·5	0 0·4	0 1·1	0 0·85	0 1	0 1
Pancreas ("sweetbread")	0 2·1	0 3·5	0 3·1	0 3·4	0 3·3	0 3·3	0 0·4	0 0·85	0 5·5	0 9·5	2 10
Thymus gland ("heartbread")	0 2·3	0 4	0 11	0 14	0 11·1		0 5·4*	0 1·1	0 1·1		
Glands about the throat ("throatbread")								0 0·1			
Milt or spleen	0 2·6	0 4	0 4·4	0 36	0 47	0 40	0 26	0 2·5	0 29	0 33	0 62
Bladder	0 0·8	0 0·7	0 0·9	0 36	0 0·8	0 0·8		0 1	0 1·1	0 0·9	0 5·7*
Head	3 5·9	4 5·2	4 12·3	4 9·7	4 12·2	4 8·1	2 10·1	3 9·3	4 2·8	3 14	6 0·5
Skin							3 1·7	5 8·6	6 10·6	7 0·6	8 0·9
Wool	13 1·8	18 9·6	20 0·9	16 4·5	18 7·9	18 0·4	3 12·7	1 0·7	0 8·6 with skin	8 1·9 with skin	25 8 with skin
Feet, hoofs, &c.	0 4·1	0 3·4	0 3·0		0 2·0	0 3·4	0 4·8	0 3·4	0 8·6		
Diaphragm ("skirts")	0 1·4	0 2·1									
Miscellaneous trimmings											
Total "offal" parts	42 12·0	58 13·2	68 12·1	60 8·2	64 6·4	61 11·5	33 9·1	43 4·6	47 3·6	53 3	93 3·2
Carcass	49 11·8	85 11·1	122 14·9	80 6·3	106 5·7	91 12·5	50 8	52 1	56 4·1	73 1	159 4
Loss by evaporation, error in weighing, &c.	0 9·0	0 13·0	0 5·3	0 8·2	0 0·1	0 2·2	0 5·4	2 4·4	1 9·3	0 14·5	0 0·8
Live-weight after fasting	93 0·8	145 5·3	192 0·3	141 6·7	170 12·2	153 10·2	84 6·5	97 10	105 1	127 2·5	252 8

Separate parts of the "Offal."

* In these cases it is doubtful whether the amounts include the Thymus Gland, and Glands about the Throat, or whether they refer to the Pancreas only.

TABLE XIX.—Showing the Mean *Actual* Weights (lbs. and ozs.) of the different Organs and Parts of Pigs.

Description of parts.	9 Pigs. Food; bran, with limited quantity of bean and lentil meal, or Indian meal, or both.	12 Pigs. Food; bean and lentil meal, with limited quantity of Indian meal, or bran, or both.	15 Pigs. Food; Indian meal, with limited quantity of bean and lentil meal, or bran, or all.	12 Pigs. Food; sugar, or starch, or both, with limited quantity of bran and lentil meal.	6 Pigs. Food; dried cod-fish, with Indian and, or bran and Indian meal.	2 Pigs. Put to feed in store condition and only half fattened.	3 Pigs. Put to feed when half-fat on same food as last and moderately fattened.	Means of 59 fattened pigs.	Store Pig.	Fat Pig.
	lbs. ozs.	lbs. ozs.	lbs. ozs.	lbs. ozs.	lbs. ozs.	lbs. ozs.	lbs. ozs.	lbs. ozs.	lbs. ozs.	lbs. ozs.
Original weight	140 12.5	142 9.4	143 7.5	55 5.3	163 13.3	130 8	135 10.7	134 5.1	100 0	103 0
Final-weight unfasted	191 7.1	239 9.4	245 10.7	185 4	297 13.3	180 8	181 5.3	292 9.8	93 15	191 0
Fasted live-weight	188 12.4	297 6.5	234 12.7	177 6.6	278 0	170 8	172 10.8	212 12		185 0
Stomachs										
Stomachs	3 0.6	2 13	2 11.4	2 0.4	3 2.9	2 15.3	1 11.3	2 10.4	1 3.3	1 3.5
Contents of stomachs	0 15.2	1 9	1 5.2	1 0.9	1 6.8	0 12.8	0 14.3	1 2.3	0 4.2	0 11.8
Caul fat	5 10.3	4 11.6	3 14.9	3 13.2	4 8.1	6 10	3 15.1	4 8.4	3 9.8	3 12.6
Small intestines and contents	9 14	5 9.4	7 10.8	4 14.3	7 9.6	7 1.8	5 10.3	8 3.7	3 9.3	6 14.6
Large intestines and contents	1 10.8	3 9.4	3 3.6	1 1.7	2 14.3	1 2.6	1 8.2	2 5.6	1 5.8	4 1.3
Intestinal fat, "midgren," &c.										
Heart and aorta	0 8.5	0 9.9	0 10.4	0 8.9	0 11.1	0 7.5	0 8.1	0 9.6	0 7.8	0 8.8
Lungs and windpipe	1 9.7	1 10.2	1 9.5	1 6.4	1 9.4	1 6.5	1 12.3	1 9.1	1 5.7	1 11.7
Blood	7 3.8	9 2	8 0.4	6 5.2	3 9.4	5 3.3	5 12.7	7 10.1	2 9.8	6 13.3
Liver	2 13.5	3 14.3	3 5.6	3 9.1	3 7.8	3 1.6	2 10.1	3 4.6	2 4.1	3 0.8
Gall-bladder and contents	0 2.1	0 2.1	0 1.7	0 1.4	0 2.1	0 4.5	0 2.4	0 2.6	0 4.1	0 2.1
Pancreas ("sweetbread")	0 5.1	0 9.1	0 2.5	0 3	0 3.1	0 4.6	0 5.1	0 3.6	0 2.7	0 4.9
Milk or spleen	0 4.7	0 5.4	0 4.7	0 3.7	0 5.6	0 4.6	0 4.5	0 4.7		
Bladder	0 1.9	0 3.1	0 2.7	0 2.2	0 2.7	0 1.8	0 2.6	0 2.5	0 2.3	0 2.5
Penis	0 6.8	0 8.1	0 8	0 5.6	0 9.2	0 5.1	0 6.8	0 7.1	0 8.4	0 12.9
Tongue	0 15.7	1 0.3	1 0.8	0 15.2	1 3.3	0 13.2	0 13.6	1 0.2		
Toes	0 2.9	0 3.3	0 2.9	0 2.3	0 2.1		0 5.1	0 2.9	0 6.6	
Miscellaneous trimmings	0 5.1	0 11.8	0 11.7	0 3.5	0 9.1	0 9.3	0 10.4	0 8.6	0 6.6	0 0
Total "Offal" parts	35 6.1	40 4.2	35 15.8	30 11.4	37 10.4	31 10.2	27 3.8	35 4.6	25 10.6*	31 4.2*
Carcass (including head, with brains, feet and tail)	146 7.5	186 14.4	197 12.5	144 9.5	239 6	135 9.5	144 6.2	176 5.3	71 2.3*	153 2.8*
Loss by evaporation, error in weighing, &c.	0 14.8	0 4.3	1 0.4	2 1.7	0 15.6	3 4.3	1 0.8	1 2.1	+ 2 13.9	0 9
Live-weight after fasting	188 12.4	227 6.9	234 12.7	177 6.6	278 0	170 8	179 10.8	212 12	93 15	185 0

* For comparison with the other results in this Table, the head (with brains), feet, and tail of the two analysed Pigs, are here excluded from the Offal, and included with the Carcass, according to the usual custom of the Butcher with Pigs.

TABLE XX.—Showing the Mean *Percentage* Proportion of the different Organs and Parts, in the Fasted Live-weight of CALVES, HEIFERS and BULLOCKS.

Description of parts.	Means of all slaughtered.				The animals selected for further analysis.		
	2 Fat Calves.	2 Fat Heifers.	14 Fat Bullocks.	Means of 16 Heifers and Bullocks.	Fat Calf.	Half-fat Ox.	Fat Ox.
Stomachs	1·37	3·75	3·09	3·17	1·09	2·60	2·56
Contents of stomachs	2·39	8·40	8·44	8·44	2·18	7·14	5·44
Caul fat	1·03	2·69	1·93	2·02	0·96	1·35	2·38
Small intestines and contents	2·13	1·80	1·49	1·52	2·39	2·14	1·03
Large intestines and contents	1·30	1·44	1·18	1·22	1·12		0·44
Intestinal fat	1·13	3·02	2·12	2·24	1·62	1·60	2·60
Heart and aorta	0·60	0·49	0·50	0·50	0·57	0·47	0·52
Heart fat	0·08	0·22	0·32	0·31	0·16	0·20	0·44
Lungs and windpipe	1·32	0·75	0·82	0·81	1·30	0·63	0·63
Blood	4·68	3·60	4·07	4·01	5·24	4·41	3·72
Liver	1·67	1·52	1·28	1·31	1·63	1·27	1·24
Gall-bladder and contents	0·05	0·08	0·09	0·09	with bladder	0·08	0·06
Pancreas ("sweetbread")	0·67	0·07	0·09	0·09	0·70	0·08	0·07
Thymus gland ("heartbread")		0·05	0·06	0·06		0·06	0·05
Glands about the throat ("throatbread")			0·03	0·03		0·03	0·03
Milt or spleen	0·32	0·15	0·17	0·16	0·29	0·17	0·16
Bladder	0·15	0·06	0·05	0·05	0·17	0·03	0·12
Penis			0·04			0·03	0·06
Brains			0·07	0·06		0·07	0·24
Tongue						0·61	
Head	5·46	2·51	2·71	2·69	4·43	2·56	2·82
Hide	6·94	7·74	7·46	7·49	6·87	6·50	5·65
Feet and hoofs	2·18	1·72	1·78	1·77	1·69	1·64	1·59
Tail	0·13	0·09	0·69	0·10	0·13	0·14	0·10
Diaphragm ("skirts")	0·44	0·53	0·39	0·41	0·43	0·46	0·53
Miscellaneous trimmings		0·49	0·27	0·30		0·12	
Total "Offal" parts	34·04	41·25	38·54	38·65	32·97	34·39	32·48
Carcass	62·53	55·58	59·84	59·31	62·05	64·75	66·20
Loss by evaporation, error in weighing, &c.	3·43	3·17*	1·62	1·84	4·98	0·86	1·32
	100·00	100·00	100·00	100·00	100·00	100·00	100·00

Left-margin bracket labels: "Offal." and "Separate parts of the 'Offal.'"

* This amount includes the Wombs of the Heifers, one of which was with Calf.

TABLE XXI.—Showing the Mean *Percentage* Proportion of the different Organs and Parts, in the Fasted Live-weight of SHEEP.

| Description of parts. | Means of all slaughtered. | | | | | | The animals selected for further analysis. | | | | |
| | Gradinatory Series. | | | Miscellaneous. | | | | | | | |
	5 sheep of different breeds, killed in store condition, for a standard of comparison.	100 sheep of different breeds, moderately fattened. About 1¾ year old.	45 sheep of different breeds, excessively fattened. About 1¾ year old.	78 Hants down sheep, moderately fattened, on different foods. 1¼ to 1½ year old.	21 sheep of various breeds and modes of feeding, of more than average fatness. About 1¾ year old.	Means of 249 sheep of different breeds, conditions of fatness, age, &c.	Fat Lamb.	Store Sheep.	Half-fat Sheep.	Fat Sheep.	Very fat Sheep.
Stomachs	2·94	2·49	2·14	2·72	2·17	2·46	1·822	3·316	2·719	2·489	1·641
Contents of stomachs	6·16	4·49	3·62	6·83	3·62	4·98	6·079	4·981	7·252	3·908	4·158
Caul fat	2·92	4·13	4·99	4·97	5·31	4·63	3·830	3·946	2·945	3·161	6·733
Small intestines and contents	2·32	1·92	1·19	1·63	1·75	1·61	......	1·735	2·084	2·625	1·015
Large intestines and contents	2·93	1·60	1·59	2·23	2·56	1·92	......	1·636	2·231	2·408	1·282
Intestinal fat.	1·28	1·70	2·10	2·23	2·55	2·04	1·984		2·231	2·626	2·921
Heart and aorta	0·48	0·40	0·36	0·51	0·41	0·43	0·400	0·531	0·440	0·428	0·322
Heart fat	0·32	0·90	0·35	0·42	0·92	0·62	0·341	0·250	0·476	0·393	0·235
Lungs and windpipe	1·17	1·04	0·83	1·06	2·84	0·99	1·244	1·465	1·035	0·911	0·743
Blood	4·81	4·14	3·73	3·95	1·37	2·97	2·428	5·199	3·879	3·578	4·059
Liver	1·61	1·75	1·33	1·44	1·05	1·52	1·392	1·392	1·634	1·514	1·040
Gall-bladder and contents	0·07	0·06	0·06	0·07	0·12	0·06	0·039	0·064	0·506	0·049	......
Pancreas ("sweetbread")	0·13	0·15	0·10	0·15	......	0·14	0·185*	0·070	0·155*	0·167*	0·143*
Thymus gland ("heartbread")	......	......	......	......	......	......	......	0·070	......	......	......
Glands about the throat ("throatbread")	0·06	0·06	......	0·16	......	......	......	0·064	......	......	......
Milt or spleen	0·17	0·17	0·14	......	0·17	0·16	0·193	0·160	0·172	0·163	0·153
Bladder	0·05	0·03	0·03	......	0·03	0·03	......	0·064	0·064	0·044	......
Head	3·64	3·90	2·53	3·27	2·74	2·93	3·117	3·658	3·974	3·047	2·389
Skin	14·09	12·83	10·46	11·50	10·84	11·73	5·865	5·672	6·686	5·535	10·099
Wool	......	......	......	......	......	......	3·680	7·382	6·341	6·385	......
Feet and hoofs	0·30	0·30	0·12	......	......	......	0·940	1·059	......	......	......
Diaphragm ("skirts")	0·10	0·13	0·11	0·07	0·07	0·14	0·355	0·218	0·511	0·305	......
Miscellaneous trimmings	......	......	......	......	......	0·12	......	......	......	......	......
Total "Offal" parts	45·55	40·52	35·78	42·84	37·71	40·17	39·770	44·341	44·948	41·828	26·911
Carcass	53·42	58·97	64·05	56·85	62·28	59·74	59·930	53·329	53·546	57·459	63·069
Loss by evaporation, error in weighing, &c.	1·03	0·51	0·17	0·31	0·01	0·09	0·400	2·330	1·506	0·713	0·020
	100·00	100·00	100·00	100·00	100·00	100·00	100·000	100·000	100·000	100·000	100·000

Separate parts of the "Offal."

* In these cases it is doubtful whether the amounts include the Thymus Gland, and Glands about the Throat, or whether they refer to the Pancreas only.

TABLE XXII.—Showing the Mean *Percentage* Proportion of the different Organs and Parts, in the Fasted Live-weight of Pigs.

Description of parts.	Moderately fattened in different descriptions of food.					Means of all slaughtered.			The animals selected for further analysis.	
	9 Pigs. Food; bran, with limited quantity of bean and lentil meal, or Indian meal, or both.	12 Pigs. Food; bean and lentil meal, with limited quantity of Indian meal, or bran, or both.	15 Pigs. Food; Indian meal, with limited quantity of bean and lentil meal, or bran, or all.	12 Pigs. Food; sugar, or starch, or both, with limited quantity of bran and lentil meal.	6 Pigs. Food; dried codfish, with Indian meal, or bran and Indian meal.	2 Pigs. Put to feed in store condition, and only half fattened.	3 Pigs. Put to feed when half-fat, on same food as last, and moderately fattened.	Means of 59 fattened pigs.	Store pig.	Fat pig.
Stomachs	1·66	1·27	1·18	1·16	1·17	1·81	0·99	1·28	1·28	0·66
Contents of stomachs									0·28	0·40
Caul fat	0·52	0·49	0·57	0·59	0·51	0·47	0·52	0·54	0·37	0·30
Small intestines and contents	3·05	2·19	3·28	2·15	1·66	3·98	2·36	2·30	3·85	2·05
Large intestines and contents	4·91	4·16		5·05	2·76	4·34	3·38	4·04	6·27	3·74
Intestinal fat, " midgeon," &c.	0·91	1·35	1·37	0·53	1·03	0·67	0·87	1·06	1·45	2·21
Heart and aorta	0·29	0·27	0·27	0·31	0·25	0·28	0·29	0·29	0·52	0·30
Lungs and windpipe	0·88	0·73	0·68	0·79	0·57	0·85	1·06	0·76	1·44	0·94
Blood	3·97	4·08	3·43	3·59	3·11	3·04	3·37	3·63	7·51	3·69
Liver	1·55	1·71	1·43	1·70	1·36	1·87	1·56	1·57	2·66	1·65
Gall-bladder and contents	0·07	0·05	0·05	0·06	0·06	0·06	0·09	0·06	0·08	0·07
Pancreas (" sweetbread ")	0·18	0·22	0·20	0·18	0·19	0·17	0·18	0·19	0·27	0·22
Milt or spleen	0·16	0·15	0·13	0·14	0·12	0·17	0·15	0·14	0·18	0·17
Bladder	0·07	0·09	0·07	0·06	0·06	0·06	0·10	0·08	0·15	0·08
Penis	0·23	0·22	0·21	0·20	0·21	0·18	0·24	0·21		
Tongue	0·54	0·46		0·53	0·43	0·49	0·51	0·48	0·56	0·43
Toes	0·69	0·69	0·08	0·09	0·07			0·08		
Miscellaneous trimmings	0·18	0·32	0·29	0·12	0·21	0·35	0·40	0·26	0·44	
Total " Offal " parts	19·26	17·85	15·38	17·38	13·67	18·78	16·07	16·87	27·31*	16·91*
Carcass (including head, with brains, feet, and tail)	80·22	82·07	84·18	81·44	85·98	79·26	83·39	82·57	75·74*	80·79*
Loss by evaporation, error in weighing, &c.	0·52	0·08	0·44	1·18	0·35	1·96	0·54	0·56	+3·05	0·30
	100·00	100·00	100·00	100·00	100·00	100·00	100·00	100·00	100·00	100·00

(Left margin label: Separate parts of the " Offal.")

* For comparison with the other results in this Table, the head (with brains), feet, and tail, of the two analysed Pigs, are here excluded from the Offal, and included with the Carcass, according to usual custom of the Butcher with Pigs.

TABLE XXIII.—*Summary* of the Mean *Actual* Weights (lbs. and ozs.), and of the Mean *Percentage* Proportion, of the different Organs and Parts of different Descriptions of Animals.—BULLOCKS, SHEEP, and PIGS.

Description of parts.	Mean Actual Weights (lbs. and ozs.).			Mean Percentage Proportion in the Fasted Live-weights.		
	Means of 16 heifers and bullocks.	Mean of 249 sheep of different breeds, conditions of fatness, age, &c.	Means of 59 fattened pigs.	Means of 16 heifers and bullocks.	Means of 249 sheep of different breeds, conditions of fatness, age, &c.	Means of 59 fattened pigs.
Stomachs	35 13.9	3 12.3	2 10.4	3.17	2.46	1.28
Contents of stomachs (and vomit)	93 15.8	7 10.4	1 2.3	8.44	4.98	0.54
Caul fat	23 2.9	7 1.8	4 8.4	2.02	4.63	2.20
Small intestines and contents	16 13.6	2 7.6	8 5.7	1.52	1.61	4.04
Large intestines and contents	13 2.3	2 15.2	2 5.6	1.22	1.92	1.06
Intestinal fat	26 5.4	3 2.2	0 9.6	2.24	2.04	0.29
Heart and aorta	5 10.6	0 10.4		0.50	0.43	
Heart fat	3 3.8	0 7.8	1 9.1	0.32	0.32	0.76
Lungs and windpipe	9 3.6	1 8.3	7 10.1	0.81	0.99	3.63
Blood	45 12.8	6 1.6	3 4.5	4.01	3.97	1.57
Liver	14 13.3	2 5.4	2 2.1	1.31	1.52	1.52
Gall-bladder and contents	0 15.7	0 1.5	0 6.6	0.09	0.06	0.06
Pancreas ("sweetbread")	1 1	0 3.3		0.09	0.14	0.19
Thymus gland ("heartbread")	0 10.7			0.06		
Glands about the throat ("throatbread")	0 5.5		0 4.7	0.03		0.14
Milt or spleen	1 13.9	0 4.0		0.16	0.16	
Bladder	0 9.1	0 0.8	0 2.5	0.05	0.03	0.08
Penis	0 12.0		0 7.1			0.21
Brains			1 *	0.06		*
Tongue	30 10.7	4 8.1	0 0.2	2.69	2.93	0.48
Head		18 0.4			11.73	*
Hide, or Skin and Wool	84 9.5		0 2.9†	7.49		0.08†
Feet and hoofs	20 0.6		0 *	1.77		*
Tail	1 1.9	0 3.4		0.10	0.14	
Diaphragm ("skirts")	5 2	0 3.0	0 8.8	0.41	0.12	0.26
Miscellaneous trimmings	3 15.3			0.30		
Total "Offal" parts	439 13.9	61 11.5	35 4.6*	38.85	40.17	16.87*
Carcass	680 12	91 12.5	176 5.3*	59.31	59.74	82.57*
Loss by evaporation, error in weighing, &c.	20 7.2‡	1 2.2	1 2.1	1.84	0.09	0.56
Live-weight after fasting	1141 1.1	153 10.2	212 12	100.00	100.00	100.00

(The rows from Stomachs to Miscellaneous trimmings are grouped as "Separate parts of the 'Offal.'")

* In the case of the Pigs, the head (with brains), feet, and tail, are included with Carcass, and not with the Offal as with the other animals.

† These quantities relate to the toes only.   ‡ Penis or Womb included here.

On the condensed, though still voluminous record of facts, relating to this branch of the inquiry, which these Tables (XVII.—XXIII. inclusive) provide, our space and more special objects will allow but a few short comments.

A few words may first be offered directing attention to the more prominent points of distinction between the different descriptions of animal—Oxen, Sheep, and Pigs—as regards the amount, and the proportion in the whole body, of their respective organs and parts.

An examination of Table XXIII. will show, that the stomachs and contents, constituted in the Oxen about $11\frac{1}{2}$, in the Sheep about $7\frac{1}{2}$, and in the Pig only about $1\frac{1}{4}$ per cent. of the entire weight of the body. The intestines and their contents, on the other hand, stand in an opposite relation. Thus, of the entire body of the Pig, these amounted to about $6\frac{1}{4}$ per cent., of that of the Sheep to about $3\frac{1}{3}$ per cent., and of that of Oxen to only about $2\frac{3}{4}$ per cent. These facts are of considerable interest, when it is borne in mind, that in the food of the Ruminant there is so large a proportion of indigestible Woody-fibre, and in that of the well-fed Pig a comparatively large proportion of Starch —the primary transformations of which are supposed to take place chiefly after leaving the stomach, and more or less throughout the intestinal canal. Again, of the masses of *internal* " loose fat," with its connecting membrane, the Bullocks yielded about $4\frac{1}{2}$ per cent., the Sheep about $7\frac{3}{4}$, and the Pig little more than $1\frac{1}{2}$ per cent. The Pig, therefore, with its much less proportion of alimentary organs, has also a much less proportion to the whole body, of the fat which surrounds them. With regard to the much larger amount of this sort of fat indicated in the Sheep than in the Oxen, it may be remarked, that a considerable proportion of the Sheep which contribute to these recorded averages, were, compared with the Oxen, in more than a corresponding degree of maturity and fatness.

Taking together, stomachs, small intestines, large intestines, and their respective contents, the Oxen yielded rather more than 14 per cent., the Sheep a little less than 11 per cent., and the Pigs about $7\frac{1}{2}$ per cent. With these great variations in the proportion in the different animals, of these receptacles and first laboratories of the food, with their contents, the further elaborating organs (if we may so say) with their fluids, appear to be much more equal in their proportion in the three cases. This is approximately illustrated in the fact, that, taking together the recorded percentages of " heart and aorta," " lungs and windpipe," " liver," " gall-bladder and contents," " pancreas," " milt or spleen," and the " blood," the sum indicated is for the Bullocks about 7 per cent., for the Sheep about $7\frac{1}{4}$ per cent., and for the Pigs about $6\frac{2}{3}$rds per cent. If from this list we were to exclude the blood, which was more than one-third of a per cent. lower in the Pig than in the other animals, the sums of the percentages of the other items enumerated would agree even much more closely for the three descriptions of animal.

A rapid survey may next be taken of the general indications as to the influence of *progression* in the maturity and fatness of the fattening animal, upon the relative development of its several organs or parts.   An examination of the Tables shows, that the internal organs, and other offal parts, pretty generally *increase* in *actual weight* as the animal passes from the store or lean, to the fat, or to the very fat condition.   Excluding the fat, however, their *percentage proportion to the whole live-weight*, as invariably *diminishes* as the animal matures and fattens.   Of the internal offal parts, the loose fat alone increases, not only in *actual weight*, but in *percentage proportion*.   The *carcasses*, on the other hand, invariably *increase* in both *actual* and *percentage* amount as the animals mature.   These remarks apply generally to Oxen, Sheep, and Pigs; but the data relating to the Sheep comprise the most complete gradationary series for their illustration.

To go a little into detail: the average *actual* weights per head of the collective stomachs, and intestines, and their contents, *increased* from about $13\frac{3}{4}$ lbs. in the five *store* or *lean* sheep, to about $15\frac{3}{4}$ lbs. in the 100 *fat* Sheep, and to about $16\frac{1}{4}$ lbs. among the forty-five *very fat* ones.   The *percentage* of these parts in the entire weight of the animal, *diminished* from 14·35 for the *store* sheep, to 10·79 for the *fat* ones, and to 8·54 for the *very fat* ones.   Again, the "heart and aorta," the "lungs and windpipe," the "blood," the "liver," the "gall-bladder and contents," the "pancreas," and the "milt or spleen," taken together, give an average *actual* weight per head, for the five *store* Sheep of $7\frac{3}{4}$ lbs., for the 100 *fat* ones of $11\frac{1}{4}$ lbs., and for the forty-five *very fat* ones of $12\frac{1}{8}$ lbs. The proportional *increase* in *actual* weight as the animals fatten, is rather greater therefore for these organs and parts than for the collective stomachs and intestines, and contents.   Still they *decrease* (though not so much as the collective stomachs, &c.) in *percentage* to the whole body with the increase in weight and fatness of the animals. Thus the *percentage* of the heart and other parts here classed with it, is for the average of the five *store* Sheep 8·44, for that of the 100 *fat* ones 7·71, and for that of the forty-five *very fat* ones 6·55.   As already said, of the internal parts the *loose fat alone* increases in both *actual weight* and *percentage relation* to the whole body with the progress of the animals.   It averages in *actual weight*, for the store or lean Sheep about $4\frac{1}{4}$ lbs., for the fat ones about $8\frac{3}{4}$ lbs., and for the very fat ones about $14\frac{1}{2}$ lbs.; and in *percentage proportion to the whole body*, 4·52 for the lean Sheep, 6·03 for the fat, and 7·44 for the very fat ones.

Turning from this more detailed view to notice the actual, and relative development of the collective or *total Offal parts*, and the *total Carcass parts*, respectively, the result is as follows:—The average *actual weights* per head, of the total Offal parts, increased from $42\frac{3}{4}$ lbs. in the *store* or *lean* condition, to $58\frac{3}{4}$ lbs. in the *fat*, and to $68\frac{3}{4}$ lbs. in the *very fat* condition.   The increase in actual weight of the corresponding Carcasses was much greater; namely, from $49\frac{3}{4}$ lbs. in the *store*, to $85\frac{3}{4}$ lbs. in the *fat*, and to nearly 123 lbs. in the *very fat* condition.   That is to say, although the collective Offal parts increase considerably as the animals fatten, the Carcass—or frame, with its muscles, membranes, vessels and fat—increases proportionally very much more.   The result of this much greater proportional rate of increase, in the so-called Carcass parts, than in the collective internal organs and other Offal parts, is, of course, that there is a *diminishing percentage* in the entire body of the total Offal parts, and an *increasing percentage* of the total Carcass parts as the animals mature and fatten. Thus, the percentage of the collective Offal parts, is, in round numbers, for the average of the *lean* sheep 45·5, for that of the *fat* ones 40·5, and for that of the *very fat* ones 35·8. The percentages of Carcass parts were, on the other hand, 53·4 for the corresponding *lean* animals, 58·9 for the *fatter* ones, and 64·0 for the *very fat* ones*.

Without going into more of numerical illustration of the points above alluded to, it may be mentioned, that the same general indications as to the comparative development of the different parts during the fattening process, are traceable in the results of the comparable cases of the individual animals selected for Analysis as the types of the different conditions, as in those of the Gradationary Series, from which the illustrations given have been drawn.

From the few summary statements that have been adduced, it is sufficiently obvious—though the details are worthy the closer attention of the Physiologist—that in the feeding or fattening of animals, the apparatus which subserves for the reception, the elaboration, and the transmission, of the food, does not increase so rapidly as those parts which it is the object of the feeder to store up from that food. These parts constitute the saleable "*Carcass*"—or framework, with its covering of flesh and fat. The Tables of ultimate and proximate composition have shown, that of the *flesh* and *fat* of the Carcass, which thus constitute the greater portion of the increase, the former—the *flesh* or *nitrogenous* portion—increases but little during the fattening process; whilst the latter—the *fat*—increases in a very much greater proportion. Of the internal parts again, it is also the *fat* which increases the most rapidly.

The maturing process consists, then, in *diminishing* the proportional amount in the whole body, of the collective muscles, membranes, vessels, internal fleshy organs, and gelatigenous matters—or motive and functional, or, so to speak, working parts of the body—the constituents of which may increase the amount, or replace the transformed portions, of similar matters in the human body. It consists further, in *increasing* very considerably the deposition of *fat*—the most concentrated of the respiratory, and *non*-flesh-forming constituents of human food.

It is then, in our *meat-diet*, of recognized good quality, to which is generally attributed such a high relative "*flesh-forming*" capacity, that we carefully store up such a large proportion of *non*-flesh-forming, but concentrated respiratory material.

---

* It will probably be noticed, that the sums of the percentages of the corresponding total offal, and total carcass-parts here quoted, do not quite make up the 100. The complementary amounts represent the "Loss by evaporation, error in weighing, &c."

Section X.—SUMMARY, AND CONCLUSION: RELATION OF THE NON-NITROGENOUS OR NON-FLESH-FORMING, TO THE NITROGENOUS CONSTITUENTS, IN ANIMAL FOOD, AND IN BREAD.

It has been established by analysis that the *entire bodies* of some of the most important animals fed and slaughtered for human food, even when in a reputed *lean* condition, may contain more *dry Fat* than *dry Nitrogenous substances*. This was the case with a half-fat Bullock, a store or lean young Sheep, a half-fat old Sheep, and a store or lean young Pig. Of these, the two last, indeed—namely, the half-fat old Sheep, and the lean Pig, contained in their Entire Bodies, nearly one and three quarter time as much *dry Fat* as *dry Nitrogenous matter*.

Of the animals "ripe" for the butcher, a Bullock contained rather more than twice as much *dry Fat* as *Nitrogenous substance*; a moderately fat Sheep nearly three times as much; and a very fat one more than four times as much. A moderately fat Pig contained in its entire body also about four times as much *dry Fat* as *dry Nitrogenous matter*. Even a fat Lamb yielded more than twice as much *Fat* as *Nitrogenous substance*. Of the professedly *fattened* animals, the fat Calf alone contained rather *less* Fat than nitrogenous matter.

Of the 10 animals analysed, the store Sheep, and the store Pig, respectively, were certainly in a much leaner condition than Sheep and Pigs are usually, if ever, slaughtered for food in this country. Sometimes, though seldom, Oxen and Sheep may be killed in as lean a state as the "half-fat Ox," and "half-fat old Sheep." The "fat Calf," the "fat Ox," the "fat Lamb," and the "fat Sheep," may perhaps be taken as fairly representing the average conditions, respectively, of such animals of reputed good quality, and admitted to be properly fattened. The "extra-fat Sheep" was undoubtedly considerably fatter than mutton as usually killed. The "fat Pig" was probably about as fat as the average of the animals consumed in large proportion as fresh pork; but certainly less so, than the average of those fed and slaughtered more exclusively for curing.

One of the most important applications which can be made of a knowledge of the composition of the animals which constitute the chief sources of our *animal* food, is to determine the main points of distinction between such food, and the staple *vegetable* substances which it substitutes or supplements, in an ordinary mixed diet. Of the latter, *Wheaten Bread* is, in this country at least, undoubtedly the most important. This substance therefore—*Wheaten Bread*—is the best that can be taken as the type of our current *vegetable* food-stuffs, for the purposes of any general view of the comparative characters of our chief *animal* and *vegetable* aliments. Obviously too, the first and main point is to attempt to gain some insight into the relative characters of these two prominently contrasted classes of human food-stuffs, in regard to the average proportions which they will probably respectively contain, of *non*-flesh-forming to "*flesh-forming*" constituents. And, for the purposes of the merely general view here contemplated, we shall, in accordance with the usual practice in such discussions of late years, assume the "*non*-flesh-forming" or more specially respiratory and fat-forming capacity of the foods, to be represented, approximately, by the *collective* or *total non-nitrogenous constituents*, and the "*flesh-forming*" capacity to be indicated, conditionally, by the *collective* or *total nitrogenous* constituents of the respective foods. Indeed—neither is our existing knowledge of the adaptation to the various exigencies of the animal œconomy of the different compounds which our foods supply, so far advanced—nor are our special facts in regard to the composition of the animal aliments we have analysed, of such a character—as to render it desirable to attempt, at present, any more exact mode of classification. With regard to the varying capacity for the purposes of the system of the different *non*-nitrogenous constituents, we shall, however, make some numerical estimates further on. But, so far as the several *nitrogenous* constituents are concerned, we are not in a position to reduce to the form of numerical illustration any distinctions that might be drawn between them. In fact, as already stated, we are not even prepared to give an estimate of how much of the nitrogen of the animal substances we have analysed was due to gelatin and chondrin-yielding matters, and how much to the so-called protein-compounds; yet, on the assumption that the former substances are not to be reckoned as "*flesh-forming*," our estimates of the amounts of such material in the animal substances in question, would be in excess by at least the quantity of gelatin and chondrin-yielding matters which the *total* or *collective* nitrogenous substance may contain.

It is proposed, then, on the present occasion, to confine attention to the contrast between the composition of the *estimated consumable portions* of the animals analysed, and that of *Bread*, in regard alone to the relation in each, of the *non-flesh-forming* to the assumed "*flesh-forming*" constituents—and in regard to this point, so far only, as this can be taken to be illustrated by the relation of the *non-nitrogenous* to the *collective nitrogenous* constituents, in the respective foods.

It is sufficiently obvious, that the composition of the *entire bodies* of our slaughtered animals cannot be taken as representing that of the *consumable portions* only. The composition of the *collective Carcass parts*, and of the *collective Offal parts*, respectively, of the animals analysed, was therefore also determined. As already alluded to, however, a considerable amount of the nitrogen of the *Carcass* will be found in its *bones*, and probably little of this will be consumed as food. On the other hand, a considerable proportion of the *internal organs* rich in nitrogen, will be so consumed. It has been estimated too, that of the *Fat* of the slaughtered animals, the amount contained in the Carcasses cannot always be taken as representing the proportion of the whole Fat of the body which will be consumed. It will be well, therefore, to state briefly here, the basis and mode of computation adopted, and the general result arrived at, in forming an estimate of the probable proportions of the total Nitrogenous compounds, and of the total Fat respectively, of the slaughtered animals, which will, on the average, be applied in some form as *human food*.

In the Calf and Bullocks analysed, about two-thirds of the entire Nitrogenous substances of the body were contained in the so-called *Carcasses*. Of this, say 66⅔rds per cent. of the whole *nitrogen* of the body thus found in the Carcasses, somewhere about 12 parts were contained in the Carcass-*bones*. Supposing none of this were eaten, there would remain only about 54⅔rds per cent. of the whole *nitrogen* of the body, in the *soft edible portions* of the Carcass. Of the 33⅓rd per cent. of the *nitrogen* which is accumulated in the Offal parts, in the Calf perhaps 7 to 8 parts, and in the Oxen perhaps from 4 to 5 parts will be consumed as human food*. Adding this to the portion eaten in the soft parts of the Carcass, it would appear, that in Calves rather more, and in Oxen rather less, than 60 per cent. of the *total nitrogen* of the bodies will be *consumed*. Of the total *Fat* of the same animals, about 70 per cent. in the case of the Calf, and rather over 75 per cent. in the case of the Oxen, were found in the Carcasses. Of the 30 per cent. of the whole Fat of the Calf, which were found in its Offal, all but about 5 parts may be estimated as eaten—that is to say, 95 per cent. of the whole Fat of the animal. Of the 25 per cent. of the Fat in the Offal of the Oxen, about one-fifth is supposed to be consumed. This, with the whole of the Carcass-fat, will show 80 per cent. of the total Fat of Oxen to be applied as food. In estimating the proportion of the consumed *Fat*, to the consumed *Nitrogenous compounds* in *Calves* and *Oxen*, it is assumed then, that in the former 95 per cent. of the total Fat, and 60 per cent. of the total Nitrogenous compounds, will be applied as food; and that in the latter (oxen), 80 per cent. of the total Fat of the body, and 60 per cent. of the Nitrogenous matters will be so applied.

Of the Lamb and Sheep analysed, owing to the large amount of *nitrogen* in the *wool*, little more than half—from 52 to 53 per cent.—of the total amount of the nitrogenous compounds of the body was found in the *Carcass*. About 10 per cent. were contained in the *bones* of the Carcass, of which but little would be consumed as food. To make up for the nitrogen in the bones of the carcass that will not be consumed, from 6 to 7 parts of the 47 or 48 per cent. of the whole nitrogen included in the Offal may be considered as eaten. Thus, in round numbers, it may be estimated, that of the whole of the *Nitrogenous compounds* of the body of the Lamb and Sheep, 50 per cent. are applied as human food. Of the total *Fat* of the Lamb and Sheep, about 75 per cent. will be contained in the Carcass-parts; and this is the proportion of the whole, which, in the case of Sheep, should be taken as eaten. Of the Lamb, however, 95 per cent. of the whole *Fat* of the body is supposed to be consumed.

---

* For the amounts, and distribution, of the *Bones* in the different animals, see Tables I. to X., inclusive, in the Appendix, pp. 580--589; also the discussion at pp. 523, 524. For the distribution of the *Nitrogen* in the different parts of the body, see Tables V. and VI., pp. 514 and 515, and the discussion upon them. And for the estimates as to which portions of the Offal parts will usually be consumed as food, see p. 524 and context.

In the fattened Pig, supposing its parts to be classified in the same manner as those of the other animals *, about three-fourths of the total *nitrogen* were found in the Carcass. Of these—say 74 to 75 parts—about 4 to 5 parts would be contained in the Carcass-*bones*. This leaves about 70 parts of the total *Nitrogenous compounds* of the fat Pig accumulated in the *soft edible parts* of the Carcass. But 8 parts at least of the whole nitrogen of its body will be consumable from the here reckoned Offal of the Pig. It may be estimated, therefore, that of the whole *Nitrogenous compounds* of the body of this animal, about 78 per cent. will be consumed as human food. Of the total *Fat* of the body of the Pig, about 90 per cent. were found in the parts classified as Carcass. Reckoning that a portion of this, from the "flare," may go for medicinal and perfumery purposes, but that the amount so lost to food is compensated by an equivalent portion of the Offal-fat consumed, it may be estimated that 90 per cent., or somewhere about the proportion of the whole which is contained in the Carcass, will be consumed as food.

The results of these estimates of the proportions of the total Nitrogenous Compounds, and total Fat respectively, of the several descriptions of animals which will be consumed as human food, may be arranged for convenience, at one view, as follows:—

	Per cent. consumed as human Food.	
	Of the Total Nitrogenous Compounds of the body.	Of the Total Fat of the body.
Calves.............................	60	95
Oxen	60	80
Lambs	50	95
Sheep..............................	50	75
Pigs	78	90

Adopting these estimates, it would result, that, in Calves and Lambs particularly, but also in Oxen and Sheep, the *proportion of Fat to nitrogenous compounds* in the *consumed portions*, will be somewhat higher than in the *entire Carcasses* including bone. In Pigs, on the other hand, the proportion of fat to nitrogenous matters will be slightly higher in the entire Carcasses as here classified (excluding head and feet), than in the estimated total consumed portions. The exact proportion to one another of the constituents in question, in the entire Carcasses, and in the total estimated consumed portions, respectively, of each animal, is shown in the first two columns of Table XXIV., which will shortly follow.

* It has already been sufficiently explained, that, in the cases of the Pigs killed for *analysis*, there was adopted for the convenience of comparison, as nearly as possible the same classification of the parts into *Carcass* and *Offal*, respectively, as with the other descriptions of animal. The deviation from the usual practice consisted, in the cases in question, in classing the Head and Feet with the Offal, instead of with the Carcass. This will not, of course, in any way affect the final result arrived at in the estimates under consideration in the text

Before any legitimate comparison can be drawn between the composition of our *Animal-food* and that of *Bread*, in regard to the proportion in each, of the *Non*-nitrogenous or *Non*-flesh-forming, to the *Nitrogenous* (or so-called "*Flesh-forming*") constituents, it is, of course, necessary to form an estimate of the probable relative values, for the purposes of the system, of a given amount of the *Fat* in the one, and of the *Starch* which predominates in the other.   In calculating the amount of *Starch* which would be required to produce a given amount of the *mixed Fats* of the animal body, it was decided on grounds that were stated (p. 551), that 2·5 parts of *Starch* might be assumed to be requisite for the formation of 1 part of *Fat*.   It was stated, that assuming the *mixed fats* of the fattening animal to contain, in round numbers, 77 per cent. of carbon, 12 per cent. of hydrogen, and 11 per cent. of oxygen, it would take pretty exactly 2·45 parts of pure Starch to supply the necessary carbon and hydrogen for 1 part of such a *mixed Fat*, and to yield, at the same time, oxidable material (carbon and hydrogen), to carry off the whole of the super-fluous oxygen of the Starch, as carbonic acid and water.   But, this being the *minimum* amount of Starch required, and owing also to other considerations stated, the convenient number 2·5 was taken as the amount of Starch required to produce 1 part of the mixed Fats, in the fattening animals.   The *non*-nitrogenous substance (not fat) in *Bread* con-sists chiefly of *Starch*—part of it in a more or less altered condition.   There is also a small but variable amount of indigestible matter, and of compounds having a some-what lower percentage of carbon than Starch itself.   We may safely take, then, for our present purpose, the number 2·5 as representing the amount of the *mixed Starch and the other non-nitrogenous substances in Bread* (excluding fat), which will be equivalent to 1 part of *Fat*, for the purposes of storing up Fat in the human body.   It would, of course, be quite out of place in such a calculation, to take into account any slight difference between the composition of the mixed Fats in the human body, and of those of the slaughtered animals used as its food.

In the converse estimate to the above, namely, that of how much pure Starch would be equivalent to 1 part of the mixed Fats in oxygen-saturating capacity—that is, for the purposes of respiration—we get of course the same figure 2·45.   But for the equivalent of the mixed Starch and other non-nitrogenous constituents, excluding fat, we take the number 2·5.   In this purely chemical point of view, therefore, we take 1 part of *Fat in Animal-food*, as equal, in respiratory and fat-forming capacity, to 2½ parts of the *Starch, &c., in Bread*.

The amount of *fat* in the Carcasses—or in the estimated total consumed portions of the entire animals—has then only to be multiplied by 2·5 to bring it to its *starch-equivalent* ; or rather, to its equivalent of the *mixed starch and the other non-nitrogenous matters in Bread*.   This "starch-equivalent" of the Fat, divided by the amount of nitrogenous constituents, gives, of course, the relation of the more specially respiratory and Fat-forming constituents to 1 of Nitrogenous matters, in the *animal substances*, in such a form that these can be compared, in this respect, with *Bread*.

From all the information at command, we take the average composition of good *wheat-*

flour-bread (whole loaves, crust and crumb together), at 64 per cent. total dry substance*. Of this, 1·5 is reckoned as mineral matter (mineral constituents of the flour and salt); 8·2 per cent. nitrogenous compounds (=1·3 per cent. nitrogen); 1 per cent. fat; and the remainder, or 53·3 starch, and allied non-nitrogenous matters. If the 1 per cent. of fat be multiplied by 2·5, and the result added to the 53·3 of starch, &c., we get 55·8 for the per cent. of *starch* or "*starch-equivalent*," in Bread. If this be then divided by 8·2—the amount of the nitrogenous compounds—we get the result 6·8† as the *proportion of non-nitrogenous or respiratory and fat-forming matters* (reckoned into "starch-equivalent") to 1 of *nitrogenous* or so-called "*flesh-forming*" *compounds in Bread*. This, then, is the standard by which is compared the composition of the several Carcasses, and that of the estimated *total consumed portions*, of the different slaughtered animals, in order to arrive at an approximate judgment as to the comparative characters of our staple *Animal* and *Vegetable* food-stuffs.

In conformity with the explanations which have been given, the First Division of Table **XXIV.**, which now follows, shows the proportion of actual dry *Fat* to 1 of dry *Nitrogenous compounds*, in—

  1st. The *Carcasses* as analysed (including bone).

  2nd. The estimated *total consumed portions* of the Entire Animals.

The Second Division of the Table shows the proportion of "*starch-equivalent*" to 1 of *Nitrogenous substances*, in—

  1st. The *Carcasses* as analysed (including bone).

  2nd. The estimated *total consumed portions* of the Entire Animals.

  3rd. *Wheat-flour Bread* (whole loaves, crust and crumb together).

---

 * See Paper, by the authors, " On some Points in the Composition of Wheat-Grain, its Products in the Mill, and Bread," in the Quarterly Journal of the Chemical Society of London, vol. x. part 1.

 † Since the above estimates were made, we have been favoured by Dr. J. Forbes Watson with a view of some unpublished results obtained in his own Laboratory. These show, taking the average of 43 loaves of London bread purchased at nearly as many different shops, 63·63 per cent. of total dry matter; 1·44 per cent. of mineral matter; and 1·306 per cent. nitrogen=8·23 nitrogenous compounds. Adopting these data, and allowing 1 per cent. of fat in the bread, we get 6·74 parts of " starch-equivalent " to 1 of nitrogenous matter in bread. Taking again the mean of analyses of 25 different specimens of bread by Dr. Odling (Journal of the Society of Arts, vol. vi. No. 281), we get, on the same plan of calculation, 6·15 parts of " starch-equivalent " to 1 of nitrogenous compounds in bread. It may be mentioned, however, that the probable average amount of *fatty-matter* in Wheaten Bread is perhaps nearer 0·5 than 1 per cent.; and taking it at 0·5 per cent., the relation of the " starch-equivalent " to 1 of nitrogenous compounds in Bread, would be, according to our own estimate of composition, 6·71; according to the results of Dr. J. F. Watson, 6·65 ; and according to those of Dr. Odling, 6·07.

TABLE XXIV.—Showing the Relation of the Non-nitrogenous or Non-flesh-forming to the Nitrogenous Constituents, in Animal Food, and in Bread.

	Proportion of Dry Fat to 1 of Dry Nitrogenous Compounds.		Proportion of Starch, or of "Starch-equivalent" of Fat, to 1 of Dry Nitrogenous Compounds.	
	In Carcasses including Bone.	In the Estimated Total Consumed Portions of the Animals.	In Carcasses including Bone.	In the Estimated Total Consumed Portions of the Animals.
Store or Lean, and Half-fat Animals.				
Store Sheep	1·64	......	4·09	......
Store Pig	2·01	......	5·02	......
Half-fat Ox	1·27	1·53	3·17	3·83
Half-fat old Sheep.....................	2·11	2·51	5·27	6·28
Fat and very Fat Animals.				
Fat Calf	1·00	1·54	2·49	3·85
Fat Ox	2·31	2·76	5·78	6·91
Fat Lamb	3·39	4·40	8·49	11·01
Fat Sheep	3·96	4·37	9·89	10·93
Very Fat Sheep.........................	6·07	6·28	15·18	15·69
Fat Pig	4·71	4·48	11·77	11·20
Means.				
Of Store and Half-fat Animals......	1·76	2·02	4·39	5·05
Of Fat and very Fat Animals	3·57	3·97	8·93	9·93
Of the 10 Animals Analysed	2·85	3·48	7·11	8·71
Wheat-flour Bread.				
Whole Loaves, Crust and Crumb together			6·8	

To the first Division of this Table, which shows only the relation of *fat itself* to the nitrogenous compounds in the staple of our animal food, and without any assumptions as to its probable equivalent food-value compared with other substances, little exception can be taken. The striking fact appears, that, whether we take the composition of the *entire carcasses* including bone, or that of the estimated *total consumed portions* of the animals, the average of those of them supposed to be sufficiently fattened, shows from $3\frac{1}{2}$ to 4 parts of dry Fat, to 1 of dry nitrogenous substances. Taking the estimates of the *total consumed portions* to be pretty near the truth, the fat Calf shows $1\frac{1}{2}$ time, the fat Ox $2\frac{3}{4}$ times, the fat Lamb, fat Sheep, and the fat Pig nearly $4\frac{1}{2}$ times, and the very fat Sheep $6\frac{1}{4}$ times as much *dry fat*, as *dry nitrogenous* or so-called "*flesh-forming*" constituents. The average of the 10 entire Carcasses even, including bone, and of which several were certainly in a leaner condition than as usually sold, gives 2·85 parts of dry fat to 1 of dry nitrogenous compounds. And lastly, the average of 8 of the animals—that is, excluding only the store Sheep and store Pig—shows in the estimated consumed portions about $3\frac{1}{2}$ parts (3·48) of *dry fat* for 1 of *dry nitrogenous compounds*.

It would perhaps be hardly anticipated, that in the staple of our *meat-diet*, to which such a high relative flesh-forming capacity is generally attributed, there should be found such a large proportion of fat or *non*-flesh-forming, to nitrogenous or assumed flesh-forming constituents, as the figures in the first Division of the Table would show. The result of such a comparison as present knowledge enables us to institute on the point in question, between our staple articles of *Animal*-food, and *Bread*, will certainly not be less surprising.

With regard to the second Division of the Table, in which the Fat of the animal matters is calculated to its supposed respiratory and fat-forming equivalent of the starch and other non-nitrogenous matters occurring in Bread, it is freely granted to the Physiologist, that it is only in a certain broad sense, that such an assumption of equivalency can be admitted. It is nevertheless maintained, that for our present purpose, it is both useful and legitimate to adopt it. Without it, the important comparison sought to be instituted cannot be made; and there is evidence enough both of a practical and scientific kind to show, that, at least to a certain degree, *Fat* and the *starch series of compounds* are really thus mutually replaceable in our foods.

The Table shows, then, that in *Bread*, there are 6·8 parts of *Starch*, or "*starch-equivalent*," to 1 part of *Nitrogenous compounds*. Taking the relation of the one class of constituents to the other in the estimated *total consumed portions* of those animals assumed to be in fit condition for the butcher, there is only one case—that of the fat Calf—in which the proportion of the so-measured respiratory or fat-forming constituents, to the so-measured flesh-forming ones, was, in this our *meat-diet*, lower than in *Bread*. In the estimated total consumed portions of the fat Ox, the proportion of the "starch-equivalent" of the *non*-flesh-forming material (fat), to 1 of nitrogenous compounds, is 6·9; or rather higher than in Bread. In the estimated consumed portions of the Fat Lamb, the Fat Sheep, and the Fat Pig, the proportion of the thus estimated respiratory and fat-forming material to the nitrogenous matters, was rather more than $1\frac{1}{2}$ time as great as in Bread. In the Extra-fat Sheep, it was more than twice as great.

The average of the six cases in which the animals were supposed to be "ripe" for the butcher, shows, in the *estimated consumable portions*, nearly 10 parts of the "starch-equivalent" of specially respiratory or fat-forming material, to 1 of nitrogenous compounds; that is, nearly $1\frac{1}{2}$ time as much as in *Bread*. In the Half-fat Ox, and the Half-fat old Sheep, neither of which, however, were in the condition of fatness of Oxen and Sheep as usually killed, the relation of the "starch-equivalent" to the nitrogenous compounds (in the consumable portions), was lower than in Bread; namely, as 3·83 to 1 in the Half-fat Ox, and as 6·28 to 1 in the Half-fat old Sheep.

Taking the *carcasses as analysed*, including bone, the relation of the *non*-nitrogenous (starch-equivalent) to the nitrogenous constituents, is, in them also, in most cases *higher*

4 F 2

than in Bread. In the Fat Calf and Fat Ox, however, it is lower, namely, only 2·49 to 1 in the former, and 5·78 to 1 in the latter.   On the other hand, in the Carcass of the Fat Lamb, the proportion of the "starch-equivalent" is 8·49, in that of the Fat Sheep 9·89, in that of the Fat Pig 11·77, and in that of the Extra-fat Sheep 15·18 to 1 of the nitrogenous matters.   The *average* of the 6 *matured* Carcasses gives 8·93, and that of those of the 10 animals analysed 7·11 of *non*-nitrogenous matter, reckoned as "starch-equivalent," to 1 of nitrogenous substance—that is, *rather more than in Bread.*

Of the fact of the *increase* in the proportion (so far as its respiratory and fat-forming capacity is concerned) of the *non*-nitrogenous to the nitrogenous matter of our food, by the use of these *Animal* aliments, the evidence adduced can hardly leave a doubt.   It will perhaps be maintained, that when animals are so far fattened as to attain the result here supposed, the feeder is simply inducing .disease in the animals themselves, and frustrating that which it is considered should be the special advantage of a *meat-diet*—namely, the increase in the relative supply of the *nitrogenous* constituents in our food. It is not denied, that occasionally animals are over-fed, and that a condition bordering on disease is so induced.   But such is certainly not the rule.   There can, indeed, be little doubt, that in animals that would be admitted, by both producer and consumer, to be in only a proper condition of fatness, there would be a *higher relation* of respiratory and fat-forming capacity, so to speak, in their total consumed portions, than in the average of our *staple Vegetable* foods.   It may be true, that with the modern system of bringing animals very early to the knife, by means of abundance of food and the avoidance of cold and exercise, the development of *Fat* will be *greater*, and that of the *muscles and other nitrogenous parts less*, than would otherwise be the case.   But it is at the same time certain, that if *meat* is to be economically produced, so as to be within the reach of the masses of the population, it can only be so on the plan of "*early maturity.*"   Nor can it be questioned, that the admixture of the meat *so produced*, with their otherwise vegetable diet, is, in practice, of great advantage to the health and vigour of those who consume it.

It is not to be assumed, that in every dish of fresh meat, the relation of the Fat to the Nitrogenous matter will be as high as in the estimated consumed portions of the animals to which our Table refers.   The collective joints, as sold, will frequently have a less proportion of fat, than the whole carcasses from which they are taken.   A further amount will be removed in the process of cooking; though this portion will generally be consumed in some form or other.   But the consumers of fresh meat generally consume also suet, lard, and butter; which either add to the fatness of the cooked meats, or are used further to reduce the relation of the nitrogenous constituents in the collaterally consumed vegetable foods.   But, even were it granted, that the proportions of Fat to Nitrogenous substance which our Table shows were too high, it must on the other hand be remembered, that a considerable portion of the Nitrogenous matter of the animals will be gelatin or chondrin-yielding substance, the applicability of which, at any rate for strictly speaking flesh-forming, is, to say the least, doubted.

It would appear to be unquestionable, therefore, that the influence of the introduction of our staple *animal foods*, to supplement our otherwise mainly farinaceous diet, is, on the large scale, to *reduce*, and *not to increase*, the relation of the *assumed* flesh-forming material, to the more peculiarly respiratory and fat-forming capacity, so to speak, of the food consumed.

That, nevertheless, a dietary containing a due proportion of *animal food*, is, for some reason or other, better adapted to meet the collective requirements of the human organism, at least under many conditions, than an *exclusively Bread*, or *other vegetable one*, the testimony of common experience may be accepted as sufficient evidence. Independently of any difference in the physical, and perhaps even chemical relations of the supposed flesh-forming nitrogenous compounds in *animal food*, which may render them, at least in limited quantity, more easily available to the purposes of the system than the assumed analogous *vegetable products*, it is at any rate clear, that the main and characteristic distinction between a *Bread*—and a *mixed Bread and Meat diet*—consists, not only in the quantitatively higher relation of the respiratory and fat-forming capacity to a given amount of assumed flesh-forming material in the latter, but in the fact, that the *non*-flesh-forming constituents in the *animal* portions of the food, are in the form of *fat itself*—and not as in *Bread*, of mainly *starch*.

In *fat*, we have the most concentrated respiratory—and of course *fat*-storing material also—which our food-stuffs supply. But independently of the far greater capacity, so far as the supply of constituents is concerned, of a given weight and bulk of *Fat* compared with *Starch* and the other substances of its class—would it not seem probable, that the tax upon the system would be less, at least for *Fat-storing*, if not in a degree for respiration also, in the case of the *ready-formed Fat*, than in that of the *Starch from which it may be formed*?

Again, it has been shown that *Fat* subserves important purposes in aiding the digestion, and preparation for assimilation, of the matters ingested with it. And certainly the natural distribution and blending of the *Fat* with the nitrogenous compounds in *meat*, is such as is not met with in our staple vegetable foods. May it not too be supposed, that its liberal distribution with the transforming nitrogenous matters throughout the body, will modify the character of the changes constantly going forward, from that which would obtain, were the needed oxidable material kept up in larger proportion through the means, more or less directly, of the current supplies of Starch, and other matters not Fat, in the food?

But whatever may prove to be the exact explanations of the benefits arising from a mixed animal and vegetable diet, it is at any rate clear, that they are essentially connected with the *amount*, the *condition*, and the *distribution*, of the *Fat* in the *animal* portions of the food. It is true, that the very basis of some of our illustrations has been the assumption, that *Starch* and its analogues on the one hand, and *Fat* on the other, are, in a certain sense, and within certain limits indifferently, mutually replaceable; —and further, that they are so, in approximately measurable proportions. It is, however, certain, that independently of the mere *supply* of constituents, the conditions of *concentration*, and *digestibility*, and consequently of *assimilability* of our different foods, must have their share in determining the relative values for the varying exigencies' of the system, of substances which, in a more general, or more purely chemical sense, may still justly be looked upon as mutually replaceable. It would, indeed, hardly be supposed, that substances so distinct, both morphologically and chemically, as *Fat* and *Starch*, will, under all circumstances, be equally adapted to the conditions supplied within the living organism, and be so at an equal cost to its energies ;—even though they may each eventually subserve the Fat-storing and respiratory requirements of the body.

It is, then, fully granted, that in the study of this branch of Physiological Chemistry, as in that of others, the facts peculiar to *Physiology herself* must be allowed an important place; though, it is at the same time claimed, that those of *Chemistry* be not excluded. By the aid of *Chemistry* it may be established—that, in the admixture of *Animal* food with *Bread*, the relation, in estimated respiratory and fat-forming capacity, of the non-nitrogenous to the Nitrogenous substance, will be increased; and further—that, in such a mixed diet, the proportion of the non-nitrogenous constituents which will be in the concentrated condition, so to speak, of *fat itself*, will be considerably greater than in Bread alone. Common experience testifies, moreover, that certain advantages are so derived. It is for Physiology to lend her aid to the full explanation of the facts and conclusions which Chemistry and common usage may in their turn determine.

APPENDIX.

APPENDIX.

TABLE I.—Showing the Fresh Weights of the various Organs and Parts of A FAT CALF, killed for Analysis, September 12, 1849; also the results of the Determinations of *Dry Matter* and *Ash* in the same.

Designation of Parts.	Original fresh weights.	Dry matter at 212°.			Mineral matter (ash).		
		Exclusive of melted fat.	Melted fat.	Total dry matter.	Proportion of whole, and calculated weights, of dry matters taken for burning.	Actual ashes obtained.	Ashes calculated for the whole dry matters.

CARCASS.

		lbs. oz.	lbs. oz.	lbs. oz.	lbs. oz.		oz.	oz.	lbs. oz.
Half-carcass... { Flesh and kidney	65 13·46	13 9·70	6 1·50	21 11·20	$\frac{7}{8}$	21·770	0·994	0 9·94
Kidney fat	2 12·94	0 1·58	2 1·11	2 2·69	$\frac{1}{4}$	0·792	0·024	0 0·05
Bones......................	11 14·66	6 8·58	....	6 8·58	$\frac{1}{16}$	10·458	4·780	2 15·80
Totals of half-carcass operated on	80 9·06	20 3·86	10 2·61	30 6·47	...	......	......	3 9·79
Other half-carcass (dry, &c., calculated)......	79 15·94	20 1·57	10 1·46	30 3·03	...	......	......	3 9·38
Whole carcass......................	160 9·00	40 5·43	20 4·07	60 9·50	...	......	......	7 3·17

ORGANS OR PARTS CONSTITUTING " OFFAL."

		lbs. oz.	lbs. oz.	lbs. oz.	lbs. oz.		oz.	oz.	lbs. oz.
Stomachs (washed)	2 13·10	0 4·68	......	......	$\frac{1}{4}$	2·329	0·111	0 0·22
Caul-fat and membrane	2 7·56	0 5·01*	......	......	$\frac{1}{4}$	2·015	0·070	0 0·28
Small intestines (washed)......................	4 8·30	} 0 15·44	......	......	$\frac{1}{4}$	7·717	0·380	0 0·76
Large intestines (washed)	2 0·50		......	......				
Intestinal fat and membrane	4 3·11	0 3·05	......	......	$\ddagger$	$\ddagger$	$\ddagger$	$\ddagger$
Heart and aorta...........................	1 7·56	0 5·05	......	......	$\frac{1}{4}$	2·527	0·215	0 0·43
Heart-fat (with membrane)......................	0 6·80	†	......	......		$\ddagger$	$\ddagger$	$\ddagger$
Lungs and windpipe	3 5·70	0 13·56	......	......	$\frac{1}{8}$	6·777	0·257	0 0·51
Blood......................................	13 8·79	2 8·13	......	......	$\frac{1}{8}$	20·064	1·192	0 2·39
Liver....................................	4 3·57	1 0·34	......	......	$\frac{1}{8}$	8·172	0·432	0 0·86
Pancreas ("sweetbread")......								
Thymus gland ("heartbread")....	} 1 12·90	0 5·31	8 4·04	27 0·64 {	$\frac{1}{4}$	2·652	0·112	0 0·22
Glands about the throat ("throatbread") ...								
Milt or spleen	0 12·01	0 2·72	......	......	$\frac{1}{4}$	1·362	0·082	0 0·16
Bladder, &c............................	0 7·20	0 1·58	......	......	$\frac{1}{4}$	0·787	0·034	0 0·07
Head flesh	7 13·84	1 7·86	......	......	$\frac{1}{4}$	5·965	0·229	0 0·92
Head bones	3 9·46	1 14·98	......	......	$\frac{1}{8}$	15·490	8·560	1 1·12
Pelt...........................	16 13·71	4 5·96	......	......	$\frac{1}{4}$	13·972	0·419	0 2·10
Hair	0 14·78	0 10·58	......	......	$\frac{1}{8}$	5·292	0·090	0 0·18
Feet, hoofs, &c......................	4 5·99	2 14·11	......	......	$\frac{1}{8}$	9·222	3·082	0 15·41
Tail flesh	0 3·48	0 0·97	......	......	$\frac{1}{4}$	0·487	0·016	0 0·03
Tail bones	0 1·86	0 0·94	......	......	$\frac{1}{4}$	0·471	0·159	0 0·32
Diaphragm ("skirts")	1 1·60	0 4·45	......	......	$\frac{1}{4}$	1·112	0·040	0 0·16
Total offal	77 1·82	18 12·60	8 4·04	27 0·64	...	......	......	2 10·14

SUMMARY;—ENTIRE ANIMAL.

		lbs. oz.	lbs. oz.	lbs. oz.				lbs. oz.
Total carcass	160 9·00	40 5·43	20 4·07	60 9·50	...	......	......	7 3·17
Total "offal" parts	77 1·82	18 12·60	8 4·04	27 0·64	...	......	......	2 10·14
Contents of stomachs	5 10·20	......	......	......	...	......	......	... ..
Contents of intestines	2 8·70	......	......	......	...	......	......	... ..
Loss by evaporation, error in weighing, &c...	12 14·28	......	......	......	...	......	......	... ..
Entire animal (live-weight after fasting)......	258 12·00	59 2·03	28 8·11	87 10·14	...	......	......	9 13·31

Amount and distribution of the fat obtained by melting and expression (lbs., ozs., and tenths).				Amount and distribution of bones (including hoofs), lbs., ozs., and tenths.		
In carcass (including kidney fat)......................		20 4·07	In carcass {	First half (by experiment) 11 14·66 }	23 11·97	
				Second half (by calculation) 11 13·31		
In offal... {	From caul	} 5 7·78	} 8 4·04	In offal... {	Head .... 3 9·46	} 8 1·31
	From intestines				Feet and hoofs .... 4 5·99	
	From region of heart......				Tail .... 0 1·86	
	From remaining parts ...... 2 12·26					
	Total .... 28 8·11				Total .... 31 13·28	

* Including dry matter of heart-fat with membrane.   † With caul-fat and membrane.   ‡ With caul-fat-membrane.

APPENDIX.—TABLE II. Showing the Fresh Weights of the various Organs and Parts of A HALF-FAT OX, killed for Analysis, November 14, 1849; also the results of the Determinations of *Dry Matter* and *Ash* in the same.

Designation of Parts.	Original fresh weights.	Dry matter at 212°.			Mineral matter (ash).		
		Exclusive of melted fat.	Melted fat.	Total dry matter.	Proportion of whole, and calculated weights, of dry matters taken for burning.	Actual ashes obtained.	Ashes calculated for the whole dry matters.

CARCASS.

Designation of Parts.		lbs. oz.	lbs. oz.	lbs. oz.	lbs. oz.		oz.	oz.	lbs. oz.
Half-carcass...	Flesh and fat...............	332 0·98	82 6·79	47 14·65	130 5·44	$\frac{1}{10}$	131·300	{4·285 / 0·054}	2 11·39
	Kidney fat and membrane	13 9·54	0 8·96	12 4·00	12 12·96	$\frac{1}{4}$	4·480	0·183	0 0·37
	Kidney	1 2·71	0 4·84	......	0 4·84	$\frac{1}{4}$	1·210	0·049	0 0·20
	Flesh juice.............		2 4·00	......	2 4·00	$\frac{1}{4}$	9·000	1·846	0 7·38
	Bones................	52 5·77	37 12·23	......	37 12·23	$\frac{1}{10}$	60·423	30·402	19 9·02
Totals of half-carcass operated on	399 3·00	123 4·82	60 2·65	183 7·47	...	......	......	22 3·36
Other half-carcass (dry, &c., calculated)......	398 8·00	123 1·42	60 0·99	183 2·41	...	......	......	22 2·75
Whole carcass............	797 11·00	246 6·24	120 3·64	366 9·88	...	......	......	44 6·11

ORGANS OF PARTS CONSTITUTING "OFFAL"

Designation of Parts.	Original fresh weights.	Exclusive of melted fat.	Melted fat.	Total dry matter.		Proportion.	Actual ashes.	Ashes calculated.
Stomachs (washed)	32 1·00	6 1·17	......	......	$\frac{1}{10}$	9·717	0·493	0 4·93
Caul-fat and membrane	16 9·50	0 4·99	......	......	$\frac{1}{4}$	2·496	0·098	0 0·19
Small intestines (washed).......	8 5·00	} 2 10·48	......	......	$\frac{1}{10}$	4·248	0·138	0 1·38
Large intestines (washed)........	6 0·00							
Intestinal fat and membrane	19 11·50	1 11·65	......	......	$\frac{1}{4}$	6·912	0·180	0 0·72
Heart and aorta.............	5 13·50	1 9·46	......	......	$\frac{1}{4}$	6·365	0·220	0 0·98
Heart-fat with membrane........	2 6·75	0 1·61	......	......	$\frac{1}{4}$	0·804	0·033	0 0·07
Lungs and windpipe............	7 12·75	1 13·63	......	......	$\frac{1}{4}$	7·382	0·398	0 1·59
Blood............................	54 5·00	11 11·41	......	......	$\frac{1}{10}$	18·741	0·812	0 8·12
Liver	15 11·00	4 7·34	......	......	$\frac{1}{10}$	7·134	0·380	0 3·80
Pancreas ("sweetbread")......	1 0·00	0 3·84	......	......	$\frac{1}{4}$	1·920	0·096	0 0·19
Thymus gland ("heartbread") ...	0 10·75	0 0·99	......	......	$\frac{1}{4}$	0·498	0·034	0 0·07
Glands about the throat ("throatbread") ...	0 6·25	0 1·30	......	......	$\frac{1}{4}$	0·650	0·042	0 0·08
Milt or spleen	2 2·25	0 8·46	......	......	$\frac{1}{4}$	4·232	0·263	0 0·52
Bladder	0 5·00							
Gall-bladder	0 3·00	0 4·22	} 38 13·88	130 5·81	{ $\frac{1}{4}$	2·109	0·071	0 0·14
Penis	0 6·50							
Brains	0 14·25	0 3·17	......	......	$\frac{1}{4}$	1·583	0·109	0 0·22
Tongue	7 7·50	1 12·75	......	......	$\frac{1}{4}$	7·187	0·349	0 1·40
Head flesh	17 6·50	3 5·12	......	......	$\frac{1}{10}$	5·312	0·275	0 2·75
Head bones	14 2·00	10 14·00	......	......	$\frac{1}{10}$	17·400	10·141	6 5·41
Hide (and horns, &c.)	72 7·98	{ 12 12·95 / 12 12·25 }	......	......	$\frac{1}{40}$	20·425	0·492	0 9·84
Hair	7 7·38	4 10·16	......	......	$\frac{1}{10}$	18·540	0·459	0 1·84
Leg bones	13 0·00	7 3·93	......	......	$\frac{1}{10}$	11·523	5·250	3 4·50
Hoofs and heels	7 2·00	3 12·34	......	......	$\frac{1}{4}$	15·085	3·327	0 13·31
Tail flesh	1 5·24	0 6·71	......	......	$\frac{1}{4}$	1·677	0·053	0 0·21
Tail bones	0 7·15	0 5·80	......	......	$\frac{1}{4}$	2·898	1·110	0 2·22
Diaphragm ("skirts")	5 11·50	1 8·82	......	......	$\frac{1}{4}$	6·205	0·187	0 0·75
Miscellaneous trimmings	1 7·00	0 2·88	......	......	$\frac{1}{4}$	1·438	0·016	0 0·09
Total offal	322 12·25	91 7·93	38 13·88	130 5·81	...	......	......	13 1·22

SUMMARY:—ENTIRE ANIMAL.

Total carcass	797 11·00	246 6·24	120 3·64	366 9·88	......	......	44 6·11
Total offal parts.....................	322 12·25	91 7·93	38 13·88	130 5·81	......	......	13 1·22
Contents of stomachs, and vomit	86 0·00	......	......	......	......	......	......
Contents of intestines, and bile	12 14·00	......	......	......	......	......	......
Loss by evaporation, error in weighing, &c.	10 10·75	......	......	......	......	......	......
Entire animal (live-weight after fasting) ..	1232 0·00	337 14·17	159 1·52	496 15·69	......	......	57 7·33

Amount and distribution of the fat obtained by melting and expression (lbs., ozs., and tenths).			Amount and distribution of bones (including hoofs), lbs., ozs., and tenths.		
In carcass (including kidney fat)..............	120 3·64		In carcass { First half (by experiment) 52 5·77	} 104 10·10	
In offal... { From caul .... 14 14·97			Second half (by calculation) 52 4·33 }		
{ From intestines............... 15 0·50	} 38 13·88		Head .... 14 2·00		
{ From region of heart ..... 2 13·36			In offal... { Legs .... 13 0·00	} 34 11·15	
{ From remaining parts ...... 6 1·05			{ Feet, hoofs, and heels .... 7 2·00		
Total ....159 1·52			{ Tail........................ 0 7·15		
			Total ....139 5·25		

APPENDIX.—TABLE III. Showing the Fresh Weights of the various Organs and Parts of A FAT OX, killed for Analysis, October 30, 1849; also the results of the Determinations of *Dry Matter* and *Ash* in the same.

Designation of Parts.	Original fresh weights.	Dry matter at 212°. Exclusive of melted fat.	Melted fat.	Total dry matter.	Mineral matter (ash). Proportion of whole, and calculated weights, of dry matters taken for burning.		Actual ashes obtained.	Ashes calculated for the whole dry matters.
CARCASS.								
	lbs. oz.	lbs. oz.	lbs. oz.	lbs. oz.		oz.	oz.	lbs. oz.
Half-carcass… Flesh and fat	386 10·32	72 5·70	115 5·16	187 10·86	$\frac{1}{10}$	115·770	4·275	2 10·75
Half-carcass… Kidney	1 8·77	0 6·07	……	……	$\frac{1}{2}$	3·034	0·134	0 0·27
Half-carcass… Kidney fat and membrane	26 11·40	0 14·56	25 9·50	27 10·72	$\frac{1}{4}$	7·280	0·245	0 0·49
Half-carcass… Flesh juice	……	0 12·59	……	……	$\frac{1}{4}$	6·295	1·110	0 2·22
Half-carcass… Bones	55 8·01	40 11·20	……	40 11·20	$\frac{1}{16}$	40·700	18·594	18 9·50
Totals of half-carcass operated on	470 6·50	115 2·12	140 14·66	256 0·78	…	……	……	21 7·23
Other half-carcass (dry, &c., calculated)	468 15·50	114 12·49	140 7·77	255 4·26	…	……	……	21 6·18
Whole carcass	939 6·00	229 14·61	281 0·43	511 5·04	…	……	……	42 13·41
ORGANS OF PARTS CONSTITUTING "OFFAL."								
Stomachs (washed)	36 6·00	6 9·05	……	……	$\frac{1}{4}$	26·262	1·130	0 4·52
Caul-fat and membrane	29 13·00	0 14·52* (Caul-fat and Heart, trimmings)	……	……	$\frac{1}{4}$	3·630	0·089	0 0·28
Heart, trimmings, &c.	3 15·50		……	……				
Small and large intestines (washed)	13 14·25	1 12·59	……	……	$\frac{1}{4}$	7·147	0·285	0 1·14
Intestinal fat and membrane	36 14·00	1 5·88	……	……	$\frac{1}{2}$	10·940	0·480	0 0·96
Heart and aorta	7 6·00	1 7·12	……	……	$\frac{1}{4}$	5·780	0·245	0 0·98
Heart-fat (with membrane)	6 3·00	0 3·91	……	……	$\frac{1}{4}$	1·955	0·061	0 0·13
Lungs and windpipe	8 14·50	2 0·29	……	……	$\frac{1}{4}$	8·072	0·404	0 1·62
Blood	52 11·75	10 12·46	……	……	$\frac{1}{10}$	17·240	0·723	0 7·23
Liver	17 10·00	5 0·70	……	……	$\frac{1}{10}$	8·070	0·385	0 3·85
Pancreas ("sweatbread")	0 15·50	0 2·39	……	……	$\frac{1}{4}$	0·598	0·040	0 0·16
Thymus gland ("heartbread")	0 10·50	0 1·15	……	……	$\frac{1}{2}$	0·575	0·047	0 0·09
Glands about the throat ("throatbread")	0 6·50	0 1·03	……	……	[illegible]	0·744	0·052	0 0·07
Milt or spleen	2 4·00	0 8·77	……	……	$\frac{1}{4}$	2·192	0·116	0 0·46
Gall-bladder, Bladder, Penis	1 15·08	0 7·32	83 13·05 (Stomachs to Miscellaneous trimmings)	177 4·34 (Stomachs to Miscellaneous trimmings)	$\frac{1}{4}$	1·830	0·061	0 0·24
Brains	0 14·00	0 3·14	……	……	$\frac{1}{2}$	1·569	0·110	0 0·22
Tongue	3 7·50	0 15·49	……	……	$\frac{1}{4}$	3·872	0·148	0 0·59
Head flesh	25 9·50	5 6·56	……	……	$\frac{1}{10}$	8·656	0·300	0 3·00
Head bones	14 6·00	10 4·40	……	……	$\frac{1}{10}$	16·440	9·350	5 13·50
Hide (and horns, &c.)	73 15·49	25 13·44	……	……	$\frac{1}{20}$	20·672	0·525	0 10·50
Hair	6 4·21	4 14·60	……	……	$\frac{1}{4}$	19·650	0·315	0 1·26
Leg bones	13 13·00	8 2·30	……	……	$\frac{1}{10}$	13·030	5·711	3 9·11
Hoofs and heels	8 10·80	4 1·98	……	……	$\frac{1}{10}$	6·598	1·370	0 13·70
Tail flesh	1 0·70	0 4·45	……	……	$\frac{1}{2}$	2·227	0·055	0 0·11
Tail bones	0 6·80	0 5·40	……	……	$\frac{1}{2}$	2·700	1·054	0 2·11
Diaphragm ("skirts")	7 9·00	1 8·35	……	……	$\frac{1}{4}$	6·087	0·193	0 0·77
Miscellaneous trimmings †	……	……	……	……	…	……	……	……
Total offal	376 0·58	93 7·29	83 13·05	177 4·34	…	……	……	12 12·60
SUMMARY:—ENTIRE ANIMAL.								
Total carcass	939 6·00	229 14·61	281 0·43	511 5·04	…	……	……	42 13·41
Total offal parts	376 0·58	93 7·29	83 13·05	177 4·34	…	……	……	12 12·60
Contents of stomachs, and vomit; Contents of intestines, and bile	84 12·67	……	……	……	…	……	……	……
Loss by evaporation, error in weighing, &c.	18 12·75	……	……	……	…	……	……	……
Entire animal (live-weight after fasting)	1419 0·00	323 5·90	365 3·48	688 9·38	…	……	……	55 10·01

Amount and distribution of the fat obtained by melting and expression (lbs., ozs., and tenths).

In carcass (including kidney fat)			281 6·43
In offal…	From caul	29 13·00	83 13·05
	From intestines	33 1·00	
	From region of heart	6 6·00	
	From remaining parts	14 9·05	
Total			365 3·48

Amount and distribution of bones (including hoofs), lbs., ozs., and tenths.

In carcass	First half (by experiment)	55 8·10	110 13·30
	Second half (by calculation)	55 5·29	
In offal…	Head	14 6·00	37 4·60
	Legs	13 13·00	
	Feet, hoofs, and heels	8 10·80	
	Tail	0 6·80	
Total			48 1·90

* These parts accidentally mixed.

† Accidentally mixed with caul-fat.

APPENDIX.—TABLE IV. Showing the Fresh Weights of the various Organs and Parts of A FAT LAMB, killed for Analysis, August 17, 1849; also the results of the Determinations of *Dry Matter* and *Ash* in the same.

Designation of Parts.	Original fresh weights.	Dry matter at 212°. Exclusive of melted fat.	Melted fat.	Total dry matter.	Mineral matter (ash). Proportion of whole, and calculated weights, of dry matters taken for burning.		Actual ashes obtained.	Ashes calculated for the whole dry matters.
CARCASS.								
	lbs. oz.	lbs. oz.	lbs. oz.	lbs. oz.		oz.	oz.	lbs. oz.
Half-carcass... Flesh and fat	21 1·34	3 3·66	6 8·10	9 11·76	½	25·830	0·960	0 1·92
Half-carcass... Kidney fat	1 11·29	0 0·46	1 9·20	1 9·66	½	0·230	0·008	0 0·02
Half-carcass... Bones	2 9·41	1 11·17	......	1 11·17	½	13·585	6·405	0 12·81
Totals of half-carcass operated on	25 6·04	4 15·29	8 1·30	13 0·59	...	......	......	0 14·75
Other half-carcass (dry, &c., calculated)	25 1·96	4 14·49	8 0·00	12 14·49	...	......	......	0 14·60
Whole carcass	50 8·00	9 13·78	16 1·30	25 15·08	...	......	......	1 13·35
ORGANS OR PARTS CONSTITUTING "OFFAL."								
Stomachs (washed)	1 8·64	0 5·01	......	......	½	2·505	0·088	0 0·18
Caul-fat and membrane	3 4·02	0 1·18*	......	......	½	0·590*	0·038*	0 0·08*
Small intestines } Large intestines	2 0·35	0 6·49	......	......	½	3·245	0·157	0 0·31
Intestinal fat and membrane	1 10·63	†	......	......	...	‡	‡	‡
Heart and aorta	0 5·37	0 1·17	......	......	½	0·585	0·022	0 0·04
Heart-fat and membrane	0 4·64	†	......	......	...	‡	‡	‡
Lungs and windpipe	1 0·80	0 5·10	......	......	½	2·550	0·083	0 0·17
Blood	2 14·27	0 10·12	......	......	½	5·062	0·245	0 0·49
Liver	1 2·85	0 5·68	3 14·80	10 14·77	½	2·840	0·137	0 0·27
Pancreas ("sweetbread") } Thymus gland ("heartbread") } Glands about the throat ("throatbread")	0 2·47§	0 0·57§	......	......	½	0·285§	0·017§	0 0·03§
Milt or spleen	0 2·58	0 0·66			½	0·330	0·019	0 0·04
Head flesh	1 11·60	0 5·41	......	......	½	2·705	0·150	0 0·30
Head bones	0 14·49	0 9·00	......	......	½	4·498	2·534	0 5·07
Pelt	4 15·19	1 7·36	......	......	½	11·678	0·580	0 1·16
Wool	3 1·71	1 15·10	......	......	½	7·775	0·256‖	0 1·02‖
Feet, hoofs, &c.	0 12·70	0 5·74	......	......	½	1·435	0·278	0 1·11
Diaphragm ("skirts")	0 4·78	0 1·38	......	......	½	0·692	0·018	0 0·04
Total offal	26 5·29	6 15·97	3 14·80	10 14·77		......	......	0 10·31
SUMMARY:—ENTIRE ANIMAL.								
Total carcass	50 8·00	9 13·78	16 1·30	25 15·08	...	......	......	1 13·35
Total offal parts	26 5·29	6 15·97	3 14·80	10 14·77	...	......	......	0 10·31
Contents of stomachs	5 2·06	......	......	......	...	......	......	......
Contents of intestines	2 1·35	......	......	......	...	......	......	......
Loss by evaporation, error in weighing, &c.	0 5·80	......	......	......	...	......	......	......
	84 6·50	16 13·75	20 0·10	36 13·85	...	......	......	2 7·66

Amount and distribution of the fat obtained by melting and expression (lbs., ozs., and tenths).

In carcass (including kidney fat)			16 1·30
In offal...	From caul } From intestines } From region of heart	3 10·40	3 14·80
	From remaining parts	0 4·40	
	Total		20 0·10

Amount and distribution of bones (including hoofs), lbs., ozs., and tenths.

In carcass	First half (by experiment)	2 9·41	5 2·40
	Second half (by calculation)	2 8·99	
In offal...	Head	0 14·49	1 11·19
	Feet and hoofs	0 12·70	
	Total		6 13·59

* Including dry matters of intestinal and heart-fat and their membranes. † With caul-fat. ‡ With caul-fat-membrane.

§ It is doubtful whether these amounts refer to the Pancreas, Thymus Gland, and Glands about the Throat collectively, or to the Pancreas alone.

‖ The amounts of Mineral Matter in the Wool are stated too high, owing to adherent dirt.

APPENDIX.—TABLE V. Showing the Fresh Weights of the various Organs and Parts of A STORE SHEEP, killed for Analysis, February 28, 1850; also the results of the Determinations of *Dry Matter* and *Ash* in the same.

Designation of Parts.	Original fresh weights.	Dry matter at 212°. Exclusive of melted fat.	Melted fat.	Total dry matter.	Mineral matter (ash). Proportion of whole, and calculated weights, of dry matters taken for burning.	Actual ashes obtained.	Ashes calculated for the whole dry matters.
CARCASS.							
	lbs. oz.	lbs. oz.	lbs. oz.	lbs. oz.	oz.	oz.	lbs. oz.
Half-carcass — Flesh and fat	21 9·91	3 10·96	4 6·50	8 3·46	14·740	1·286	0 5·14
Half-carcass — Kidney	0 2·17	0 0·48	......	0 0·48	0·120	0·006	0 0·02
Half-carcass — Kidney fat and membrane	0 6·85	0 0·45	0 7·00	0 7·45	0·114	0·002	0 0·01
Half-carcass — Bones	3 8·01	2 4·85	......	2 4·85	9·212	3·207	0 12·83
Totals of half-carcass operated on	25 12·94	6 0·74	4 16·50	11 0·24	...	......	1 2·00
Other half-carcass (dry, &c., calculated)	26 4·06	6 2·41	5 0·87	11 3·28	...	......	1 2·31
Whole carcass	52 1·00	12 3·15	10 0·37	22 3·52	...	......	2 4·31
ORGANS OR PARTS CONSTITUTING "OFFAL."							
Stomachs (washed)	3 3·63	0 5·98			2·243	0·105	0 0·28
Caul-fat and membrane	3 2·70	0 1·08			0·406	0·016	0 0·04
Small intestines (washed)	1 1·04	} 0 4·71			1·767	0·078	0 0·21
Large intestines (washed)	1 7·09						
Intestinal fat and membrane	1 9·40	0 1·24			0·465	0·020	0 0·05
Heart and aorta	0 8·30	0 1·78			0·687	0·026	0 0·07
Heart-fat (with membrane)	0 3·90	0 0·12			0·044	0·004	0 0·01
Lungs and windpipe	1 6·95	0 6·44			2·413	0·091	0 0·24
Blood	5 1·25	0 13·76			5·158	0·208	0 0·56
Liver	1 10·60	0 8·46			3·173	0·138	0 0·37
Pancreas ("sweetbread")	0 1·13						
Thymus gland ("heartbread")	0 1·10	} 0 0·62	4 5·05	13 9·25	0·235	0·021	0 0·06
Glands about the throat ("throatbread")	0 1·00						
Milt or spleen	0 2·50	0 0·50			0·187	0·011	0 0·03
Gall-bladder	0 0·11	} 0 0·22			0·083	0·008	0 0·02
Bladder	0 1·00						
Head flesh	2 6·00	0 6·06			2·280	0·131	0 0·35
Head bones	1 3·25	0 12·68			4·755	2·059	0 5·49
Pelt	5 8·57	1 10·00			9·750	0·543	0 1·45
Wool	7 3·25	3 1·80			24·900	1·202*	0 2·40*
Feet, hoofs, &c.	1 0·58	0 7·79			2·920	0·539	0 1·44
Diaphragm ("skirts")	0 3·37	0 0·94			0·354	0·013	0 0·03
Total offal	37 6·92	9 4·20	4 5·05	13 9·25	...	......	0 13·10
SUMMARY:—ENTIRE ANIMAL.							
Total carcass	52 1·00	12 3·15	10 0·37	22 3·52	...	......	2 4·31
Total offal parts	37 6·92	9 4·20	4 5·05	13 9·25	...	......	0 13·10
Contents of stomachs	4 13·80	......					
Contents of intestines, and bile	0 15·90	......					
Loss by evaporation, error in weighing, &c.	2 4·38	......					
Entire animal (live-weight after fasting)	97 10·00	21 7·35	14 5·42	35 12·77	...	......	3 1·41

Amount and distribution of the fat obtained by melting and expression (lbs., ozs., and tenths).		Amount and distribution of bones (including hoofs), lbs., ozs., and tenths.	
In carcase (including kidney fat)	10 0·37	In carcase { First half (by experiment) ... 3 8·01; Second half (by calculation)... 3 8·97	7 0·98
In offal... { From caul ... 1 14·80; From intestines ... 1 2·43; From region of heart ... 0 2·60; From remaining parts... 1 1·22 }	4 5·05	In offal ... { Head ... 1 3·25; Feet and hoofs ... 1 0·68 }	2 3·93
Total	14 5·42	Total	9 4·91

* The amounts of Mineral Matter in the Wool are stated too high, owing to adherent dirt.

APPENDIX.—TABLE VI. Showing the Fresh Weights of the various Organs and Parts of A HALF-FAT OLD SHEEP, killed for Analysis, May 8, 1849; also the results of the Determinations of *Dry Matter* and *Ash* in the same.

Designation of Parts.	Original fresh weights.	Dry matter at 212°.			Mineral matter (ash).		
		Exclusive of melted fat.	Melted fat.	Total dry matter.	Proportion of whole, and calculated weights, of dry matters taken for burning.	Actual ashes obtained.	Ashes calculated for the whole dry matters.
	lbs. oz.	lbs. oz.	lbs. oz.	lbs. oz.	oz.	oz.	lbs. oz.
CARCASS.							
Half-carcass ... { Flesh and fat	25 7·87	5 3·01	5 11·59	10 14·60	⅛ 16·602	0·568	0 2·84
Kidney fat	......	0·47	1 0·20	3 3·94	₁⁄₇₂ 0·188	0·004	0 0·01
Bones	2 10·20	2 3·27			¼ 7·054	3·151	0 15·75
Totals of half-carcass operated on	28 2·07	7 6·75	6 11·79	14 2·54	...	......	1 2·60
Other half-carcass (dry, &c., calculated)	28 2·07	7 6·75	6 11·79	14 2·54	...	......	1 2·61
Whole carcass	56 4·14	14 13·50	13 7·58	28 5·08	...	......	2 5·21
ORGANS OR PARTS CONSTITUTING "OFFAL."							
Stomachs (washed)	2 13·75	0 7·78			₁⁄₇₂ 3·112	0·129	0 0·32
Caul-fat and membrane	3 1·50	0 0·63			₁⁄₇₂ 0·250	0·044†	0 0·11†
Small intestines	1 0·80	0 6·33			₁⁄₇₂ 2·532	0·092	0 0·23
Large intestines	1 3·00						
Intestinal fat and membrane	2 5·50	0 1·36			₁⁄₇₂ 0·542	§	§
Heart and aorta	0 7·35	0 1·51			₁⁄₇₂ 0·605	0·025	0 0·06
Heart-fat and membrane	0 8·00	0 0·93			₁⁄₇₂ 0·374	§	§
Lungs and windpipe	1 1·40	0 4·43			₁⁄₇₂ 1·772	0·082	0 0·20
Blood	4 1·93	0 11·21			₁⁄₇₂ 3·362	0·184	0 0·61
Liver	1 11·30	0 6·33	} 5 8·50	14 6·91	₁⁄₇₂ 2·532	0·124	0 0·31
Pancreas ("sweetbread")							
Thymus gland ("heartbread")	} 0 2·58‖	0 0·51‖			₁⁄₇₂ 0·204‖	0·014‖	0 0·03‖
Glands about the throat ("throatbread")							
Milt or spleen	0 2·95	0 0·80			₁⁄₇₂ 0·318	0·019	0 0·05
Head flesh	2 10·44	0 7·54			₁⁄₇₂ 3·016	0·122	0 0·31
Head bones	1 8·36	1 1·30			₁⁄₇₂ 1·730	0·868	0 8·68
Pelt	7 0·44*	0 15·37			₁⁄₇₂ 6·148	0·370	0 0·93
Wool	6 10·56	3 4·50			₁⁄₇₂ 5·250	0·310¶	0 3·10¶
Feet, hoofs, &c.		0 5·60			₁⁄₇₂ 0·840	0·165	0 1·10
Diaphragm ("skirts")	0 8·60	0 2·28			₁⁄₇₂ 0·911	0·034	0 0·09
Total offal	37 1·76	8 14·41	5 8·50	14 6·91	...	......	1 0·13
SUMMARY:—ENTIRE ANIMAL.							
Total carcass	56 4·14	14 13·50	13 7·58	28 5·08	...	......	2 5·21
Total "offal" parts	37 1·76	8 14·41	5 8·50	14 6·91	...	......	1 0·13
Contents of stomachs	7 9·35	......	......	......	...	......	......
Contents of intestines	1 14·90	......	......	......	...	......	......
Loss by evaporation, error in weighing, &c.	2 2·85	......	......	......	...	......	......
Entire animal (live-weight after fasting)	105 1·00	23 11·91	19 0·08	42 11·99	...	......	3 5·34

Amount and distribution of the fat obtained by melting and expression (lbs., ozs., and tenths).				Amount and distribution of bones (lbs., ozs., and tenths).			
In carcass (including kidney-fat)		13 7·58		In carcass { First half (by experiment)... 2 10·20	Second half (by calculation) 2 10·20 }		5 8·40
In offal ... { From caul	2 6·66			In offal ... { Head	1 8·36		
From intestines	2 1·80			{ Feet and hoofs (with pelt, not weighed separately)	......		
From region of heart ...	0 6·58	} 5 8·50					
From remaining parts...	0 9·46						
Total		19 0·08		Total			7 0·76

* Including feet and hoofs.   † Including intestinal and heart-fat, and their membranes.

‡ With pelt.   § With caul-fat-membrane.

‖ It is doubtful whether these amounts refer to the Pancreas, Thymus Gland, and Glands about the Throat collectively, or to the Pancreas alone.

¶ The amounts of Mineral Matter in the Wool are stated too high, owing to adherent dirt.

APPENDIX.—TABLE VII. Showing the Fresh Weights of the various Organs and Parts of A FAT SHEEP, killed for Analysis, May 7, 1849; also the results of the Determinations of *Dry Matter* and *Ash* in the same.

Designation of Parts.	Original fresh weights.	Dry matter at 212°.			Mineral matter (ash).		
		Exclusive of melted fat.	Melted fat.	Total dry matter.	Proportion of whole, and calculated weights, of dry matters taken for burning.	Actual ashes obtained.	Ashes calculated for the whole dry matters.
CARCASS.							
	lbs. oz.	lbs. oz.	lbs. oz.	lbs. oz.	oz.	oz.	lbs. oz.
Half-carcase ... { Flesh and fat	33 1·00	4 1·49	12 4·60	16 6·09	¼	13·097	0·538	0 2·61
Kidney		0 0·51	......	0 0·51	1/15	0·204		0 0·07
Kidney fat		0 1·17	3 0·66	3 1·83	1/10	0·469	} 0·028	
Bones	3 4·00	2 6·20		2 6·20	¼	7·650	3·456	1 1·28
Totals of half-carcass operated on	36 5·00	6 9·37	15 5·26	21 14·63	...	......	......	1 4·04
Other half-carcass (dry, &c., calculated)......	36 12·00	6 10·64	15 8·21	22 2·85	...	......	......	1 4·28
Whole carcass......................	73 1·00	13 4·01	30 13·47	44 1·48	...	......	......	2 8·32
ORGANS OR PARTS CONSTITUTING "OFFAL."							
Stomachs (washed)	3 2·50	0 6·92	......		1/10	2·769	0·204	0 0·51
Caul-fat and membrane	6 9·00	0 1·84	......		1/10	0·737	0·058 †	0 0·14†
Small intestines..........	1 5·80	} 0 5·90	......		1/10	2·360	0·120	0 0·30
Large intestines..........	2 5·50		......					
Intestinal fat and membrane	3 9·50	0 1·57	......		1/10	0·626	§	§
Heart and aorta..........	0 8·70	0 1·86	......		1/10	1·115	0·040	0 0·07
Heart-fat and membrane..........	0 8·00	0 0·48	......		1/10	0·190	§	§
Lungs and windpipe..........	1 0·50	0 4·38	......		1/10	2·628	0·107	0 0·18
Blood	4 8·80	0 13·02	......		1/10	5·208	0·220	0 0·55
Liver	1 14·80	0 9·36	} 10 2·00	20 5·50	1/10	5·746	0·180	0 0·45
Pancreas ("sweetbread ")..........	} 0 3·40‖	0 0·51‖	......		1/10	0·205‖	0·014‖	0 0·03‖
Thymus gland ("heartbread ") Glands about the throat ("throatbread ") ...								
Milt or spleen	0 3·33	0 0·78	......		1/10	0·469	0·034	0 0·06
Head flesh	2 10·20	0 6·12	......		1/10	2·446	0·149	0 0·37
Head bones	1 3·80	0 13·42	......		1/10	1·341	0·709	0 7·09
Pelt	7 0·60*	1 11·87	......		1/10	11·148	0·613	0 1·53
Wool	8 1·90	3 13·10	......		1/10	6·110	0·404¶	0 4·04¶
Feet, hoofs, &c.	‡	0 6·66	......		1/10	0·666	0·150	0 1·50
Diaphragm ("skirts")	0 6·20	0 1·71	......		1/10	1·027	0·032	0 0·05
Total offal	45 6·53	10 3·50	10 2·00	20 5·50	...	......	......	1 0·87
SUMMARY :—ENTIRE ANIMAL.							
Total carcase	73 1·00	13 4·01	30 13·47	44 1·48	...	......	......	2 8·32
Total "offal" parts	45 6·53	10 3·50	10 2·00	20 5·50	...	......	......	1 0·87
Contents of stomachs	4 15·50	......	......	......				
Contents of intestines	2 11·10	......	......	......				
Loss by evaporation, error in weighing, &c.	1 0·37	......	......	......				
Entire animal (live-weight after fasting) ...	127 2·50	23 7·51	40 15·47	64 6·98	...	......	......	3 9·19

Amount and distribution of the fat obtained by melting and expression (lbs., ozs., and tenths).		Amount and distribution of bones (lbs., ozs., and tenths).	
In carcass (including kidney fat)......................	30 13·47	In carcase ... { First half (by experiment) ... 3 4·00 Second half (by calculation)... 3 4·62 }	6 8·62
In offal ... { From caul .... 3 15·80 From intestines .... 2 15·70 From region of heart ... 0 0·00 From remaining parts... 1 2·50 }	10 2·00	In offal ... { Head Feet and hoofs (with pelt, not weighed separately) }	1 3·80 ......
Total	40 15·47	Total	7 12·42

* Including feet and hoofs.   † Including ash of intestinal and heart-fat, and their membranes.

‡ With pelt.   § With caul-fat.

‖ It is doubtful whether these amounts refer to the Pancreas, Thymus Gland, and Glands about the Throat collectively, or to the Pancreas alone.

¶ The amounts of Mineral Matter in the Wool are stated too high, owing to adherent dirt.

APPENDIX.—TABLE VIII. Showing the Fresh Weights of the various Organs and Parts of AN EXTRA-FAT SHEEP *, killed for Analysis, December 13, 1848; also the results of the Determinations of *Dry Matter* and *Ash* in the same.

Designation of Parts.	Original fresh weights.	Dry matter at 212°.			Mineral matter (ash).		
		Exclusive of melted fat.	Melted fat.	Total dry matter.	Proportion of whole, and calculated weights, of dry matters taken for burning.	Actual ashes obtained.	Ashes calculated for the whole dry matters.
	lbs. oz.	*lbs. oz.*	*lbs. oz.*	*lbs. oz.*	*oz.*	*oz.*	*lbs. oz.*
CARCASS.							
Half-carcass ... { Flesh and fat .... / Fat-membrane .... / Bones .... }	79 10·00	7 7·36 / 2 0·94 / 4 3·08	39 9·10	53 4·49 {	¾ / ½ / ½	44·760 / 12·350 / 25·158	1·220 / 0·332 / 11·890	0 3·25 / 0 0·89 / 1 15·17
Totals of half-carcass operated on	79 10·00	13 11·39	39 9·10	53 4·49	...	....	....	2 3·31
Other half-carcass (dry, &c., calculated)......	79 10·00	13 11·39	39 9·10	53 4·49	...	....	....	2 3·31
Whole carcass......................	159 4·00	27 6·78	79 2·20	106 8·98	...	....	....	4 6·62
ORGANS OR PARTS CONSTITUTING "OFFAL."							
Stomachs (washed)	4 2·30						
Caul-fat and membrane	24 6·00†						
Small intestines (washed)...................	1 14·70						
Large intestines (washed)..................	1 3·90						
Intestinal fat and membrane	‡						
Heart and aorta.............................	0 13·00						
Heart-fat and membrane	0 0·50						
Lungs and windpipe..........................	1 14·00	6 0·64	24 1·00	30 1·64	⅐	18·120	0·698	0 3·72
Blood	10 4·00	(2 4·84)			(⅐)	(6·907)	(0·278)	(0 1·48)
Liver, with mill...........................	3 0·20						
Pancreas ("sweetbread ")...................	....						
Thymus gland ("heartbread ")	0 5·70§						
Glands about the throat ("throatbread ") ...	....						
Head flesh	3 10·00	1 6·00	......	1 6·00	¹⁄₇	4·125	2·310	0 12·32
Head bones	2 6·50	3 13·46	......	3 13·46	¹⁄₇	11·523	0·560	0 2·99
Pelt..	} 25 8·00	7 15·76	......	7 15·76	¹⁄₇	23·955	4·667‖	1 8·89
Wool		0 11·40	......	0 11·40	¹⁄₇	2·136	0·515	0 2·75
Feet and hoofs, &c.							
Total offal	80 1·90	19 15·26	24 1·00	44 0·26	...	....	....	2 14·67
SUMMARY:—ENTIRE ANIMAL.							
Total carcass	159 4·00	27 6·78	79 2·20	106 8·98	...	....	....	4 6·62
Total "offal" parts	80 1·90	19 15·26	24 1·00	44 0·26	...	....	....	2 14·67
Contents of stomachs	10 8·00	......	......	......	...	....	....	
Contents of intestines	2 9·40	......	......	......	...	....	....	
Loss by evaporation, error in weighing, &c.	0 0·80	......	......	......	...	....	....	
Entire animal (live-weight after fasting) ..	252 8·00	47 6·04	103 3·20	150 9·24	...	....	......	7 5·29

Amount and distribution of the fat obtained by melting and expression (lbs., ozs., and tenths).

In carcass (including kidney-fat)	79 2·20	
In offal ... { From caul .... / From intestines .... / From remaining parts...........	15 10·00 / 5 15·00 / 2 8·00 }	24 1·00
Total	103 3·20	

* This was the first of the ten animals analysed; and, as the Table on comparison will show, the plan of operation and separation of the parts was less complete and systematic, than in the other cases.

† Including intestinal fat and membrane.   ‡ With caul-fat and membrane.

§ It is doubtful whether this amount refers to the Pancreas, Thymus Gland, and Glands about the Throat collectively, or to the Pancreas only.

‖ The amounts of Mineral Matter in the Wool are stated too high, owing to adherent dirt.

APPENDIX.—TABLE IX. Showing the Fresh Weights of the various Organs and Parts of A STORE PIG, killed for Analysis, May 12, 1850; also the results of the Determinations of *Dry Matter* and *Ash* in the same.

Designation of Parts.	Original fresh weights.	Dry matter at 212°.			Mineral matter (ash).		
		Exclusive of melted fat.	Melted fat.	Total dry matter.	Proportion of whole, and calculated weights, of dry matters taken for burning.	Actual ashes obtained.	Ashes calculated for the whole dry matters.
	lbs. oz.	lbs. oz.	lbs. oz.	lbs. oz.	oz.	oz.	lbs. oz.
CARCASS.							
Half-carcase { Flesh and fat	26 0·96	4 1·18	7 0·00	11 1·18	16·295	0·654	0 2·61
Kidney	0 2·62	0 0·64		0 0·64	0·160	0·009	0 0·04
Kidney fat and membrane	0 12·97	0 1·02	0 8·30	0 9·32	0·255	0·004	0 0·02
Flesh juice		0 1·91		0 1·91	0·955	0·210	0 0·42
Skin and diaphragm	1 8·01	0 10·47		0 10·47	2·617	0·031	0 0·12
Bones	2 7·50	1 6·66		1 6·66	5·585	2·394	0 9·58
Totals of half-carcase operated on	31 1·26	6 5·88	7 8·30	13 14·18	...	......	0 12·79
Other half-carcase (dry, &c., calculated)	31 5·18	6 6·68	7 9·25	13 15·93	...	......	0 12·89
Whole carcase	62 6·44	12 12·56	15 1·55	27 14·11	...	......	1 9·68
ORGANS OR PARTS CONSTITUTING "OFFAL."							
Stomach (washed)	1 3·30	0 3·60	......	......	1·425	0·065	0 0·17
Caul-fat and membrane	0 5·55	0 0·34	......	......	0·127	0·003	0 0·01
Small intestines (washed)	2 9·00	0 9·47	......	......	3·551	0·152	0 0·40
Large intestines (washed)	2 5·74						
Intestinal fat, "mudgeon," &c.	1 5·77	0 1·62	......	......	0·607	0·024	0 0·06
Heart and aorta	0 7·85	0 1·86		......	0·706	0·032	0 0·08
Lungs and windpipe	1 5·70	0 3·82	......		1·432	0·086	0 0·23
Blood	7 0·85	0 13·21	......		4·955	0·270	0 0·72
Liver	2 8·00	0 11·47	......		4·309	0·231	0 0·62
Pancreas ("sweetbread")	*0 4·05	*0 1·02	......		*0·127	*0·009	*0 0·07
Milt or spleen	0 2·75	0 0·65			0·245	0·013	0 0·03
Gall-bladder	0 0·20						
Bladder	0 2·30	0 0·53	3 7·10	9 6·83	0·198	0·010	0 0·03
Brains	0 3·56	0 0·68	......		0·254	0·017	0 0·05
Tongue	0 8·40	0 1·85	......		0·231	0·020	0 0·16
Head flesh	12·54	0 10·56	......		3·956	0·175	0 0·47
Head bones	1 11·25	0 15·55	......		5·631	3·112	0 8·30
Head-skin and ears	0 10·62	0 3·47	......		1·301	0·012	0 0·03
Hair		0 1·76	......		0·876	0·011	0 0·02
Scurf		0 1·92			0·240	0·010	0 0·08
Feet and toes	{ 1 3·57 / 0 1·75 }	0 10·88		......	2·720	0·705	0 2·82
Tail and bones	0 0·57	0 0·31	......	......	0·114	0·013	0 0·04
Œsophagus and trimmings	0 6·55	0 0·94			0·354	0·017	0 0·05
Total offal	29 7·87	5 15·73	3 7·10	9 6·83	...	......	0 14·44
SUMMARY:—ENTIRE ANIMAL.							
Total carcase	62 6·44	12 12·56	15 1·55	27 14·11	...	......	1 9·68
Total offal parts	29 7·87	5 15·73	3 7·10	9 6·83	...	......	0 14·44
Contents of stomachs	0 4·25	......	......	......	...	......	......
Contents of intestines and bile	4 10·36	......	......	......	...	......	......
Loss by evaporation, error in weighing, &c.	— 2 13·92	......	......	......	...	......	......
Entire animal (live-weight after fasting)	93 15·00	18 12·29	18 8·65	37 4·94	...	......	2 8·12

Amount and distribution of the fat obtained by melting and expression (lbs., ozs., and tenths).			Amount and distribution of the bones (including toes), lbs., ozs., and tenths.		
In carcase (including kidney fat)		15 1·55	In carcase { First half (by experiment)... 2 7·50 / Second half (by calculation) 2 7·81 }		4 15·31
In offal... { From caul ... 0 3·35 / From intestines, "mudgeon,"&c. 0 6·65 / From remaining parts (including head) 2 13·10 }		3 7·10	In offal { Head ... 1 11·25 / Feet and toes ... 1 5·32 }		3 0·57
Total		18 8·65	Total		7 15·88

* It is doubtful whether these amounts refer to the Pancreas, Thymus Gland, and Glands about the Throat collectively, or to the Pancreas alone.

APPENDIX.—TABLE X. Showing the Fresh Weights of the various Organs and Parts of A FAT PIG, killed for Analysis, July 18, 1850; also the results of the Determinations of *Dry Matter* and *Ash* in the same.

Designation of Parts.	Original fresh weights.	Dry matter at 212°.			Mineral matter (ash).		
		Exclusive of melted fat.	Melted fat.	Total dry matter.	Proportion of whole, and calculated weights, of dry matters taken for burning.	Actual ashes obtained.	Ashes calculated for the whole dry matters.

CARCASS.

		lbs. oz.	lbs. oz.	lbs. oz.	lbs. oz.	oz.	oz.	lbs. oz.
Half-carcass...	Flesh and fat	60 1·22	7 0·46	29 15·00	36 15·46	28·114	0·641	0 2·56
	Kidney	0 4·50	0 1·02	......	0 1·02	0·254	0·013	0 0·05
	Kidney fat and membrane	3 11·52	0 1·70	3 0·75	3 2·45	0·425	0·012	0 0·05
	Flesh juice	......	0 0·54	......	0 0·54	0·136	0·027	0 0·11
	Skin and diaphragm	3 2·88	1 1·99	......	1 1·99	4·498	0·061	*0 0·36
	Bones	3 4·21	2 0·20	......	2 0·20	8·050	3·160	0 12·64
Totals of half-carcass operated on	70 8·33	10 5·91	32 15·75	43 5·66	...	......	......	0 15·77
Other half-carcass (dry, &c., calculated)	70 0·40	10 4·74	32 12·04	43 0·78	...	......	......	0 15·66
Whole carcass	140 8·73	20 10·65	65 11·79	86 6·44	...	......	......	1 15·43

ORGANS OR PARTS CONSTITUTING "OFFAL."

	lbs. oz.	lbs. oz.	lbs. oz.	lbs. oz.	oz.	oz.	lbs. oz.
Stomach (washed)	1 3·48	0 3·90	......		1·462	0·019	0 0·05
Caul-fat and membrane	0 8·95	0 0·30	......		0·112	0·005	0 0·01
Small intestines (washed)	2 8·54	0 8·62			3·232	0·135	0 0·36
Large intestines (washed)	1 10·74				1·145	0·057	0 0·15
Intestinal fat, "mudgeon," &c.	4 1·31	0 3·05					
Heart and aorta	0 8·80	0 1·87	......	......	0·703	0·033	0 0·09
Lungs and windpipe	1 11·73	0 5·64	......		1·880	0·087	0 0·26
Blood	6 13·30	1 7·26	......		8·724	0·455	0 1·21
Liver	3 0·77	0 14·34	......		5·377	0·350	*0 0·93
Pancreas ("sweetbread")	*0 6·44	*0 1·00	......	7 0·45	14 13·11	*0·375	*0·017	*0 0·05
Milt or spleen	0 4·93	0 0·85			0·318	0·018	0 0·05
Gall-bladder	0 0·21	0 0·59			0·222	0·009	0 0·02
Bladder	0 2·45						
Brains	0 3·31	0 0·68			0·171	0·013	0 0·05
Tongue	0 12·90	0 2·66			0·996	0·040	0 0·11
Head flesh	7 1·98	0 12·86			4·822	0·182	0 0·49
Head bones	1 13·50	1 2·01			6·754	3·498	0 0·31
Head-skin and ears	1 5·00	0 5·12			1·920	0·053	0 0·14
Hair	......	0 3·54			1·339	0·054	0 0·14
Scurf	1 14·47						
Feet and toes	0 2·84	1 1·96			6·733	1·463	0 3·90
Tail and bones	0 1·01	0 0·41	......	......	0·151	0·015	0 0·01
Total offal	36 8·66	7 12·66	7 0·45	14 13·11	...	......	......	1 1·36

SUMMARY:—ENTIRE ANIMAL.

	lbs. oz.	lbs. oz.	lbs. oz.	lbs. oz.			lbs. oz.
Total carcass	140 8·73	20 10·65	65 11·79	86 6·44	...	......	......	1 15·43
Total offal parts	36 8·66	7 12·66	7 0·45	14 13·11	...	......	......	1 1·36
Contents of stomachs	0 11·82	......	......	......	...	......	......	......
Contents of intestines and bile	6 9·80	......	......	......	...	......	......	......
Loss by evaporation, error in weighing, &c.	0 8·99	......	......	......	...	......	......	......
Entire animal (live-weight after fasting)	185 0·00	28 7·31	72 12·24	101 3·55	...	......	......	3 0·79

Amount and distribution of the fat obtained by melting and expression (lbs., ozs., and tenths).		Amount and distribution of bones (including toes), lbs., ozs., and tenths.	
In carcass (including kidney fat)	65 11·79	In carcass { First half (by experiment) ... 3 4·21 / Second half (by calculation) 3 3·84 } 6 8·05	
In offal... { From caul	0 8·05	In offal... { Head ... 1 13·50 / Feet and toes ... 2 1·31 } 3 14·81	
From intestines, "mudgeon," &c. 2 8·75 / From remaining parts (including head) 3 15·55 } 7 0·45			
Total	72 12·24	Total	10 6·86

* It is doubtful whether these amounts refer to the Pancreas, Thymus Gland, and Glands about the Throat collectively, or to the Pancreas alone.

APPENDIX.—TABLE XI. Showing the Percentages of *Crude Dry Matter** in the Individual Organs, and other separated Parts, of 10 Animals of different Description, Age, or condition of Fatness.

Designation of Parts	Calf and Oxen			Lamb and Sheep					Pigs	
	Fat calf	Half-fat ox	Fat ox	Fat lamb	Store sheep	Half-fat old sheep	Fat sheep	Extra fat sheep	Store pig	Fat pig
Carcase { Flesh and fat	20·655	24·622	18·714	15·316	17·044		12·697		15·639	11·499
Kidney	†	25·854	24·477	1·691	22·659	20·469		17·290	22·727	22·750
Kidney fat and membrane	3·514	4·117	3·407		5·985				7·870	2·856
Flesh juice		4·677	0·303			83·499	73·461		0·460	0·456
Skin and diaphragm	54·834			66·311	65·903				41·947	35·358
Bones		72·124	23·933						57·338	61·733
Total carcass	25·124	20·868	24·475	19·597	23·428	26·384	18·136	17·220	20·489	14·704
Stomachs (washed)	10·230	18·941	19·050	29·333	11·540	17·006	13·703		19·689	20·020
Caul-fat and membrane	19·907	11·889	11·986	1·413	2·138	1·273	1·752		6·196	3·330
Small and large intestines (washed)	14·728	18·550	13·664	29·061	11·740	17·681	9·949		19·027	19·812
Intestinal fat and membrane	4·544	8·764	3·798	†	4·682	3·627	2·730		7·441	4·570
Heart and aorta	21·451	27·220	19·593	21·787	21·446	20·544	21·379		23·974	21·295
Heart-fat with membrane		4·150	3·949		3·926	11·625	6·090			
Lungs and windpipe	25·242	23·671	23·658	30·357	23·896	25·460	39·645	22·403	17·603	20·339
Blood	18·510	21·566	20·440	21·872	16·929	12·185	17·884		11·709	21·283
Liver	24·188	28·452	29·617	30·132	31·932	23·186	30·390		28·675	29·403
Pancreas ("sweetbread")	18·354	24·000	15·445	23·076**	19·195	19·767**	15·000***		25·185**	15·638**
Thymus gland ("heartbread")		9·256	10·952							
Glands about the throat ("throatbread")		20·800	15·784							
Milk or spleen	22·681	24·712	24·855	25·581	20·000	27·118	23·423		23·636	17·241
Gall-bladder and bladder	21·875	29·090	29·352		19·923	‡‡‡	‡‡‡	8·908††	21·130	22·256
Bile	†	9·200	22·414	‡‡‡	‡	‡	‡		†	
Brains		22·917	27·910						19·101	20·531
Tongue	18·909	24·058	21·138	19·401	16·000	17·766	14·502		23·024	20·589
Head flesh		19·074	71·480						12·607	11·282
Head bones	53·915	70·991	34·934	62·112	65·870	71·018	67·778	57·142	57·169	81·174
Head-skin and ears		33·493	78·435	29·499	29·355	18·650	30·666		33·661	24·427
Pelt	25·902	62·119	59·959	62·563	43·210	49·288	47·036	49·171	§	§
Hair or wool	71·582	51·599	47·596	45·196	46·684	¶	¶		51·128	53·917
Feet bones and hoofs	66·680	52·930	96·670	¶	¶	¶	¶		53·806	40·594
Tail flesh	27·988	31·599	79·412	28·870	28·012	26·512	27·581		§	§
Tail bones	50·645	81·074	30·124	¶	¶	¶	¶		14·427	
Diaphragm ("skirts")	25·272	27·196	†							
Miscellaneous trimmings		12·569								
Total offal	24·363	28·347	24·853	26·578	24·745	23·984	23·504	24·907	20·287	21·329
Entire animal	22·951	27·436	23·788	19·974	21·981	22·600	18·457	18·763	19·979	15·382

* The so-called "*Crude Dry Matter*" is exclusive of the fat removable by melting and expression; but still retains, in most cases, 20 to 30 per cent. of fat extractable by ether.

† With caul-fat and membrane.   ‡ Thrown away.   § With carcase.   ‖ With pelt.

** It is doubtful whether these amounts refer to the Pancreas, Thymus Gland, and Glands about the Throat collectively, or to the Pancreas alone.

†† This is the per cent. of *Crude Dry Matter* (that is the Dry Matter exclusive of melted and expressed Fat) in all those parts taken collectively, to which the other figures in the column do not apply.

APPENDIX.—TABLE XII. Showing the Percentages of *Mineral Matter* (Ash) in the Individual Organs, and other separated Parts (fresh), of 10 Animals of different Description, Age, or condition of Foetuses.

Designation of Parts.	Calf and Oxen.			Lamb and Sheep.					Pigs.	
	Fat calf.	Half-fat ox.	Fat ox.	Fat lamb.	Store sheep.	Half-fat old sheep.	Fat sheep.	Extra-fat sheep.	Store pig.	Fat pig.
Carcass										
Flesh and fat	0·943	0·816	0·691	0·569	1·486	0·699	0·552		0·695	0·266
Kidney		1·068	1·088		0·919				1·430	1·116
Kidney fat and membrane	0·111	0·170	0·115	0·073	0·113			2·772	0·154	0·084
Flesh juice		0·139	0·435						0·101	0·011
Skin and diaphragm	+			+		+	+		0·481	0·707
Bones	25·053	36·289	33·321	30·793	22·910	37·287	33·231		24·941	24·233
Total carcass	4·483	5·563	4·569	3·632	4·359	4·134	3·449	2·772	2·572	1·398
Separate parts of the "offal."										
Stomachs (washed)	0·492	0·961	0·777	0·730	0·540	0·689	1·009		0·896	0·962
Caul-fat and membrane	0·603	0·074	0·051	0·096	0·097	0·116	0·062	0·902	0·180	0·145
Small and large intestines (washed)	0·725	0·603	0·513	0·958	0·518	0·642	0·506		0·514	0·535
Intestinal fat and membrane	+	0·226	0·163	+	0·209	+	+		0·276	0·230
Heart and aorta	1·895	0·941	0·830	0·745	0·831	0·816	0·964		1·083	1·000
Heart-fat with membrane	0·957	0·170	0·127	1·012	0·256	1·145	1·691		1·655	0·938
Lungs and windpipe	1·020	2·717	2·427	1·069	2·640	0·935	0·755		0·638	1·110
Blood	1·278	0·934	0·857	1·437	0·683	1·143	1·461		1·540	1·913
Liver	+	1·514	1·365		1·392					
Pancreas ("sweetbread")	0·775	1·200	1·032	1·214**	2·844	1·163**	0·862**		1·778**	0·776**
Thymus gland ("heartbread")		0·632	0·895		0·454					
Glands about the throat ("throatbread")	1·365	1·280	1·103	1·550	1·900	1·695	1·602		1·273	0·974
Milk or spleen		1·586	1·290		1·160					
Gall-bladder and bladder	0·944	0·970	0·785		1·885			0·378††	1·080	0·902
Bile	+	1·234	+						+	+
Brains		1·530	1·571						1·404	1·510
Tongue	0·728	1·168	1·067	1·086	0·918	0·730	0·877		1·905	0·829
Head flesh		0·987	0·733						0·614	0·420
Head bones	29·794	44·872	40·652	34·989	98·525	36·632	35·806	32·000	30·515	31·623
Head-skin and ears	0·778	0·807	0·887	1·465	1·635	1·805	2·691		0·282	0·667
Pelt	1·218	1·538	1·257	2·052	2·086	2·909	3·110	7·507	§	§
Hair or wool*	22·017	25·240	25·841	8·740	8·616	¶	¶	¶	13·248	11·708
Leg bones		11·674	9·870							
Feet bones and hoofs	0·919	0·998	0·659	0·637	1·089	1·046	0·806		8·944	3·960
Tail flesh	17·097	31·053	31·000							
Tail bones	0·969	0·817	0·638						0·687	§
Diaphragm ("skirts")		1·264								
Miscellaneous trimmings										
Total offal	3·415	4·061	3·401	2·447	2·187	2·717	2·322	3·641	3·060	2·969
Entire animal	3·900	4·664	3·920	2·937	3·163	3·173	2·811	2·903	2·669	1·648

* The amounts of mineral matter in wool are stated too high, owing to adherent dirt.   † With carcass.   ‡ Thrown away.

§ With pelt.   ¶ With carcass in case of all the sheep.

** It is doubtful whether these amounts refer to the Pancreas, Thymus Gland, and Glands about the Throat collectively, or to the Pancreas alone.

†† With caul-fat and membrane.

†† This is the per cent of Ash in all those parts taken collectively, to which the other figures in the column do not refer.

4 H 2

APPENDIX.—TABLE XIII. Showing the Results of the individual Determinations of *Fat* (by extraction with Ether), in the "Crude Dry Substance *" of certain collective portions, and of the entire bodies, of 10 Animals of different Description, Age, or condition of Fatness.

	Percentages of Fat remaining in the "Crude Dry Substance."				
	Experiment 1.	Experiment 2.	Experiment 3.	Experiment 4.	Mean.
1. COLLECTIVE CARCASS PARTS (INCLUDING BONE).					
Fat calf	15·98	15·84	......	......	15·91
Half-fat ox	24·67	23·94	......	......	24·30
Fat ox	19·99	19·85	......	......	19·92
Fat lamb	25·61	25·93			25·77
Store sheep	19·34	19·43			19·39
Half-fat old sheep	27·43	27·74			27·59
Fat sheep	17·64	17·67			17·66
Extra-fat sheep	31·34	31·16			31·25
Store pig	18·98	19·19			19·09
Fat pig	18·70	19·16			18·93
Store pig (head and feet without tongue and brains)	18·02	18·17	......	......	18·09
Fat pig (head and feet without tongue and brains) ...	21·72	21·65	......	......	21·68
2. COLLECTIVE OFFAL PARTS (INCLUDING BONE).					
Fat calf	16·52	16·31	......	......	16·42
Half-fat ox	13·54	13·51	14·22	13·33	13·66
Half-fat ox (without bone)	15·78	15·31	......	......	15·55
Half-fat ox (offal bones only)	9·16	8·52	......	......	8·84
Fat ox	17·24	16·19	17·27	......	16·90
Fat lamb	23·89	23·80	......	......	23·85
Store sheep	22·38	22·15	......	......	22·27
Half-fat old sheep	18·40	18·27	......	......	18·34
Fat sheep	20·93	21·05	20·76	......	20·91
Extra-fat sheep	22·90	22·62	......	......	22·76
Store pig	15·47	15·35	......	......	15·41
Fat pig	13·41	13·49	......	......	13·45
3. WOOL †.					
Fat lamb	8·69	9·28	......	......	8·99
Store sheep	11·18	8·98	11·38	12·75	11·07
Half-fat old sheep	8·95	8·85	......	......	8·90
Fat sheep	14·40	12·69	14·81	......	13·97
Extra-fat sheep	11·65	9·70	10·38	9·84	10·44
4. ENTIRE ANIMAL (EXCLUDING WOOL).					
Fat calf	17·10	16·52	......	......	16·81
Half-fat ox	22·74	22·79	......	......	22·77
Fat ox	19·10	19·10	......	......	19·10
Fat lamb	25·70	25·83			25·77
Store sheep	19·35	19·38			19·37
Half-fat old sheep	26·17	26·48			26·33
Fat sheep	19·42	19·35			19·39
Extra-fat sheep	29·42	29·46			29·44
Store pig	18·18	18·08	......	......	18·13
Fat pig	19·08	18·49	......	......	18·78

* After the removal of as much fat as possible by melting and expression.

† The agreement of the separate determinations is not so good in the case of the wool, as in that of the other parts, owing to the adherent dirt, which rendered it difficult to secure even samples for analysis.

APPENDIX.—TABLE XIV. Showing the Results of the individual Determinations of *Nitrogen* in the " Crude Dry Substance *" of certain collective portions, and of the entire bodies, of 10 Animals of different Description, Age, and condition of Fatness.

	Percentages of Nitrogen in the "Crude Dry Substance."				
	Experiment 1.	Experiment 2.	Experiment 3.	Experiment 4.	Mean.
1. COLLECTIVE CARCASS PARTS (EXCLUDING BONE).					
Fat calf	12·49	12·44	......	......	12·47
Half-fat ox	10·90	10·86	......	......	10·88
Fat ox	12·20	12·05	......	......	12·13
Fat ox (with bones)	9·62	9·59	......	......	9·60
Fat lamb	10·63	10·72	......	......	10·68
Store sheep	13·04	13·09	......	......	13·07
Half-fat old sheep	10·33	10·43	......	......	10·38
Fat sheep	12·65	12·73	......	......	12·69
Extra-fat sheep	9·55	9·45	......	......	9·50
Store pig (with bones)	11·38	11·26	......	......	11·32
Fat pig (with bones)	11·61	11·55	11·58	......	11·64
Store pig (head and feet without tongue and brains)	8·70	8·88	......	......	8·79
Fat pig (head and feet without tongue and brains) ...	8·68	8·66	......	......	8·67
2. CARCASS BONES.					
Fat calf	5·94	6·06			6·00
Half-fat ox	4·88	4·90			4·89
Fat ox	4·95	5·02			4·99
Fat lamb	5·17	5·02	......	......	5·10
Store sheep	5·08	5·09	......	......	5·09
Half-fat old sheep	4·62	4·65	......	......	4·64
Fat sheep	4·92	4·94	......	......	4·93
Extra-fat sheep	4·97	4·93	......	......	4·95
3. COLLECTIVE OFFAL PARTS (INCLUDING BONE).					
Fat calf	11·35	11·30	11·43	......	11·36
Half-fat ox	11·95	11·71	11·95	......	11·87
Fat ox	11·25	11·29	11·29	......	11·28
Fat lamb	10·21	9·89	9·97		10·02
Store sheep	10·51	10·60	10·43		10·51
Half-fat old sheep	10·52	10·35	10·51		10·46
Fat sheep	10·61	10·60	10·28		10·50
Extra-fat sheep	10·58	10·33	10·29		10·40
Store pig (no bones)	12·96	12·82	......	......	12·89
Fat pig (no bones)	13·10	13·23	......	......	13·17
4. HAIR OR WOOL†.					
Fat calf	16·46	16·60	......		16·53
Half-fat ox	16·74	16·90	......		16·82
Fat ox	16·16	16·82	16·57		16·52
Fat lamb	14·80	14·97	......	......	14·89
Store sheep	14·30	13·86	15·20	14·03	14·35
Half-fat old sheep	16·52	14·38	14·70	......	15·20
Fat sheep	14·49	13·56	13·60	13·08	13·43
Extra-fat sheep	12·49	11·83	12·08	12·54	12·24
5. ENTIRE ANIMAL (EXCLUDING HAIR OR WOOL).					
Fat calf	10·79	10·70	......	.....	10·75
Half-fat ox	10·04	10·06	......	......	10·05
Fat ox	10·15	10·13	......	......	10·14
Fat lamb	9·24	9·22	......	......	9·23
Store sheep	10·33	10·02	10·34	......	10·23
Half-fat old sheep ‡ {	9·33	9·23	......	......	9·28
{	8·85	9·26	9·50	......	9·20
Fat sheep ‡ {	9·92	10·05	......	......	9·99
{	10·69	10·24	10·76	......	10·56
Extra-fat sheep ‡ {	8·71	8·72	......	......	8·72
{	9·10	9·13	9·21	......	9·15
Store pig	11·10	11·16	......	......	11·13
Fat pig	11·52	11·77	11·57	......	11·62

* After the removal of as much fat as possible by melting and expression.

† The agreement of the separate determinations is not so good in the case of the wool, as in that of the other parts, owing to the adherent dirt, which rendered it difficult to secure even samples for analysis.

‡ In these cases a second set of determinations was made as a check, some months after the first, and with different reagents.

APPENDIX.—TABLE XV. Showing the Actual Weights (lbs. and ozs.) of the

Designation of Parts.	Calves.		Heifers.		Bullocks.				
	No. 1.	No. 2.	No. 1.	No. 2.	No. 1.	No. 2.	No. 3.	No. 4.	No. 5.
	Short horned; milk-fed; killed Aug. 11, 1849.	Durham breed; (analysed as fat) taken from dam feeding on grass; killed Sept. 12, 1849.	Welsh; three to four years old; killed Aug. 23, 1849.	Welsh; three years old; lately oil-cake fed; killed Aug. 30, 1849.	Mixed breed; killed Aug. 2, 1849.	Mixed breed; killed Aug. 9, 1849.	Welsh, horned; four years old; killed Aug. 16, 1849.	Scotch, long-horned; four years old; grass-fed; killed Aug. 30, 1849.	Dutch; lately grass-fed in Norfolk; killed Aug. 23, 1849.
	lbs. oz.	lbs. oz.	lbs. oz.	lbs. oz.	lbs. oz.	lbs. oz.	lbs. oz.	lbs. oz.	lbs. oz.
Stomachs	4 0	2 13	33 0	31 0	40 8	37 2	28 8	36 0	33 8
Contents of stomachs and vomit	3 14	8 3	51 0	90 8	157 14	83 14	81 2	99 0	79 8
Caul-fat	2 11	2 7·5	31 11	14 13	18 7	15 8	11 9	21 9	19 0
Small intestines and contents	4 8	6 3	13 0	17 8	24 10	19 0	13 2	20 10	19 8
Large intestines and contents	8 9·5	2 14·5	9 4	15 0	18 0	21 12	12 10	16 6	13 12
Intestinal fat	1 9	4 3	36 0	16 6	17 4	15 14	12 12	17 6	24 1
Heart and aorta	1 8	1 7·5	4 3	3 13	6 4	5 2	4 14·5	6 1	6 8
Heart-fat	.....	0 6·8	2 0	1 12	1 14	3 0	1 14·5	1 15	1 14
Lungs and windpipe	3 4	3 5·5	5 7	7 6	12 8	0 0	7 2·5	11 4	11 12
Blood	10 0	13 8·8	32 4	29 4	48 9	46 8	25 13·5	49 0	44 8
Liver	4 2	4 3·5	13 12	12 2	15 3	14 4	10 5	16 14	13 10
Gall-bladder and contents	0 2	*	0 10	0 11·5	0 6	0 3	0 15	1 4·5	1 14
Pancreas ("sweetbread")	0 4·5	.....	0 12	0 14	1 1	1 2·5	0 12	0 12·5	0 14
Thymus gland ("heartbread")	0 11·5	1 13	0 9	0 9·5	1 0	0 8	0 7	0 10·5	1 0
Glands about the throat ("throatbread")	0 9		0 5	0 6·5	0 5	.....	0 4	0 3·5	0 11
Milt or spleen	0 14	0 12	1 8	1 0	2 0	2 0	0 15	1 11	2 0
Bladder, with penis, or womb	0 4·5	0 7·2	9 12†	1 6	0 9	0 8	0 4·5	0 7·5	0 8
Brains				0 10	1 2·5	0 8	0 11·8	0 12	0 10
Head and tongue	15 12	11 7·2	20 4	22 0	31 0	26 12	24 7·5	31 12	35 2
Hide and horns	17 0	17 12·5	64 12	67 0	91 0	68 8	73 7	98 12	81 0
Feet, hoofs, &c.	6 9	4 6	13 12	15 8	22 8	18 7	17 10·5	18 2	20 12
Tail	.....	0 5·2	0 8	1 1·5	1 8	0 14	0 13	0 13	1 4
Diaphragm ("skirts")	.....	1 1·5	4 12	4 7	5 12	2 4·5	1 10	2 1	1 14·5
Miscellaneous trimmings	.....	.....	7 4	1 8	.....	1 2	2 5·5	2 1	3 12
Total "offal" parts	81 4	87 12·7	356 5	356 10	519 4·5	393 13	334 7·8	455 7·5	418 14·5
Carcass	155 14	157 7·5	498 6	451 4	665 8	550 4	527 4	629 8	713 13
Loss by evaporation, error in weighing, &c.	5 10	13 7·8	37 7	8 2	27 11·5	20 0	20 0	23 0·5	36 4·5
Live-weight after fasting	242 12	258 12	891 12	816 0	1212 8	964 1	881 11·6	1108 0	1169 0

(Rows from "Stomachs" to "Milt or spleen" bracketed as "Separate parts of the 'offal.'")

* With bladder.   † Including calf.

individual Organs, and other separated Parts, of CALVES, HEIFERS, and BULLOCKS.

	Bullocks.									Means of			
	No. 6.	No. 7.	No. 8.	No. 9.	No. 10.	No. 11.	No. 12.	No. 13.	No. 14.	The two calves.	The two heifers.	The fourteen bullocks.	The sixteen heifers and bullocks.
	Scotch, long-horned: four years old; grass-fed; killed Sept. 6, 1849.	Welsh, five years old; killed Sept. 13, 1849.	Mixed breed; killed Sept. 20, 1849.	Durham, short-horned; three to four years old; grass-fed; killed Sept. 27, 1849.	Irish, lately grass-fed in Leicestershire; killed Sept. 27, 1849.	Mixed breed; three years old; killed Oct. 4, 1849.	Scotch; (analysed as fat) four years old; killed Oct. 30, 1849.	Scotch; (analysed as half-fat) three to four years old; killed Nov. 14, 1849.	Devon: working ox; afterwards fed on oilcake, &c.; seven years old; killed April 6, 1853.				
	lbs. oz.	lbs. oz.	lbs. oz.	lbs. oz.	lbs. oz.	lbs. oz.	lbs. oz.	lbs. oz.	lbs. oz.	lbs. oz.	lbs. oz.	lbs. oz.	lbs. oz.
	34 0	31 11	36 0	41 12	30 10	33 4	36 6	32 1	58 8	3 6·5	32 0	36 6·7	35 13·9
	117 12	104 7	93 0	92 0	108 6	100 9·5	84 4	100 1	60 8	6 0·5	70 12	97 4·7	93 15·8
	13 10	22 9·5	24 2	24 8·5	19 0·5	35 0	29 13	16 9·5	53 0	2 9·2	23 4	23 2·7	23 2·9
	19 0	20 0	17 0	20 4	17 0·5	16 15·5	8 11·7	8 5	14 15	5 5·5	15 4	17 1·3	16 13·6
	22 4	16 2	11 7	8 5	11 15·5	14 10	5 2·5	6 0	7 11	3 4	12 2	13 4·6	13 2·3
	10 12	21 14	27 0	27 14	19 10	39 0	36 14	19 11·5	79 0	2 14	26 3	26 5·8	26 5·4
	5 13	4 13	5 10	5 14·5	5 3	5 1·5	7 6	5 13·5	8 2	1 7·7	4 0	5 14·4	5 10·6
	1 9	3 5	3 14	2 14·5	3 14	4 7	6 3	2 6·8	8 14	0 3·5	1 14	3 6·9	3 3·8
	9 12	8 1	8 3	9 6	10 0	8 11·5	6 14·5	7 12·6	12 6	4 4·8	6 6·5	9 10·1	9 3·6
	44 10	49 8	56 6	57 6	42 3·5	45 5	52 11·8	54 5	54 7	11 12·5	30 12	47 15·2	45 12·8
	13 12	13 2	15 0	17 11	13 12	14 6·5	17 10	15 11	20 2	4 2·6	12 15	15 1·6	14 13·3
	0 13·5	1 7	1 5	1 1·8	0 15	0 14·5	0 13	1 0	1 6	0 2	0 10·8	1 0·5	0 15·7
	0 13·5	0 12·5	0 15	1 3	1 1	1 5	0 15·5	1 0	2 10	......	0 13	1 1·6	1 1
	0 13	0 8	0 9	0 8	0 9·5	......	0 10·5	0 10·8	1 11	1 11	0 9·2	0 11	0 10·7
	0 7·5	0 2	0 5	0 7·2	0 4·8	0 5·5	0 6·5	0 6·2	0 8	......	0 5·7	0 5·5	0 5·5
	1 13	1 14	2 9	1 13·8	2 1·5	1 6·5	2 4	3 2·2	2 12	0 13	1 4	1 15·3	1 13·9
	0 7	0 8	0 9	0 15·5	0 15	1 2·5	1 10·7	0 11·5	1 5	0 6	5 ·94	0 16·7	0 9·1
	0 10·5	0 12·5	0 11	0 15·2	0 12·2	0 11·8	0 14	0 14·2	0 8	} 13 9·5	0 5	0 12·1	0 12·0
	32 0	27 0	26 6	30 12	30 11	23 10	43 7	39 0	40 8		21 2	32 0·5	30 10·7
	105 0	84 8	91 8	90 8	80 4	83 14	80 3·8	79 15·4	113 4	17 6·2	65 14	87 4·3	84 9·5
	20 14	17 14	21 13	23 11	20 9	21 7	22 7·7	20 2	25 0	5 7·5	14 10	20 13	20 0·6
	1 0	1 1	1 3	1 6·5	1 0	1 0	1 7·5	1 12·4	} † 13 0	0 5·2	0 12·8	1 1·3	1 1·9
	4 11	6 12	5 3	7 1	4 7	4 12	7 9	5 11·5		1 1·5	4 9·5	5 3·2	5 2
	3 11	1 3	2 3	2 5·3	3 2	11 9·5	3 6·2	3 8	8 11	......	4 6	3 14·3	3 15·3
	466 0	439 14·5	452 13	470 11·8	428 7	475 8·8	465 14·2	426 9·5	588 12	35 4·9	356 7·5	452 13·3	439 13·9
	639 4	630 0	693 12	762 12	666 12	701 1·2	939 6	797 11	1095 12	156 10·8	474 10	710 3·1	680 12
	6 12	15 1·5	15 7	32 8·2	16 13	-2 10	13 11·8	8 11·5	37 8	8 12·3	22 12·5	19 1·1	20 7·2
	1112 0	1085 0	1162 0	1266 0	1112 0	1174 0	1419 0	1232 0	1652 0	250 12	853 14	1182 1·5	1141 1·1

‡ With hide.   § In one case Womb with Calf.

APPENDIX.—TABLE XVI. Showing the *Actual Weights* (lbs. and ozs.) of the individual Organs, and other separated Parts, of SHEEP.

CLASS I.—5 Sheep of different Breeds, killed in Store condition (at Rothamsted), for standards of comparison.

Designation of Parts.	Cotswold Wethers; killed Nov. 25, 1851. No. 1 (lbs. oz.)	No. 2 (lbs. oz.)	Leicester Wether; killed Nov. 22 1852 (lbs. oz.)	Cross-bred Wether (Leicester and South Down); killed Nov. 22, 1852 (lbs. oz.)	Cross-bred Ewe (Leicester and South Down); killed Nov. 22, 1852 (lbs. oz.)	Means of the 5 Store Sheep (lbs. oz.)
Original weight	115 0	109 0	94 0	87 0	84 0	97 12·8
Final weight, unfasted	112 0	112 0	95 0	89 0	87 0	99 0
Final weight after fasting	105 12	104 8	89 0	84 0	82 0	93 0·8
Stomachs	2 12·6	3 2·5	2 9·7	2 11·5	2 5·5	2 11·5
Contents of stomachs	5 14·1	7 3	5 6·3	†	†	6 2·5
Caul-fat	3 15·5	3 0	1 8·6	2 15·5	2 3·8	2 11·9
Small intestines and contents	3 8·2	2 9·8	3 2	1 14·4	1 13·5	2 2·6
Large intestines and contents	3 4	2 6·5	1 3·6	2 8	2 5	2 11·5
Intestinal fat	1 0·6	1 0·3	0 6·8	1 9·1	0 15·5	1 2·6
Heart and aorta	0 7·8	0 8·3	0 3·7	0 6·7	0 5·9	0 7·1
Heart-fat	0 6·8	0 6·5	0 14·9	0 4	0 3·5	0 4·9
Lungs and windpipe	1 4	1 5	4 1	0 13·2	1 2·3	1 1·5
Blood	5 3·5	4 11·2	1 3·5	3 15·5	4 5·5	4 7·3
Liver	1 13	1 13·3	0 0·4	1 6	1 4·8	1 8·1
Gall-bladder and contents	0 0·7	0 0·3	0 2·3	0 0·5	0 1·5	0 1
Pancreas ("sweetbread")	0 2·1	0 3		0 1	0 1·9	0 2·1
Glands about the throat ("throatbread")			0 2·2	0 0·8		0 0·8
Milt or spleen	0 3·9	0 2·2		0 2	0 2·7	0 2·6
Bladder	0 0·8	0 0·8	0 0·6	0 1·3	0 0·5	0 0·8
Womb					0 1·5	
Head	3 10	3 9	3 6	3 2·7	3 1·7	3 5·9
Skin (with feet, &c.)	14 11	14 4	15 2	10 12	10 12	13 1·8
Wool						
Diaphragm ("skirts")			0 1·6	0 4·1	0 1·3	0 4·1
Miscellaneous trimmings						1 1·4
Total "offal" parts	47 6·6	46 7·4	41 10·2	33 0·3	31 8·4	42 12·0
Carcase	56 15	56 11·6	45 10·5	45 7·5	43 14·5	49 11·8
Loss by evaporation, error in weighing, &c.	1 6·4*	1 5*	1 11·3	5 8·2†	6 9·1†	0 9·0
Live-weight after fasting	105 12	104 8	89 0	84 0	82 0	93 0·8

* Inclusive of contents of bladder.   † Including contents of stomachs.   ‡ Included with loss, &c.

TABLE XVII.

APPENDIX.—TABLE XVII. Showing the *Actual Weights*

Class II.—20 Wether Sheep of *Cotswold Breed*, about 1½ year old, in *moderately* Fat condition.

Designation of Parts.	The 5 giving the Largest amount of Increase during Fattening.					The 5 giving the Smallest amount of Increase during Fattening.				
	No. 1.	No. 2.	No. 3.	No. 4.	No. 5.	No. 6.	No. 7.	No. 8.	No. 9.	No. 10.
	lbs. oz.	lbs. oz.	lbs. oz.	lbs. oz.	lbs. oz.	lbs. oz.	lbs. oz.	lbs. oz.	lbs. oz.	lbs. ozs.
Original weight	112 0	127 0	108 0	146 0	119 0	128 0	109 0	133 0	120 0	129 0
Final weight, unfasted (including shorn wool)	201 0	207 1	185 0	222 12	194 2	177 2	155 12	176 9	160 8	166 8
Final weight, fasted (including shorn wool)	188 0	196 1	178 0	208 12	182 2	166 2	148 12	168 9	151 8	162 8
Separate parts of the "offal." Stomachs	5 1	4 12.5	4 9	5 14	4 5	4 2	5 3	4 3	4 0	4 0
Contents of stomachs	8 11.5	10 15.5	7 15	9 4	9 8	7 0	6 9	7 7	7 5	8 0
Caul-fat	7 8	5 6	4 9	8 3	6 6.5	8 1	6 0	5 9	4 9	7 14
Small intestines and contents	3 7	3 7	3 10	3 10.5	3 11	3 0	4 4	3 3	2 13	2 12
Large intestines and contents	3 5.5	3 7	2 2.5	3 6.5	4 2.5	2 3	4 3	3 2	2 9	3 11.5
Intestinal fat	1 14	2 7	2 13	2 2	2 6	2 1	1 4.5	1 12.5	1 10	1 14
Heart and aorta	0 11.3	0 12.3	0 11	0 12	0 11.5	0 9	0 10.8	0 11	0 8.5	0 9
Heart-fat	0 6	0 7.3	0 4.5	0 11.5	0 3	0 8	0 4.6	0 4	0 4.7	0 2
Lungs and windpipe	1 8.5	2 2.5	2 0	2 3	1 12.5	1 9.5	1 12	1 9	1 7	1 8
Blood	7 5.5	7 12.5	6 10.5	8 10	7 4.5	6 9	8 1.5	7 11.5	6 0.5	6 13
Liver	3 5.5	3 4	2 13	3 15	3 1	2 10.5	2 15	3 2	2 9	2 9
Gall-bladder and contents	0 1.9	0 2.2	0 1.1	0 2.2	0 3	0 1.6	0 0.2	0 2.3	0 1.2	0 1.4
Pancreas ("sweetbread")	0 2.5	0 4.3	0 3	0 3.5	0 4	0 3.5	0 3.5	0 3.5	0 3.5	0 3.5
Milt or spleen	0 4.5	0 5	0 3.8	0 5.8	0 5.5	0 4	0 5	0 6	0 3.7	0 4
Bladder	0 1	0 0.8	0 0.7	0 0.8	0 1	0 0.6	0 1.1	0 0.6	0 0.8	0 0.8
Head	4 9	5 4	4 13	5 5	5 0	4 13	4 13.5	5 0	4 6	4 7
Skin (with feet, &c.)	14 0	15 8	14 0	14 6	13 4	12 6	14 0	13 8	12 4	12 0
Wool previously shorn	10 0	11 1	8 0	8 12	9 2	9 2	8 12	11 9	8 8	8 8
Total "offal" parts	72 6.7	77 6.9	65 7.1	77 14.8	72 0	65 5.6	69 6.7	69 7.4	59 6.9	65 5.2
Carcass	115 5.8	117 14	110 6	131 6.5	109 14.5	101 0.5	78 6	98 4.5	91 14.8	95 5.2
Loss by evaporation, error in weighing, &c.	0 7.8	0 12.1	2 2.9	−0 9.3	0 3.5	−0 4.1	0 15.3	0 13.1	0 2.3	1 13.6
Live-weight after fasting	188 0	196 1	178 0	208 12	182 2	166 2	148 12	168 9	151 8	162 8

* For particulars of the feeding experiment, see article on the "Comparative Fattening Qualities of

(lbs. and ozs.) of the individual Organs, and other separated Parts, of SHEEP.

Fattening food—Oilcake, Clover Chaff, and Swedish Turnips*.   Killed at Rothamsted, April 19, 1852.

										Means of			
The 10 giving the Medium amount of Increase during Fattening.										The 5 of Largest Increase.	The 5 of Smallest Increase.	The 10 of Medium Increase.	The 20 Cotswolds.
No. 11.	No. 12.	No. 13.	No. 14.	No. 15.	No. 16.	No. 17.	No. 18.	No. 19.	No. 20.				
lbs. oz.	lbs. oz.	lbs. oz.	lbs. oz.	lbs. oz.	lbs. oz.	lbs. oz.	lbs. oz.	lbs. oz.	lbs. oz.	lbs. oz.	lbs. oz.	lbs. oz.	lbs. oz.
108 0	125 0	119 0	116 0	123 0	128 0	121 0	105 0	108 0	112 0	122 6·4	123 12·8	116 8	119 12·8
176 3	191 8	185 1	181 13	188 11	193 1	184 8	168 2	168 13	172 5	201 15·8	167 4·6	189 0·1	182 13·1
164 3	180 8	176 1	173 13	180 11	180 1	173 8	161 2	162 13	161 5	190 9·4	159 7·8	171 6·5	173 3·5
4 5	4 6	4 13	4 13	4 5	4 13	4 14	4 12	4 4	4 9·5	4 6	4 14·7	4 4·6	4 8·7	4 9·3
7 3	8 7	8 13	8 14	7 7	8 11	8 4	5 10	5 4·5	6 2	9 4·4	7 4·2	7 12·3	8 0·3
7 4	8 11	7 12·5	9 3	8 8	8 10	7 5	7 0	5 11·5	5 14	6 6·5	6 6·6	7 9·5	7 0
2 14·5	3 7	4 0	3 3	3 7·5	3 6	3 4	2 9·5	3 3	3 5	3 9·1	3 3·2	3 4·3	3 5·2
4 0	3 10·5	3 13	3 1	3 15	3 2·5	3 1	2 10	3 12	3 15	3 4·8	3 2·5	3 6·4	3 5·2
2 5	2 10·2	1 8	2 3	1 10	2 9	1 7	1 12·5	1 10	1 11	2 5·2	1 11·6	1 15	1 15·7
0 10	0 10	0 10·5	0 11	0 10·9	0 9·5	0 10·5	0 10	0 11	0 10	0 11·6	0 9·7	0 10·3	0 10·5
0 4	0 5·3	0 6	0 9·5	0 4	0 6·5	0 4·5	0 8	0 4	0 5·7	0 7·4	0 4·6	0 5·8	0 5·9
1 15·5	2 1·5	2 6	1 13	2 2	2 5	1 15·5	1 15	1 13	2 0	1 14·9	1 9·1	2 0·7	1 14·3
6 8·5	7 9	7 0·5	7 4	7 4·5	7 14	7 1	6 2	8 0·5	7 4	7 8·6	7 0·7	7 3·2	7 3·9
X3 0	3 6	3 2·5	3 2	3 0	3 6	3 3	2 10	3 5	3 3	3 4·5	2 12·3	3 2·1	3 1·3
0 1·6	0 1	0 1·3	0 1·5	0 2	0 1·7	0 1·5	0 1·6	0 0·8	0 1·5	0 2·1	0 1·4	0 1·5	0 1·6
0 3·5	0 3·2	0 4	0 3	0 3·5	0 3·3	0 3·2	0 3·5	0 3	0 4	0 3·5	0 3·5	0 3·4	0 3·4
0 4·5	0 4·5	0 4·7	0 4·5	0 4·3	0 3·8	0 4·2	0 4·6	0 8·5	0 5	0 4·9	0 4·5	0 4·7	0 4·7
0 0·6	0 0·8	0 0·5	0 0·7	0 0·5	0 0·7	0 0·7	0 0·7	0 0·8	0 0·8	0 0·9	0 0·8	0 0·7	0 0·7
4 10	4 8·5	5 2	4 8	5 0	5 2	4 14	4 12·5	5 1·5	5 0	4 15·8	4 11·1	4 13·9	4 13·6
12 8	13 8	13 0	11 8	13 0	13 8	13 0	11 8	15 0	13 8	14 3·6	12 13·6	13 0	13 4·3
7 3	9 8	10 1	8 13	8 11	10 1	9 8	8 2	8 13	9 5	9 6·2	9 4·6	9 0·1	9 2·7
65 4·6	73 5·5	73 2·5	69 11·2	70 7·2	75 2	69 3·1	60 12·1	70 13·5	66 4	73 0·7	65 12·8	69 6·6	69 6·6
93 7·5	106 9	104 4	105 5·5	109 0	104 11·5	102 6·5	98 14·5	91 14·7	94 6	116 14·9	92 15·8	101 9·5	103 4·4
0 8·9	0 9·5	−1 5·5	−1 3·7	1 3·8	0 3·5	1 14·4	1 7·4	0 0·8	0 11	0 9·8	0 11·2	0 6·4	0 8·5
164 3	180 8	176 1	173 13	160 11	180 1	173 8	161 2	162 13	161 5	190 9·4	159 7·8	171 6·5	173 3·5

different Breeds of Sheep," Journal of the Royal Agricultural Society of England, vol. xiii. part 1.

APPENDIX.—TABLE XVIII. Showing the *Actual Weights* (lbs. and ozs.)

CLASS III.—16 Wether Sheep of *Leicester Breed*, about 1¼ year old, in *moderately*
Killed at Rothamsted,

Designation of Parts.	The 4 giving the Largest amount of Increase during Fattening.								The 4 giving the Smallest amount of Increase during Fattening.							
	No. 1.		No. 2.		No. 3.		No. 4.		No. 5.		No. 6.		No. 7.		No. 8.	
	lbs.	oz.	lbs.	oz.	lbs.	oz.	lbs.	oz.	lbs.	oz.	lbs.	oz.	lbs.	oz.	lbs.	oz.
Original weight	119	0	121	0	117	0	108	0	96	0	92	0	93	0	84	0
Final weight, unfasted (including shorn wool)	185	4	183	12	179	0	164	0	127	0	123	9	118	12	107	11
Final weight, after fasting (including shorn wool)	170	4	168	12	165	0	150	0	116	0	112	9	109	12	98	11
Separate parts of the "offal.":																
Stomachs	4	12	3	14	3	12	3	15	3	6	3	7	3	1	2	11
Contents of stomachs	7	0·5	5	14	6	8	7	1	4	15	6	0	5	1	5	1
Caul-fat	6	3	6	13	7	4	5	5	4	8	2	0	2	8·5	1	11
Small intestines and contents	3	10	3	0	3	9	2	13	2	4	4	1	2	11	2	12·5
Large intestines and contents	3	3·5	2	11	3	1	2	9	1	14	2	11	2	2	2	6
Intestinal fat	2	0	1	15	1	16	1	6	1	6	1	10	0	12·5	1	5·5
Heart and aorta	0	10	0	12	0	10 5	0	10	0	7·5	0	9·5	0	7	0	9
Heart-fat	0	5·7	0	3	0	8·5	0	3	0	2	0	2·5	0	2	0	2·4
Lungs and windpipe	1	6	1	11	1	3	1	5	1	4	2	0	1	1	1	14
Blood	6	13	6	10	7	2	5	11	4	8	5	7	4	15	4	13
Liver	3	0	2	10	3	1	2	14	2	3·5	2	4	1	15·5	2	0·4
Gall-bladder and contents	0	1·3	0	1·5	0	0·5	0	1	0	0·8	0	1·2	0	0·8	0	1
Pancreas ("sweetbread")	0	4	0	4·5	0	4	0	3	0	3·2	0	3·3	0	3	0	2·5
Milt or spleen	0	3·5	0	3·5	0	3·3	0	3	0	2·5	0	3·6	0	3	0	3
Bladder	0	1	0	0·9	0	0·9	0	1	0	0·7	0	0·7	0	0·9	0	1
Head	4	3	4	11	4	1	4	4	3	9	3	15	3	9·5	3	7·5
Skin (with feet, &c.)	12	15	12	1	11	10	10	14	9	1	10	0	9	8	9	0
Wool previously shorn	10	4	8	12	10	0	10	0	6	0	8	9	9	12	6	11
Miscellaneous trimmings	......		......		......		......		......		......		......		......	
Total "offal" parts	66	15·5	62	3·4	64	13·7	59	6	45	15·2	53	4·8	48	1·7	44	15·8
Carcass	99	9·5	101	13	96	5	88	6	66	13·5	59	2·5	69	14·5	51	15
Loss by evaporation, error in weighing, &c.	3	11	4	11·6	3	13·3	2	4	3	3·3	1	7	1	11·8	1	12·2
Live-weight after fasting	170	4	168	12	165	0	150	0	116	0	112	9	109	12	98	11

* For particulars of the feeding experiment, see article on the "Comparative Fattening Qualities of

of the individual Organs, and other separated Parts, of SHEEP.

Fat condition.   Fattening Food—Oilcake, Clover Chaff, and Swedish Turnips*.
April 23, 1853.

| The 8 giving the Medium amount of Increase during Fattening. | | | | | | | | Means of | | | |
No. 9.	No. 10.	No. 11.	No. 12.	No. 13.	No. 14.	No. 15.	No. 16.	The 4 of Largest Increase.	The 4 of Smallest Increase.	The 8 of Medium Increase.	The 16 Leicesters.
lbs. oz. 114 0	lbs. oz. 100 0	lbs. oz. 89 0	lbs. oz. 105 0	lbs. oz. 105 0	lbs. oz. 95 0	lbs. oz. 105 0	lbs. oz. 91 0	lbs. oz. 116 4	lbs. oz. 91 4	lbs. oz. 100 8	lbs. oz. 102 2
160 3	145 14	134 7	150 3	149 2	138 4	146 10	132 8	178 0	119 4	144 10·4	146 10·2
148 3	132 14	121 7	138 3	139 2	122 4	134 10	123 8	163 8	109 4	132 8·4	134 7·2
3 9	3 8	3 8	3 2·5	3 11	3 5	3 14	3 5	4 1·2	3 2·2	3 7·8	3 8·8
5 7·5	4 12	7 1	4 9·5	5 11	4 11	4 6	7 1	6 9·9	5 4·2	5 7·4	5 11·2
5 6·5	4 13	3 4	7 1	5 2	4 4·5	3 11	5 2	6 6·2	2 10·9	4 13·5	4 11
2 15	2 14	3 6	2 9·5	2 13	3 1	2 10·5	3 0	3 4	2 15·1	2 14·6	3 0·1
2 4·5	2 5	2 2	2 8·5	3 6·5	2 5·5	2 8	2 4·5	2 14·1	2 4·3	2 7·6	2 8·4
1 7·5	1 7·5	1 7	2 4	1 9·7	1 14	1 5·5	1 13	1 13	1 4·5	1 10·5	1 9·6
0 9·5	0 9	0 9	0 7·5	0 8	0 8	0 9·5	0 8·5	0 10·6	0 8·3	0 8·6	0 9
0 3·8	0 4	0 2·3	0 4·5	0 4	0 2	0 3·5	0 1·5	0 5·1	0 2·2	0 3·2	0 3·4
1 5	1 6	2 0	1 4·5	1 5·5	1 1	1 8	1 3	1 6·2	1 8·8	1 6·1	1 6·8
5 8	5 0	5 12	5 2·5	5 15·5	4 11	5 6	5 4	6 9	4 14·8	5 5·4	5 8·6
2 8·5	2 12	2 10	2 5·5	2 10	2 4	2 13	2 10·5	2 14·3	2 1·9	2 5·2	2 8·6
0 1·3	0 2	0 2·2	0 1	0 1	0 1·6	0 1	0 0·8	0 1·1	0 0·9	0 1·4	0 1·2
0 3·5	0 3·7	0 3	0 3·5	0 4	0 4	0 3·5	0 3	0 3·9	0 3	0 3·5	0 3·5
0 3·2	0 3·5	0 3·5	0 3	0 3	0 2·5	0 3	0 3	0 3·3	0 3	0 3·1	0 3·1
0 0·5	0 0·8	0 0·8	0 0·7	0 0·8	0 1·7	0 0·7	0 0·5	0 1	0 0·8	0 0·8	0 0·9
4 1·5	4 0·5	4 1·5	3 12	4 1	3 11	4 3	3 10	4 4·7	3 10·3	3 15·1	3 15·3
11 8	10 1	10 7	10 0	11 4	9 14	11 11	9 8	11 14	9 6·2	10 8·6	10 9·4
8 3	6 14	8 7	8 3	9 2	7 4	6 10	6 8	9 12	7 12	7 10·4	8 3·2
0 3	0 2·5	0 1·2	0 2	0 1·8	0 1	0 4	0 3	......	......	0 2·3	0 2·3
55 12·8	51 6·5	55 7·5	54 4·7	58 1·8	49 10·7	52 3·2	52 9·3	63 5·6	48 1·4	53 11·1	54 12·4
90 7	79 5·5	65 1	81 5·5	79 11·5	72 12	80 14	70 7·5	96 8·4	59 7·4	77 8	77 11·9
1 15·2	2 2	0 14·5	2 8·8	1 4·7	−0 2·7	1 8·8	0 7·2	3 10	1 11·2	1 5·3	1 14·9
148 3	132 4	121 7	138 3	139 2	132 4	134 10	123 8	163 8	109 4	132 8·4	134 7·2

APPENDIX.—TABLE XIX. Showing the *Actual Weights* (lbs. and oz.)

CLASS IV.—16 Wether Sheep of *Cross-breed* (Leicester and South Down), about 1¼ year old, Killed at Rothamsted,

Designation of Parts.	The 4 giving the Largest amount of Increase during Fattening.				The 4 giving the Smallest amount of Increase during Fattening.			
	No. 1.	No. 2.	No. 3.	No. 4.	No. 5.	No. 6.	No. 7.	No. 8.
	lbs. oz.	lbs. oz.	lbs. oz.	lbs. oz.	lbs. oz.	lbs. oz.	lbs. oz.	lbs. oz.
Original weight	88 0	93 0	99 0	102 0	91 0	88 0	100 0	98 0
Final weight, unfasted (including shorn wool)	144 12	149 0	154 10	155 12	127 13	124 5	134 8	131 7
Final weight, after fasting (including shorn wool)	134 12	138 0	142 10	141 12	115 13	111 6	122 8	122 7
Separate parts of the "offal"								
Stomachs	3 11	3 12	3 15	3 14	3 1	3 2	3 8	3 2
Contents of stomachs	7 6	5 15	9 5	5 12	4 15	5 12	5 12	7 3
Caul-fat	4 12	6 12·5	4 5·5	5 12	4 0	4 4	5 6	6 1
Small intestines and contents	1 14	2 7·5	2 6	2 7	1 15	2 3	2 9	2 7·5
Large intestines and contents	2 4	2 12	3 4	3 6	2 10·5	2 7	2 15	2 11
Intestinal fat	1 7	2 3	1 9	1 11	1 0	1 0·5	1 9·5	1 7
Heart and aorta	0 9·3	0 8·5	0 10	0 9	0 7	0 9·5	0 8	0 7·5
Heart-fat	0 4	0 3·5	0 4·5	0 3·5	0 4	0 3	0 2·2	0 4
Lungs and windpipe	1 8	1 4·5	1 14	1 8	1 9	1 2	1 7	1 8
Blood	5 5	5 8	5 9	6 9	4 12	4 14	5 12·5	5 5·3
Liver	2 7	2 7·5	2 15	2 3	2 1	2 4·	2 4	2 2·5
Gall-bladder and contents	0 2·5	0 1·5	0 3	0 1·6	0 2	0 1·5	0 1·1	0 1·2
Pancreas ("sweetbread")	0 3·3	0 4	0 3·5	0 4	0 3·5	0 3·5	0 3·5	0 3·5
Milt or spleen	0 3·5	0 3	0 3	0 4	0 3	0 3·5	0 4·4	0 3·3
Bladder	0 1	0 0·8	0 1·3	0 0·8	0 0·7	0 0·8	0 0·7	0 0·9
Head	4 4	4 1	4 6·5	4 6	3 14·5	3 12·5	4 2·5	4 0
Skin (with feet, &c.)	11 0	8 12	13 2	12 0	10 8	10 0	9 11	10 4
Wool previously shorn	8 12	7 0	7 10	6 12	5 13·	5 6	7 8	6 7·
Miscellaneous trimmings	0 5·5	0 1·6	......	0 5·5	0 2	0 3·5	0 3·5	0 2·5
Total "offal" parts	56 7·1	54 6·1	61 14·3	58 0·6	47 9·2	47 12·3	53 15·9	54 1·2
Carcass	77 13·5	85 5	83 0	83 12	67 15·5	64 6·5	65 12	68 14·5
Loss by evaporation, error in weighing, &c.	0 7·4	−1 11·1	−2 4·3	−0 0·6	0 4·3	−0 12·8	2 12·1	−0 8·7
Live-weight after fasting	134 12	138 0	142 10	141 12	115 13	111 6	122 8	122 7

* For particulars of the feeding experiment, see article on the "Comparative Fattening Qualities of

of the individual Organs, and other separated Parts, of SHEEP.

in *moderately* Fat condition. Fattening food—Oilcake, Clover Chaff, and Swedish Turnips*.
April 23, 1853.

| | The 8 giving the Medium amount of Increase during Fattening. | | | | | | | Means of | | | |
| | | | | | | | | The 4 of Largest Increase. | The 4 of Smallest Increase. | The 8 of Medium Increase. | The 16 Cross-bred Wethers. |
No. 9.	No. 10.	No. 11.	No. 12.	No. 13.	No. 14.	No. 15.	No. 16.				
lbs. oz.	lbs. oz.	lbs. oz.	lbs. oz.	lbs. oz.	lbs. oz.	lbs. oz.	lbs. oz.	lbs. oz.	lbs. oz.	lbs. oz.	lbs. oz.
95 0	102 0	88 0	98 0	101 0	89 0	96 0	100 0	95 8	94 4	96 2	95 8
140 12	147 4	132 12	142 9	145 8	133 5	139 13	142 8	151 0·5	129 8·5	140 8·9	140 6·7
126 12	139 4	120 12	133 9	131 8	123 5	132 13	126 8	139 4·5	118 0·5	129 4·9	128 15·7
3 6	3 12	2 14	3 1·5	3 7	3 2	3 14	3 5	3 13	3 3·3	3 5·7	3 6·9
4 15	6 4	5 9	6 8·5	3 13	5 6	7 10·5	3 9	7 1·5	5 14·5	5 7·4	5 15·7
5 11	7 5·5	5 1	5 8	4 9·5	3 12·5	4 10	5 9·5	5 6·5	4 14·7	5 4·4	5 3·5
1 11	3 1	1 13	2 3·5	2 8·5	1 11	2 9	2 3	2 4·6	2 4·6	2 3·5	2 4·1
2 2	2 9	2 0	2 8	2 9·5	2 13	3 9	2 5·5	2 14·5	2 10·9	2 9	2 10·9
2 3·5	2 12	1 12	2 8·5	1 10·8	1 0	1 7·5	2 2	1 11·5	1 4·2	1 15	1 11·5
0 9	0 8·7	0 7·7	0 8·5	0 8·5	0 8·2	0 8·8	0 9·5	0 9·2	0 8	0 8·6	0 8·6
0 4·4	0 5·5	0 5	0 3	0 7·5	0 3·1	0 6·7	0 4·5	0 3·9	0 3·3	0 5	0 4·3
1 4	1 6·2	1 2·5	1 4·5	1 10	1 5·5	1 8	1 5	1 8·6	1 6·5	1 5·7	1 6·6
5 9·5	5 11·3	4 7	5 3	4 12	4 15	5 13·5	5 5	5 11·7	5 2·9	5 3·6	5 5·4
2 5	2 9	2 1	2 6	2 5·5	2 1	2 5	2 7	2 8·1	2 2·9	2 4·9	2 5·2
0 1·8	0 1·3	0 2·2	0 2	0 0·8	0 0·7	0 2·2	0 1·2	0 2·2	0 1·5	0 1·5	0 1·7
0 2·7	0 4·7	0 3·5	0 3·2	0 3·7	0 3	0 4·2	0 3·7	0 3·7	0 3·5	0 3·6	0 3·6
0 3·7	0 3·8	0 3	0 3	0 3·5	0 2·7	0 3	0 3	0 3·4	0 3·6	0 3·2	0 3·3
0 0·6	0 0·9	0 0·7	0 0·7	0 0·9	0 0·6	0 0·9	0 0·8	0 1	0 0·8	0 0·8	0 0·8
4 0	4 4·7	3 10	3 14	4 1·8	4 2·5	4 1·5	4 2	4 4·4	3 15·4	4 0·5	4 1·2
9 6	10 12	9 6	10 14	11 3	11 12	11 11	9 10	11 3·5	10 1·7	10 9·2	10 9·9
4 12	5 4	6 12	6 9	5 6	8 5	6 13	6 8	7 8·5	6 4·5	6 4·9	6 0·7
0 2·5	0 2	0 2·5	0 1	0 3	0 2·8	0 3·5	0 1·8	0 4·3	0 2·9	0 2·4	0 2·9
48 13·7	57 5·6	48 0·1	53 13·9	49 14·5	51 10·6	57 13·3	49 15·5	57 12·1	50 13·7	52 2·9	53 3·8
78 14	80 7·5	72 0	78 12	80 13·2	68 4·5	72 10	76 9·5	83 7·6	66 12·1	76 0·8	75 5·4
-0 15·7	1 6·9	0 11·9	0 15·1	0 12·3	3 5·9	2 5·7	-0 1	-0 15·2	0 6·7	1 1·2	0 6·5
126 12	139 4	120 12	133 9	131 8	123 5	123 5	126 8	139 4·5	118 0·5	129 4·9	128 15·7

different Breeds of Sheep,"

APPENDIX.—TABLE XX. Showing the *Actual Weights* (lbs. and ozs.)

Class V.—16 Ewe Sheep of *Cross-breed* (Leicester and South Down), about 1¼ year old, in

Killed at Rothamsted,

Designation of Parts.	The 4 giving the Largest amount of Increase during Fattening.				The 4 giving the Smallest amount of Increase during Fattening.			
	No. 1.	No. 2.	No. 3.	No. 4.	No. 5.	No. 6.	No. 7.	No. 8.
	lbs. oz.	lbs. oz.	lbs. oz.	lbs. oz.	lbs. oz.	lbs. oz.	lbs. oz.	lbs. oz.
Original weight	84 0	91 0	95 0	91 0	90 0	91 0	92 0	89 0
Final weight, unfasted (including shorn wool)	143 14	142 6	145 14	140 4	124 12	124 8	125 6	118 7
Final weight, after fasting (including shorn wool)	129 14	129 6	131 14	125 4	112 12	112 8	114 6	108 7
Stomachs	3 2·5	3 0	3 7	2 15	3 4	2 15	2 13	2 10·5
Contents of stomachs	5 11·5	3 6	5 6	6 2	4 2	3 0	5 4	4 6·5
Caul-fat	6 4	5 3·5	6 8	4 7	5 3·5	6 0	3 15·5	4 4·5
Small intestines and contents	2 0	2 4·5	2 4	2 5	1 12	1 11	2 0	2 1·5
Large intestines and contents	1 12	2 7·5	2 4	1 15	2 ·4	1 5	2 6	2 4·5
Intestinal fat	1 8·3	1 5	2 10·5	1 14·5	1 12	2 1·5	1 7	1 0
Heart and aorta	0 8·5	0 9	0 9	0 9	0 8	0 8	0 6·5	0 7
Heart-fat	0 4·5	0 2	0 3·7	0 2·5	0 4·5	0 3	0 2·5	0 2
Lungs and windpipe	1 6	1 2·5	1 3·7	1 2	1 2·6	1 1	1 6	1 8·5
Blood	5 12	5 6·5	5 5	4 6	5 7·5	4 12	4 11	4 1
Liver	2 8·5	2 5·5	2 9	2 2·5	1 12·5	1 14	1 15·5	1 13
Gall-bladder and contents	0 2	0 1·2	0 0·5	0 2	0 1·4	0 1·8	0 0·7	0 0·9
Pancreas ("sweetbread")	0 3·5	0 3·3	0 3·5	0 3	0 2·5	0 3	0 3	0 3
Milt or spleen	0 3·2	0 3·2	0 4·5	0 3	0 3	0 2·5	0 2·5	0 2·5
Bladder	0 0·5	0 0·8	0 0·7	0 0·5	0 0·6	0 0·9	0 0·8	0 0·9
Womb	0 0·7	0 1·2	0 1	0 1	0 1·2	0 ·07	0 0·7	0 0·7
Head	3 13·5	4 0	4 0	3 11·5	3 6·5	3 7·5	3 7·5	3 3
Skin (with feet, &c.)	11 3	10 7	9 8	10 0	8 12	8 4	9 0	9 8
Wool previously shorn	7 14	7 6	6 14	7 4	6 12	5 8	6 6	6 7
Miscellaneous trimmings	0 3	......	0 2·5	0 4·5	0 2	......	......	0 4
Total "offal" parts	54 9·2	49 10·7	53 8·6	50 0	47 2	43 2·9	45 12·2	44 9
Carcass	76 11·0	77 5·5	77 13	71 12	65 5	67 6·0	68 1	62 11
Loss by evaporation, error in weighing, &c.	-1 6·2	2 5·8	0 8·4	3 8	0 5	1 15·1	0 6·8	1 3
Live-weight after fasting	129 14	129 6	131 14	125 4	112 12	112 8	114 6	108 7

(Left margin label for offal rows: "Separate parts of the 'offal.'")

* For particulars of the feeding experiment, see article on the "Comparative Fattening Qualities of

of the individual Organs, and other separated Parts, of SHEEP.

moderately Fat condition. Fattening food—Oilcake, Clover Chaff, and Swedish Turnips*.
April 23, 1853.

| | The 8 giving the Medium amount of Increase during Fattening. | | | | | | | | Means of— | | | |
	No. 9.	No. 10.	No. 11.	No. 12.	No. 13.	No. 14.	No. 15.	No. 16.	The 4 of Largest Increase.	The 4 of Smallest Increase.	The 8 of Medium Increase.	The 16 Cross-bred Ewes.
	lbs. oz.	lbs. oz.	lbs. oz.	lbs. oz.	lbs. oz.	lbs. oz.	lbs. oz.	lbs. oz.	lbs. oz.	lbs. oz.	lbs. oz.	lbs. oz.
	86 0	98 0	86 0	98 0	87 0	96 0	91 0	92 0	90 4	90 8	91 12	91 1
	129 10	141 8	129 8	140 10	129 .3	137 12	132 6	133 4	143 1.5	123 4.3	134 3.6	133 11.3
	119 10	129 .8	118 8	129 10	117 3	125 12	122 6	120 4	129 1.5	112 0.3	122 13.6	121 11.2
	3 2	3 6	2 15.5	3 0	2 13.5	3 3.5	3 0	3 2.5	3 2.1	2 14.6	3 1.4	3 0.9
	6 9	6 4	5 14.5	4 11.5	3 10.5	4 13.5	5 2	2 7.5	5 2.3	4 3.1	4 15	4 12.9
	5 12	5 10	5 10.5	5 12	5 9.5	5 10	4 10	5 1	5 9.6	4 13.9	5 7.4	5 5.6
	2 2.5	2 3	2 4	2 3	1 8.5	2 2.5	2 1	2 2.5	2 3.3	1 14.1	2 1.4	2 1.1
	2 6	2 9	2 4.5	2 5	2 1	2 11	2 2	2 3.5	2 1.6	2 0.9	2 5.3	2 3.2
	1 5.5	1 7.5	1 5	2 4	1 2	2 5.5	2 3.5	1 10	1 13.6	1 9.1	1 11.4	1 11.4
	0 8	0 7	0 7	0 8.3	0 8.5	0 7.7	0 8.3	0 8	0 8.8	0 7.4	0 7.8	0 8
	0 2	0 3	0 4	0 4.4	0 5.5	0 4.5	0 4.3	0 3	0 3.1	0 3	0 3.8	0 3.5
	1 3.5	1 5	1 3	1 2.6	1 5	1 3.8	1 3.3	1 1.7	1 3.5	1 4.6	1 3.6	1 3.8
	5 0	4 8	4 14.5	4 6.5	5 3	5 2.5	4 14	4 14.5	5 3.8	4 11.9	4 13.9	4 14.9
	1 14.5	2 1.5	2 2.5	2 2	2 3.5	2 1.5	2 3	2 1	2 6.3	1 13.6	2 1.7	2 1.9
	0 1.5	0 1.3	0 2.1	0 1.3	0 2	0 1.2	0 1.2	0 1.6	0 1.4	0 1.2	0 1.5	0 1.4
	0 3.5	0 3	0 2.7	0 4	0 3	0 3	0 3.2	0 3.3	0 3.3	0 2.9	0 3.2	0 3.1
	0 4	0 3	0 3	0 3.5	0 3.3	0 2.8	0 3	0 3.5	0 3.4	0 2.6	0 3.3	0 3.1
	0 0.6	0 0.5	0 0.5	0 0.8	0 0.7	0 0.7	0 0.6	0 0.7	0 0.6	0 0.6	0 0.6	0 0.7
	0 1.5	0 1	0 0.8	0 1	0 1.2	0 1.4	0 0.9	0 1	0 0.9	0 0.8	0 1.1	0 1
	4 0	4 0	3 8.5	3 10	3 10.5	3 11.5	3 14	3 8	3 14.2	3 6.1	3 11.8	3 11
	10 2	10 8	9 10	9 10	10 4	11 0	9 7	9 14	10 4.5	8 14	10 0.9	9 13
	7 10	6 8	7 8	5 10	7 3	7 12	6 6	8 4	7 5.5	6 4.2	7 1.6	6 15.2
	0 4.4	0 1.7	0 3	0 2.4	0 2	0 1.8	0 2.8	0 1.5	0 3.3	0 3	0 2.4	0 2.7
	52 12.5	51 10.5	50 11.6	48 6.2	48 4.2	53 4.4	48 10.1	47 12.8	51 15.1	45 4	50 3	49 6.4
	65 10	75 11.5	67 8.5	79 8.2	68 12	71 2	73 1	71 9	75 14.4	65 13.6	71 9.8	71 3.9
	1 3.5	2 2	0 3.9	1 11.6	0 2.8	1 5.6	0 10.9	0 14.2	1 4	0 14.5	1 0.8	1 0.9
	119 10	129 8	118 8	129 10	117 3	125 12	122 6	120 4	129 1.5	112 0.3	122 13.6	121 11.2

different Breeds of Sheep," Journal of the Royal Agricultural Society of England, vol. xvi. part 1.

APPENDIX.—TABLE XXI. Showing the *Actual Weights* (lbs. and ozs.)

CLASS VI.—16 Wether Sheep of *Hampshire Down Breed*, about 1¼ year old, in mode-
Killed at Rothamsted,

Designation of Parts.	The 4 giving the Largest amount of Increase during Fattening.				The 4 giving the Smallest amount of Increase during Fattening.			
	No. 1.	No. 2.	No. 3.	No. 4.	No. 5.	No. 6.	No. 7.	No. 8.
	lbs. oz.	lbs. oz.	lbs. oz.	lbs. oz.	lbs. oz.	lbs. oz.	lbs. oz.	lbs. oz.
Original weight	119 0	124 0	112 0	116 0	105 0	96 0	119 0	105 0
Final weight, unfasted (including shorn wool)	218 8	220 8	207 8	204 0	159 0	150 12	174 4	160 8
Final weight, after fasting (including shorn wool)	202 8	205 8	192 8	191 0	151 0	140 12	164 4	151 8
Stomachs	4 15	4 11	4 2	4 6	3 7	3 10	3 10	3 6
Contents of stomachs	8 15	10 7	10 0	10 6	8 5	6 6	7 14	6 12
Caul-fat	8 3	8 15.6	7 2.4	7 8	8 11	5 11	8 12.1	6 2.3
Small intestines and contents	4 0	3 15	3 4	3 0	2 12	2 10	2 10	2 4
Large intestines and contents	4 7	3 0	2 13	3 1	2 8	2 9	3 0	2 10
Intestinal fat	5 0.4	5 2	5 4	4 10	3 14.1	2 4.3	5 6.5	4 7.2
Heart and aorta	0 13	0 11.5	0 10.8	0 10.5	0 9.1	0 8.5	0 9.7	0 8.6
Heart-fat	0 10.6	0 7.4	0 8.6	0 5.9	0 3.5	0 4.5	0 6	0 4.2
Lungs and windpipe	1 14.3	1 13	1 6.1	1 9.3	1 9	1 13	1 9.5	1 5.6
Blood	9 1	9 2.5	7 12.5	7 10.8	6 7	6 10.3	5 8.5	6 4.5
Liver	3 7.6	3 9.6	2 9.9	3 5.6	2 6	2 9	2 5.6	2 0.8
Gall-bladder and contents	0 1.1	0 0.5	0 0.6	0 0.9	0 1.4	0 0.6	0 1.2	0 0.4
Pancreas ("sweetbread")	0 4	0 4	0 3.1	0 4.1	0 4.7	0 4	0 4.3	0 3
Milt or spleen	0 4.4	0 5.1	0 4.2	0 4.1	0 3.4	0 4.2	0 3.7	0 3.1
Bladder	......	0 3.2	0 2.4	0 0.8	0 0.5	0 0.5	0 1	0 0.6
Head	6 4	6 0.5	5 10.5	5 1	4 8	4 14	5 0.1	4 4.8
Skin (with feet, &c.)	17 11	17 8	15 14	16 2	11 0	11 8	11 5	12 2
Wool previously shorn	5 8	5 8	6 8	8 0	6 0	5 12	4 4	7 8
Miscellaneous trimmings	0 4.9	0 1.9	0 2.1	0 4	0 4.5	0 5	0 4.3	0 3.4
Total "offal" parts	81 12.4	81 14	74 6.4	76 10.2	63 2.2	57 15.9	63 3.5	60 10.5
Carcass	120 10.5	123 13	118 13.5	114 5.5	86 14	80 6	99 8.5	69 15
Loss by evaporation, error in weighing, &c.	0 1.1	-0 3	-0 11.9	0 0.3	0 15.8	2 6.1	1 8	0 14.5
Live-weight after fasting	202 8	205 8	192 8	191 0	151 0	140 12	164 4	151 8

(Left margin label: Separate parts of the "offal.")

* For particulars of the *feeding* experiment, see Article on the "Comparative Fattening

of the individual Organs, and other separated Parts, of SHEEP.

rately Fat condition.   Fattening food—Oilcake, Clover Chaff, and Swedish Turnips*.
May 8, 1851.

The 8 giving the Medium amount of Increase during Fattening.								Means of—			
No. 9.	No. 10.	No. 11.	No. 12.	No. 13.	No. 14.	No. 15.	No. 16.	The 4 of Largest Increase.	The 4 of Smallest Increase.	The 8 of Medium Increase.	The 16 Hampshire Downs.
lbs. oz.	lbs. oz.	lbs. oz.	lbs. oz.	lbs. oz.	lbs. oz.	lbs. oz.	lbs. oz.	lbs. oz.	lbs. oz.	lbs. oz.	lbs. oz.
108 0	125 0	108 0	113 0	131 0	100 0	120 0	112 0	117 12	106 4	114 10	113 5
177 8	194 4	177 0	181 8	199 8	168 0	187 8	178 8	212 10	161 2	182 15·5	184 14·8
168 8	184 4	164 0	173 8	188 8	156 0	176 8	163 8	197 14	151· 14	171 13·5	173 5·8
3 14	3 10	3 9	3 8	4 2	3 8	3 12	3 10	4 8·5	3 8·3	3 11·1	3 13·8
8 10	10 10	7 11	8 8	6 14	7 0	8 10	7 6	9 15	7 5·3	8 2·6	8 6·4
8 3·5	6 15·7	7 1	9 10	9 5·5	6 3·4	6 8	7 8·5	7 15·3	7 5·1	7 11	7 10·6
2 14	3 3	4 8	3 0	3 4	3 2	2 12	3 2	3 8·8	2 9	3 3·6	3 2·3
2 14	4 2	3 0	3 4	4 8	2 8	3 12	3 2	3 5·3	2 10·7	3 6·2	3 3·1
5 0·5	4 10	5 2	5 2·5	4 14	3 8	4 3·5	5 9	5 0·1	4 0	4 12·2	4 10·1
0 12·8	0 12·3	0 9·5	0 9·8	0 13·8	0 9	0 12·1	0 10·2	0 11·5	0 9	0 11·2	0 10·7
0 3·3	0 7·6	0 5·5	0 4·8	0 10·5	0 6	0 5·7	0 4·2	0 8·1	0 4·5	0 6	0 6·1
1 12·5	1 7·5	1 10·5	1 6·8	1 11·5	1 9·5	1 9·2	1 9·2	1 10·7	1 9·3	1 9·6	1 9·8
6 14	7 7·5	7 1·5	6 5·5	8 10·5	5 14·5	7 4·5	6 15	8 6·7	6 3·5	7 1·1	7 3·1
2 12·5	1 15·7	2 8	2 9·5	2 11·8	2 7·5	3 0·5	2 12	3 4·3	2 5·3	2 9·7	2 11·2
0 0·7	0 2·6	0 .1·4	0 2·9	0 1·4	0 1·1	0 1·3	0 0·9	0 0·8	0 0·9	0 1·5	0 1·2
0 4·3	0 3·5	0 3·5	0 3·3	0 3·6	0 4·5	0 4	0 3·1	0 3·8	0 4	0 3·7	0 3·8
0 4·8	0 4·1	0 5·1	0 4·5	0 5·3	0 3·7	0 4·7	0 3·5	0 4·4	0 3·6	0 4·5	0 4·2
0 1	0 1	0 1·1	0 0·7	0 1	0 0·6	0 0·9	0 1	0 2·1	0 0·7	0 0·9	0 1·1
5 2·2	5 2	4 13	5 4	5 12	4 15·5	5 11·5	5 4	5 12	4 10·7	5 4	5 3·7
12 3	15 12	12 12	11 12	14 4	12 14	16 0	12 0	16 12·7	11 7·6	13 7·1	13 13·7
5 8	6 4	7 0	5 8	6 8	6 0	5 8	4 8	6 6	5 14	5 13·6	5 15·8
0 2	0 3·8	0 3	0 2·6	0 4·5	0 4	0 3	0 7	0 3·2	0 4·3	0 3·8	0 3·8
67 9·1	73 6·3	68 9·1	67 11·1	75 1·4	61 7·3	70 10·9	65 3·6	78 11·3	61 4	68 11·3	69 5·5
100 0	106 12·5	94 12	105 3·5	111 10	94 3	196 6·5	98 13	119 6·6	89 2·9	102 7·6	103 6·2
0 14·9	2 1·2	0 10·9	0 9·4	1 12·6	0 5·7	−0 9·4	−0 8·6	−0 3·9	1 7·1	0 10·6	0 10·1
168 8	184 4	164 0	173 8	188 8	156 0	176 8	163 8	197 14	151 14	171 13·5	173 5·8

Qualities of Sheep," Journal of the Royal Agricultural Society of England, vol. xii. part 2.

APPENDIX.—Table XXII. Showing the *Actual Weights* (lbs. and ozs.)

CLASS VII.—16 Wether Sheep of *Sussex Down Breed*, about 1¼ year old, in *moderately* Killed at Rothamsted,

Designation of Parts.	The 4 giving the Largest amount of Increase during Fattening.								The 4 giving the Smallest amount of Increase during Fattening.							
	No. 1.		No. 2.		No. 3.		No. 4.		No. 5.		No. 6.		No. 7.		No. 8.	
	lbs.	oz.	lbs.	oz.	lbs.	oz.	lbs.	oz.	lbs.	oz.	lbs.	oz.	lbs.	oz.	lbs.	oz.
Original weight	99	0	97	0	84	0	80	0	86	0	88	0	86	0	78	0
Final weight, unfasted (including shorn wool)	167	4	163	8	147	8	142	12	121	4	123	8	126	4	121	8
Final weight, after fasting (including shorn wool)	154	4	151	8	137	8	132	12	117	4	116	8	119	4	116	8
Stomachs	3	13	3	1	3	2	3	0	2	10	2	14	2	13	2	9
Contents of stomachs	5	13	4	12	7	5	7	0	3	14	5	0	6	3	6	14
Caul-fat	7	0·4	6	3	6	9	6	5	6	2·3	4	7·5	6	8·3	5	2
Small intestines and contents	3	10	2	12	2	14	2	13	1	12	2	8	3	4	2	8
Large intestines and contents	2	5	2	7	2	6	2	4	1	14	2	7	2	6	2	3
Intestinal fat	4	9	4	4	3	4·6	2	14·3	3	9·5	2	3	3	1	2	9·6
Heart and aorta	0	9·5	0	9·3	0	9·5	0	8·6	0	8	0	7·5	0	7·5	0	7·8
Heart-fat	0	10·1	0	10·1	0	9·4	0	4·5	0	5·6	0	8	0	4·5	0	3·8
Lungs and windpipe	1	5·9	1	3·5	1	3·8	1	5	1	2·5	1	4·5	1	5	1	2·6
Blood	8	13·8	6	1·6	5	15·8	5	8·9	4	8·3	4	11·8	4	12	4	9·5
Liver	2	3·8	2	5·8	2	2	2	2	1	14·5	2	1·4	2	0	2	1·3
Gall-bladder and contents	0	0·3	0	0·5	0	0·8	0	0·8	0	1	0	0·7	0	0·4	0	0·8
Pancreas ("sweetbread")	0	2·7	0	4	0	4	0	3·6	0	2·4	0	2·5	0	3·1	0	3·9
Milt or spleen	0	4·6	0	5·9	0	5·9	0	4·7	0	5·5	0	5·5	0	4·9	0	6
Bladder	0	0·6	0	0·9	0	0·5	0	0·5	0	0·6	0	0·5	0	1	0	0·8
Head	4	3·3	4	8	4	8·5	4	2·5	3	10·3	3	12·8	3	14·5	3	11·5
Skin (with feet, &c.)	12	4	10	4	10	6	9	2	9	8	9	0	8	7	9	5
Wool previously shorn	6	4	6	8	6	8	4	12	5	4	4	8	6	4	4	8
Miscellaneous trimmings	0	2·1	0	3·9	0	0·8	0	3·4	0	4·5	0	5	0	2·3	0	3·3
Total "offal" parts	64	3·2	56	8·5	58	2·6	52	14·8	47	9	46	11·7	52	5·5	48	14·3
Carcass	92	12	94	6	79	10	80	11	68	6	68	6·5	67	0	67	5
Loss by evaporation, error in weighing, &c	−2	11·2	0	9·4	−0	4·6	−0	13·8	1	4·9	1	5·7	−0	1·5	0	3·7
Live-weight after fasting	154	4	151	8	137	8	132	12	117	4	116	8	119	4	116	8

The left-margin label for the middle group of rows reads: Separate parts of the "offal."

* For particulars of the *feeding* experiment, see Article on the "Comparative Fattening

of the individual Organs, and other separated Parts, of SHEEP.

Fat condition.   Fattening food—Oilcake, Clover Chaff, and Swedish Turnips*.
May 8, 1851.

| The 8 giving the Medium amount of Increase during Fattening. | | | | | | | | Means of— | | | |
No. 9.	No. 10.	No. 11.	No. 12.	No. 13.	No. 14.	No. 15.	No. 16.	The 4 of Largest Increase.	The 4 of Smallest Increase.	The 8 of Medium Increase.	The 16 Sussex Downs.
lbs. oz. 89 0	lbs. oz. 96 0	lbs. oz. 86 0	lbs. oz. 87 0	lbs. oz. 85 0	lbs. oz. 89 0	lbs. oz. 93 0	lbs. oz. 93 0	lbs. oz. 90 0	lbs. oz. 84 8	lbs. oz. 89 10	lbs. oz. 88 8
143 8	149 0	139 12	140 8	138 8	142 4	145 8	145 4	155 4	123 2	143 0·5	141 1·6
139 8	142 0	132 12	134 8	129 8	136 4	137 8	135 4	144 0	117 6	135 14·5	133 4·7
2 14	3 0	2 12	2 14	3 2	3 0	3 2	3 0	3 4	2 11·5	2 15·5	2 15·6
6 6	4 10	5 8	6 10	5 4	9 0	6 2	5 4	6 3·5	5 7·8	5 15·5	5 14·6
6 13	7 5	7 6	6 15	4 14	5 13·5	7 6	6 5·5	6 8·3	5 9	6 9·8	6 5·2
3 4	2 8	2 10	3 0	2 12	2 10	2 2	2 4	3 0·3	2 8	2 10·3	2 11·2
2 6	2 2	2 5	2 8	3 0	3 6	2 8	2 4	2 5·5	2 3·5	2 8·9	2 6·7
3 2	5 6·5	4 2·5	2 14·5	2 13	2 13	3 12·8	3 5·2	3 11·9	2 13·8	3 8·7	3 6·8
0 9·3	0 9·5	0 7·2	0 8·1	0 8·5	0 9	0 7·8	0 8	0 9·2	0 7·7	0 8·4	0 8·4
0 3·3	0 1·9	0 4	0 4·5	0 7	0 4	0 5	0 6	0 6·3	0 5·5	0 4·5	0 5·7
1 11·4	1 10	1 3·8	1 2·5	1 6·5	1 6·3	1 3·5	1 7·7	1 4·6	1 3·7	1 8·5	1 6·3
6 0·8	5 6·6	5 2·5	5 9·5	5 8·9	5 15	5 8·5	4 13·8	6 10	4 10·4	5 6·2	5 8·2
2 8·5	2 6·4	2 3·5	2 0	2 6	1 15·5	1 15·3	2 9	2 3·4	2 0 ·3	2 4	2 2·9
0 1·1	0 0·4	0 1·8	0 1·3	0 1·9	0 2·6	0 2·7	0 3·1	0 0·6	0 0·7	0 1·9	0 1·3
0 3·5	0 2·8	0 3·5	0 3	0 2·3	0 4·1	0 3	0 3·3	0 3·6	0 3	0 3·2	0 3·2
0 6	0 4·7	0 6	0 3·7	0 6·2	0 4·5	0 4	0 4·5	0 5·3	0 5·5	0 4·9	0 5·2
0 0·5	0 0·6	0 0·5	0 0·7	0 0·5	0 0·7	0 0·5	0 0·8	0 0·6	0 0·7	0 0·6	0 0·6
4 0·5	3 12·5	3 14	3 11	3 15·7	4 2·9	4 0·5	4 6·5	4 5·6	3 12·3	3 15·9	4 0·4
12 4	10 8	10 0	10 2	10 10	9 10	10 0	10 6	10 8	9 1	10 7	10 1·8
5 8	5 0	5 12	6 8	6 8	5 4	5 8	5 4	6 0	5 2	5 10·5	5 9·8
0 2	0 3	0 4	0 3·5	0 3	0 2·9	0 4·5	0 4·1	0 2·6	0 3·6	0 3·3	0 3·8
58 7·9	55 1·9	54 10·3	55 7·3	54 1·5	55 12	55 0·1	53 3·5	57 15·3	48 14·2	55 3·6	54 5·2
80 2	85 14·5	77 13	78 7·5	76 0·5	79 12·5	81 13·5	82 1·5	86 13·7	67 12·6	80 3·9	78 12·6
0 14	0 15·6	0 4·6	0 9·2	−0 10	0 11·5	0 10·4	−0 1	−0 13	0 11·2	0 7	0 2·9
139 8	142 0	132 12	134 8	129 8	136 4	137 8	135 4	144 0	117 6	135 14·5	133 4·7

APPENDIX.—TABLE XXIII. Showing the *Actual Weights* (lbs. and ozs.) of the individual Organs, and other separated Parts, of SHEEP.

CLASS VIII.—6 Wether Sheep of *Cotswold Breed*, about 1¼ year old, in *excessively* Fattened condition. Fattening food—Oilcake, Clover Hay, and Swedish Turnips, under cover, until "moderately" fattened; afterwards, Oilcake (or Lentils), with Grass or Green Clover, or with Meadow-hay and Roots, in the field. Killed at Rothamsted, December 18, 1852.

Designation of Parts.	No. 1.		No. 2.		No. 3.		No. 4.		No. 5.		No. 6.		Means of the 6 Cotswolds.	
	lbs.	oz.	lbs.	oz.	lbs.	oz.	lbs.	oz.	lbs.	oz.	lbs.	oz.	lbs.	oz.
Original weight	121	0	132	0	112	0	121	0	121	0	121	0	121	0
Final weight, unfasted	262	0	254	0	252	0	242	0	234	0	228	0	245	5·3
Final weight, after fasting	252	0	245	0	242	0	233	0	224	0	220	0	236	0
Separate parts of the "offal."														
Stomachs	5	7	4	11	4	9	4	5	4	6	4	0		9
Contents of stomachs	11	3	8	4	10	13	8	9	7	10	7	11	9	4·6
Caul-fat	8	2	9	12	6	13	12	15	8	11·7	3	2	9	0·1
Small intestines and contents	3	7·6	3	3	2	12	2	2	3	5	3	8	2	15·1
Large intestines and contents	5	0	4	6	3	9	3	6	3	2	3	3	3	13·7
Intestinal fat	4	14	3	14·5	3	5·5	3	2·5					3	6·9
Heart and aorta	0	12·9	0	15	0	13	0	11·5	0	13	0	13	0	13·1
Heart-fat	1	0	0	14·5	0	15	0	10·5	0	7	0	10·5	0	12·3
Lungs and windpipe	2	1·2	2	3	1	14	1	10·5	2	1·5	1	12·5	1	15·1
Blood	10	3	10	5	8	10	7	13	8	1	8	8·5	8	14·7
Liver	3	15	3	7	3	2	2	9	2	9·6	8	9	3	0·6
Gall-bladder and contents	0	1·8	0	3·7	0	1·4	0	1·1	0	1·7	0	1·3	0	1·8
Pancreas ("sweetbread")	0	3·5	0	2·7	0	4·5	0	2·5	0	3·3	0	3	0	3·3
Milt or spleen	0	6·4	0	5·5	0	5	0	6·5	0	4	0	5·5	0	5·5
Bladder	0	0·8	0	0·7	0	1	0	0·9	0	0·9	0	1·2	0	0·9
Head	5	7·5	5	3·5	5	4	5	3·5	5	11	4	15·3	5	4·8
Skin and wool (with feet, &c.)	29	10	24	4	27	12	26	0	26	4	24	14	26	7·3
Wool shorn in Spring*	(10	7)	(10	0)	(16	8)	(11	8)	(10	0)	(9	12)	(11	5·8)
Diaphragm ("skirts")	0	3·2	0	0	0	0			0	3·5	0	2·5	0	3·5
Miscellaneous trimmings			0	4·5	0	4·5	0	3	0	5·5	0	2·9	0	4·2
Total "offal" parts	92	2·8	88	7·6	81	3·9	80	1·5	76	2·6	66	11·2	81	9·4
Carcass	158	10·5	156	12·5	156	2·5	150	11·7	145	2·5	139	11·2	151	3·2
Loss by evaporation, error in weighing, &c.	1	2·7	5	11·9	4	9·6	2	2·8	2	10·9	13	9·6	3	3·4
Live-weight after fasting	252	0	245	0	242	0	233	0	224	0	220	0	236	0

* It should be mentioned, that in the case of these animals killed in December, the weight of wool shorn in the previous Spring, is not included either in the recorded "Final Weight," or in the sum of items at the time of slaughter. Nor, is it taken into account in calculating the *Percentage proportions* of the different parts, which are recorded in Appendix-Table XLVIII. It is, however, given above, parenthetically, as Memorandum.

APPENDIX.—TABLE XXIV. Showing the *Actual Weights* (lbs. and ozs.) of the individual Organs, and other separated Parts, of SHEEP.

CLASS IX.—7 Wether Sheep of *Leicester Breed*, about 1¼ year old, in *excessively* Fattened condition. Fattening food—Oilcake, Clover Hay, and Swedish Turnips, under cover, until "moderately" fattened; afterwards, Oilcake, with Grass or Green Clover, or with Meadow-hay and Roots, in the field. Killed at Rothamsted, December 20, 1853.

Designation of Parts.	No. 1. lbs. oz.	No. 2. lbs. oz.	No. 3. lbs. oz.	No. 4. lbs. oz.	No. 5. lbs. oz.	No. 6. lbs. oz.	No. 7. lbs. oz.	Means of the 7 Leicesters. lbs. oz.
Original weight	94 0	88 0	112 0	91 0	100 0	94 0	112 0	98 11·4
Final weight, unfasted	188 0	184 0	224 0	182 0	189 0	199 0	201 0	195 4·6
Final weight, after fasting	176 0	171 0	212 0	170 0	176 0	186 0	187 0	182 9·1
Separate parts of the "offal."								
Stomachs	3 10	4 6	5 0	4 0	4 6	4 2	4 1	4 2·7
Contents of stomachs	4 6	6 6	10 4	6 4	7 14	6 14	5 15	6 13·6
Caul-fat	6 10·5	5 8	8 6	5 5	12 0	7 4	10 6	7 14·8
Small intestines and contents	2 8	2 8	3 3	1 8	2 14	2 3	2 11	2 7·1
Large intestines and contents	3 2	2 14	3 12	3 0	3 8	3 0	2 9	3 2·2
Intestinal fat	3 0·5	2 12·4	3 10	1 5·5	3 0	3 0		2 12·2
Heart and aorta	0 10	0 11·5	0 13	0 9	0 12·5	0 10	0 9·3	0 10·7
Heart-fat	0 10·5	0 7·3	0 1·3	0 8	0 9	0 11·5	0 14	0 11·3
Lungs and windpipe	1 6·3	1 5·5	1 15	1 7·5	1 9·5	1 7·5	1 8·5	1 8·6
Blood	6 7	7 1·5	7 6·5	6 11	6 13	6 10	8 5·5	6 12·8
Liver	2 7·5	2 11·5	3 0·5	2 4	2 13	2 7	2 5	2 9·3
Gall-bladder and contents	0 1·8	0 1·7	0 2	0 1·2	0 1·8	0 1·3	0 2·3	0 1·7
Pancreas ("sweetbread")	0 2·5	0 2·5	0 2	0 2·2	0 1·7	0 1·7		0 2·1
Milt or spleen	0 5·5	0 3·5	0 4	0 3·5	0 3·5	0 4	0 4·2	0 4
Bladder	0 1	0 1	0 1·5	0 1	0 1	0 0·8	0 0·9	0 1
Head	4 8	4 3	5 0	4 4	4 4·5	4 8·5	4 4·5	4 6·9
Skin and wool (with feet, &c.)	20 4	16 4	25 0	18 8	19 12	19 4	19 12	19 13·2
Wool shorn in Spring*	(9 13)	(6 14)	(9 9)	(7 12)	(8 4)	(7 14)	(9 4)	(8 7·7)
Diaphragm ("skirts")								0 2·3
Miscellaneous trimmings	0 1·5		0 1·5	0 15·1	0 14·5	0 2·3		0 1·5
Total "offal" parts	60 6·6	57 5·4	79 2·5	56 1·9	70 11·5	62 11·6	64 7·7	64 10
Carcass	115 8·5	112 2·5	133 5·5	112 15	106 3	124 1·7	120 9	117 13·3
Loss by evaporation, error in weighing, &c.	0 0·9	1 8·1	— 8	0 15·1	— 14·5	— 13·3	1 15·3	0 1·8
Live-weight after fasting	176 0	171 0	212 0	170 0	176 0	186 0	187 0	182 9·1

* It should be mentioned, that in the case of these animals killed in December, the weight of wool shorn in the previous Spring, is not included either in the recorded "Final Weight," or in the sum of items at the time of slaughtering. Nor, is it taken into account in calculating the *Percentage proportions* of the different parts, which are recorded in Appendix-Table XLIX. It is, however, given above, parenthetically, as Memorandum.

APPENDIX.—TABLE XXV. Showing the *Actual Weights* (lbs. and ozs.) of the individual Organs, and other separated Parts, of SHEEP.

CLASS X.—8 Wether Sheep of *Cross-breed* (Leicester and South Down), about 1¾ year old, in *excessively* Fattened condition. Fattening food—Oilcake, Clover Hay, and Swedish Turnips, under cover, until "moderately" fattened; afterwards, Oilcake, with Grass or Green Clover, or with Meadow-hay and Roots, in the field. Killed at Rothamsted, December 20, 1853.

Designation of Parts.	8 Very Fat Cross-bred Wether Sheep (Leicester and South Down).																	Means of the 8 Cross-bred Wethers.	
	No. 1.		No. 2.		No. 3.		No. 4.		No. 5.		No. 6.		No. 7.		No. 8.			
	lbs.	oz.	lbs.	oz.	lbs.	oz.	lbs.	oz.	lbs.	oz.	lbs.	oz.	lbs.	oz.	lbs.	oz.	lbs.	oz.
Original weight	97	0	93	0	96	0	98	0	91	0	89	0	86	0	98	0	92	4
Final weight, unfatted	172	0	181	0	190	0	203	0	179	0	186	0	183	0	196	0	186	4
Final weight, after fasting	162	0	170	0	182	0	191	0	168	0	176	0	171	0	184	0	175	8
Stomachs	3	9	3	12	4	1	3	15	4	6	3	12	3	14	4	1	3	14·7
Contents of stomachs	6	11·5	7	6	9	8	7	5	7	1	6	12	3	14	6	1	6	13·3
Caul-fat	7	0	9	4	8	7	11	12·5	7	7·5	7	9·5	9	1·5	6	13·5	8	6·9
Small intestines and contents	1	14	1	13	2	0	1	12·5	1	13	1	14	2	1	2	0	1	14·4
Large intestines and contents	2	13	2	4	3	10	2	15	3	0	2	10	2	13	2	11	2	13·5
Intestinal fat	2	12	3	9·5	3	11·5	4	11	2	4	1	15	3	12	2	9	3	2·5
Heart and aorta	0	8	0	9·8	0	9	0	9·5	0	9	0	9·5	0	9	0	10·5	0	9·3
Heart-fat	0	15	0	9·5	0	13·6	0	14	0	10·5	0	14	0	8	0	15·6	0	12·5
Lungs and windpipe	1	4·5	1	1	1	8	1	7	1	7·5	1	6·7	1	8	1	6·5	1	7
Blood	6	4	6	7	5	13·5	6	13	6	15	6	7	6	8	6	6·5	6	7·2
Liver	2	1	2	2·5	2	3	2	7	2	3·5	2	3·5	2	6	2	6	2	4·1
Gall-bladder and contents	0	1·7	0	1·5	0	1·3	0	1·5	0	2·5	0	2	0	1·8	0	1·2	0	1·7
Pancreas ("sweetbread")	0	2·5	0	2·4	0	2·8	0	2·7	0	3·5	0	2·7	0	2·2	0	1·5	0	2·5
Milt or spleen	0	3·3	0	3·5	0	4	0	4	0	4	0	4	0	4·7	0	4·5	0	4
Bladder	0	1	0	1	0	1	0	1·1	0	1	0	1·1	0	0·7	0	1·7	0	1·1
Head	3	13·5	4	2	4	9	4	2·5	4	8·5	4	6·5	4	6	4	4	4	4·5
Skin and wool (with feet, &c.)	14	4	17	8	18	0	15	0	18	10	18	4	18	8	17	8	17	3·3
Wool shorn in Spring*	(6	4)	(5	10)	(5	9)	(4	4)	(5	8)	(5	7)	(6	14)	(5	12)	(5	10·5)
Miscellaneous trimmings	0	4	0	4·2			0	2	0	1					0	2	0	2·6
Total "offal" parts	54	10	61	11·4	65	6·6	64	7·3	61	11·5	59	7·5	60	3·9	68	7·4	60	13·1
Carcass	107	13	107	10	112	12	126	3·5	105	5	115	12·5	109	14	125	2·5	113	13·1
Loss by evaporation, error in weighing, &c.	−0	7·0	0	10·6	3	13·4	0	5·2	0	15·5	0	12	0	14·1	0	6·1	0	13·8
Live-weight after fasting	162	0	170	0	182	0	191	0	168	0	176	0	171	0	184	0	176	8

Separate parts of the "offal."

* It should be mentioned, that in the case of these animals killed in December, the weight of wool shorn in the previous Spring, is not included either in the recorded "Final Weight," or in the sum of items at the time of slaughtering. Nor, is it taken into account in calculating the *Percentage proportions* of the different parts, which are recorded in Appendix-Table L. It is, however, given above, parenthetically, as Memorandum.

APPENDIX.—TABLE XXVI. Showing the *Actual Weights* (lbs. and ozs.) of the individual Organs, and other separated Parts, of SHEEP.

CLASS XI.—8 Ewe Sheep of Cross-bred (Leicester and South Down), about 1½ year old, in *excessively* Fattened condition. Fattening food—Oilcake, Clover Hay, and Turnips, under cover, until "moderately" fattened; afterwards, Oilcake, with Grass or Green Clover, or with Meadow-hay and Roots, in the field. Killed at Rothamsted, December 20, 1853.

Designation of Parts.	No. 1		No. 2		No. 3		No. 4		No. 5		No. 6		No. 7		No. 8		Means of the 8 Cross-bred Ewes.	
	lbs.	oz.	lbs.	oz.	lbs.	oz.	lbs.	oz.	lbs.	oz.	lbs.	oz.	lbs.	oz.	lbs.	oz.	lbs.	oz.
Original weight	94	2	89	6	86	0	88	0	98	0	92	0	78	0	98	0	90	6
Final weight, unfasted	186	0	178	0	175	0	171	0	209	0	188	0	164	0	186	0	182	2
Final weight, after fasting	177	0	167	0	168	0	163	0	197	0	176	0	154	0	176	0	172	4
Stomachs	4	2	4	6	3	6	3	5	5	0	3	12	3	5	4	6	3	15·2
Contents of stomachs	5	12	5	6	5	6	5	4	8	14	4	3	5	8	6	2	5	12·9
Caul-fat	9	5	8	14	8	12·5	6	9·5	9	8	7	7	7	12	9	10	8	7·1
Small intestines and contents	3	2	1	12	2	1	2	3	2	10	3	0	2	3	1	10	2	3·5
Large intestines and contents	2	10	2	10	2	14	2	14	3	12	2	13·5	2	5	2	10	2	15·9
Intestinal fat	4	0·5	5	0	3	10·5	2	6·5	4	0	4	0·5	2	14	2	10	3	9·5
Heart and aorta	0	9	0	11	0	9	0	9·5	0	10·8	0	10·5	0	9·3	0	10·5	0	9·9
Heart-fat	1	1·5	0	15	0	11	0	8	0	12·5	0	15	0	9·3	0	1·2	0	13·3
Lungs and windpipe	1	5·5	1	8·5	1	3·5	1	10	1	7	1	6·5	1	3·5	1	9	1	6·7
Blood	6	1	6	1	6	4·5	6	2·5	7	6·5	5	9·4	5	11	7	3	6	10·8
Liver	2	4	2	2	2	2	2	5·5	2	12	2	9·8	2	3·5	2	5	2	6·2
Gall-bladder and contents	0	0·5	0	7·5	0	1·1	0	2·6	0	3·7	0	1	0	1·5	0	2·5	0	2
Pancreas ("sweetbread")	0	2	0	2·3	0	1·5	0	2·2	0	3	0	1·8	0	1·8	0	2·3	0	2·2
Milt or spleen	0	4	0	4	0	3	0	4	0	4	0	2·5	0	3·3	0	3·5	0	3·7
Bladder	0	1	0	1	0	0·9	0	1	0	0·8	0	1·5	0	0·7	0	1	0	1
Head	4	3	4	11·5	4	11·5	4	6	5	0·5	4	8·5	3	14	4	7	4	6·5
Skin and wool (with feet, &c.)	17	14	18	4	17	4	19	10	24	0	19	12	16	8	19	0	19	0·5
Wool shorn in Spring*	(6	4)	(7	0)	(6	1)	(6	14)	(9	12)	(7	4)	(7	13)	(6	14)	(7	3·8)
Womb	0	2·5	0	2·5	0	2·5	0	2·5	0	2·5	0	2	0	1·7	0	3	0	2·4
Miscellaneous trimmings	……		……		……		……		……		……		0	3·5	……		0	3·5
Total "offal" parts	63	11·5	63	6·3	58	14·5	58	10·8	76	11·3	64	6·7	55	6·1	64	11·3	63	4·8
Carcass	114	12	104	14	109	10·5	106	2	119	5	116	5·7	100	8·5	113	4·5	110	9·8
Loss by evaporation, error in weighing, &c.	-0	7·5	-1	4·3	-0	9	-1	12·8	0	15·7	-4	12·4	-1	14·6	-1	15·8	-1	10·6
Live-weight after fasting	177	0	167	0	168	0	163	0	197	0	176	0	154	0	176	0	172	4

Separate parts of the "offal."

* It should be mentioned, that in the case of these animals killed in December, the weight of wool shorn in the previous Spring, is not included either in the recorded "Final Weight," or in the sum of items at the time of slaughtering. Nor, is it taken into account in calculating the *Percentage proportions* of the different parts, which are recorded in Appendix-Table LI. It is, however, given above, parenthetically, as Memorandum.

APPENDIX.—TABLE XXVII. Showing the *Actual Weights* (lbs. and ozs.) of the individual Organs, and other separated Parts, of SHEEP.

CLASS XII.—8 Wether Sheep of *Hampshire Down Breed*, about 1¾ year old, in *excessively* Fattened condition. Fattening food—Oilcake, Clover Hay, and Swedish Turnips, under cover, until "moderately" fattened; afterwards, Oilcake, with Grass or Green Clover, or with Meadow-hay and Roots, in the field. Killed at Rothamsted, December 17, 1851.

Designation of Parts.	8 Very Fat Hampshire Down Sheep.								Means of the 8 Hampshire Downs.
	No. 1. (lbs. oz.)	No. 2. (lbs. oz.)	No. 3. (lbs. oz.)	No. 4. (lbs. oz.)	No. 5. (lbs. oz.)	No. 6. (lbs. oz.)	No. 7. (lbs. oz.)	No. 8. (lbs. oz.)	(lbs. oz.)
Original weight	114 0	112 0	112 0	117 0	109 0	120 0	113 0	117 0	114 4
Final weight, unfasted	228 0	226 0	234 0	235 0	238 0	262 0	236 0	238 0	237 2
Final weight, after fasting	218 0	214 0	224 0	226 0	227 0	250 0	225 0	227 0	226 6
Stomachs	4 8	4 7	5 8	4 10	4 14	5 4·5	5 0	4 0	4 12·5
Contents of stomachs	9 0	7 3	7 2	8 15	9 14	8 5·5	8 4	6 4	8 1·9
Caul-fat	18 12	10 13	11 14	13 2	12 10·5	12 7	17 6	11 6	13 9·1
Small intestines and contents	2 8·5	1 13	3 2	2 0	2 12	2 9	1 8	2 8	2 3·6
Large intestines and contents	2 12	1 14	4 6	3 11	4 3	3 13·5	3 8	3 3	3 4·9
Intestinal fat	5 12	6 4	7 10	7 9	6 10	7 13	6 9	7 2	6 14·5
Heart and aorta	0 12	0 12·5	0 13	1 0	0 12	0 12·5	0 13	0 13·2	0 13
Heart-fat	0 9	0 3·2	0 3·5	0 7·3	0 14·5	0 9	0 12	0 13	0 8·9
Lungs and windpipe	1 9·5	1 11·5	3 2	1 10·5	1 13·5	1 14·5	1 9·5	1 15	1 12·8
Blood	7 1	7 7	7 10	8 4	8 14·5	9 9·5	8 11	8 7	8 3·8
Liver	2 6	2 11	2 10	2 13	2 5·5	3 3·5	2 7	3 8	2 12
Gall-bladder and contents	0 2	0 1·7	0 1·9	0 2·3	0 0·8	0 0·8	0 0·3	0 1·9	0 2·1
Pancreas ("sweetbread")	0 5·7	0 4·7	0 3·5	0 4·8	0 4·8	0 3·7	0 5·5	0 4·5	0 4·7
Milk or spleen		0 4·3	0 4·5	0 4·5	0 5·6	0 5·6	0 4·5	0 5	0 4·8
Bladder	0 0·8	0 0·9	0 0·5	0 1	0 0·7	0 0·8	0 1	0 0·7	0 0·8
Head	5 7	5 10	5 10	5 8	5 10	5 13	5 15	5 13·5	5 10·8
Skin and wool (with feet, &c.)	20 12	23 14	21 10	23 0	22 14	24 4	23 12	21 0	22 10·3
Wool shorn in Spring*	(6 0)	(7 0)	(6 4)	(7 8)	(6 8)	(5 8)	(5 12)	(6 8)	(6 6)
Miscellaneous trimmings	....	....	....	....	....	....	....	0 3	0 3
Total "offal" parts	82 10	75 6·8	79 0·9	83 5·4	84 15·4	87 3·8	87 0·5	77 12·3	82 5·5
Carcass	134 7·1	135 14·5	143 10	142 10	142 6·5	161 6·5	137 5·5	148 5	143 4·1
Loss by evaporation, error in weighing, &c.	0 14·9	2 10·7	1 5·1	0 0·6	-0 5·9	1 5·7	0 10	0 14·7	0 12·4
Live-weight after fasting	218 0	214 0	224 0	226 0	227 0	250 0	225 0	227 0	226 6

(Separate parts of the "offal.")

* It should be mentioned, that in the case of these animals killed in December, the weight of wool shorn in the previous Spring, is not included either in the recorded "Final Weight," or in the sum of items at the time of slaughtering. Nor, is it taken into account in calculating the *Percentage proportions* of the different parts, which are recorded in Appendix-Table LIII. It is, however, given above, parenthetically, as Memorandum.

APPENDIX.—TABLE XXVIII. Showing the *Actual Weights* (lbs. and ozs.) of the individual Organs, and other separated Parts, of SHEEP.

CLASS XIII.—8 Wether Sheep of *Sussex Down Breed*, about 1½ year old, in *excessively* Fattened condition. Fattening food—Oilcake, Clover Hay, and Swedish Turnips, under cover, until "moderately" fattened; afterwards, Oilcake, with Grass or Green Clover, or with Meadow-hay and Roots, in the field. Killed at Rothamsted, December 17, 1851.

Designation of Parts	No. 1		No. 2		No. 3		No. 4		No. 5		No. 6		No. 7		No. 8		Means of the 8 Sussex Downs	
	lbs.	oz.	lbs.	oz.	lbs.	oz.	lbs.	oz.	lbs.	oz.	lbs.	oz.	lbs.	oz.	lbs.	oz.	lbs.	oz.
Original weight	82	0	82	0	79	0	84	0	87	0	80	0	81	0	91	0	83	4
Final weight, unfasted	160	0	179	0	167	0	178	0	189	0	184	0	182	0	189	0	178	8
Final weight, after fasting	152	0	170	0	158	0	168	0	178	0	175	0	172	0	181	0	169	4
Stomachs	2	9	3	5	3	3	3	14	4	0	3	6.5	3	7	3	12	3	7
Contents of stomachs	5	9	6	11	3	13	6	6	6	4	5	3.5	3	9	6	14.5	5	8.5
Caul-fat	9	14	11	5	10	8	10	10	10	4	9	5	11	12	7	14	10	3
Small intestines and contents	1	12	2	1	1	15.5	2	1	2	8	2	0	1	15	1	13	2	0.3
Large intestines and contents	2	0.5	2	9	1	15	1	14	2	14	2	7	2	4	3	6	2	6.8
Intestinal fat	4	2	4	6	5	0	3	9	5	1	2	7	6	2.5	7	4.5	5	1.8
Heart and aorta	0	8.5	0	11	0	10.2	0	9.7	0	9.5	0	10.8	0	11.2	0	13	0	10.5
Heart-fat	0	4	0	6	0	4.2	0	4.5	0	6.8	0	5.9	0	11.2	0	8	0	6.3
Lungs and windpipe	1	5	1	9	1	6.4	1	9	1	9.5	1	9	1	11.5	1	6.5	1	8.2
Blood	5	12	6	8	5	5	6	5	6	7	6	12.5	5	5.9	6	12.5	6	3.5
Liver	2	1	2	8	2	2	2	6	2	10	2	8	2	10.5	2	8	2	6.7
Gall-bladder and contents	0	1.8	0	1.1	0	0.7	0	2	0	1.5	0	1.1	0	2	0	2.2	0	1.5
Pancreas ("sweetbread")	0	3.2	0	3.5	0	3.3	0	4	0	3.5	0	3.8	0	4.4	0	4.1	0	3.7
Milt or spleen	0	4	0	5	0	3.7	0	4	0	4.5	0	5.5	0	4.7	0	5.5	0	4.6
Bladder	0	0.7	0	0.5	0	0.5	0	0.5	0	0.7	0	0.6	0	0.6	0	0.6	0	0.6
Head	4	10	4	4	4	9	4	5	4	11	4	8	4	8	5	0	4	9.8
Skin and wool (with feet, &c.)	15	0	17	0	16	8	16	2	16	0	17	0	16	12	20	4	16	12
Wool shorn in Spring *	(5	12)	(6	8)	(5	12)	(5	8)	(6	0)	(5	0)	(4	8)	(6	4)	(5	10.5)
Total "offal" parts	56	14.7	63	4.1	57	11.5	60	9.7	63	15	62	5.2	63	9.5	69	0.4	61	14.8
Carcass	96	7.5	107	2.5	100	2	105	12	114	6	112	12.5	109	14.5	111	12	107	4.6
Loss by evaporation, error in weighing, &c.	-0	6.2	-0	6.6	0	2.5	1	10.3	-0	5	-0	1.7	-0	8	0	3.6	0	0.6
Live-weight after fasting	152	0	170	0	158	0	168	0	178	0	175	0	172	0	181	0	169	4

(Rows from "Stomachs" down to "Wool shorn in Spring *" are bracketed under the label "Separate parts of the 'offal'.")

* It should be mentioned, that in the case of these animals killed in December, the weight of wool shorn in the previous Spring, is not included either in the recorded "Final Weight," or in the sum of items at the time of slaughtering. Nor, is it taken into account in calculating the *Percentage proportions* of the different parts, which are recorded in Appendix-Table LIII. It is, however, given above, parenthetically, as Memorandum.

APPENDIX.—TABLE XXIX. Showing the *Actual Weights* (lbs. and ozs.)

CLASS XIV.—19 Sheep of *Hampshire Down Breed*, divided into 4 Lots, each with different Food*.
Killed April

Designation of Parts.	Lot 1.—Food:— Oilcake—in fixed quantity. Swedish Turnips—*ad libitum*.					Lot 2.—Food:— Oats—in fixed quantity. Swedish Turnips—*ad libitum*.				
	No. 1.	No. 2.	No. 3.	No. 4.	No. 5.	No. 6.	No. 7.	No. 8.	No. 9.	No. 10.
	lbs. oz.	lbs. oz.	lbs. oz.	lbs. oz.	lbs. oz.	lbs. oz.	lbs. oz.	lbs. oz.	lbs. oz.	lbs. oz.
Original weight	118 8	112 8	111 0	110 0	106 0	117 8	112 8	112 0	110 0	96 0
Final weight, unfasted	155 0	147 0	143 0	123 0	120 0	153 0	148 8	144 0	121 0	123 0
Final weight, after fasting	151 0	144 0	139 0	121 0	116 8	146 0	145 0	139 0	119 0	118 0
Separate parts of the "offal." Stomachs	3 7	3 14	3 10	3 6·5	3 4·5	4 2·5	4 2	3 12·5	3 6	3 7
Contents of stomachs	8 6	9 12	9 5	11 1	7 14	12 4	13 8	10 8	9 12	9 12
Caul, intestinal, and heart-fat	13 2	13 11·1	12 14	9 7	7 3·5	12 4	11 11	11 14	8 1·5	7 10
Small intestines and contents	1 14	2 1·4	1 9	2 1	2 12·5	1 10·5	1 8·5	2 1·5	1 7·5	2 8
Large intestines and contents	2 14·5	2 13	2 2·5	2 8 5	2 1	2 7·5	3 2	3 5 5	2 15	2 11
Intestinal fat (included with caul-fat).										
Heart and aorta	1 1·4	1 4·5	1 1	0 13	0 13	1 4·5	1 5	1 1·5	1 1	0 14
Heart-fat (included with caul-fat).										
Lungs and windpipe	1 14	1 12	1 8·5	1 6·7	1 11	1 15	2 0	1 11·5	1 9	1 2
Blood	6 7	5 0	5 15	4 4·5	4 9·5	5 11	5 6·5	5 11	4 8·5	4 11·5
Liver	2 5	2 3·5	2 6	1 3·2	1 12·7	2 0·5	1 15·5	2 11	1 11	1 14
Gall-bladder and contents	0 1·1	0 1·4	0 2	0 2·5	0 0·5	0 1	0 2	0 4	0 2	0 1·5
Head	4 15·5	4 11·1	4 7	4 4	4 6·5	4 8·5	4 15·5	4 12	4 10·5	4 8
Skin and wool (with feet, &c.)	17 7	17 0	14 12·5	12 13	15 10	14 14	17 4	15 4	13 13	17 0
Total "offal" parts	63 14·5	64 4	59 12·5	53 6·9	52 2·7	63 3	67 0	63 0·5	53 1	56 3
Carcass	89 0	81 8	77 0	68 8	64 8	86 4	80 0	78 8	68 8	64 0
Loss by evaporation, error in weighing, &c.	−1 14·5	−1 12	2 3·5	− 14·9	− 2·7	−3 7	−2 0	−2 8·5	−2 9	−2 3
Live-weight after fasting	151 0	144 0	139 0	121 0	116 8	146 0	145 0	139 0	119 0	118 0

* For particulars of the *feeding* experiment, refer, under the head of "Experiments with Sheep—Series 1,"

of the individual Organs, and other separated Parts, of SHEEP.

Moderately Fattened. Bred, Fed, and killed at Rothamsted—Period of Feeding Experiment 97 days. 11, 1848.

	Lot. 3.—Food:— Clover Chaff —in fixed quantity. Swedish Turnips—*ad libitum*.					Lot 4.—Food:— Oat-straw Chaff } Swedish Turnips } *ad libitum*.				Means of—				
	No. 11.	No. 12.	No. 13.	No. 14.	No. 15.	No. 16.	No. 17.	No. 18.	No. 19.	Lot 1.	Lot 2.	Lot 3.	Lot 4.	The 19 Sheep.
	lbs. oz.	lbs. oz.	lbs. oz.	lbs. oz.	lbs. oz.	lbs. oz.	lbs. oz.	lbs. oz.	lbs. oz.	lbs. oz.	lbs. oz.	lbs. oz.	lbs. oz.	lbs. oz.
	117 0	114 0	110 8	110 0	107 0	115 0	114 8	112 0	110 4	111 9·6	109 9·6	111 11·2	112 15	111 6·1
	142 0	144 0	138 0	141 0	149 0	136 0	138 0	124 0	129 0	137 9·6	137 14·4	142 12·8	131 12	137 13
	142 0	143 0	135 8	139 0	145 0	129 0	134 0	121 0	127 0	134 4·8	133 8·4	140 14·4	127 12	134 6·7
	4 8	4 3	4 2	4 6·5	4 6	3 12	4 2	3 8	3 8	3 8·4	3 12·4	4 5·1	3 12·1	3 13·6
	19 0	13 6	14 2·5	14 11	15 6·5	10 13	11 9·5	8 5·5	12 15·5	9 4·4	11 2·4	15 5·2	10 14·9	11 11·3
	8 11	10 4·5	10 9·5	11 1	10 10	11 9	11 2·5	11 4·5	10 9	11 4·3	10 4·9	10 4	11 2·2	10 11·5
	4 1·5	2 2·5	1 14·5	2 2	1 15·5	2 7	2 9·5	1 8·5	2 10·5	2 1·2	1 13·6	2 7·2	2 4·9	2 9·6
	4 14·5	3 13·5	3 10·5	3 13	2 10	2 9·5	3 4	2 4	2 12·5	2 7·9	2 14·6	3 12·3	2 11·5	2 15·8
	1 2	1 3	1 8	1 2	1 4	1 1·5	1 3	0 14	0 13	1 0·2	1 2	1 3·8	0 15·9	1 1·6
	1 12	1 12	1 15	1 15	1 14	1 9	1 14	1 10	1 10	1 10·5	1 10·7	1 13·6	1 10·8	1 11·4
	5 11	5 6	4 7	5 5	5 8·5	3 13	5 1·5	4 8·5	4 15·5	5 4	5 3·3	5 4·3	4 9·6	5 1·7
	2 8	2 2·5	2 7·5	2 8	2 7	1 15	2 5	1 7·5	2 1·5	1 15·6	2 0·8	2 6·6	1 15·2	2 1·7
	0 0·3	0 2·5	0 0·9	0 0·7	0 1·9	0 1·2	0 2	0 0·5	0 0·6	0 1·3	0 2·1	0 1·2	0 1·1	0 1·5
	4 3·5	4 8	4 11	4 10·5	5 0	4 6	4 6·5	4 8	4 4	4 8·8	4 10·9	4 9·8	4 6·1	4 9·1
	16 0	15 2	15 0	14 12	16 9	14 0	13 4	15 0	14 10	15 8·5	15 10·2	15 7·8	14 3·5	15 4·3
	72 7·8	64 1·5	64 8·4	66 6·7	67 12·4	58 0·2	60 15·5	54 15	61 0·6	58 11·3	60 7·9	67 0·9	58 11·8	61 6·1
	71 0	81 8	72 8	73 12	76 8	72 0	74 8	67 8	66 8	76 1·6	75 7·2	75 0·8	70 2	74 6·3
	−1 7·8	−2 9·5	−1 8·4	−1 2·7	0 11·6	−1 0·2	−1 7·5	−1 7	−0 8·6	−0 8·1	−2 8·7	−1 3·3	−1 1·8	−1 5·7
	142 0	143 0	135 8	139 0	145 0	129 0	134 0	121 0	127 0	134 4·8	133 8·4	140 14·4	127 12	134 6·7

to Article—"Sheep Feeding and Manure," Journal of the Royal Agricultural Society of England, vol. x. part 1.

APPENDIX.—TABLE XXX. Showing the *Actual Weights* (lbs. and oz.)

CLASS XV.—20 Sheep of *Hampshire Down Breed*, divided into 4 Lots, each with different
Experiment 134 days.

Designation of Parts.	Lot 1.—Food:— Oilcake—in fixed quantity. Clover Chaff—*ad libitum.*										Lot 2.—Food:— Linseed—in fixed quantity. Clover Chaff—*ad libitum.*									
	No. 1.		No. 2.		No. 3.		No. 4.		No. 5.		No. 6.		No. 7.		No. 8.		No. 9.		No. 10.	
	lbs.	oz.	lbs.	oz.	lbs.	oz.	lbs.	oz.	lbs.	oz.	lbs.	oz.	lbs.	oz.	lbs.	oz.	lbs.	oz.	lbs.	oz.
Original weight....................	120	0	124	0	125	0	121	0	117	0	125	0	123	0	117	0	123	0	119	0
Final weight, unfasted	147	0	157	0	157	0	151	0	147	8	141	0	146	0	161	0	151	0	151	0
Final weight, after fasting	142	2·6	148	8·8	149	15·9	141	13·7	143	10·2	132	2·7	136	13·3	151	8·9	142	0·6	138	15
Stomachs	3	11·5	4	8	4	5	3	10	3	15	3	6	3	6	3	15	3	5	3	14
Contents of stomachs	13	2·5	13	3	14	10	12	2	14	3	7	14	9	0	11	13	10	12	10	2
Caul-fat........................	4	2·5	7	1	6	8	7	11	7	0	9	25	6	13	7	14	6	13·5	8	8
Small intestines and contents	2	9·5	2	12	2	11·5	2	5·5	2	3	2	14	8	0	2	11	2	1	2	10
Large intestines and contents	4	14	4	1·5	5	0	3	11	4	0	2	13	2	2	4	15	3	6	3	3
Intestinal fat....................	2	7·5	3	10	2	10·5	2	5	2	4	2	15	2	7	3	10	3	2	2	2
Heart and aorta	0	9	0	7·5	0	8	0	9	0	9	0	9	0	7	0	9	0	9·5	0	9
Heart-fat	0	6·3	0	8·5	0	6·5	0	10·5	0	7	0	8	0	8·5	0	9	0	8·5	0	10
Lungs and windpipe	1	4	1	3	1	3·5	1	3·5	2	6	1	3	1	3	1	4	1	2	1	6
Blood............................	6	4·5	5	15	5	10	5	9	5	12	5	4	5	7	6	2	5	6	5	0
Liver............................	1	13	2	1	1	15·5	1	14	2	4	1	11	1	8	2	2	1	15	1	13
Gall-bladder and contents	0	1	0	1·5	0	0·7	0	1	0	1·1	0	1·7	0	2·3	0	3·3	0	2·1	0	2·1
Pancreas ("sweetbread")	0	2·3	0	2·8	0	3·2	0	2·7	0	1·2	0	27	0	2·1	0	3·6	0	2·8	0	3·4
Milt or spleen			0	3·2	0	2·5	0	3	0	2·9	0	2·8	0	2·9	0	4	0	3·2	0	2·5
Head............................	4	9	4	3	4	12	4	10·5	4	8	4	6	4	6·5	5	0	4	7	4	12
Skin and wool (with feet, &c.)	13	2	15	0	17	5	13	10	12	14	10	10	13	0	13	6	13	5	13	2
Total "offal" parts	59	2·6	65	1	67	15·9	60	5·7	62	10·2	53	10·7	52	11·3	64	8·9	57	4·6	58	3
Carcass........................	83	0	83	8	82	0	81	8	81	0	78	8	84	2	87	0	84	12	80	12
Loss by evaporation, error in weighing, &c.	0	0	-0	0·2	0	0	0	0	0	0	0	0	0	0	0	0	0	0	0	0
Live-weight after fasting...........	142	2·6	148	8·8	149	15·9	141	13·7	143	10·2	132	2·7	136	13·3	151	8·9	142	0·6	138	15

(Rows "Stomachs" through "Skin and wool" are grouped under the side heading *Separate parts of the "offal."*)

* For particulars of the *feeding* experiment, refer, under the head of "Experiments with Sheep—Series 2,"

of the individual Organs, and other separated Parts, of SHEEP.

Food *. *Moderately* Fattened. Bred, fed, and killed at Rothamsted.—Period of Feeding Killed October 17, 1848.

Lot 3.—Food:—Barley—in fixed quantity. Clover Chaff—*ad libitum.*					Lot 4.—Food:—Malt—in fixed quantity. Clover Chaff—*ad libitum.*					Means of:—				
No. 11.	No. 12.	No. 13.	No. 14.	No. 15.	No. 16.	No. 17.	No. 18.	No. 19.	No. 20.	Lot 1.	Lot 2.	Lot 3.	Lot 4.	The 20 Sheep.
lbs. oz.	lbs. oz.	lbs. oz.	lbs. oz.	lbs. oz.	lbs. oz.	lbs. oz.	lbs. oz.	lbs. oz.	lbs. oz.	lbs. oz.	lbs. oz.	lbs. oz.	lbs. oz.	lbs. oz.
122 0	117 0	120 0	118 0	125 0	117 0	122 0	120 0	119 0	124 0	121 6·4	121 6·4	120 6·4	120 6·4	120 14·4
150 0	134 0	149 0	154 0	154 0	140 0	144 0	141 0	143 0	155 0	151 14·4	150 0	148 3·2	144 9·6	148 10·8
142 7·1	129 7·7	140 15·7	140 1·1	142 9·2	133 6	136 10	130 2	133 7·7	144 9·2	145 0·6	140 4·9	139 1·7	135 10·2	140 0·3
4 3	3 13	4 5	4 3·5	4 14	3 2	3 8	3 3	3 7	4 3	4 0·3	3 9·2	4 4·5	3 7·8	3 13·4
13 5	9 9	15 6	14 0·5	14 14	11 14	11 4	7 5	10 3·5	12 14	13 7·3	9 14·6	13 6·9	10 11·3	11 14
6 1	4 11	6 15	5 5	6 2	4 7	4 9	5 2·5	5 1	8 1·5	6 7·7	7 13·4	5 13·2	5 7·4	6 6·4
2 2	1 8	1 13	1 14	1 13	2 2	2 1	1 12	1 15	1 15	2 8·3	2 7·2	1 13·2	1 15·4	2 3
3 11	3 8	4 5	2 12	3 14·5	3 2	3 6	2 14	3 5·5	3 14	4 5·3	3 4·6	3 10·1	3 5·1	3 10·3
2 5	2 3	2 5·5	2 6	1 12	2 11	2 11	2 11	2 7	3 0	2 10·6	2 13·6	2 3·1	2 11·2	2 9·6
0 7	0 9	0 8·5	0 8·5	0 9·5	0 7·5	0 9	0 8	0 8	0 9	0 8·5	0 8·7	0 8·5	0 8·3	0 8·5
0 4·3	0 9	0 7	0 9·5	0 7	0 7·5	0 8·5	0 9·5	0 9	0 9	0 7·7	0 8·8	0 7·3	0 8·7	0 8·1
1 9·5	0 13	1 4	1 1·5	1 4	1 2	1 5	1 1·5	1 4	1 5	1 7·1	1 3·6	1 3·2	1 3·5	1 4·4
6 0	6 2	5 9	5 4	5 15	5 6	5 10	5 8	5 15	6 3	5 13·3	5 7	5 12·4	5 11·6	5 11·1
1 13	1 11	1 10	1 12·5	1 14	ʼ1 10	1 12	1 12	1 10	2 4	1 15·8	1 13	1 12·1	1 12·8	1 13·4
0 0·9	0 1·7	0 1·4	0 2·8	0 1·7	0 1·2	0 1	0 1·5	0 1·2	0 2	0 1	0 2·3	0 1·7	0 1·4	0 1·6
0 2·7	0 2·4	0 2·9	0 2·8	0 2·2	0 1·7	0 2·5	0 2·7	0 2·7	0 3·3	0 2·4	0 2·9	0 2·6	0 2·6	0 2·6
0 3·7	0 3·1	0 3·4	0 2·5	0 3·3	0 3·1	0 3	0 3·3	0 2·8	0 3·4	0 2·9	0 3·1	0 3·2	0 3·1	0 3·1
4 9	4 1·5	4 10	4 11	5 4	4 3	4 13	4 8	4 7	4 12	4 8·5	4 9·5	4 10·3	4 8·6	4 9·2
13 2	11 15	13 6	14 13	13 7	11 10	15 3	15 4	14 9	11 11	14 6·1	12 11	13 5·4	13 10·6	13 8·3
59 15·1	51 7·7	62 15·7	59 13·1	62 9·2	52 10	57 10	52 10	55 11·7	61 13·2	63 0·8	57 4·5	59 5·7	56 1·4	58 15
82 8	78 0	79 0	80 4	80 0	80 12	79 0	77 8	77 12	81 12	82 0	83 0·4	79 15·2	79 5·6	81 1·3
0 0	0 0	−1 0	0 0	0 0	0 0	0 0	0 0	0 0	1 0	−0 0·2	0 0	−0 3·2	0 3·2	0 0
142 7·1	129 7·7	140 15·7	140 1·1	142 9·2	133 6	136 10	130 2	133 7·7	144 9·2	145 0·6	140 4·9	139 1·7	135 10·2	140 0·3

to Article—"Sheep Feeding and Manure," Journal of the Royal Agricultural Society of England, vol. x. part 1.

APPENDIX.—TABLE XXXI. Showing the *Actual Weights* (lbs. and ozs.)

CLASS XVI.—25 Sheep of *Hampshire Down Breed*, divided into 6 Lots, each with different Food*.

Killed

Designation of Parts.	Lot 1.—Food:— Barley (ground)—in fixed quantity. Mangolds—*ad libitum.*								Lot 2.—Food:— Malt (ground), and Malt-dust—in fixed quantity. Mangolds—*ad libitum.*								Lot 3.—Food:— Barley (ground and *steeped*)—in fixed quantity. Mangolds—*ad libitum.*						
	No. 1.		No. 2.		No. 3.		No. 4.		No. 5.		No. 6.		No. 7.		No. 8.		No. 9.		No. 10.		No. 11.		No. 12.
	lbs. oz.		lbs. oz.		lbs. oz.		lbs. oz.		lbs. oz.		lbs. oz.		lbs. oz.		lbs. oz.		lbs. oz.		lbs. oz.		lbs. oz.		lbs. oz.
Original weight	136	0	136	0	136	0	111	0	121	0	133	0	130	0	123	0	139	0	133	0	127	0	137	0
Final weight, unfasted (including shorn wool)	147	12	152	8·5	150	12·5	147	8	150	7·5	143	15·5	153	8·5	148	8·5	177	1	154	8·5	147	9·5	153	12
Final weight, after fasting (including shorn wool)	140	12	143	0·5	142	12·5	139	12	140	7·5	138	15·5	144	8·5	138	12·5	166	1	144	8·5	139	13·5	147	0
Stomachs	3	8	4	0	4	2	3	11	3	15·5	3	13·5	3	6	3	10	4	6·5	3	11	3	9	3	12
Contents of stomachs	4	11·5	4	12	6	4	5	6	5	14·5	7	1·5	6	14·5	4	11·5	9	6·5	6	7	6	4	4	11·5
Caul-fat	7	6	5	10·5	6	5·2	6	13·5	6	2	7	5·8	7	0	7	9·5	5	3	5	10	7	11·5	8	2
Small intestines and contents	2	7	1	15·5	2	7	2	10	2	0·7	2	10	1	8	1	15	3	0	1	13·5	1	15	2	10·5
Large intestines and contents	2	5	3	7·5	3	10	2	15·5	2	12·7	3	5·5	2	8·8	2	11	3	7	2	3·5	2	9	2	10·2
Intestinal fat	3	3·5	4	12	4	3	3	13	2	11·7	2	13	4	2·8	3	5·5	3	12	2	8·3	2	9	3	9·5
Heart and aorta	0	9	0	11	0	12·5	0	8·5	0	11·4	0	9·5	0	9·5	0	8·5	0	11·5	0	10·3	0	9·1	0	10·2
Heart-fat	0	7·4	0	8	0	10·4	0	8·7	0	13·7	0	8·1	0	13·8	0	13·4	0	11·3	1	3·2	0	9·7	0	14·2
Lungs and windpipe	1	8·5	1	7	1	15	1	6	1	6	1	8·8	1	7·7	1	10	1	12·7	1	6·7	1	5·6	1	12
Blood	5	8	5	7	5	14	6	1	5	14	5	8	5	10	4	15	7	11	6	1	5	3	6	6
Liver	2	0·8	2	2·4	1	15	2	2·2	2	2·2	1	14	2	0	1	11·5	2	11	1	15	1	13	2	1·7
Gall-bladder and contents	0	1·2	0	0·8	0	0·6	0	0·7	0	1·4	0	1·2	0	0·5	0	1·8	0	1·8	0	1·7	0	0·8	0	1·1
Pancreas ("sweetbread")	0	3·7	0	4·5	0	4·3	0	4	0	4	0	4·4	0	3·2	0	4·2	0	4·2	0	3·2	0	4·7	0	3·7
Milt or spleen	0	3·6	0	3	0	4·5	0	4	0	4	0	3·7	0	3·2	0	2·4	0	6·4	0	4·2	0	4·4	0	4·2
Head	4	12	4	9	4	11	4	5·5	4	12·5	4	12·3	4	3	4	2	5	3·5	4	8·6	4	6·7	4	10·6
Skin (with feet, &c.)	9	14	10	14·5	11	9	10	3	8	15	10	10	10	2	9	8	12	1·5	10	11	9	10·5	10	15
Wool previously shorn	6	12	7	8·5	5	12·5	7	8	5	7·5	6	15·5	10	8·5	9	8·5	9	1	6	8·5	7	9·5	7	12
Total "offal" parts	55	9·2	58	5·2	60	12	58	8·6	54	4·8	60	0·8	61	5·5	57	3·8	69	14·9	55	14·7	56	6·5	61	2·8
Carcass	84	0	85	0	81	0	80	0	85	0	76	0	80	0	80	0	95	0	86	0	80	0	85	0
Loss by evaporation, error in weighing, &c.	1	2·8	−0	4·7	1	0·5	1	3·4	1	2·7	2	14·7	3	3	1	8·7	1	2·1	2	9·8	3	7	0	13·7
Live-weight after fasting	140	12	143	0·5	142	12·5	139	12	140	7·5	138	15·5	144	8·5	138	12·5	166	1	144	8·5	139	13·5	147	0

(Left margin label, rows Stomachs through Milt or spleen: "Separate parts of the 'offal.'")

* For particulars of the *feeding* experiment, refer, under the head of "Experiments with Sheep—Series 4," to Article—"Sheep exact *feeding* experiment concluded on May 29th. Between that date and the date of killing (June 13), the animals either gained diately after the conclusion of the feeding experiment. The facts here stated, will of course account for the differences that occur feeding experiment, in the Paper referred to.

of the individual Organs, and other separated Parts, of SHEEP.

Moderately Fattened.   Bred, fed, and killed at Rothamsted.   Period of Feeding Experiment 70 days.
June 13, 1849.

Food:—steeped), and Malted quantity. ifum.		Lot 5.—Food:—Malt (ground), and Malt-dust—in fixed quantity. Mangolds—*ad libitum.*					Lot 6.—Food:—Oilcake—in fixed quantity. Mangolds—*ad libitum.*				Means of—				
No. 15.	No. 16.	No. 17.	No. 18.	No. 19.	No. 20.	No. 21.	No. 22.	No. 23.	No. 24.	No. 25.	Lot 1.	Lot 2.	Lot 3.	Lot 4.	Lot 5.
lbs. oz. 135 0	lbs. oz. 137 0	lbs. oz. 134 0	lbs. oz. 145 0	lbs. oz. 134 0	lbs. oz. 136 0	lbs. oz. 117 0	lbs. oz. 150 0	lbs. oz. 135 0	lbs. oz. 131 0	lbs. oz. 130 0	lbs. oz. 129 12	lbs. oz. 126 12	lbs. oz. 134 0	lbs. oz. 140 0	lbs. oz. 133 3·2
163 12	153 15	152 4	158 12	150 7	154 3·5	155 10	156 8·5	155 11	148 9	144 10	149 10·2	148 2	156 3·7	156 15·7	154 4·1
149 12	143 3	146 4	152 0	143 11	149 11·5	152 6	151 8·5	149 11	144 1	137 10	141 9·3	140 11	149 5·7	148 0·7	149 3·3
4 0	3 7	3 13	3 13	4 13	3 12·5	4 7·5	3 10·4	4 6	5 10	3 14	3 13·3	3 11·3	3 13·8	3 12·2	4 9·2
7 3	6 15	7 5	9 15	7 14	12 4	11 4·5	6 8·6	6 10	6 13·5	6 11·5	5 4·4	6 2·5	6 11·3	6 14·7	9 11·7
8 1	6 5·5	5 12	5 9·5	6 11·5	7 14	4 13·5	7 10·5	7 8·3	6 2	6 10·2	6 8·8	7 0·3	8 10·7	7 3·3	6 2·5
1 14·9	2 7	1 14·5	2 8·7	2 6·8	4 3	2 8·7	1 8	2 1	1 8·5	2 1·5	2 5·9	2 0·4	2 5·9	2 0·6	2 11·5
2 7·7	2 15	3 0·5	3 10	2 1	3 4·5	3 4	3 6·6	3 1	2 8	3 2	3 1·5	2 13·5	2 11·5	2 9·9	3 0·8
4 11·5	2 14	4 6·5	4 7	2 4	2 10·3	3 2	3 5·6	4 9	2 8	2 10·5	3 15·9	3 4·3	3 1·8	3 9·3	3 6·4
0 10	0 10	0 10·6	0 10·3	0 10·3	0 10	0 9·5	0 9·9	0 10·5	0 10·3	0 11	0 10·2	0 9·7	0 10·3	0 9·6	0 10·1
0 13·5	0 11	0 11·6	0 11·4	0 10·4	0 10·5	0 11	0 12·5	0 11·4	0 7·7	0 7	0 8·6	0 12·3	0 12·1	0 12	0 11
1 7·3	1 6·7	1 13	1 6·5	1 7·3	1 4·5	1 10	1 6	1 5·5	1 8·6	1 6·5	1 9·1	1 8·1	1 9·3	1 7·0	1 8·2
5 14	5 15·5	5 3·5	5 7	6 3	6 0	6 6	5 12	5 6	5 11	5 15	5 11·5	5 7·8	6 5·4	5 19·7	5 13·5
2 6	1 13·7	2 11·6	1 13	2 0·6	1 13·6	2 3·7	2 3	2 9	2 2	2 6·3	2 1·1	1 14·9	2 2·2	1 15·5	2 9·2
0 2·7	0 0·6	0 1·7	0 2·3	0 2·2	0 2·4	0 2·2	0 1·9	0 2·4	0 1·6	......	0 0·8	0 1·2	0 1·4	0 1·7	0 2·2
0 4	0 4	0 3·8	0 4	0 4	0 2·6	0 4·7	0 2·7	0 4·4	0 3·5	0 3·3	0 4·1	0 3·9	0 4·1	0 4	0 3·8
0 4·7	0 3	0 3·4	0 3	0 4·5	0 4·4	0 4·3	0 3·6	0 4	0 4	0 3·4	0 3·8	0 3·3	0 4·9	0 3·7	0 3·9
4 8·5	4 7	4 10	4 15	4 9	4 5·5	5 3·5	4 11	4 5·5	4 9	4 11	4 9·4	4 7·5	4 11·5	4 10	4 11·6
9 11	10 5	10 11	9 10·4	11 14	11 4	12 0	11 4·5	10 8	11 0	11 13·5	10 10·1	9 19·7	10 13·6	10 6·1	11 1·5
5 12	6 15	11 4	6 12	8 7	7 3·5	5 10	6 8·5	8 11	6 8	6 10	6 14·3	8 2	7 11·7	7 7·7	8 4·1
61 10·8	57 11	64 8·9	63 14·1	62 10·6	67 13·5	64 9·1	59 13·5	63 0	56 4·6	59 7·7	58 4·6	58 3·7	60 13·5	59 12·9	64 11·4
67 0	64 0	61 0	69 0	60 0	62 0	65 0	69 0	65 0	66 0	76 0	62 8	60 4	66 8	66 12	83 0·4
1 8·2	1 8	2 10·1	–0 14·1	1 0·4	–0 2	2 12·0	2 11	1 11	1 12·4	2 2·3	0 12·5	2 3·3	2 0·2	1 7·8	1 1·5
149 12	143 3	146 4	152 0	143 11	149 11·5	152 6	151 8·5	149 11	144 1	137 10	141 9·3	140 11	149 5·7	148 0·7	149 3·3

Feeding and Manure," Journal of the Royal Agricultural Society of England, vol. x. part 1.   By reference it will be seen that the but little, or in some cases even lost.   This was owing to the influence of losing their wool, which was shorn on May 29th, immediately between the final weights (unfasted) have given, in the Table, and those given for the respective animals at the conclusion of the

APPENDIX.—TABLE **XXXII.** Showing the *Actual Weights* (lbs. and ozs.)

CLASS XVII.—14 Sheep of *Hampshire Down Breed*, divided into 3 Lots—Fed respectively, for 63 days, and Mangolds, and Lot 3 with Oilcake and Mangolds.   Total period of Feeding Experiment 96 days;

Designation of Parts.	Lot 1.—Food:— Clover Chaff—in fixed quantity. Swedish Turnips, highly manured, or Mangolds—*ad libitum.*				
	No. 1.	No. 2.	No. 3.	No. 4.	No. 5.
	lbs. oz.	lbs. oz.	lbs. oz.	lbs. oz.	lbs. oz.
Original weight	140 0	134 0	135 0	129 0	128 0
Final weight, unfasted (including shorn wool)*	158 6	153 0	161 13	150 0	150 15
Final weight, after fasting (including shorn wool)*	146 6	145 0	151 13	142 0	142 15
Stomachs	4 8	3 4·5	3 6	3 12	4 2
Contents of stomachs	9 12	8 5·5	6 13	7 4	9 9
Caul-fat	6 14	5 11	7 4	6 7	6 0
Small intestines and contents	3 7	2 2	3 0	2 9	2 10·6
Large intestines and contents	3 12·4	3 1·5	3 3	2 13	4 0
Intestinal fat	2 13	2 13	3 12	2 13·5	3 2
Heart and aorta	0 11	0 9	0 9	0 8·7	0 9·1
Heart-fat	0 9·5	0 10·7	0 12	0 10·1	0 11
Lungs and windpipe	1 13	1 4	1 6	1 7·3	1 6·6
Blood	3 13·5	5 10·5	6 3·5	5 8	6 1
Liver	2 2	1 15	2 7	1 15	2 1·3
Gall-bladder and contents	0 0·8	......	......	0 0·9	0 0·7
Pancreas ("sweetbread")	0 3·5	0 3·6	0 3·9	0 4	0 4
Milt or spleen	0 4·5	0 3·8	0 4	0 3·4	0 3·6
Head	4 15	4 14	4 9	4 10·7	4 10·5
Skin (with feet, &c.)	10 14·5	10 7	10 13	9 11	10 1
Wool previously shorn*	7 6	5 0	7 13	8 0	7 15
Total "offal" parts	63 15·7	56 3·1	62 6·4	58 9·6	63 7·4
Carcase	79 8	86 0	86 0	81 0	76 0
Loss by evaporation, error in weighing, &c.	2 14·3	2 12·9	3 6·6	2 6·4	3 7·6
Live-weight after fasting	146 6	145 0	151 13	142 0	142 15

* Wool shorn May 29.

of the individual Organs, and other separated Parts, of SHEEP.

with Clover-chaff, and Turnips differently manured; then, for 33 days, Lots 1 and 2 with Clover-chaff namely, from March 7 to June 11. Bred, fed, and killed at Rothamsted. Killed June 12, 1849.

Lot 2.—Food:— Clover Chaff—in fixed quantity. Swedish Turnips, manured with Superphosphate of Lime alone, or Mangolds—ad libitum.				Lot 3.—Food:— Clover Chaff—in fixed quantity. Swedish Turnips, unmanured—ad libitum, or Oilcake—in fixed quantity. Mangolds—ad libitum.					Means of—			
No. 6.	No. 7.	No. 8.	No. 9.	No. 10.	No. 11.	No. 12.	No. 13.	No. 14.	Lot 1.	Lot 2.	Lot 3.	The 14 Sheep.
lbs. oz.	lbs. oz.	lbs. oz.	lbs. oz.	lbs. oz.	lbs. oz.	lbs. oz.	lbs. oz.	lbs. oz.	lbs. oz.	lbs. oz.	lbs. oz.	lbs. oz.
139 0	130 0	129 0	127 0	140 0	130 0	134 0	124 0	130 0	133 3·2	131 4	131 9·6	132 1·1
158 12	154 12	157 2	146 13	167 0·5	152 10·5	157 1	143 9	143 12	154 13·2	154 5·8	152 13	153 15·6
149 4	144 0	145 14	138 5	159 8·5	146 6·5	145 5	135 13	136 0	145 10	144 5·7	144 9·8	144 14·4
4 4	3 10	4 11	3 13	3 12	3 5	3 13	3 7	3 11	3 12·9	4 1·5	3 9·6	3 13
9 7·5	8 2·5	8 1	7 12	8 7	8 3	7 3	5 8	10 3	8 5·5	8 5·7	7 14·4	8 3
5 3·4	9 9	5 12	4 8·5	8 7·5	6 5	6 13·5	10 5	4 4	6 7·2	6 4·2	7 3·8	6 10·8
2 8·6	2 9	2 13·5	2 14	2 4	3 1·5	2 14	2 4·5	3 3·8	2 12·1	2 11·3	2 12	2 11·8
4 0	3 3	2 12·3	3 1·5	2 0·4	3 2	3 3	2 7	2 12·5	3 6	3 4·2	2 11·4	3 1·6
2 12	2 10	2 13·3	4 0·8	4 13·5	2 14·2	2 10	5 0·5	3 3·5	3 1·1	3 1	3 11·5	3 4·8
0 12·2	0 7·3	0 9·2	0 10·4	0 9·4	0 10·5	0 10·2	0 9	0 10	0 9·3	0 9·9	0 9·6	0 9·6
0 8·7	0 8·7	0 6·3	0 8·3	0 12·4	0 10	0 11·5	0 5·5	0 6·5	0 10·6	0 8	0 9·2	0 9·4
1 13	1 5·7	1 7·6	1 9·7	1 4·7	1 12	1 8·3	1 8	1 8·5	1 7·4	1 9·1	1 8·3	1 8·2
5 8·5	5 11	6 13	5 13	5 8·5	6 8·5	5 10	5 7	5 11·5	5 7·3	5 15·4	5 12·3	5 11·4
2 3	1 14	2 0	1 15·4	2 5·2	2 5	2 4·5	2 2	2 2	2 1·7	2 0·1	2 3·7	2 1·9
0 2·1	0 1·3	0 2	......	0 1	0 2·3	0 2	......	0 1	0 0·8	0 1·8	0 1·6	0 1·4
0 3	0 4·4	0 3·6	0 3·4	0 4·1	0 3·5	0 3·3	0 2·3	0 5	0 3·8	0 3·6	0 3·6	0 3·7
0 4·3	0 4·3	0 4·3	0 3·7	0 4·5	0 3	0 3·4	0 3·8	0 3·8	0 3·9	0 4·2	0 3·7	0 3·9
5 0	4 8	4 5	4 12·5	4 2·5	4 9	4 14·5	4 9·5	5 0	4 11·8	4 10·4	4 10·3	4 10·8
10 13	10 1	10 13	10 7·5	11 14·5	14 2	11 11	8 14	9 9	10 6·1	10 8·6	11 3·7	10 11·7
8 12	6 12	7 2	7 13	6 0·5	5 10·5	10 1	6 9	6 12	7 3·6	7 9·7	7 0·2	7 4·5
64 3·3	61 10	61 1·3	60 2·7	62 15·7	63 11	64 8·2	59 6·1	59 11·1	60 15·1	61 12·7	62 1·1	61 9·5
82 0	81 0	85 0	75 0	95 0	84 0	79 0	75 0	74 0	81 11·2	80 12	81 6·4	81 5·2
3 0·7	1 6	-0 3·3	3 2·3	1 8·8	-1 4·5	1 12·8	1 6·9	2 4·9	2 15·7	1 13	1 2·3	1 15·7
149 4	144 0	145 14	138 5	159 8·5	146 6·5	145 5	135 13	136 0	145 10	144 5·7	144 9·8	144 14·4

APPENDIX.—TABLE XXXIII. Showing the *Actual Weights* (lbs. and ozs.)

CLASS XVIII.—21 Sheep of various Breeds and Modes of

Designation of Parts.	Hampshire Down Breed. Killed December 18, 1851.				Sussex Down Breed.					
	No. 1.	No. 2.	No. 3.	No. 4.	No. 5.	No. 6.	No. 7.	No. 8.	No. 9.	No. 10.
	lbs. oz.	lbs. oz.	lbs. oz.	lbs. oz.	lbs. oz.	lbs. oz.	lbs. oz.	lbs. oz.	lbs. oz.	lbs. oz.
Original weights	......	......	......	......	76 0	85 0	91 0	81 0	79 0	81 0
Final weight, unfasted	224 0	224 0	243 0	218 0	158 0	166 0	184 0	163 0	150 0	184 0
Final weight, after fasting	211 0	214 0	231 0	209 0	150 0	158 0	176 0	155 0	142 0	174 0
Stomachs	4 1	4 11	2 8	4 2	3 4	3 11	4 0	3 1·5	2 8	3 13
Contents of stomachs	2 13	10 15	9 12	5 8	5 0	4 13	4 14	4 0·5	4 9	5 8
Caul-fat	14 14	11 13	13 8	13 12	8 0	7 13	13 10	11 11	7 7·5	9 14
Small intestines and contents	1 13	2 3	2 14	2 4	2 2	2 9	2 0	1 15	1 6	2 1
Large intestines and contents	2 8	3 10	3 0	2 10	2 6·5	2 6	2 11	2 2·5	2 11	2 8·5
Intestinal fat	6 9	4 4	6 13	6 10	4 1	5 13	5 5	6 0	3 7	5 2
Heart and aorta	0 12	0 12·5	0 14·5	0 12	0 9	0 14	0 10	0 10·5	0 12	0 11
Heart-fat	0 7	0 8	0 13·5	1 4	0 6	0 9	0 10·5	0 8	0 4	0 11·5
Lungs and windpipe	2 1	2 0	1 15	1 7·5	1 3	1 10·5	1 5	1 5	1 10	1 3·5
Blood	7 3·5	8 .0	8 8	7 2·5	5 9	6 8·5	5 15	6 0	5 14	7 11
Liver	3 1·5	2 9·5	3 3·5	2 2	2 2	2 5·5	2 3	2 2·5	1 8·3	2 6
Gall-bladder and contents	0 2·3	0 2·6	0 0·3	0 1·6	0 0·9	0 0·7	0 2·2	0 1	0 0·9	0 1·5
Pancreas ("sweetbread")	0 4·5	0 3·5	0 4·5	0 4	0 2·6	0 4·3	0 3·5	0 2	0 4·8	0 3·8
Milt or spleen	0 4·5	0 5·5	0 6·5	0 5·5	0 5	0 5	0 5	0 4	0 6·5	0 6
Bladder	0 1	0 0·7	0 1·3	0 0·9	0 0·5	0 0·5	0 1	0 0·7	0 0·5	0 0·8
Head	5 7·5	5 14	6 4	5 9	4 6	4 4·5	4 5	4 5	4 13	4 14
Skin and wool (with feet, &c.)	20 0	24 0	20 8	15 12	16 8	18 8	15 8	15 6	18 0	18 4
Wool shorn in Spring*	(6 0)	(5 0)	(5 4)	(7 8)	(6 0)	(6 0)	(7 8)	(9 0)	(8 0)	(7 8)
Miscellaneous trimmings	......	......	......	......	......	......	......	......	......	......
Total "offal" parts	72 6·8	82 0·3	81 6·1	69 11	56 1·5	62 7·5	63 12·2	59 13·2	55 10·7	65 8·6
Carcass	137 8	130 4·5	149 10·5	139 14·5	95 5	96 4	113 6·5	96 6·5	86 9	109 1·5
Loss by evaporation, error in weighing, &c.	1 1·2	1 11·2	—0 0·6	—0 9·5	—1 6·5	—0 11·5	—1 2·7	—1 3·7	—0 3·7	—0 10·1
Live-weight after fasting	211 0	214 0	231 0	209 0	150 0	158 0	176 0	155 0	142 0	174 0

Separate parts of the "offal".

* It should be mentioned, that in the case of these animals killed in December, the weight of wool shorn in the previous Spring, is not included *proportions* of the different parts, which are recorded in Appendix-

of the individual Organs, and other separated Parts, of SHEEP.

Feeding, about 1¾ year old; of more than Average Fatness.

				Leicesters and Cross-breds. Killed December 21, 1853.							Means of—			
Killed December 18, 1851.				Cross-bred Ewe.	Cross-bred Wether.	Leicester Wethers.					The 4 Hants Downs.	The 10 Sussex Downs.	The 7 Leicesters and Cross-breds.	The 21 Sheep.
No. 11.	No. 12.	No. 13.	No. 14.	No. 15.	No. 16.	No. 17.	No. 18.	No. 19.	No. 20.	No. 21.				
lbs. oz.	lbs. oz.	lbs. oz.	lbs. oz.	lbs. oz.	lbs. oz.	lbs. oz.	lbs. oz.	lbs. oz.	lbs. oz.	lbs. oz.	lbs. oz.	lbs. oz.	lbs. oz.	lbs. oz.
89 0	79 0	83 0	81 0	95 0	82 0	84 0	88 0	88 0	77 0	86 0	......	82 8	85 11·4	96 11·4
189 0	165 0	192 0	182 0	158 0	171 0	195 0	152 0	173 0	140 0	148 0	227 4	173 4·8	162 6·8	179 15·3
182 0	157 0	184 0	173 0	150 0	159 0	184 0	143 0	163 0	132 0	139 0	216 4	165 4	152 13·7	170 12·2
3 10	3 6	3 12	3 11	3 9	3 14	4 6	3 11	4 4	3 12	4 0	3 13·5	3 7·7	3 15·2	3 11·3
5 14	......	7 6	4 10	7 12	7 10	9 1	6 9	6 2	8 12	8 2	7 4	4 10·6	7 11·4	6 2·6
12 9·5	9 10	10 1	10 11	5 8·5	6 3·5	6 11	3 15·5	5 3	3 10	3 14	13 7·7	10 2·3	5 0·2	9 1·1
1 13·5	1 15	1 15	2 0	2 2	2 6	3 6	2 6	2 10	3 2	2 11	2 4·5	1 15·6	2 10·7	2 4·3
3 2	3 6	3 3	2 15	2 14	3 14·5	3 8·5	3 2	3 4	3 8	3 8	2 15	2 11·9	3 6·2	2 15·9
6 4	3 12	5 3	5 4	3 5·5	1 13	3 0	2 4·2	2 13	1 9·7	2 2	6 1	5 0·3	2 6·8	4 5·7
0 10·5	0 10	0 13	0 13	0 8·7	0 10·8	0 10·6	0 11	0 11·5	0 9	0 9	0 12·7	0 11·3	0 10·1	0 11·2
0 12	0 9·5	1 2	0 9	0 12	0 12·7	1 1·9	0 13·5	0 12·5	0 13·5	0 11	0 12·1	0 9·7	0 13·3	0 11·4
1 5·5	1 4	1 7·5	1 6	1 3·7	1 4	2 10	1 8·5	1 11	1 9·5	1 12·5	1 13·9	1 6	1 10·8	1 9·1
6 7·5	6 9	7 0·5	7 2·5	5 3	6 9	6 14	5 12·5	5 15·5	5 8	6 0	7 11·4	6 7·8	5 15·8	6 8·9
2 6	2 3	2 7	2 4·5	2 0	2 0	2 12·5	2 2	2 7·5	2 7	2 3	2 12·1	2 3·2	2 4·6	2 5·4
0 0·8	0 1·1	0 2·5	0 1·5	0 0·5	0 0·4	0 0·7	0 1·5	0 1·9	0 1·3	0 1·5	0 2·1	0 1·3	0 1·1	0 1·4
0 3·3	0 3·5	0 3·5	0 4·3	0 2·3	0 2·3	0 2·8	0 2·3	0 2·7	0 2·8	0 2	0 4·1	0 3·6	0 2·4	0 3·3
0 5	0 5	0 6	0 6·3	0 2·9	0 3·5	0 4	0 3·5	0 3·7	0 3	0 3·5	0 5·5	0 5·4	0 3·5	0 4·8
0 0·5	0 0·8	0 0·7	0 0·6	0 1	0 0·8	0 1·4	0 0·7	0 1	0 1	0 1	0 0·9	0 0·7	0 1	0 0·9
4 9	4 7	4 13	4 14	4 2·5	4 8·5	4 5·5	4 3·5	4 7·5	4 2·5	4 4	5 12·6	4 9·1	4 4·8	4 10·9
18 4	16 8	17 6	18 4	17 12	19 4	21 5	20 4	20 8	17 4	19 4	20 1	17 4·2	19 5·9	18 8·1
(7 0)	(9 0)	(6 8)	(7 4)	(7 0)	(6 8)	(8 0)	(8 0)	(8 0)	(8 0)	(8 0)	(5 15)	(7 6)	(7 10·3)	(7 3)
......	......	......	......	......	0 1	......	......	......	0 3	......	......		0 2	0 2
68 5·1	54 13·9	67 5·7	65 4·7	57 5·6	61 6	70 6·9	57 14·7	61 6·8	57 6·3	59 9·5	76 6·1	61 14·7	60 13·8	64 6·5
113 8·5	96 7	116 2·5	108 4	93 7	98 14·7	112 12	85 7·5	99 3	74 6	80 9	139 5·4	103 2·2	92 1·6	106 5·7
0 2·4	5 11·1	0 7·8	-0 8·7	-0 12·6	-1 4·7	0 13·1	-0 6·2	2 6·2	0 3·7	-1 1·5	0 8·5	0 0·7	-0 1·7	......
182 0	157 0	184 0	173 0	150 0	159 0	184 0	143 0	163 0	132 0	139 0	216 4	165 1·6	152 13·7	170 12·2

either in the recorded "Final Weight," or in the sum of items at the time of slaughtering. Nor, is it taken into account in calculating the *Percentage* Table LVIII. It is, however, given above, parenthetically, as Memorandum.

APPENDIX.—TABLE XXXIV. Showing the *Actual Weights* (lbs. and oz.)

CLASS I.—9 Pigs, divided into 3 Lots, each with rather different Food *.

Designation of Parts.	Lot 1.—Food:— Bean and Lentil meal—in fixed quantity. Bran—*ad libitum.*			Lot 2.—Food:— Indian meal—in fixed quantity. Bran—*ad libitum.*		
	No. 1.	No. 2.	No. 3.	No. 4.	No. 5.	No. 6.
	lbs. oz.	lbs. oz.	lbs. oz.	lbs. oz.	lbs. oz.	lbs. oz.
Original weight	156 0	142 0	130 0	149 0	138 0	129 0
Final weight, unfasted	210 0	151 0	188 0	186 0	190 0	183 0
Final weight, after fasting	200 0	144 0	175 0	178 0	178 0	175 0
Stomach and contents	4 6	2 2	2 4·5	2 7	3 6	3 4
Caul-fat	0 11	0 10	0 11	1 5	1 1·5	0 13·5
Small intestines and contents	9 2	2 12	5 14	3 12	6 10	5 4
Large intestines and contents	15 1	5 3	8 12	5 6·5	10 0	8 4
Intestinal fat, "mudgeon," &c.	1 13·5	1 1·5	1 2·5	2 7·5	1 11·5	1 6·5
Heart and aorta	0 10·5	0 8	0 8·5	0 9	0 5	0 9
Lungs and windpipe	1 9	1 8	1 11·5	1 8	1 4·5	1 8
Blood	8 13	6 11	5 9	7 11	7 2	6 0
Liver	3 8	2 0	3 0	2 5	2 14	2 10
Gall-bladder and contents	0 4·5	0 2·8	0 1·8	0 2·2	0 1·5	0 1·8
Pancreas ("sweetbread")	0 4·5	0 5·5	0 4·5	0 6·5	0 5	0 4·5
Milt or spleen	0 5	0 4·5	0 7	0 4·5	0 3·5	0 4
Bladder	0 1·8	0 1·2	0 1·5	0 2·8	0 1·5	0 1·5
Penis (or uterus)	0 8	0 6·8	0 5	......	......	0 6
Tongue	1 2·5	1 0	0 13·5	1 2	0 14	0 13·5
Toes	0 4	0 2·5	0 3	0 3	0 2	0 2·2
Miscellaneous trimmings	0 13	0 5	0 3	0 1·8	0 9	0 3
Total "offal" parts	49 5·3	25 3·8	32 0·3	29 13·8	36 11	31 15·5
Carcass (including head and feet)	147 14	117 14	139 4·5	148 12·5	138 14·5	142 7·5
Loss by evaporation, error in weighing, &c.	2 12·7	0 14·2	3 11·2	−0 10·3	2 6·5	0 9
Live-weight after fasting	200 0	144 0	175 0	178 0	178 0	175 0

* For particulars of the *feeding* experiment, refer to Pens 9, 10, and 11, under the head of "Experiments

of the individual Organs, and other separated Parts, of PIGS.

Somewhat *under* Fattened—the Food containing a considerable portion of Bran.

| Lot 3.—Food:— Bean and Lentil meal, and Indian meal —in fixed quantity. Bran—*ad libitum*. | | | Means of— | | | |
No. 7.	No. 8.	No. 9.	Lot 1. 3 Pigs.	Lot 2. 3 Pigs.	Lot 3. 3 Pigs.	The 9 Pigs.
lbs. oz.	lbs. oz.	lbs. oz.	lbs. oz.	lbs. oz.	lbs. oz.	lbs. oz.
137 0	150 0	136 0	142 10·7	138 10·7	141 0	140 12·5
201 0	204 0	210 0	183 0	186 5·3	205 0	191 7·1
196 0	198 0	201 0	173 0	177 0	198 5·3	182 12·4
3 12	3 1	2 11	2 14·8	3 0·3	3 2·7	3 0·6
1 5	1 1	0 15	0 10·7	1 1·3	1 1·7	0 15·2
5 7	6 4	5 12	5 14·7	5 3·3	5 13	5 10·3
9 0	10 1	10 1	9 10·7	7 14·2	9 11·4	9 1·4
2 0·5	1 15	1 6	1 5·6	1 13·9	1 12·6	1 10·8
0 9	0 8·5	0 9	0 9	0 7·7	0 6·9	0 8·5
1 15	1 10·3	1 13	1 9·5	1 6·8	1 12·6	1 9·7
7 8	7 5	8 7	7 0·4	6 15	7 12	7 3·6
3 0	2 12	3 6	2 13·3	2 9·7	3 1·4	2 13·5
0 2·8	0 1·2	0 2	0 3	0 1·8	0 1·4	0 2·1
0 6·5	0 4·5	0 4·5	0 4·8	0 5·3	0 5·2	0 5·1
0 5	0 4	0 5	0 5·5	0 4	0 4·7	0 4·7
0 3	0 2	0 2	0 1·5	0 1·9	0 2·4	0 1·9
......		0 8	0 6·6	0 6	0 8	0 6·8
1 15	1 3	0 14	1 0	0 15·2	1 0	0 15·7
0 2·5	0 3	0 3·5	0 3·2	0 2·4	0 3	0 2·9
0 1·5	0 3·3	0 5	0 7	0 4·6	0 3·6	0 5·1
36 12·8	36 14·8	37 15	35 8·5	33 1·4	37 8·8	35 6·1
157 5	162 6	163 5·5	135 0·1	143 6·2	161 0·2	146 7·5
1 14·2	−1 4·8	−0 4·5	2 7·4	0 8·4	−0 3·7	0 14·8
196 0	198 0	201 0	173 0	177 0	198 5·3	182 12·4

APPENDIX,—TABLE XXXV. Showing the *Actual Weights* (lbs. and ozs.)
CLASS II.—12 Pigs, divided into 4 Lots, each with rather different Food*. *Moderately*

Designation of Parts.	Lot 1.—Food:— Bean and Lentil meal—*ad libitum.*			Lot 2.—Food:— Indian meal—in fixed quantity. Bean and Lentil meal—*ad libitum.*		
	No. 1.	No. 2.	No. 3.	No. 4.	No. 5.	No. 6.
	lbs. oz.	lbs. oz.	lbs. oz.	lbs. oz.	lbs. oz.	lbs. oz.
Original weight	176 0	135 0	129 0	157 0	142 0	123 0
Final weight, unfasted	283 0	231 0	239 0	304 0	246 0	238 0
Final weight, after fasting	266 2·5	224 0	230 0	292 0	237 0	224 0
Stomach and contents	3 15·5	2 4	3 4·5	2 3·2	2 10	1 9
Caul-fat	1 3·5	1 9	0 13·5	1 11·5	0 15·2	1 1·5
Small intestines and contents	4 11·5	4 11	5 0	5 1	5 0	4 8
Large intestines and contents	9 10	8 6·5	11 14	10 2	9 8	6 3
Intestinal fat, "mudgeon," &c.	4 9·8	3 12·8	3 3·3	6 5	3 0	3 2
Heart and aorta	0 10·8	0 9	0 11	0 11·3	0 9·8	0 11·5
Lungs and windpipe	1 13·2	1 8	1 10·5	1 15·5	1 7	1 7·1
Blood	9 13·8	8 9·5	9 13·2	10 11	9 8·5	10 0
Liver	4 15	4 6	3 15	4 11	3 6	4 0
Gall-bladder and contents	0 3·2	0 2·2	0 2	0 2·5	0 1·7	0 3
Pancreas ("sweetbread")	0 4·2	0 7·5	0 9·2	0 14·2	0 8·2	0 9·2
Milt or spleen	0 6·5	0 5	0 5·8	0 5·8	0 6·5	0 5
Bladder	0 2·5	0 2·8	0 4	0 4	0 2·8	0 1·8
Penis (or uterus)	0 12·8	......	......	0 8·2	......	0 5·8
Tongue	1 3	1 0·2	1 3·5	1 2·5	1 0·6	0 14·5
Toes	0 3·5	0 3·5	0 3	0 3	0 3·5	0 3
Miscellaneous trimmings	0 13·2	0 11·5	0 11·5	0 9	0 11·5	0 6·8
Total "offal" parts	45 8	38 12·5	43 12	47 8·7	39 3·5	35 11·2
Carcass (including head and feet)	223 2	184 12	182 10	240 15	195 8·5	188 4
Loss by evaporation, error in weighing, &c.	−2 7·5	0 7·5	3 10	3 8·3	2 4	0 0·8
Live-weight after fasting	266 2·5	224 0	230 0	292 0	237 0	224 0

* For particulars of the *feeding* experiment, refer to Pens 1, 2, 3, and 4, under the head of "Experiments

of the individual Organs, and other separated Parts, of PIGS.

Fattened—the Food containing a considerable proportion of Bean and Lentil Meal.

Lot 3.—Food:— Bran—in fixed quantity. Bean and Lentil meal—ad libitum.			Lot 4.—Food:— Indian meal and Bran—in fixed quantity. Bean and Lentil meal—ad libitum.			Means of—				
No. 7.	No. 8.	No. 9.	No. 10.	No. 11.	No. 12.	Lot 1. 3 Pigs.	Lot 2. 3 Pigs.	Lot 3. 3 Pigs.	Lot 4. 3 Pigs.	The 12 Pigs.
lbs. oz.	lbs. oz.	lbs. oz.	lbs. oz.	lbs. oz.	lbs. oz.	lbs. oz.	lbs. oz.	lbs. oz.	lbs. oz.	lbs. oz.
163 0	131 0	128 0	173 0	131 0	123 0	146 10·7	140 10·7	140 10·7	142 5·3	142 9·4
248 0	183 0	202 0	302 0	207 0	189 0	251 0	262 10·7	211 0	232 10·7	239 5·4
238 0	173 0	194 0	281 8	191 8	178 0	240 0·8	251 0	201 10·7	217 0	227 6·9
2 14	3 0·5	2 13	3 4	2 14	3 0	3 2·7	2 2·1	2 14·5	3 0·7	2 13
1 7	0 15·3	0 11	1 4·5	1 3	0 9·5	1 3·3	1 4·1	1 0·4	1 0·3	1 2
6 12	4 7	4 7·5	6 9	4 0	3 15	4 12·8	4 13·7	5 3·5	4 13·3	4 14·8
10 4	8 0	8 15·5	12 4	8 10	8 3	9 15·5	8 9·7	9 1·2	9 11	9 5·4
2 7	1 0	2 7	3 4·5	2 15	1 10	3 14	4 2·3	1 15·3	2 9·8	3 2·4
0 6·2	0 9	0 7·7	0 14·3	0 8·3	0 9·6	0 10·3	0 10·9	0 7·6	0 10·8	0 9·9
1 11·5	1 8	1 3·5	2 0	1 14·5	1 8	1 10·6	1 9·9	1 7·7	1 12·8	1 10·2
8 13	7 4	7 13	8 6·5	9 4	9 7	9 6·8	10 1·2	7 15·4	9 0·5	9 2
4 4	2 10	2 15·5	5 2	3 12	2 11·5	4 6·7	4 0·3	3 4·5	3 13·8	3 14·3
0 3	0 1·5	0 1	0 1·8	0 2·5	0 1	0 2·5	0 2·4	0 1·6	0 1·8	0 2·1
0 9	0 6	0 6·8	0 9·2	0 7·3	0 6	0 7	0 10·5	0 7·3	0 7·5	0 8·1
0 5	0 4·5	0 4	0 6·5	0 5·2	0 5·2	0 5·8	0 5·8	0 4·5	0 5·6	0 5·4
0 2·6	0 3·2	0 3	0 3·5	0 3·2	0 3·5	0 3·1	0 2·9	0 3	0 3·4	0 3·1
......	......	......	0 5·8	......	......	0 12·6	0 7	......	0 5·8	0 8·1
1 4	0 15	0 12·8	1 0	0 14	0 13·5	1 2·2	1 0·6	0 15·9	0 14·5	1 0·3
0 3·5	0 3	0 3	0 4	0 3·5	0 3	0 3·3	0 3·2	0 3·2	0 3·5	0 3·3
·1 8	0 13	0 11·5	0 9·2	......	0 9	0 12·1	0 9·1	1 0·2	0 9·1	0 11·8
43 2	32 4	34 7·8	46 8·6	37 4·5	34 3	43 3·5	40 15·7	36 10	39 12·2	40 4·2
192 6·5	141 3	157 6	235 7	158 6·3	142 12	196 13·3	208 3·6	163 10·5	178 13·8	186 14·4
2 7·5	−0 7	2 2·2	−0 7·8	−4 2·6	1 1	......	1 12·5	1 6·2	−1 10	0 4·3
238 0	173 0	194 0	281 8	191 8	178 0	240 0·8	251 0	201 10·7	217 0	227 6·9

with Pigs—Series 1," Article—"Pig Feeding," Journal of the Royal Agricultural Society of England, vol. xiv. part 2.

APPENDIX.—TABLE XXXVI. Showing the *Actual Weights* (lbs. and ozs.)

CLASS III.—15 Pigs, divided into 5 Lots, each with rather different Food*.

Designation of Parts.	Lot 1.—Food:— Indian meal—*ad libitum.*			Lot 2.—Food:— Bean and Lentil meal—in fixed quantity. Indian meal—*ad libitum.*			Lot 3.—Food:— Bran—in fixed quantity. Indian meal—*ad libitum.*		
	No. 1.	No. 2.	No. 3.	No. 4.	No. 5.	No. 6.	No. 7.	No. 8.	No. 9.
	lbs. oz.	lbs. oz.	lbs. oz.	lbs. oz.	lbs. oz.	lbs. oz.	lbs. oz.	lbs. oz.	lbs. oz.
Original weight	168 0	128 0	135 0	157 0	144 0	144 0	148 0	126 0	141 0
Final weight, unfasted	263 0	187 0	210 0	266 0	235 0	255 0	254 0	196 0	292 0
Final weight, after fasting	253 8	181 8	208 0	262 0	223 0	248 0	244 0	190 0	279 0
Stomach and contents	2 15	3 0·5	2 2	2 0	2 3	2 2	2 9·5	1 15	2 12·5
Caul-fat	1 10	0 14·3	1 1·2	1 7	0 14·5	1 13	1 4·5	1 3·5	1 4
Small intestines and contents	4 10	3 0·5	4 1·5	3 8	3 13	3 14	3 2	3 2	4 14
Large intestines and contents	7 0·5	5 11·5	5 6	9 1	6 8	7 5	11 0	7 8	7 11
Intestinal fat, "mudgeon," &c.	4 10·5	2 8·5	1 11·8	4 10·8	2 8·5	5 9	2 10	3 3	4 0
Heart and aorta	0 11	0 9·2	0 10·5	0 11	0 10·5	0 10	0 10·5	0 9·5	0 13
Lungs and windpipe	1 13	1 5	1 11	1 10	1 7·3	1 14	1 5	1 5	2 4
Blood	9 1	6 9	7 13	9 10·5	6 8	8 14	7 6·5	6 14	8 3
Liver	3 6·5	2 10	2 15·2	3 14	3 0·5	3 4	4 5	3 0	3 15
Gall-bladder and contents	0 1·5	0 0·5	0 2·2	0 2·5	0 1·8	0 2·5	0 1·5	0 0·8	0 2·2
Pancreas ("sweetbread")	0 8·8	0 5·3	0 9	0 7·5	0 4·5	0 10	0 6·2	0 5·2	0 11·5
Milt or spleen	0 4·2	0 4·3	0 4·5	0 4·5	0 5·2	0 5·5	0 4	0 5	0 5·5
Bladder	0 1·8	0 2	0 1·5	0 3·2	0 3·2	0 2·2	0 2·5	0 2·8	0 4·5
Penis (or uterus)	0 8·5	......	0 8·5	0 8·3	......	......	0 9·5	......	......
Tongue	1 1·5	0 13	0 15·5	1 0·5	0 14·5	1 2·5	1 2	1 1·5	1 3
Toes	0 3·2	0 3·2	0 2·8	0 3	0 3	0 3·5	0 2·5	0 2·5	0 3·5
Miscellaneous trimmings	0 11·5	0 9	0 1	1 3	1 5·3	0 12	1 6	0 4	0 10·5
Total "offal" parts	39 6·5	28 9·8	30 5·2	40 8·8	30 14·8	38 11·2	38 7·2	31 1·8	39 5·2
Carcass (including head and feet)	217 6	156 2·5	175 11·5	219 7·5	190 14·5	208 1·5	204 11	157 8·5	235 1·5
Loss by evaporation, error in weighing, &c.	−3 4·5	−3 4·3	1 15·3	1 15·7	1 2·7	1 3·3	0 13·8	1 5·7	4 9·3
Live-weight after fasting	253 8	181 8	208 0	262 0	223 0	248 0	244 0	190 0	279 0

(Left margin vertical label: Separate parts of the "offal.")

* For particulars of the *feeding* experiment, refer to Pens 5, 6, 7, 8, and 12, under the head of "Experiments with

of the individual Organs, and other separated Parts, of Pigs.

Well Fattened—the Food containing a considerable proportion of Indian-corn Meal.

	Lot 4.—Food:— Bean and Lentil meal, and Bran—in fixed quantity. Indian meal—*ad libitum.*			Lot 5.—Food:— Bean and Lentil meal, Indian meal, and Bran—each *ad libitum.*			Means of—					
	No. 10.	No. 11.	No. 12.	No. 13.	No. 14.	No. 15.	Lot 1. 3 Pigs.	Lot 2. 3 Pigs.	Lot 3. 3 Pigs.	Lot 4. 3 Pigs.	Lot 5. 3 Pigs.	The 15 Pigs.
	lbs. oz.	lbs. oz.	lbs. oz.	lbs. oz.	lbs. oz.	lbs. oz.	lbs. oz.	lbs. oz.	lbs. oz.	lbs. oz.	lbs. oz.	lbs. oz.
	145 0	144 0	143 0	149 0	130 0	150 0	143 10·7	144 5·3	138 5·3	144 0	143 0	143 7·5
	294 0	250 0	255 0	271 0	163 0	244 0	220 0	252 0	247 5·3	266 5·3	226 0	235 10·7
	284 0	242 0	239 0	267 0	165 0	236 0	214 5·3	244 5·3	237 10·7	255 0	222 10·7	234 12·7
	2 11	3 2	2 14	4 5	3 0	2 12	2 11·1	2 1·6	2 7	2 14·4	3 8·7	2 11·4
	1 11·5	1 4·5	1 8·5	1 5	1 9·5	0 14·5	1 3·2	1 6·2	1 4	1 8·2	1 4·3	1 5·2
	5 2	4 2	5 5	3 14	3 6	3 2	3 14·7	3 11·7	3 11·3	4 13·7	3 7·3	3 14·9
	9 10	10 8	7 10	8 0	5 10	6 9	6 0·7	7 10	8 11·7	9 4	6 11·7	7 10·8
	5 2	2 8·5	1 12	2 9·3	2 14·5	2 1	2 15·5	4 4·1	3 4·3	3 2·1	2 8·3	3 3·6
	0 13	0 10·5	0 9·5	0 12	0 7·5	0 9	0 10·2	0 10·5	0 11	0 11	0 9·5	0 10·4
	1 10	1 12	1 10	1 13	1 4·5	1 3	1 9·7	1 10·4	1 10	1 10·7	1 6·8	1 9·5
	8 14	9 4	8 11	8 10	5 14	8 1	7 13	8 5·5	7 7·9	8 15·1	7 8·3	8 0·4
	4 2	3 4	3 5	3 6	2 8	3 4	2 15·9	3 6·2	3 12	3 9	3 0·7	3 5·6
	0 2	0 1·5	0 3·7	0 1·5	0 0·5	0 1·5	0 1·4	0 2·3	0 1·5	0 2·2	0 1·2	0 1·7
	0 12·5	0 7·5	0 6·8	0 5	0 5	0 7	0 7·7	0 7·3	0 7·6	0 8·9	0 5·7	0 7·5
	0 5	0 5·5	0 5	0 5	0 3	0 4·5	0 4·3	0 5·1	0 4·6	0 5·2	0 4·2	0 4·7
	0 3·5	0 2·5	0 1·8	0 2·8	0 1·3	0 4	0 1·8	0 2·9	0 3·3	0 2·6	0 2·7	0 2·7
	......	0 8·5	0 9	0 6	0 5·5	......	0 8·5	0 8·3	0 9·5	0 8·7	0 5·7	0 8
	1 1·5	1 0	1 1	1 8	0 12·5	0 15	0 15·3	1 0·5	1 2·2	1 0·9	1 1·2	1 0·8
	0 3	0 3	0 2·5	0 3·2	0 3	0 3	0 3·1	0 3·2	0 2·6	0 2·8	0 3	0 2·9
	1 3	0 5·5	0 9·7	0 12	0 9	0 9·5	0 7·2	1 1·4	0 12·2	0 11·4	0 10·2	0 11·7
	43 10	39 9·5	36 12·5	38 8·6	29 1·8	31 4	32 15·3	37 1·2	36 11·1	40 2·9	33 1·5	35 15·8
	238 3	209 6	200 6	226 12·5	133 4·5	202 11	183 1·3	206 2·5	199 1·7	212 15·7	187 9·3	197 12·5
	2 3	2 0·5	1 13·5	1 10·7	2 9·7	2 1	−1 11·3	1 1·6	1 13·9	1 13·4	1 15·9	1 0·4
	284 0	242 0	239 0	267 0	165 0	236 0	214 5·3	244 5·3	237 10·7	255 0	222 10·7	234 12·7

Pigs—Series 1," Article—" Pig Feeding," Journal of the Royal Agricultural Society of England, vol. xiv. part 2.

APPENDIX.—TABLE XXXVII. Showing the *Actual Weights* (lbs. and ozs.)

CLASS IV.—12 Pigs, divided into 4 Lots, according to the Food*.   *Moderately* Fattened.

Designation of Parts.	Lot 1.—Food:— Lentils, and Bran—in fixed quantity. Sugar—*ad libitum*.			Lot 2.—Food:— Lentils, and Bran—in fixed quantity. Starch—*ad libitum*.		
	No. 1.	No. 2.	No. 3.	No. 4.	No. 5.	No. 6.
	lbs. oz.	lbs. oz.	lbs. oz.	lbs. oz.	lbs. oz.	lbs. oz.
Original weight	109 0	82 0	95 0	89 0	105 0	91 0
Final weight, unfasted	181 0	168 0	184 0	167 0	204 0	162 0
Final weight, after fasting	173 0	163 0	175 0	160 0	198 0	153 0
Stomach and contents	1 8	1 12	2 3·5	2 5	1 13·5	1 6·5
Caul-fat	1 1	1 2·5	0 14·3	1 0·5	1 1·3	0 12
Small intestines and contents	3 2	3 9	3 3	3 10	3 14	3 2
Large intestines and contents	8 2	7 13	7 4	9 6	10 1	10 6
Intestinal fat, "mudgeon," &c.	0 15·7	1 1	1 0	1 0	0 14	0 14·5
Heart and aorta	0 8·8	0 9	0 8·7	0 7·3	0 9·5	0 .9
Lungs and windpipe	1 3·2	1 6	1 9·5	1 4	1·11·5	1 10
Blood	5 6·5	5 12	6 5	6 2	7 6	6 14·5
Liver	2 8·5	3 4·5	2 13	2 12·5	3 0	2 11·5
Gall-bladder and contents	0 1·8	0 2·3	0 0·7	0 3	0 3·4	0 3
Pancreas ("sweetbread")	0 4	0 6	0 4	0 4·8	0 5·8	0 4·5
Milt or spleen	0 3·5	0 4	0 4·5	0 3	0 4	0 3·8
Bladder	0 3·3	0 1·5	0 1·5	0 3	0 1·5	0 2
Penis (or uterus)	......	0 4·5	......	0 4·8	0 5	0 4·5
Tongue	1 2·5	1 0·5	1 2·5	1 0	0 14·5	0 13
Toes				0 2·5	0 2	0 2·5
Miscellaneous trimmings	......	......	......	0 2·5	0 2·5	0 2
Total "offal" parts	26 6·8	28 7·8	27 12·7	30 6·4	32 14	30 8·8
Carcass (including head and feet)	144 15	132 5	147 6·7	125 5·7	163 5·5	121 11·5
Loss by evaporation, error in weighing, &c.	1 10·2	2 3·2	−0 3·4	4 3·2	1 12·5	0 11·7
Live-weight after fasting	173 0	163 0	175 0	160 0	198 0	153 0

(*Separate parts of the "offal".*)

* For particulars of the *feeding* experiment, see Article—" On the Equivalency of Starch and

of the individual Organs, and other separated Parts, of PIGS.

The Food consisted, in considerable proportion, of either Starch or Sugar.

	Lot 3.—Food:— Lentils, and Bran—in fixed quantity. Sugar, and Starch—ad libitum.			Lot 4.—Food:— Lentils, Bran, Sugar, and Starch —each ad libitum.			Means of—				
	No. 7.	No. 8.	No. 9.	No. 10.	No. 11.	No. 12.	Lot 1. 3 Pigs.	Lot 2. 3 Pigs.	Lot 3. 3 Pigs.	Lot 4. 3 Pigs.	The 12 Pigs.
	lbs. oz.	lbs. oz.	lbs. ozs.	lbs. oz.	lbs. oz.	lbs. oz.	lbs. oz.	lbs. oz.	lbs. oz.	lbs. oz.	lbs. oz.
	86 0	87 0	108 0	98 0	100 0	94 0	95 5·3	95 0	93 10·6	97 5·3	95 5·3
	177 0	172 0	204 0	211 0	208 0	185 0	177 10·6	177 10·6	184 5·3	201 5·3	185 4
	168 0	163 0	196 0	205 0	193 0	182 0	170 5·3	170 5·3	175 10·6	193 5·3	177 6·6
	2 2	1 15	2 4·7	1 11	2 11	2 13·5	1 13·2	1 13·7	2 1·9	2 6·5	2 0·8
	1 0	1 1	1 0·5	1 5·5	1 0·5	1 3·5	1 0·6	0 15·3	1 0·5	1 3·2	1 0·9
	3 1	3 6	4 13	4 3	5 2	4 13	3 4·7	3 8·7	3 12	4 11·3	3 13·2
	7 9	8 14	8 9	9 8	8 8	10 12	7 11·7	9 15	8 5·3	9 9·3	8 14·3
	1 6	0 14	1 7	1 6·5	1 7	0 15	1 0·2	0 14·8	1 3·7	1 4·2	1 1·7
	0 8·5	0 8·5	0 10	0 9·5	0 9	0 9	0 8·8	0 8·6	0 9	0 9·2	0 8·9
	1 4	1 2·7	1 7	1 6·8	1 8	1 4	1 6·2	1 8·5	1 4·6	1 6·3	1 6·4
	5 10	6 1	6 0	7 6·5	6 2	6 13	5 13·1	6 12·8	5 14·3	6 12·5	6 5·2
	2 11·5	2 7	2 15·5	3 6	4 0·5	3 7	2 14	2 13·3	2 11·3	3 9·8	3 0·1
	0 1·8	0 2·3	0 2	0 3	0 3·2	0 2	0 1·6	0 3·1	0 2	0 2·7	0 2·4
	0 5·2	0 4·3	0 4·5	0 5·8	0 5	0 6	0 4·7	0 5	0 4·7	0 5·6	0 5
	0 4	0 3·5	0 3·5	0 4	0 3·5	0 3·5	0 4	0 3·6	0 3·7	0 3·7	0 3·7
	0 2	0 2·5	0 2·3	0 2·5	0 2·5	0 2·5	0 2·1	0 2·2	0 2·3	0 2·5	0 2·2
	......	......	......	0 6	0 8·5	......	0 4·5	0 4·8		0 7·2	0 5·6
	0 14·5	0 14	0 15	0 15	0 13·5	0 12·8	1 1·8	0 14·5	0 14·5	0 13·8	0 15·2
	0 2	0 2	0 3	0 0	0 2·5	0 2·5	0 2·5	0 2·2	0 2·3	0 2·5	0 2·3
	0 3·7	0 3·5	0 5	0 5	0 6	0 1·3	......	0 2·3	0 4·1	0 4·1	0 3·5
	27 5·2	28 5·3	31 6	33 8·1	33 12·7	34 8·6	27 13·7	31 4·4	29 0·2	34 2·4	30 11·4
	137 6	132 9·7	160 14	168 9·3	155 14·5	144 11·5	141 9	136 12·9	143 9·8	156 6·4	144 9·5
	3 4·8	2 1	3 12	2 14·6	3 4·8	2 11·9	0 14·6	2 4	3 0·6	2 12·5	2 1·7
	168 0	163 0	196 0	205 0	193 0	182 0	170 5·3	170 5·3	175 10·6	193 5·3	177 6·6

Sugar in Food "—Report of the British Association for the Advancement of Science for 1854.

APPENDIX.—TABLE XXXVIII. Showing the *Actual Weights* (lbs. and ozs.) of the individual Organs, and other separated Parts, of PIGS.

CLASS V.—6 Pigs, divided into 2 Lots, each with rather different Food*. Well Fattened.—Food comprised a portion of dried Cod-fish.

Designation of Parts.	Lot 1.—Food: Dried Cod-fish—in fixed quantity. Bran and Indian meal, equal parts—ad libitum.						Lot 2.—Food: Dried Cod-fish—in fixed quantity. Indian meal—ad libitum.						Means of—					
	No. 1.		No. 2.		No. 3.		No. 4.		No. 5.		No. 6.		Lot 1. 3 Pigs.		Lot 2. 3 Pigs.		The 6 Pigs.	
	lbs.	oz.	lbs.	oz.	lbs.	oz.	lbs.	oz.	lbs.	oz.	lbs.	oz.	lbs.	oz.	lbs.	oz.	lbs.	oz.
Original weight	171	2	158	0	164	0	192	0	158	0	140	0	164	5·3	163	5·3	163	13·3
Final weight, unfasted	294	0	238	0	286	0	335	0	275	0	299	0	272	10·7	303	0	287	13·3
Final weight, after fasting	279	0	226	0	271	0	329	0	270	0	293	0	258	10·7	297	5·3	278	0
Stomach and contents	2	12	3	15	2	10	3	6	3	2	3	4	3	1·7	3	4	3	2·9
Caul-fat	1	8·5	1	0	1	1	1	15·5	1	11	1	6	1	2·8	1	10·8	1	6·8
Small intestines and contents	4	8	5	6	5	1	4	11·5	3	14	6	8	4	4·7	4	0·5	4	8·1
Large intestines and contents	11	2	9	2	7	0·5	7	13	6	0	2	12·5	9	6·8	5	1·2	7	9·6
Intestinal fat, "mudgeon," &c.	3	5	1	14	2	14	3	7	3	1			2	11	3	1·5	2	14·3
Heart and aorta	0	11	0	15	0	11·5	0	10	0	7·5	0	12	0	12·5	0	9·8	0	11·1
Lungs and windpipe	1	3·5	1	4	1	4	1	10·5	2	10·5	1	7·7	1	3·8	1	14·9	1	9·4
Blood	9	13·5	7	13·5	8	7·5	9	10	7	15·5	7	12	8	11·5	8	7·9	8	9·4
Liver	3	12	3	5	4	1	3	4	3	4	3	0	3	11·3	3	2·7	3	7
Gall-bladder and contents	0	8	0	2	0	2	0	10	0	2·5	0	8	0	2·4	0	3·2	0	2·8
Pancreas ("sweetbread")	0	5·5	0	8	0	7·5	0	10	0	7·5	0	6	0	7·8	0	8·5	0	8·1
Milt or spleen			0	5	0	5	0	6·5	0	5			0	5·4	0	5·8	0	5·6
Bladder	0	3·2	0	2·3	0	2·5	0	2·5	0	3	0	3	0	2·7	0	2·8	0	2·7
Penis (or uterus)	0	10	0	7·5			0	10	1	0			0	8·7	0	10	0	9·2
Tongue	1	6	1	2·2	1	4	1	9·5	0	3	0	15	1	3·7	1	3·3	1	3·3
Toes	0	2·5	0	2·5	0	3	0	4	0	10	0	3	0	2·7	0	7·2	0	3
Miscellaneous trimmings	0	11	0	5	1	1	0	2·5			0	9	0	11			0	9·1
Total "offal" parts	42	12·2	35	13·5	36	10	40	7·5	35	0·5	33	6·2	38	9·5	36	11·4	37	10·4
Carcass (including head and feet)	235	14	189	2·5	232	5	288	11·5	234	0	256	7	219	0·5	289	11·5	239	6
Loss by evaporation, error in weighing, &c.	0	5·8	1	0	2	5	−0	3	0	15·5	3	2·8	1	0·7	0	14·4	0	15·6
Live-weight after fasting	279	0	226	0	271	0	329	0	270	0	293	0	258	10·7	297	5·3	278	0

(Rows *Heart and aorta* through *Miscellaneous trimmings* are bracketed as "Separate parts of the 'offal'.")

* For particulars of the *feeding* experiment, refer to Pens 1 and 2, under the head of "Experiments with Pigs—Series 3," Article—" Pig Feeding," Journal of the Royal Agricultural Society of England, vol. xiv. part 2.

APPENDIX.—TABLE XXXIX. Showing the *Actual Weights* (lbs. and ozs.) of the individual Organs, and other separated Parts, of PIGS.

5 Pigs, divided into 2 Lots, according to condition of Maturity when put to Fatten.

CLASS VI.—Put to Fatten when in Store condition, and fed till only Half-fattened.

CLASS VII.—Put to Fatten when Half-fat, and fed till Moderately Fattened.

Designation of Parts	Class 6. Put to Fatten when in store condition, and fed till only Half-fattened				Class 7. Put to Fatten when Half-fat, and fed till Moderately fattened						Means of—					
	No. 1		No. 2		No. 3		No. 4		No. 5		Class 6.		Class 7.		The 5 Pigs.	
	lbs.	oz.	lbs.	oz.	lbs.	oz.	lbs.	oz.	lbs.	oz.	lbs.	oz.	lbs.	oz.	lbs.	oz.
Original weight	121	0	140	0	147	0	112	0	148	0	130	8	135	10·7	133	9·6
Final weight, unfasted	165	0	195	0	185	0	137	0	222	0	180	8	181	5·3	180	12·8
Final weight, after fasting	155	0	186	0	175	0	130	0	213	0	170	8	172	10·8	171	12·8
Stomach and contents	4	3	1	11·6	1	7·8	1	5·5	2	4·5	2	15·3	1	11·3	2	3·3
Caul-fat	0	12·9	0	12·7	0	14·2	0	11·2	1	1·6	0	12·8	0	14·3	0	13·7
Small intestines and contents	7	12	5	8	3	12·7	3	13·8	4	2·9	6	10	3	15·1	5	0·3
Large intestines and contents	6	14	7	14	4	11·5	5	7·5	6	12	7	6	5	10·3	6	5·4
Intestinal fat, "mudgeon," &c.	0	15·7	1	5·5	2	4·1	0	13·5	1	7·2	1	2·6	1	8·2	1	6
Heart and aorta	1	7·4	0	7·5	0	7·2	0	6·2	1	10·8	0	7·5	0	8·1	0	7·8
Lungs and windpipe	1	9·7	1	3·3	5	7·8	1	14	1	15·2	1	6·5	1	12·3	1	10
Blood	4	7	2	15·5	2	9·9	4	10	7	2	3	3·3	2	12·7	5	8·9
Liver	3	7·1	2	13·2	2	10	2	6·3	2	14	3	2·1	2	10·1	2	13·3
Gall-bladder and contents	0	1	0	2·2	0	1·7	0	2·3	0	3·1	0	1·6	0	2·4	0	2·1
Pancreas ("sweetbread")	0	3·4	0	5·6	0	5·6	0	3·8	0	6	0	4·5	0	5·1	0	4·9
Milt or spleen	0	5·1	0	4·2	0	3·2	0	2·7	0	7·5	0	4·6	0	4·5	0	4·5
Bladder	0	1·8	0	1·7	0	2	0	2·5	0	3·3	0	1·8	0	2·6	0	2·3
Penis (or uterus)	0	4·2	0	6	0	5·4	0	6	0	9	0	5·1	0	6·8	0	6·1
Tongue	0	13·5	0	12·9	0	14·3	0	12·2	0	14·2	0	13·2	0	13·6	0	13·4
Miscellaneous trimmings	0	8·9	0	9·7	1	0·7	0	9·3	0	5·1	0	9·3	0	10·4	0	9·9
Total "offal" parts	32	14·7	30	5·6	26	6·1	23	14·8	31	6·4	31	10·2	27	3·8	28	15·9
Carcass (including head and feet)	118	3	153	0	147	0	106	2·5	180	0	135	9·5	144	6·2	140	13·9
Loss by evaporation, error in weighing, &c.	3	14·3	2	10·4	1	9·9	–0	1·3	1	9·6	3	4·3	1	0·8	1	1·5
Live-weight after fasting	155	0	186	0	175	0	130	0	213	0	170	8	172	10·8	171	12·8

Appendix.—Table XL. Showing the *Percentage Proportion* of the individual Organs, and other

Designation of Parts.	Calves.		Heifers.		Bullocks.				
	No. 1.	No. 2.	No. 1.	No. 2.	No. 1.	No. 2.	No. 3.	No. 4.	No. 5.
	Short-horned; milk-fed; killed Aug. 11, 1849.	Durham breed (analysed as fat); taken from dam feeding on grass; killed Sept. 12, 1849.	Welsh; 3 to 4 years old; killed Aug. 23, 1849.	Welsh; 3 years old; lately oilcake-fed; killed Aug. 30, 1849.	Mixed breed; killed Aug. 2, 1849.	Mixed breed; killed Aug. 9, 1849.	Welsh, horned; 4 years old; killed Aug. 16, 1849.	Scotch; long-horned; 4 years old; grass-fed; killed Aug. 30, 1849.	Dutch; lately grass-fed in Norfolk; killed Aug. 23, 1849.
Stomachs	1·64	1·09	3·70	3·79	3·34	3·85	3·23	3·24	2·67
Contents of stomachs, and vomit	1·60	3·17	5·72	11·09	13·02	6·70	9·20	6·93	6·80
Caul-fat	1·11	0·96	3·55	1·82	1·82	1·61	1·31	1·94	1·63
Small intestines and contents	1·85	2·39	1·46	2·14	2·03	1·97	1·49	1·86	1·67
Large intestines and contents	1·48	1·12	1·04	1·84	1·48	2·25	1·43	1·47	1·18
Intestinal fat	0·64	1·82	4·04	2·01	1·42	1·65	1·45	1·56	2·06
Heart and aorta	0·62	0·57	0·47	0·50	0·52	0·33	0·56	0·55	0·56
Heart-fat	......	0·16	0·22	0·21	0·15	0·31	0·22	0·17	0·16
Lungs and windpipe	1·34	1·29	0·61	0·90	1·03	0·93	0·81	1·01	1·01
Blood	4·12	5·24	3·62	3·58	4·01	4·82	2·93	4·42	3·81
Liver	1·70	1·63	1·54	1·49	1·25	1·46	1·17	1·52	1·16
Gall-bladder and contents	0·05	......	0·07	0·09	0·03	0·02	0·11	0·11	0.16
Pancreas ("sweetbread")	0·12	} 0·70 {	0·08	0·11	0·09	0·13	0·08	0·07	0·07
Thymus gland ("heartbread")	0·30		0·06	0·07	0·08	0·05	0·05	0·06	0·08
Glands about the throat ("throatbread")	0·23		0·04	0·05	0·03	......	0·03	0·02	0·06
Milt or spleen	0·36	0·29	0·17	0·12	0·16	0·21	0·11	0·15	0·17
Bladder, and penis, or womb	0·12	0·18	1·09 *	0·17	0·05	0·05	0·03	0·11	0·04
Brains	} 6·49 {	} 4·43 {	} 2·27 {	0·08	0·09	0·05	0·08	0·07	0·05
Head and tongue				2·69	2·56	2·78	2·77	2·86	3·00
Hide and horns	7·00	6·87	7·26	8·21	7·50	7·10	8·33	8·91	6·93
Feet, hoofs, &c.	2·70	1·66	1·54	1·89	1·86	1·91	2·00	1·63	1·78
Tail	......	0·13	0·06	0·13	0·12	0·09	0·09	0·07	0·11
Diaphragm ("skirts")	......	0·43	0·53	0·54	0·18	0·24	0·18	0·19	0·16
Miscellaneous trimmings	......	......	0·81	0·18	......	0·12	0·27	0·19	0·32
Total "offal" parts	33·47	33·93	39·95	43·70	42·82	40·85	37·93	41·11	35·84
Carcass	64·21	60·86	55·85	55·30	54·89	57·07	59·80	56·81	61·06
Loss by evaporation, error in weighing, &c.	2·32	5·21	4·20	1·00	2·29	2·08	2·27	2·08	3·10
Live-weight after fasting	100·00	100·00	100·00	100·00	100·00	100·00	100·00	100·00	100·00

Separate parts of the "offal."

* Including calf.

separated Parts, in the Fasted Live-weight—of CALVES, HEIFERS, and BULLOCKS.

| Bullocks. | | | | | | | | | Means of— | | | |
No. 6.	No. 7.	No. 8.	No. 9.	No. 10.	No. 11.	No. 12.	No. 13.	No. 14.	The 2 Calves.	The 2 Heifers.	The 14 Bullocks.	The 16 Heifers and Bullocks.
Scotch; long-horned; 4 years old; grass-fed; killed Sept. 6, 1849.	Welsh; 5 years old; killed Sept. 13, 1849.	Mixed breed; killed Sept. 20, 1849.	Durham, short-horned; 3 to 4 years old; grass-fed; killed Sept. 27, 1849.	Irish; lately grass-fed in Leicester-shire; killed Sept. 27, 1849.	Mixed breed; 3 years old; killed Oct. 4, 1849.	Scotch (analysed as fat); 4 years old; killed Oct. 30, 1849.	Scotch (analysed as half-fat); 3 to 4 years old; killed Nov. 14, 1849.	Devon; working ox; afterwards fed on oilcake, &c.; 7 years old; killed April 6, 1853.				
3·06	2·92	3·10	3·30	2·74	2·83	2·56	2·60	3·54	1·37	3·75	3·09	3·17
10·59	9·63	8·00	7·27	9·75	8·56	5·92	8·12	3·66	2·39	8·40	8·44	8·44
1·23	2·08	2·08	1·94	1·71	2·96	2·10	1·35	3·21	1·03	2·68	1·93	2·02
1·71	1·64	1·46	1·60	1·53	1·45	0·62	0·67	0·90	2·12	1·80	1·49	1·52
2·00	1·49	0·98	0·66	1·08	1·25	0·36	0·49	0·46	1·30	1·44	1·18	1·22
0·97	2·02	2·32	2·20	1·76	3·32	2·60	1·61	4·78	1·13	3·02	2·12	2·24
0·52	0·44	0·48	0·47	0·47	0·43	0·52	0·47	0·49	0·60	0·48	0·50	0·50
0·34	0·31	0·33	0·23	0·35	0·38	0·72	0·31	0·54	0·08	0·22	0·32	0·31
0·88	0·74	0·71	0·74	0·90	0·74	0·63	0·63	0·75	1·32	0·75	0·82	0·81
4·01	4·56	4·85	4·53	3·80	3·86	3·72	4·41	3·30	4·68	3·60	4·07	4·01
1·24	1·21	1·29	1·39	1·24	1·23	1·24	1·26	1·22	1·67	1·52	1·28	1·31
0·08	0·13	0·11	0·09	0·08	0·08	0·06	0·08	0·08	0·05	0·08	0·09	0·09
0·08	0·07	0·08	0·09	0·10	0·11	0·07	0·08	0·16		0·09	0·09	0·09
0·07	0·05	0·05	0·04	0·05	......	0·05	0·05	0·10	0·67	0·07	0·06	0·06
0·04	0·01	0·03	0·03	0·03	0·03	0·03	0·03	0·03		0·05	0·03	0·03
0·16	0·17	0·22	0·15	0·19	0·12	0·16	0·17	0·17	0·32	0·15	0·17	0·16
0·04	0·05	0·05	0·07	0·08	0·10	0·12†	0·06†	0·08†	0·15	0·63§	0·09‖	0·05¶
0·06	0·07	0·06	0·08	0·07	0·06	0·06	0·08	0·03		0·04	0·07	0·06
2·87	2·49	2·27	2·43	2·76	2·52	3·06	3·17	2·45	5·46	2·48	2·71	2·69
9·44	7·79	7·88	7·15	7·22	7·15	5·67	6·49	6·86	6·94	7·74	7·46	7·49
1·67	1·65	1·83	1·87	1·85	1·83	1·57	1·63	1·51	2·18	1·72	1·78	1·77
0·09	0·09	0·10	0·11	0·09	0·09	0·10	0·14	†	0·13	0·09	0·09	0·10
0·42	0·62	0·45	0·56	0·40	0·40	0·53	0·46	0·79	0·43	0·53	0·39	0·41
0·13	0·12	0·19	0·18	0·28	0·99	0·36	0·16	0·53	......	0·49	0·27	0·30
41·90	40·55	38·97	37·18	38·53	40·51	32·83	34·54	35·64	34·02	41·82	38·54	38·85
57·49	58·06	59·70	60·25	59·96	59·72	66·20	64·75	62·09	62·53	55·58	59·84	59·31
0·61	1·39	1·33	2·57	1·51	−0·23	0·97	0·71	2·27	3·45	2·60	1·62	1·82
100·00	100·00	100·00	100·00	100·00	100·00	100·00	100·00	100·00	100·00	100·00	100·00	100·00

† In these cases bladder and penis together, and in the others bladder only.
‡ With hide.　　　§ In one case womb with calf.
‖ Sum of the mean of the bladder, and that of the penis, taken separately.
¶ Mean of bladders only, the penis or womb included with the "Loss, &c."

APPENDIX.—TABLE XLI. Showing the *Percentage Proportion* of the individual Organs, and other separated Parts, in the Fasted Live-weight of SHEEP.

CLASS I.—5 Sheep, of different Breeds, killed (at Rothamsted) in *store* or *less* condition, for standards of comparison.

Designation of Parts.	Cotswold Wethers; killed November 25, 1851.		Leicester Wether; killed November 22, 1852.	Cross-bred Wether (Leicester and South Down); killed November 22, 1852.	Cross-bred Ewe (Leicester and South Down); killed November 22, 1852.	Means of the 5 Store Sheep.
	No. 1.	No. 2.				
Stomachs	2·64	3·02	2·93	3·24	2·86	2·94
Contents of stomachs	5·55	6·97	6·06	*	*	6·16
Caul-fat	3·75	2·87	1·73	3·53	2·73	2·92
Small intestines and contents	2·38	2·50	2·18	2·26	2·25	2·32
Large intestines and contents	3·07	2·30	3·51	2·97	2·82	2·93
Intestinal fat	0·98	0·97	1·38	1·87	1·18	1·28
Heart and aorta	0·46	0·60	0·48	0·50	0·45	0·48
Heart-fat	0·40	0·39	0·26	0·30	0·26	0·32
Lungs and windpipe	1·18	1·26	1·05	0·98	1·40	1·17
Blood	4·94	4·50	4·56	4·73	5·30	4·81
Liver	1·71	1·75	1·37	1·64	1·68	1·61
Gall-bladder and contents	0·04	0·12	0·03	0·04	0·11	0·07
Pancreas ("sweetbread")	0·12	0·18	0·16	0·07	0·14	0·13
Glands about the throat ("throatbread")	......	......	......	0·06	......	0·06
Milt or spleen	0·23	0·13	0·15	0·15	0·21	0·17
Bladder	0·04	0·05	0·04	0·10	0·04	0·05
Womb	......	......	......	......	0·11	......
Head	3·43	3·41	3·79	3·77	3·79	3·64
Skin and wool (with feet, &c.)	13·90	13·64	16·99	12·80	13·11	14·09
Diaphragm ("skirts")	......	......	......	0·30	0·10	0·30
Miscellaneous trimmings	......	......	0·11	......	......	0·10
Total "offal" parts	44·83	44·46	46·78	39·31	38·44	45·55
Carcass	53·84	54·28	51·30	54·13	53·54	53·42
Loss by evaporation, error in weighing, &c.	1·33†	1·26†	1·92	6·56‡	8·02‡	1·03
	100·00	100·00	100·00	100·00	100·00	100·00

Separate parts of the "offal."

* Included with "Loss, &c."   † Including contents of bladder.   ‡ Including contents of stomachs.

TABLE XLII.

APPENDIX.—TABLE XLII. Showing the *Percentage Proportion* of the individual
CLASS II.—20 Wether Sheep of *Cotswold Breed*, about 1¼ year old, in *moderately*
Killed at Rothamsted,

Designation of Parts.	The 5 giving the Largest amount of Increase during Fattening.					The 5 giving the Smallest amount of Increase during Fattening.				
	No. 1.	No. 2.	No. 3.	No. 4.	No. 5.	No. 6.	No. 7.	No. 8.	No. 9.	No. 10.
Stomachs	2·69	2·44	2·56	2·81	2·37	2·48	3·42	2·48	2·64	2·46
Contents of stomachs	4·64	5·60	4·46	4·42	5·22	4·20	4·41	4·41	4·63	4·92
Caul-fat	3·99	2·74	2·56	3·01	3·52	4·85	4·03	3·30	3·01	4·85
Small intestines and contents	1·53	1·75	2·04	1·75	2·02	1·60	2·86	1·90	1·86	1·69
Large intestines and contents	1·78	1·75	1·21	1·63	2·28	1·32	2·82	1·85	1·69	2·29
Intestinal fat	1·00	1·24	1·58	1·03	1·30	1·24	0·86	1·06	1·07	1·15
Heart and aorta	0·37	0·39	0·39	0·36	0·39	0·34	0·45	0·41	0·35	0·33
Heart-fat	0·20	0·23	0·16	0·34	0·27	0·30	0·19	0·15	0·19	0·08
Lungs and windpipe	0·81	1·10	1·12	1·04	0·98	0·96	1·18	0·93	0·95	0·92
Blood	3·91	3·97	3·74	4·11	4·00	3·94	5·44	4·58	3·98	4·19
Liver	1·78	1·66	1·58	1·88	1·68	1·60	1·97	1·85	1·69	1·58
Gall-bladder and contents	0·06	0·07	0·04	0·07	0·11	0·06	0·01	0·09	0·05	0·06
Pancreas ("sweetbread")	0·08	0·14	0·10	0·10	0 14	0·13	0·15	0·13	0 15	0·14
Milt or spleen	0·15	0·16	0·13	0·17	0·19	0·15	0·21	0·22	0·15	0·15
Bladder	0·03	0·03	0·02	0·02	0·03	0·02	0·05	0·02	0·03	0·03
Head	2·43	2·68	2·70	2·54	2·75	2·89	3·26	2·96	2·89	2·73
Skin (with feet, &c.)	7·45	7·90	7·87	6·87	7·27	7·51	9·41	8·01	8·09	7·38
Wool previously shorn	5·32	5·64	4·49	4·18	5·01	5·49	5·88	6·66	5·61	5·23
Total "offal" parts	38·52	39·49	36·75	37·23	39·53	39·28	46·67	41·21	39·23	40·20
Carcass	61·22	60·12	62·01	62·77	60·35	60·72	52·69	58·30	60·68	58·66
Loss by evaporation, error in weighing, &c.	0·26	0·39	1·24	0·00†	0·12	0·00†	0·64	0·49	0·09	1·14
	100·00	100·00	100·00	100·00	100·00	100·00	100·00	100·00	100·00	100·00

(Left margin, rotated: Separate parts of the "offal.")

* For particulars of the *feeding* experiment, see Article on the "Comparative Fattening Qualities of
† In these cases the sum of the weights taken for the separated parts exceeded the Fasted Live-

Organs, and other separated Parts, in the Fasted Live-weight of SHEEP.

Fat condition. Fattening Food—Oilcake, Clover Chaff, and Swedish Turnips*.
April 19, 1852.

The 10 giving the Medium amount of Increase during Fattening.										Means of—			
No. 11.	No. 12.	No. 13.	No. 14.	No. 15.	No. 16.	No. 17.	No. 18.	No. 19.	No. 20.	The 5 of Largest Increase.	The 5 of Smallest Increase.	The 10 of Medium Increase.	The 20 Cotswolds.
2·63	2·42	2·71	2·46	2·66	2·71	2·74	2·64	2·82	2·71	2·57	2·71	2·65	2·65
4·38	4·67	4·97	5·07	4·12	4·83	4·75	3·49	5·09	3·80	4·87	4·55	4·52	4·65
4·42	4·81	4·39	5·25	4·70	4·79	4·21	4·34	3·51	3·64	3·34	4·01	4·41	3·92
1·77	1·90	2·26	1·82	1·92	1·87	1·87	1·61	1·96	2·05	1·88	2·02	1·90	1·93
2·44	2·03	2·15	1·75	2·18	1·75	1·77	1·63	2·30	1·82	1·73	2·00	1·99	1·91
1·41	1·46	0·84	1·25	0·90	1·42	0·83	1·10	1·00	1·05	1·23	1·08	1·12	1·14
0·38	0·35	0·37	0·39	0·38	0·33	0·38	0·39	0·42	0·39	0·38	0·38	0·38	0·38
0·15	0·18	0·21	0·34	0·14	0·23	0·16	0·31	0·15	0·22	0·24	0·16	0·21	0·21
1·20	1·16	1·34	1·04	1·18	1·26	1·13	1·20	1·11	1·24	1·01	0·99	1·19	1·06
3·97	4·19	3·96	4·15	4·02	4·37	4·07	3·80	4·24	4·50	3·95	4·42	4·20	4·19
1·83	1·87	1·78	1·78	1·66	1·87	1·84	1·63	2·05	1·98	1·72	1·74	1·83	1·77
0·06	0·04	0·05	0·06	0·07	0·06	0·06	0·07	0·03	0·05	0·07	0·05	0·05	0·06
0·13	0·11	0·14	0·10	0·12	0·12	0·12	0·14	0·12	0·16	0·11	0·14	0·13	0·13
0·17	0·16	0·16	0·16	0·15	0·13	0·15	0·18	0·25	0·19	0·16	0·18	0·17	0·14
0·02	0·03	0·01	0·02	0·02	0·02	0·02	0·02	0·03	0·03	0·03	0·03	0·02	0·03
2·82	2·51	2·89	2·58	2·77	2·85	2·81	2·97	3·13	3·10	2·62	2·95	2·84	2·80
7·61	7·48	7·33	6·57	7·19	7·50	7·49	7·14	9·21	8·37	7·47	8·08	7·59	7·72
4·38	5·26	5·67	5·03	4·81	5·59	5·48	5·04	5·41	5·77	4·93	5·81	5·23	5·33
39·77	40·63	41·23	39·82	38·99	41·72	39·88	37·70	43·51	41·07	38·31	41·32	40·43	40·02
59·97	59·04	58·77	60·18	60·33	58·16	59·02	61·39	56·46	58·50	61·29	58·21	59·18	59·56
0·26	0·33	0·00†	0·00†	0·68	0·12	1·10	0·91	0·03	0·43	0·40	0·47	0·39	0·42
100·00	100·00	100·00	100·00	100·00	100·00	100·00	100·00	100·00	100·00	100·00	100·00	100·00	100·00

different Breeds of Sheep," Journal of the Royal Agricultural Society of England, vol. xiii. part 1.
weight, and this *sum* has therefore been taken as the standard, in calculating the Percentages.

APPENDIX.—Table XLIII. Showing the *Percentage Proportion* of the individual
CLASS III.—16 Wether Sheep of *Leicester Breed*, about 1¼ year old, in *moderately*
Killed at Rothamsted,

Designation of Parts.	The 4 giving the Largest amount of Increase during Fattening.				The 4 giving the Smallest amount of Increase during Fattening.			
	No. 1.	No. 2.	No. 3.	No. 4.	No. 5.	No. 6.	No. 7.	No. 8.
Stomachs	2·79	2·30	2·27	2·63	2·91	3·05	2·79	2·72
Contents of stomachs	4·13	3·48	3·94	4·71	4·26	5·33	4·61	5·13
Caul-fat..	3·63	4·04	4·39	3·54	3·88	1·77	2·31	1·71
Small intestines and contents	2·13	1·78	2·16	1·88	1·94	3·61	2·45	2·82
Large intestines and contents	1·89	1·59	1·66	1·71	1·62	2·39	1·94	2·41
Intestinal fat....................................	1·17	1·15	1·17	0·92	1·19	1·44	0·72	1·36
Heart and aorta	0·37	0·44	0·40	0·41	0·40	0·53	0·40	0·57
Heart-fat	0·21	0·11	0·32	0·12	0·11	0·14	0·11	0·15
Lungs and windpipe	0·81	1·00	0·72	0·67	1·08	1·78	0·97	1·90
Blood	4·00	3·93	4·32	3·79	3·88	4·83	4·50	4·88
Liver...	1·76	1·55	1·86	1·92	1·91	2·00	1·79	2·05
Gall-bladder and contents	0·05	0·06	0·02	0·04	0·04	0·07	0·04	0·06
Pancreas ("sweetbread")	0·14	0·17	0·15	0·12	0·17	0·18	0·17	0·16
Milt or spleen	0·13	0·13	0·13	0·12	0·13	0·20	0·17	0·19
Bladder...	0·04	0·03	0 03	0·05	0·04	0·04	0·05	0·06
Head..	2·46	2·78	2·46	2·83	3·07	3·50	3·27	3·51
Skin (with feet, &c.)............................	7·60	7·15	7·05	7·25	7·81	8 88	8·66	9·12
Wool previously shorn	6·02	5·18	6·06	6·67	5·17	7·61	8·88	6·78
Miscellaneous trimmings......................	......	......	......	......	......	......	......	......
Total "offal" parts	39·33	36·87	39·31	39·58	39·61	47·35	43·83	45·58
Carcass	58·50	60·33	58·37	58·92	57·62	52·56	54·59	52·63
Loss by evaporation, error in weighing, &c.	2·17	2·80	2·32	1·50	2·77	0·09	1·58	1·79
	100·00	100·00	100·00	100·00	100·00	100·00	100·00	100·00

Separate parts of the "offal."

* For particulars of the *feeding* experiment, see Article on the "Comparative Fattening Qualities of
† This sheep was an Ewe, and this amount includes the womb.
‡ In this case the sum of the weights taken for the separated parts exceeded the Fasted Live-weight,

Organs, and other separated Parts, in the Fasted Live-weight of SHEEP.

Fat condition.   Fattening food—Oilcake, Clover Chaff, and Swedish Turnips*.
April 23, 1853.

The 8 giving the Medium amount of Increase during Fattening.								Means of—			
No. 9.	No. 10.	No. 11.	No. 12.	No. 13.	No. 14.	No. 15.	No. 16.	The 4 of Largest Increase.	The 4 of Smallest Increase.	The 8 of Medium Increase.	The 16 Leicesters.
2·40	2·63	2·88	2·28	2·65	2·71	2·88	2·68	2·50	2·87	2·64	2·67
3·69	3·58	5·82	3·32	4·09	3·83	3·25	5·72	4·07	4·83	4·16	4·35
3·65	3·62	2·68	5·11	3·68	3·50	2·74	4·15	3·90	2·42	3·64	3·82
1·98	2·16	2·78	1·88	2·02	2·30	1·97	2·43	1·99	2·70	2·22	2·30
1·54	1·74	1·75	1·83	2·45	1·91	1·86	1·85	1·76	2·09	1·87	1·91
0·99	1·11	1·18	1·63	1·15	1·53	1·00	1·47	1·10	1·18	1·26	1·18
0·40	0·42	0·46	0·34	0·36	0·41	0·44	0·43	0·41	0·47	0·41	0·43
0·16	0·19	0·12	0·20	0·18	0·10	0·16	0·08	0·19	0·13	0·15	0·16
0·89	1·04	1·65	0·93	0·97	0·87	1·11	0·96	0·85	1·43	1·05	1·11
3·71	3·77	4·74	3·73	4·29	3·83	3·99	4·26	4·01	4·52	4·03	4·19
1·71	2·07	2·16	1·70	1·89	1·84	2·09	2·15	1·77	1·94	1·95	1·89
0·06	0·09	0·12	0·05	0·04	0·08	0·05	0·04	0·04	0·05	0·06	0·05
0·15	0·17	0·15	0·16	0·18	0·20	0·17	0·15	0·14	0·17	0·17	0·16
0·13	0·17	0·18	0·14	0·13	0·13	0·14	0·15	0·13	0·17	0·15	0·15
0·02	0·04	0·04	0·03	0·04	0·08†	0·03	0·02	0·04	0·05	0·04	0·04
2·76	3·03	3·37	2·71	2·92	3·01	3·11	2·94	2·63	3·34	2·98	2·98
7·76	7·57	8·59	7·24	8·09	8·07	8·68	7·69	7·26	8·62	7·96	7·95
5·52	5·17	6·95	5·92	6·56	5·92	4·92	5·26	5·98	7·11	5·78	6·29
0·13	0·12	0·06	0·09	0·08	0·05	0 19	0·15	......	......	0·11	0·11
37·65	38·69	45·68	39·29	41·77	40·57	38·78	42·58	38·77	44·09	40·63	41·24
61·03	59·71	53·58	58·86	57·30	59·43	60·07	57·06	59·03	54·35	58·38	57·25
1·32	1·60	0·74	1·85	0·93	0·00†	1·15	0·36	2·20	1·56	0·99	1·51
100·00	100·00	100·00	100·00	100·00	100·00	100·00	100·00	100·00	100·00	100·00	100·00

different Breeds of Sheep," Journal of the Royal Agricultural Society of England, vol. xvi. part 1.

and this *sum* has therefore been taken as the standard, in calculating the Percentages.

APPENDIX.—TABLE XLIV. Showing the *Percentage Proportion* of the individual
CLASS IV.—16 Wether Sheep of *Cross-breed* (Leicester and South Down), about 1¼ year old,
Killed at Rothamsted,

Designation of Parts.	The 4 giving the Largest amount of Increase during Fattening.				The 4 giving the Smallest amount of Increase during Fattening.			
	No. 1.	No. 2.	No. 3.	No. 4.	No. 5.	No. 6.	No. 7.	No. 8.
Stomachs	2·74	2·68	2·72	2·73	2·65	2·79	2·86	2·54
Contents of stomachs	5·47	4·25	6·43	4·06	4·26	5·13	4·69	5·84
Caul-fat	3·53	4·85	3·00	4·06	3·45	3·79	4·39	4·93
Small intestines and contents	1·39	1·77	1·64	1·72	1·67	1·95	2·09	2·01
Large intestines and contents	1·67	1·97	2·24	2·38	2·29	2·17	2·40	2·19
Intestinal fat	1·07	1·57	1·08	1·19	0·86	0·92	1·30	1·17
Heart and aorta	0·43	0·38	0·43	0·40	0·38	0·53	0·41	0·38
Heart-fat	0·19	0·16	0·19	0·15	0·22	0·17	0·11	0·20
Lungs and windpipe	1·11	0·92	1·29	1·06	1·35	1·00	1·17	1·22
Blood	3·94	3·94	3·84	4·62	4·10	4·34	4·72	4·34
Liver	1·81	1·77	2·03	1·54	1·76	2·01	1·84	1·75
Gall-bladder and contents	0·11	0·07	0·13	0·08	0·11	0·09	0·05	0·06
Pancreas ("sweetbread")	0·15	0·18	0·15	0·18	0·19	0·19	0·18	0·18
Milt or spleen	0·16	0·13	0·13	0·16	0·16	0·19	0·23	0·17
Bladder	0·05	0·03	0·06	0·03	0·04	0·04	0·04	0·05
Head	3·16	2·91	3·04	3·09	3·37	3·37	3·39	3·25
Skin (with feet, &c.)	8·16	6·26	9·06	8·46	9·07	8·92	7·91	8·33
Wool previously shorn	6·49	5·01	5·26	4·76	5·02	4·79	6·12	5·23
Miscellaneous trimmings	0·26	0·05	0·00	0·24	0·11	0·19	0·18	0·13
Total "offal" parts	41·89	38·93	42·72	40·93	41·08	42·58	44·06	43·97
Carcass	57·77	61·07	57·28	59·07	58·69	57·42	53·67	56·03
Loss by evaporation, error in weighing, &c.	0·34	0·00†	0·00†	0·00†	0·23	0·00†	2·25	0·00†
	100·00	100·00	100·00	100·00	100·00	100·00	100·00	100·00

Separate parts of the "offal."

* For particulars of the *feeding* experiment, see Article on the " Comparative Fattening Qualities of
† In those cases the sum of the weights taken for the separated parts exceeded the Fasted Live-

Organs, and other separated Parts, in the Fasted Live-weight, of SHEEP.

in *moderately* Fat condition.   Fattening food—Oilcake, Clover Chaff, and Swedish Turnips*.
April 23, 1853.

| The 8 giving the Medium amount of Increase during Fattening. | | | | | | | | Means of— | | | |
No. 9.	No. 10.	No. 11.	No. 12.	No. 13.	No. 14.	No. 15.	No. 16.	The 4 of Largest Increase.	The 4 of Smallest Increase.	The 8 of Medium Increase.	The 16 Cross-bred Wethers.
2·64	2·70	2·38	2·32	2·61	2·53	2·92	2·62	2·72	2·71	2·59	2·67
3·87	4·49	4·61	4·89	2·90	4·36	5·77	2·81	5·05	4·98	4·21	4·75
4·45	5·28	4·19	4·12	3·49	3·07	3·48	4·42	3·86	4·14	4·06	4·02
1·32	2·20	1·50	1·66	1·93	1·37	1·93	1·73	1·63	1·93	1·71	1·76
1·66	1·64	1·66	1·87	1·97	2·28	2·68	1·85	2·06	2·26	1·98	2·10
1·74	1·98	1·45	1·89	1·27	0·81	1·10	1·68	1·23	1·06	1·49	1·26
0·44	0·39	0·40	0·40	0·40	0·42	0·41	0·47	0·41	0·43	0·42	0·42
0·22	0·25	0·26	0·14	0·36	0·16	0·32	0·22	0·17	0·17	0·24	0·19
0·98	1·00	0·96	0·96	1·24	1·09	1·13	1·04	1·09	1·19	1·05	1·11
4·38	4·10	3·67	3·89	3·61	4·00	4·41	4·20	4·08	4·38	4·03	4·16
1·81	1·84	1·71	1·78	1·78	1·67	1·74	1·93	1·79	1·85	1·78	1·81
0·09	0·06	0·11	0·09	0·04	0·04	0·10	0·06	0·10	0·07	0·07	0·08
0·13	0·21	0·18	0·15	0·18	0·15	0·20	0·18	0·16	0·18	0·17	0·17
0·18	0·13	0·16	0·14	0·17	0·14	0·14	0·15	0·15	0·19	0·15	0·16
0·03	0·04	0·04	0·03	0·04	0·03	0·04	0·04	0·04	0·04	0·04	0·04
3·13	3·09	3·00	2·90	3·13	3·37	3·08	3·26	3·05	3·35	3·12	3·17
7·34	7·72	7·76	8·14	8·51	9·53	8·80	7·60	7·99	8·56	8·18	8·25
3·72	3·77	5·59	4·91	4·18	6·74	5·13	5·13	5·39	5·29	4·90	5·19
0·12	0·09	0·13	0·05	0·14	0·14	0·16	0·09	0·19	0·15	0·11	0·14
38·25	41·18	39·76	40·33	37·95	41·90	43·54	39·48	41·16	42·93	40·30	41·45
61·75	57·79	59·63	58·96	61·46	55·37	54·68	60·52	58·80	56·45	58·77	58·01
0·00†	1·03	0·61	0·71	0·59	2·73	1·78	0·00†	0·04	0·62	0·93	0·54
100·00	100·00	100·00	100·00	100·00	100·00	100·00	100·00	100·00	100·00	100·00	100·00

different Breeds of Sheep," Journal of the Royal Agricultural Society of England, vol. xvi. part 1.
weight, and this *sum* has been taken as the standard, in calculating the Percentages.

APPENDIX.—TABLE XLV. Showing the *Percentage Proportion* of the individual
CLASS V.—16 Ewe Sheep of *Cross-breed* (Leicester and South Down), about 1¼ year old, in
Killed at Rothamsted,

	Designation of Parts.	The 4 giving the Largest amount of Increase during Fattening.				The 4 giving the Smallest amount of Increase during Fattening.			
		No. 1.	No. 2.	No. 3.	No. 4.	No. 5.	No. 6.	No. 7.	No. 8.
Separate parts of the "offal."	Stomachs	2·41	2·32	2·61	2·35	2·88	2·61	2·46	2·45
	Contents of stomachs	4·36	2·61	4·06	4·89	3·66	2·67	4·59	4·06
	Caul-fat	4·76	4·04	4·93	3·54	4·63	5·33	3·47	3·95
	Small intestines and contents	1·52	1·76	1·71	1·85	1·55	1·50	1·75	1·93
	Large intestines and contents	1·33	1·91	1·71	1·55	1·99	1·17	2·08	2·11
	Intestinal fat	1·16	1·01	2·01	1·52	1·55	1·86	1·26	0·92
	Heart and aorta	0·41	0·43	0·43	0·45	0·44	0·44	0·36	0·40
	Heart-fat	0·22	0·10	0·18	0·12	0·25	0·17	0·14	0·12
	Lungs and windpipe	1·05	0·89	0·93	0·90	1·04	0·94	1·20	1·41
	Blood	4·38	4·18	4·03	3·59	4·85	4·22	4·10	3·75
	Liver	1·93	1·81	1·94	1·72	1·58	1·67	1·72	1·67
	Gall-bladder and contents	0·09	0·06	0·02	0·10	0·08	0·10	0·04	0·05
	Pancreas ("sweetbread")	0·17	0·16	0·17	0·15	0·14	0·17	0·17	0·17
	Milt or spleen	0·15	0·15	0·21	0·15	0·17	0·14	0·14	0·15
	Bladder	0·02	0·04	0·03	0·03	0·03	0·05	0·04	0·05
	Womb	0·03	0·06	0·05	0·05	0·07	0·04	0 04	0·04
	Head	2·93	3·09	3·03	2·97	3·02	3·08	3·01	2·94
	Skin (with feet, &c.)	8·52	8·07	7·20	7·98	7·76	7·33	7·87	8·76
	Wool previously shorn	6·00	5·70	5·21	5·79	5·99	4·89	5·57	5·94
	Miscellaneous trimmings	0·14	......	0·12	0·22	0·11	......	......	0·23
Total " offal " parts		41·58	38·39	40·60	39·92	41·79	38·38	40·01	41·10
Carcass		58·42	59·78	59·00	57·29	57·93	59·89	59·51	57·81
Loss by evaporation, error in weighing, &c.		0·00†	1·83	0·40	2·79	0·28	1·73	0·48	1·09
		100·00	100·00	100·00	100·00	100·00	100·00	100·00	100·00

* For particulars of the *feeding* experiment, see Article on the "Comparative Fattening Qualities of
† In this case the sum of the weights taken for the separated parts exceeded the Fasted Live-weight,

Organs, and other separated Parts, in the Fasted Live-weight, of SHEEP.

moderately Fat condition.   Fattening food—Oilcake, Clover Chaff, and Swedish Turnips*.
April 23, 1853.

| The 8 giving the Medium amount of Increase during Fattening. | | | | | | | | Means of— | | | The 16 Crossbred Ewes. |
No. 9.	No. 10.	No. 11.	No. 12.	No. 13.	No. 14.	No. 15.	No. 16.	The 4 of Largest Increase.	The 4 of Smallest Increase.	The 8 of Medium Increase.	
2·61	2·61	2·51	2·31	2·43	2·56	2·45	2·62	2·42	2·60	2·51	2·51
5·49	4·83	4·98	3·64	3·12	3·85	4·19	2·05	3·99	3·75	4·02	3·92
4·61	4·35	4·77	4·44	4·77	4·47	3·78	4·21	4·32	4·34	4·45	4·37
1·80	1·69	1·90	1·69	1·31	1·72	1·69	1·79	1·71	1·68	1·70	1·70
1·99	1·98	1·93	1·78	1·76	2·14	1·74	1·85	1·63	1·84	1·90	1·79
1·12	1·13	1·11	1·74	0·96	1·87	1·81	1·35	1·42	1·40	1·39	1·40
0·42	0·34	0·37	0·40	0·45	0·38	0·42	0·42	0·43	0·41	0·40	0·41
0·11	0·14	0·21	0·21	0·29	0·22	0·22	0·16	0·16	0·17	0·19	0·17
1·02	1·01	1·00	0·89	1·12	0·99	0·99	0·92	0·94	1·15	0·99	1·03
4·18	3·48	4·14	3·40	4·43	4·10	3·98	4·08	4·05	4·23	3·97	4·09
1·59	1·62	1·62	1·64	1·89	1·67	1·79	1·72	1·85	1·66	1·72	1·75
0·08	0·06	0·11	0·06	0·10	0·05	0·06	0·08	0·07	0·07	0·07	0·07
0·18	0·14	0·14	0·19	0·16	0·15	0·16	0·17	0·16	0·16	0·16	0·16
0·21	0·14	0·16	0·17	0·18	0·14	0·15	0·18	0·16	0·15	0·17	0·16
0·03	0·02	0·03	0·04	0·04	0·03	0·03	0·04	0·03	0·04	0·03	0·03
0·08	0·05	0·04	0·05	0·06	0·07	0·05	0·05	0·05	0·05	0·06	0·05
3·34	3·09	2·98	2·80	3·12	2·96	3·17	2·91	3·00	3·01	3·05	3·02
8·46	8·11	8·12	7·43	8·75	8·75	7·71	8·21	7·94	7·93	8·19	8·02
6·37	5·02	6·33	4·34	6·13	6·16	5·21	6·86	5·67	5·60	5·80	5·69
0·23	0·08	0·16	0·11	0·11	0·09	0·14	0·08	0·16	0·17	0·13	0·14
44·12	39·89	42·81	37·33	41·18	42·37	39·74	39·75	40·16	40·41	40·90	40·48
54·86	58·47	56·99	61·34	58·67	56·56	59·70	59·51	58·62	58·79	58·26	58·56
1·02	1·64	0·20	1·33	0·15	1·07	0·56	0·74	1·22	0·80	0·84	0·96
100·00	100·00	100·00	100·00	100·00	100·00	100·00	100·00	100·00	100·00	100·00	100·00

different Breeds of Sheep," Journal of the Royal Agricultural Society of England, vol. xvi. part 1.
and this *sum* has been taken as the standard, in calculating the Percentages.

APPENDIX.—TABLE XLVI. Showing the *Percentage Proportion* of the individual
CLASS VI.—16 Wether Sheep of *Hampshire Down Breed*, about 1½ year old, in
Killed at Rothamsted,

Designation of Parts.	The 4 giving the Largest amount of Increase during Fattening.				The 4 giving the Smallest amount of Increase during Fattening.			
	No. 1.	No. 2.	No. 3.	No. 4.	No. 5.	No. 6.	No. 7.	No. 8.
Stomachs	2·44	2·28	2·13	2·29	2·28	2·58	2·21	2·23
Contents of stomachs	4·41	5·07	5·18	5·43	5·50	4·53	4·79	4·46
Caul-fat	4·04	4·37	3·70	3·93	5·75	4·04	5·33	4·06
Small intestines and contents	1·97	1·92	1·68	1·57	1·62	1·86	1·60	1·49
Large intestines and contents	2·19	1·46	1·46	1·60	1·66	1·62	1·63	1·73
Intestinal fat	2·48	2·49	2·72	2·42	2·57	1·61	3·29	2·94
Heart and aorta	0·40	0·35	0·35	0·34	0·38	0·36	0·37	0·35
Heart-fat	0·33	0·23	0·28	0·19	0·15	0·20	0·23	0·17
Lungs and windpipe	0·93	0·88	0·71	0·83	1·04	1·29	0·97	0·89
Blood	4·47	4·45	4·02	4·01	4·26	4·72	3·37	4·14
Liver	1·72	1·75	1·35	1·76	1·57	1·82	1·43	1·35
Gall-bladder and contents	0·04	0·02	0·03	0·03	0·06	0·03	0·04	0·01
Pancreas ("sweetbread")	0·12	0·12	0·10	0·14	0·19	0·18	0·16	0·12
Milt or spleen	0·14	0·16	0·14	0·14	0·14	0·19	0·14	0·13
Bladder	......	0·09†	0·08†	0·03	0·02	0·02	0·04	0·03
Head	3·09	2·93	2·93	2·65	2·98	3·46	3·05	2·84
Skin (with feet, &c.)	8·74	8·51	8·21	8·44	7·29	8·17	6·89	8·00
Wool previously shorn	2·72	2·67	3·36	4·19	3·97	4·09	2·59	4·95
Miscellaneous trimmings	0·15	0·06	0·07	0·13	0·18	0·22	0·16	0·14
Total "offal" parts	40·36	39·81	38·50	40·12	41·81	41·21	38·49	40·03
Carcass	59·59	60·19	61·50	59·87	57·53	57·10	60·00	59·37
Loss by evaporation, error in weighing, &c.	0·03	0·00‡	0·00‡	0·01	0·66	1·69	0·91	0·60
	100·00	100·00	100·00	100·00	100·00	100·00	100·00	100·00

Separate parts of the "offal"

* For particulars of the *feeding* experiment, see Article on the "Comparative Fattening
† In each of these cases the weight of one Testicle is included with that of the Bladder.
‡ In these cases the sum of the weights taken for the separated parts exceeded the Feated

Organs, and other separated Parts, in the Fasted Live-weight, of SHEEP.
moderately Fat condition.   Fattening food—Oilcake, Clover Chaff, and Swedish Turnips*.
May 8, 1851.

| The 8 giving the Medium amount of Increase during Fattening. | | | | | | | | Means of— | | | |
No. 9.	No. 10.	No. 11.	No. 12.	No. 13.	No. 14.	No. 15.	No. 16.	The 4 of Largest Increase.	The 4 of Smallest Increase.	The 8 of Medium Increase.	The 16 Hampshire Downs.
2·30	1·97	2·17	2·02	2·19	2·24	2·12	2·21	2·28	2·33	2·15	2·23
5·12	5·77	4·69	4·90	3·65	4·49	4·87	4·50	5·02	4·62	4·75	4·83
4·88	3·79	4·31	5·55	4·96	3·98	3·67	4·59	4·01	4·80	4·47	4·43
1·71	1·73	2·74	1·73	1·72	2·00	1·55	1·90	1·78	1·69	1·69	1·81
1·71	2·24	1·83	1·87	2·39	1·60	2·12	1·90	1·68	1·76	1·96	1·84
2·99	2·51	3·13	2·97	2·58	2·24	2·38	3·39	2·53	2·60	2·77	2·67
0·47	0·42	0·36	0·35	0·46	0·36	0·43	0·39	0·36	0·37	0·41	0·38
0·12	0·26	0·21	0·17	0·35	0·24	0·20	0·16	0·26	0·19	0·21	0·22
1·06	0·80	1·01	0·82	0·91	1·02	0·89	0·96	0·84	1·05	0·93	0·94
4·08	4·05	4·33	3·66	4·59	3·79	4·11	4·23	4·23	4·12	4·10	4·08
1·65	1·07	1·52	1·49	1·45	1·58	1·71	1·68	1·64	1·54	1·52	1·62
0·02	0·09	0·06	0·11	0·05	0·05	0·05	0·03	0·03	0·04	0·06	0·05
0·16	0·12	0·13	0·12	0·12	0·18	0·14	0·12	0·12	0·17	0·14	0·14
0·18	0·14	0·19	0·16	0·17	0·15	0·17	0·13	0·14	0·15	0·16	0·15
0·04	0·03	0·04	0·02	0·03	0·02	0·03	0·04	0·07	0·03	0·03	0·04
3·05	2·78	2·93	3·03	3·05	3·19	3·23	3·20	2·90	3·08	3·06	3·02
7·23	8·55	7·77	6·77	7·56	8·25	9·03	7·32	8·47	7·59	7·81	7·92
3·26	3·39	4·27	3·17	3·45	3·85	3·10	2·74	3·23	3·90	3·40	3·49
0·07	0·13	0·11	0·10	0·15	0·16	0·11	0·27	0·10	0·15	0·14	0·14
40·10	39·84	41·80	39·01	39·83	39·39	39·91	39·76	39·69	40·38	39·96	40·00
59·35	59·04	57·78	60·65	59·22	60·38	60·09	60·24	60·29	58·65	59·59	59·53
0·55	1·12	0·42	0·34	0·95	0·23	0·00‡	0·00‡	0·02	0·97	0·45	0·47
100·00	100·00	100·00	100·00	100·00	100·00	100·00	100·00	100·00	100·00	100·00	100·00

Qualities of Sheep," Journal of the Royal Agricultural Society of England, vol. xii. part 2.

Live-weight, and this sum has been taken as the standard, in calculating the Percentages.

APPENDIX.—TABLE XLVII. Showing the *Percentage Proportion* of the

CLASS VII.—16 Wether Sheep of *Sussex Down Breed*, about 1¼ year old, in

Killed at Rothamsted,

Designation of Parts.	The 4 giving the Largest amount of Increase during Fattening.				The 4 giving the Smallest amount of Increase during Fattening.			
	No. 1.	No. 2.	No. 3.	No. 4.	No. 5.	No. 6.	No. 7.	No. 8.
Separate parts of the "offal": Stomachs	2·43	2·02	2·27	2·25	2·24	2·47	2·36	2·20
Contents of stomachs	3·70	3·14	5·31	5·24	3·30	4·29	5·18	5·90
Caul-fat	4·48	4·08	4·76	4·72	5·24	3·84	5·46	4·40
Small intestines and contents	2·31	1·82	2·09	2·11	1·49	2·15	2·72	2·15
Large intestines and contents	1·47	1·61	1·72	1·68	1·60	2·09	1·99	1·88
Intestinal fat	2·91	2·80	2·39	2·17	3·06	1·88	2·57	2·24
Heart and aorta	0·38	0·38	0·43	0·40	0·43	0·40	0·39	0·42
Heart-fat	0·40	0·42	0·38	0·21	0·30	0·43	0·24	0·20
Lungs and windpipe	0·87	0·80	0·90	0·98	0·99	1·10	1·10	1·01
Blood	5·64	4·02	4·34	4·15	3·85	4·06	3·98	3·95
Liver	1·43	1·56	1·54	1·59	1·63	1·79	1·68	1·79
Gall-bladder and contents	0·02	0·03	0·03	0·04	0·05	0·04	0·02	0·04
Pancreas ("sweetbread")	0·11	0·17	0·18	0·17	0·13	0·13	0·16	0·21
Milt or spleen	0·18	0·24	0·27	0·22	0·29	0·29	0·26	0·32
Bladder	0·03	0·04	0·02	0·02	0·03	0·03	0·05	0·04
Head	2·68	2·97	3·29	3·11	3·11	3·26	3·27	3·19
Skin (with feet, &c.)	7·80	6·77	7·53	6·83	8·10	7·73	7·07	7·99
Wool previously shorn	3·98	4·29	4·72	3·56	4·48	3·86	5·24	3·86
Miscellaneous trimmings	0·09	0·16	0·04	0·16	0·24	0·27	0·12	0·18
Total "offal" parts	40·91	37·32	42·21	39·61	40·56	40·11	43·86	41·97
Carcass	59·09	62·29	57·79	60·39	58·32	58·72	56·14	57·83
Loss by evaporation, error in weighing, &c.	0·00†	0·39	0·00†	0·00†	1·12	1·17	0·00†	0·20
	100·00	100·00	100·00	100·00	100·00	100·00	100·00	100·00

* For particulars of the *feeding* experiment, see Article on the "Comparative Fattening

† In these cases the sum of the weights taken for the separated parts exceeded the Fasted

individual Organs, and other separated Parts, in the Fasted Live-weight, of SHEEP.

moderately Fat condition.   Fattening Food—Oilcake, Clover Chaff, and Swedish Turnips*.

May 9, 1851.

| The 8 giving the Medium amount of Increase during Fattening. | | | | | | | | Means of— | | | |
No. 9.	No. 10.	No. 11.	No. 12.	No. 13.	No. 14.	No. 15.	No. 16.	The 4 of Largest Increase.	The 4 of Smallest Increase.	The 8 of Medium Increase.	The 16 Sussex Downs.
2·06	2·11	2·07	2·14	2·40	2·29	2·27	2·22	2·24	2·32	2·18	2·23
4·57	3·26	4·14	4·93	4·03	5·87	4·46	3·88	4·35	4·67	4·39	4·45
4·88	5·15	5·56	5·16	3·75	4·29	5·36	4·69	4·51	4·74	4·85	4·74
2·33	1·76	1·98	2·23	2·11	1·93	1·55	1·66	2·08	2·13	1·94	2·02
1·70	1·50	1·74	1·66	2·31	2·48	1·62	1·66	1·62	1·89	1·88	1·82
2·24	3·81	3·13	2·16	2·16	2·06	2·77	2·46	2·57	2·44	2·60	2·55
0·42	0·42	0·34	0·38	0·41	0·41	0·35	0·37	0·40	0·41	0·39	0·38
0·15	0·06	0·19	0·21	0·34	0·18	0·23	0·28	0·35	0·29	0·21	0·27
1·23	1·14	0·93	0·86	1·06	1·02	0·89	1·09	0·89	1·05	1·03	1·00
4·34	3·81	3·89	4·15	4·27	4·36	4·02	3·59	4·53	3·96	4·05	4·15
1·81	1·69	1·67	1·49	1·83	1·45	1·42	1·89	1·53	1·72	1·66	1·64
0·05	0·02	0·08	0·06	0·09	0·12	0·12	0·14	0·03	0·03	0·09	0·06
0·16	0·12	0·16	0·14	0·11	0·19	0·14	0·15	0·16	0·16	0·15	0·15
0·27	0·21	0·28	0·17	0·30	0·21	0·18	0·21	0·23	0·29	0·24	0·24
0·02	0·03	0·03	0·03	0·02	0·03	0·02	0·04	0·03	0·04	0·03	0·03
2·89	2·66	2·92	2·74	3·06	3·07	2·93	3·26	3·01	3·21	2·94	3·03
8·78	7·39	7·53	7·53	8·17	7·06	7·27	7·67	7·23	7·72	7·67	7·58
3·94	3·52	4·33	4·83	4·99	3·85	4·00	3·88	4·14	4·36	4·17	4·21
0·09	0·13	0·19	0·16	0·14	0·13	0·21	0·19	0·11	0·20	0·15	0·16
41·93	38·81	41·16	41·23	41·57	40·91	40·01	39·33	40·01	41·63	40·62	40·71
57·44	60·50	58·62	58·34	58·43	58·56	59·52	60·67	59·89	57·75	59·01	58·92
0·63	0·69	0·22	0·43	0·00†	0·53	0·47	0·00†	0·10	0·62	0·37	0·37
100·00	100·00	100·00	100·00	100·00	100·00	100·00	100·00	100·00	100·00	100·00	100·00

Qualities of Sheep," Journal of the Royal Agricultural Society of England, vol. xii. part 2.
Live-weight, and this *sum* has been taken as the standard, in calculating the Percentages.

APPENDIX.—TABLE XLVIII. Showing the *Percentage Proportion* of the individual Organs, and other separated Parts, in the Fasted Live-weight, of SHEEP.

(CLASS VIII.—6 Wether Sheep of *Cotswold Breed*, about 1½ year old, in *excessively* Fattened condition. Fattening food—Oilcake, Clover Hay, and Swedish Turnips, under cover, until "moderately" fattened; afterwards, Oilcake (or Lentils), with Grass or Green Clover, or with Meadow-hay and Roots, in the field. Killed at Rothamsted, December 18, 1852.

Designation of Parts	6 Very Fat Cotswold Sheep.						Means of the 6 Cotswolds
	No. 1.	No. 2.	No. 3.	No. 4.	No. 5.	No. 6.	
Stomachs	2·16	1·91	1·88	1·85	1·95	1·82	1·93
Contents of stomachs	4·44	3·37	4·47	3·68	3·40	......	3·87
Caul-fat	3·92	3·98	3·81	5·55	3·90	3·49	3·83
Small intestines and contents	1·38	1·30	1·14	0·97	1·28	1·48	1·25
Large intestines and contents	1·94	1·79	1·47	1·46	1·48	1·59	1·63
Intestinal fat	1·94	1·59	1·38	1·36	0·95	1·45	1·44
Heart and aorta	0·32	0·38	0·34	0·31	0·36	0·37	0·35
Heart-fat	0·40	0·37	0·39	0·28	0·20	0·30	0·32
Lungs and windpipe	0·82	0·89	0·77	0·71	0·94	0·81	0·82
Blood	4·04	4·21	3·56	3·35	3·60	3·88	3·77
Liver	1·56	1·40	1·29	1·10	1·16	1·17	1·28
Gall-bladder and contents	0·045	0·097	0·035	0·094	0·045	0·036	0·045
Pancreas ("sweetbread")	0·09	0·07	0·12	0·07	0·09	0·08	0·09
Milk or spleen	0·16	0·14	0·13	0·17	0·11	0·16	0·14
Bladder	0·02	0·02	0·03	0·02	0·02	0·03	0·02
Head	2·17	2·13	2·17	2·24	2·54	2·25	2·25
Skin and wool * (with feet, &c.)	11·76	9·90	11·47	11·16	11·72	11·31	11·22
Diaphragm ("skirts")	0·08	0·11	0·11	0·08	0·10	0·07	0·09
Miscellaneous trimmings	......	......	......	......	0·15	0·08	0·11
Total "offal" parts	36·58	33·66	33·67	34·37	34·00	36·32	34·45
Carcass	62·96	63·99	64·53	64·69	64·80	63·50	64·08
Loss by evaporation, error in weighing, &c.	0·46	2·35	1·90	0·94	1·20	6·18	1·47
	100·00	100·00	100·00	100·00	100·00	100·00	100·00

Separate parts of the "offal."

* In the case of these animals killed in December, the wool shorn in the previous Spring is not included in the calculations. For the *actual weights* of the shorn wool, see Appendix-Table XXIII.

APPENDIX.—TABLE XLIX. Showing the *Percentage Proportion* of the individual Organs, and other separated Parts, in the Fasted Live-weight, of SHEEP.

CLASS IX.—7 Wether Sheep of *Leicester Breed*, about 1¾ year old, in *excessively* Fattened condition. Fattening food—Oilcake, Clover Hay, and Swedish Turnips, under cover, until "moderately" fattened; afterwards, Oilcake, with Grass or Green Clover, or with Meadow-hay and Roots, in the field. Killed at Rothamsted, December 20, 1858.

Designation of Parts.	7 Very Fat Leicester Sheep.							Means of the 7 Leicesters.
	No. 1.	No. 2.	No. 3.	No. 4.	No. 5.	No. 6.	No. 7.	
Separate parts of the "offal."								
Stomachs	2·06	2·34	2·36	2·35	2·49	2·22	2·17	2·28
Contents of stomachs	2·49	3·73	4·84	3·68	4·48	3·70	3·17	3·73
Caul-fat	3·78	3·22	3·95	3·13	6·82	3·90	5·55	4·34
Small intestines and contents	1·43	1·46	1·50	0·88	1·63	1·17	1·27	1·33
Large intestines and contents	1·78	1·58	1·77	1·76	1·99	1·61	1·44	1·72
Intestinal fat	1·72	1·62	1·71	0·79	1·70	1·61	1·37	1·50
Heart and aorta	0·35	0·42	0·38	0·33	0·44	0·33	0·31	0·37
Heart-fat	0·37	0·27	0·56	0·29	0·32	0·39	0·17	0·38
Lungs and windpipe	0·79	0·78	0·91	0·86	0·91	0·79	0·82	0·84
Blood	3·66	4·14	3·50	3·94	3·87	3·56	3·49	3·74
Liver	1·40	1·59	1·43	1·32	1·60	1·31	1·23	1·41
Gall-bladder and contents	0·07	0·07	0·06	0·05	0·06	0·05	0·07	0·06
Pancreas ("sweetbread")	0·09	0·09	0·06	0·08	0·06	0·06	0·08	0·07
Milt or spleen	0·19	0·13	0·12	0·13	0·12	0·13	0·14	0·14
Bladder	0·04	0·04	0·04	0·04	0·04	0·03	0·03	0·04
Head	2·56	2·45	2·36	2·50	2·43	2·43	2·29	2·43
Skin and wool * (with feet, &c.)	11·51	9·50	11·79	10·88	11·22	10·35	10·56	10·83
Diaphragm ("skirts")	....	....	....	....	....	0·08	....	0·08
Miscellaneous trimmings	0·05	....	....	....	....	....	....	0·05
Total "offal" parts	34·33	33·53	37·34	33·01	40·18	33·72	34·48	35·34
Carcass	65·64	65·59	62·90	66·43	60·33	66·72	64·47	64·58
Loss by evaporation, error in weighing, &c.	0·03	0·88	−0·24	0·56	−0·51	−0·44	1·05	0·08
	100·00	100·00	100·00	100·00	100·00	100·00	100·00	100·00

* In the case of these animals killed in December, the wool shorn in the previous Spring is not included in the calculations. For the *actual weights* of the shorn wool, see Appendix-Table XXIV.

APPENDIX.—TABLE L. Showing the *Percentage Proportion* of the individual Organs, and other separated Parts, in the Fasted Live-weight, of SHEEP.

CLASS I.—8 Wether Sheep of *Cross-breed* (Leicester and South Down), about 1¾ year old, in *excessively* Fattened condition. Fattening food—Oilcake, Clover Hay, and Swedish Turnips, under cover, until "moderately" fattened; afterwards, Oilcake, with Grass or Green Clover, or with Meadow-hay and Roots, in the field. Killed at Rothamsted, December 20, 1853.

Designation of Parts.	8 Very Fat Cross-bred Wether Sheep (Leicester and South Down).								Means of the 8 Cross-bred Wethers.
	No. 1.	No. 2.	No. 3.	No. 4.	No. 5.	No. 6.	No. 7.	No. 8.	
Separate parts of the "offal."									
Stomachs	2·20	2·21	2·23	2·06	2·60	2·13	2·27	2·21	2·24
Contents of stomachs	4·15	4·34	5·22	3·83	4·20	3·84	2·27	3·39	3·89
Caul-fat	4·39	5·54	4·64	6·17	4·45	4·31	5·32	3·72	4·80
Small intestines and contents	1·16	1·07	1·10	0·93	1·08	1·07	1·21	1·09	1·09
Large intestines and contents	1·73	1·32	1·99	1·54	1·79	1·49	1·64	1·46	1·62
Intestinal fat	1·70	2·11	2·04	2·45	1·34	1·10	2·19	1·39	1·79
Heart and aorta	0·31	0·36	0·31	0·31	0·33	0·34	0·33	0·36	0·33
Heart-fat	0·58	0·35	0·46	0·46	0·39	0·50	0·29	0·53	0·44
Lungs and windpipe	0·79	0·86	0·82	0·75	0·87	0·81	0·88	0·76	0·82
Blood	3·86	3·79	3·21	3·56	4·13	3·65	3·90	3·48	3·68
Liver	1·27	1·27	1·20	1·28	1·32	1·33	1·31	1·29	1·28
Gall-bladder and contents	0·06	0·05	0·05	0·05	0·09	0·07	0·07	0·04	0·06
Pancreas ("sweetbread")	0·10	0·09	0·10	0·09	0·13	0·10	0·08	0·05	0·09
Milt or spleen	0·13	0·13	0·14	0·13	0·15	0·14	0·17	0·15	0·14
Bladder	0·04	0·04	0·03	0·04	0·04	0·04	0·02	0·06	0·04
Head	2·37	2·43	2·51	2·18	2·70	2·50	2·56	2·31	2·45
Skin and wool * (with feet, &c.)	8·80	10·29	9·89	7·85	11·09	10·37	10·82	9·51	9·83
Miscellaneous trimmings	0·15	0·15	......	0·07	0·04	......	......	0·07	0·10
Total "offal" parts	33·72	36·30	35·94	33·75	36·74	33·79	35·23	31·77	34·69
Carcass	66·55	63·31	61·95	66·08	62·68	65·78	64·25	68·02	64·83
Loss by evaporation, error in weighing, &c	−0·27	0·39	2·11	0·17	0·58	0·43	0·52	0·21	0·48
	100·00	100·00	100·00	100·00	100·00	100·00	100·00	100·00	100·00

* In the case of these animals killed in December, the wool shorn in the previous Spring is not included in the calculations. For the *actual weights* of the shorn wool, see Appendix-Table XXV.

APPENDIX.—TABLE LI. Showing the *Percentage Proportion* of the individual Organs, and other separated Parts, in the Fasted Live-weight, of SHEEP.

CLASS XI.—8 Ewe Sheep of *Cross-breed* (Leicester and South Down), about 1¾ year old, in *excessively* Fattened condition. Fattening food—Oilcake, Clover Hay, and Swedish Turnips, under cover, until "moderately" fattened; afterwards, Oilcake, with Grass or Green Clover, or with Meadow-hay and Roots, in the field. Killed at Rothamsted, December 20, 1853.

Designation of Parts.		8 Very Fat Cross-bred Ewe Sheep (Leicester and South Down).								Means of the 8 Cross-bred Ewes.
		No. 1.	No. 2.	No. 3.	No. 4.	No. 5.	No. 6.	No. 7.	No. 8.	
Separate parts of the "offal."	Stomachs	2·33	2·62	2·01	2·03	2·54	2·13	2·19	2·49	2·29
	Contents of stomachs	3·25	3·22	3·20	3·22	4·50	2·38	3·53	3·48	3·35
	Caul-fat	5·96	5·31	5·23	4·04	4·82	4·23	5·03	5·27	4·90
	Small intestines and contents	1·31	1·05	1·23	1·34	1·33	1·70	1·42	0·92	1·29
	Large intestines and contents	1·76	1·57	1·71	1·73	1·90	1·62	1·50	2·06	1·73
	Intestinal fat	2·28	2·99	2·18	1·55	2·03	2·29	1·87	1·49	2·08
	Heart and aorta	0·32	0·41	0·33	0·36	0·34	0·37	0·38	0·37	0·36
	Heart-fat	0·62	0·56	0·41	0·31	0·40	0·53	0·38	0·64	0·48
	Lungs and windpipe	0·76	0·92	0·72	1·00	0·73	0·80	0·79	0·89	0·83
	Blood	3·43	3·63	3·74	3·78	3·76	4·68	3·70	4·09	3·88
	Liver	1·27	1·48	1·26	1·44	1·40	1·48	1·44	1·31	1·38
	Gall-bladder and contents	0·05	0·09	0·05	0·10	0·12	0·04	0·06	0·09	0·07
	Pancreas ("sweetbread")	0·07	0·07	0·05	0·08	0·10	0·09	0·07	0·08	0·07
	Milt or spleen	0·14	0·15	0·11	0·15	0·13	0·14	0·13	0·12	0·13
	Bladder	0·03	0·04	0·03	0·04	0·03	0·05	0·03	0·04	0·04
	Head	2·36	2·83	2·44	2·68	2·55	2·58	2·52	2·52	2·56
	Skin and wool * (with feet, &c.)	10·10	10·93	10·27	12·04	12·18	11·82	10·71	10·80	11·03
	Womb	0·09	0·09	0·09	0·10	0·08	0·07	0·07	0·11	0·09
	Miscellaneous trimmings	......	......	......	......	......	......	0·14	......	0·14
	Total "offal" parts	35·43	37·96	35·06	35·99	38·94	36·60	35·96	36·77	36·71
	Carcass	64·83	62·80	65·27	65·11	60·56	66·11	65·28	64·36	64·29
	Loss by evaporation, error in weighing, &c.	-0·26	-0·76	-0·33	-1·10	0·50	-2·71	-1·24	-1·13	-1·00
		100·00	100·00	100·00	100·00	100·00	100·00	100·00	100·00	100·00

* In the case of these animals killed in December, the wool shorn in the previous Spring is not included in the calculations. For the *actual weights* of the shorn wool, see Appendix-Table XXVI.

4 R 2

APPENDIX.—TABLE LII. Showing the *Percentage Proportion* of the individual Organs, and other separated Parts, in the Fasted Live-weight, of SHEEP.

CLASS XII.—8 Wether Sheep of *Hampshire Down Breed*, about 1¾ year old, in *excessively Fattened* condition. Fattening food—Oilcake, Clover Hay, and Swedish Turnips, under cover, until "moderately" fattened; afterwards, Oilcake, with Grass or Green Clover, or with Meadow-hay and Roots, in the field. Killed at Rothamsted, December 17, 1851.

Designation of Parts.	No. 1.	No. 2.	No. 3.	No. 4.	No. 5.	No. 6.	No. 7.	No. 8.	Means of the 8 Hampshire Downs.
				8 Very Fat Hampshire Down Sheep.					
Stomachs	2·06	2·07	2·46	2·05	2·14	2·11	2·22	1·76	2·11
Contents of stomachs	4·13	3·36	3·18	3·95	4·34	3·34	3·67	2·75	3·58
Caul-fat	8·61	5·05	5·30	5·82	5·57	4·98	7·78	5·01	6·01
Small intestines and contents	1·16	0·85	1·00	0·88	1·21	1·02	0·61	1·10	0·97
Large intestines and contents	1·26	0·88	1·51	1·63	1·84	1·54	1·55	1·42	1·45
Intestinal fat	2·64	2·92	3·40	3·32	2·92	3·13	2·92	3·14	3·05
Heart and aorta	0·34	0·36	0·36	0·44	0·33	0·31	0·36	0·37	0·35
Heart-fat	0·26	0·09	0·10	0·20	0·40	0·22	0·33	0·36	0·24
Lungs and windpipe	0·73	0·80	0·95	0·73	0·81	0·76	0·71	0·85	0·79
Blood	3·24	3·48	3·40	3·64	3·92	3·84	3·66	3·72	3·64
Liver	1·09	1·25	1·17	1·24	1·03	1·29	1·08	1·54	1·21
Gall-bladder and contents	0·06	0·05	0·06	0·07	0·03	0·08	0·09	0·05	0·06
Pancreas ("sweetbread")	0·16	0·14	0·10	0·13	0·13	0·09	0·15	0·12	0·12
Milt or spleen	0·13	0·12	0·13	0·12	0·15	0·14	0·13	0·14	0·13
Bladder	0·02	0·03	0·01	0·03	0·02	0·02	0·03	0·02	0·02
Head	2·49	2·63	2·51	2·43	2·47	2·33	2·64	2·58	2·51
Skin and wool * (with feet, &c.)	9·52	11·16	9·65	10·19	10·06	9·70	10·55	9·25	10·00
Miscellaneous trimmings	.....	.....	.....	.....	.....	.....	.....	0·08	0·08
Total "offal" parts	37·90	35·24	35·29	36·87	37·37	34·90	38·68	34·26	36·32
Carcass	61·68	63·51	64·12	63·11	62·63	64·56	61·04	65·34	63·25
Loss by evaporation, error in weighing, &c.	0·42	1·25	0·59	0·02	0·00†	0·54	0·28	0·40	0·43
	100·00	100·00	100·00	100·00	100·00	100·00	100·00	100·00	100·00

Separate parts of the "offal."

* In the case of these animals killed in December, the wool shorn in the previous Spring is not included in the calculations. For the *actual weights* of the shorn wool, see Appendix-Table XXVII.

† In this case the sum of the weights taken for the separated parts exceeded the Fasted Live-weight, and this *sum* has been taken as the standard, in calculating the Percentages.

APPENDIX.—TABLE LIII. Showing the *Percentage Proportions* of the individual Organs, and other separated Parts, in the Fasted Live-weight, of SHEEP.

CLASS XIII.—8 Wether Sheep of *Sussex Down Breed*, about 1½ year old, in *excessively* Fattened condition. Fattening food—Oilcake, Clover Hay, and Swedish Turnips, under cover, until "moderately" fattened; afterwards, Oilcake, with Grass or Green Clover, or with Meadow-hay and Roots, in the field. Killed at Rothamsted, December 17, 1851.

Designation of Parts.	No. 1.	No. 2.	No. 3.	No. 4.	No. 5.	No. 6.	No. 7.	No. 8.	Means of the 8 Sussex Downs.
				8 Very Fat Sussex Down Sheep.					
Stomachs	1·69	1·94	2·02	2·31	2·24	1·95	1·99	2·07	2·03
Contents of stomachs	3·57	3·92	2·41	3·79	3·51	2·98	2·07	3·82	3·26
Caul-fat	6·48	6·64	6·65	6·32	5·75	5·32	6·81	4·35	6·04
Small intestines and contents	1·15	1·21	1·25	1·23	1·40	1·14	1·12	1·00	1·19
Large intestines and contents	1·33	1·50	1·23	1·12	1·61	1·39	1·30	1·86	1·42
Intestinal fat	2·71	2·57	3·16	2·14	2·84	3·05	3·57	4·02	3·01
Heart and aorta	0·35	0·40	0·40	0·36	0·33	0·39	0·41	0·45	0·39
Heart-fat	0·16	0·22	0·17	0·17	0·24	0·21	0·41	0·28	0·23
Lungs and windpipe	0·86	0·92	0·89	0·93	0·89	0·89	1·00	0·75	0·89
Blood	3·77	3·52	3·36	3·76	3·61	3·87	3·69	3·75	3·66
Liver	1·35	1·47	1·34	1·41	1·47	1·43	1·54	1·38	1·42
Gall-bladder and contents	0·074	0·037	0·028	0·076	0·038	0·038	0·078	0·076	0·057
Pancreas ("sweetbread")	0·13	0·13	0·13	0·14	0·12	0·13	0·16	0·14	0·13
Milt or spleen	0·16	0·18	0·15	0·14	0·16	0·20	0·17	0·19	0·17
Bladder	0·03	0·02	0·02	0·02	0·02	0·02	0·02	0·02	0·02
Head	3·04	2·46	2·89	2·57	2·63	2·87	2·61	2·76	2·73
Skin and wool* (with feet, &c.)	9·84	9·98	10·44	9·60	8·97	9·35	9·35	11·19	9·89
Total "offal" parts	36·69	37·12	36·54	36·09	35·85	35·59	36·30	38·14	36·54
Carcass	63·31	62·88	63·37	62·94	64·15	64·41	63·70	61·74	63·31
Loss by evaporation, error in weighing, &c.	0·00†	0·00†	0·09	0·97	0·00†	0·00†	0·00†	0·12	0·15
	100·00	100·00	100·00	100·00	100·00	100·00	100·00	100·00	100·00

Separate parts of the "offal."

* In the case of these animals killed in December, the wool shorn in the previous Spring is not included in the calculations. For the *actual weights of* the shorn wool, see Appendix-Table XXVIII.

† In these cases the sum of the weights taken for the separated parts exceeded the Fasted Live-weight, and this *sum* has been taken as the standard, in calculating the Percentages.

APPENDIX.—TABLE LIV. Showing the *Percentage Proportion* of the individual CLASS XIV.—19 Sheep of *Hampshire Down Breed*, divided into 4 Lots, each with different Experiment 97 days.

Designation of Parts.	Lot 1.—Food:—Oilcake—in fixed quantity. Swedish Turnips—*ad libitum.*					Lot 2.—Food:—Oats—in fixed quantity. Swedish Turnips—*ad libitum.*				
	No. 1.	No. 2.	No. 3.	No. 4.	No. 5.	No. 6.	No. 7.	No. 8.	No. 9.	No. 10.
Stomachs	2·28	2·69	2·61	2·62	2·82	2·65	2·84	2·72	2·84	2·91
Contents of stomachs	5·55	6·77	6·70	9·14	6·76	8·39	9·31	7·55	8·19	8·26
Caul, intestinal, and heart-fat	8·69	9·51	9·26	7·80	6·20	8·39	8·06	8·54	6·80	6·46
Small intestines and contents	1·24	1·45	1·13	1·71	2·39	1·13	1·06	1·51	1·23	2·12
Large intestines and contents	1·93	1·95	1·55	2·09	1·77	1·69	2·15	2·41	2·47	2·28
Heart and aorta	0·72	0·89	0·76	0·67	0·70	0·88	0·90	0·79	0·69	0·74
Lungs and windpipe	1·24	1·22	1·10	1·17	1·45	1·33	1·38	1·24	1·31	0·95
Blood	4·26	3·47	4·27	3·54	3·93	3·89	3·73	4·09	3·61	4·00
Liver	1·53	1·54	1·71	0·99	1·54	1·39	1·36	1·93	1·42	1·59
Gall-bladder and contents	0·04	0·06	0·09	0·13	0·03	0·04	0·09	0·18	0·11	0·08
Head	3·29	3·26	3·19	3·51	3·78	3·10	3·43	3·42	3·91	3·81
Skin and wool (with feet, &c.)	11·55	11·81	10·63	10·59	13·41	10·19	11·90	10·97	11·61	14·41
Total "offal" parts†	42·32	44·62	43·00	44·16	44·78	43·27	46·21	45·35	44·59	47·61
Carcass	58·94	56·60	55·40	56·61	55·36	59·08	55·17	56·47	57·56	54·24
Loss by evaporation, error in weighing, &c.	−1·26	−1·22	1·60	−0·77	−0·14	−2·35	−1·38	−1·82	−2·15	−1·85
	100·00	100·00	100·00	100·00	100·00	100·00	100·00	100·00	100·00	100·00

(Leftmost vertical label: Separate parts of the "offal.")

* For particulars of the *feeding experiment*, refer, under the head of "Experiments with Sheep—Series 1,"
† In the case of these animals the Pancreas, Spleen, and Bladder were not weighed.

Organs, and other separated Parts, in the Fasted Live-weight, of SHEEP.

Food *. *Moderately* Fattened. Bred, fed, and killed at Rothamsted.—Period of Feeding Killed April 11, 1848.

Lot 3.—Food:— Clover Chaff—in fixed quantity. Swedish Turnips—ad libitum.					Lot 4.—Food:— Oat-straw Chaff, and Swedish Turnips—each ad libitum.				Means of—				
No. 11.	No. 12.	No. 13.	No. 14.	No. 15.	No. 16.	No. 17.	No. 18.	No. 19.	Lot 1.	Lot 2.	Lot 3.	Lot 4.	The 19 Sheep.
3·17	2·93	3·04	3·17	3·02	2·91	3·07	2·89	2·88	2·64	2·83	3·06	2·94	2·87
13·36	9·35	10·45	10·57	10·63	8·38	8·65	6·90	10·21	6·98	8·34	10·88	8·54	8·69
6·12	7·19	7·82	7·96	7·33	8·96	8·33	9·32	8·32	8·29	7·65	7·28	8·73	7·95
2·68	1·51	1·41	1·53	1·36	1·89	1·94	1·27	2·09	1·58	1·41	1·74	1·79	1·62
3·46	2·09	2·70	2·74	1·81	2·01	2·42	1·86	2·19	1·86	·2·20	2·68	2·12	2·22
0·79	0·63	1·11	0·81	0·86	0·85	0·89	0·72	0·64	0·75	0·64	0·88	0·78	0·81
1·93	1·22	1·43	1·39	1·29	1·21	1·40	1·34	1·28	1·24	1·24	1·31	1·31	1·27
4·00	3·76	3·27	3·82	3·81	2·96	3·80	3·75	3·91	3·90	3·91	3·73	3·60	3·79
1·76	1·61	1·82	1·80	1·68	1·50	1·72	1·21	1·65	1·46	1·54	1·71	1·52	1·56
0·02	0·11	0·04	0·03	0·08	0·06	0·09	0·02	0·03	0·07	0·10	0·00	0·05	0·07
2·97	3·15	3·46	3·35	3·45	3·39	3·29	3·72	3·35	3·41	3·53	3·28	3·44	3·41
11·27	10·57	11·07	10·61	11·42	10·85	9·89	12·40	11·51	11·60	11·82	10·99	11·16	11·41
51·05	44·82	47·62	47·78	46·74	44·97	45·49	45·40	48·06	43·78	45·41	47·60	45·98	45·67
50·00	56·99	53·50	53·06	52·76	55·81	55·60	55·78	52·36	56·58	56·50	53·26	54·89	55·33
−1·05	−1·61	−1·12	−0·84	0·50	−0·78	−1·09	−1·18	−0·42	−0·36	−1·91	−0·86	−0·67	−1·00
100·00	100·00	100·00	100·00	100·00	100·00	100·00	100·00	100·00	100·00	100·00	100·00	100·00	100·00

to Article—"Sheep Feeding and Manure," Journal of the Royal Agricultural Society of England, vol. x. part 1.

APPENDIX.—TABLE LV. Showing the *Percentage Proportion* of the individual

CLASS XV.—20 Sheep of *Hampshire Down Breed*, divided into 4 Lots, each with different Experiment 134 days.

Designation of Parts.	Lot 1.—Food:— Oilcake—in fixed quantity. Clover Chaff—*ad libitum*.					Lot 2.—Food:— Linseed—in fixed quantity. Clover Chaff—*ad libitum*.				
	No. 1.	No. 2.	No. 3.	No. 4.	No. 5.	No. 6.	No. 7.	No. 8.	No. 9.	No. 10.
Stomachs	2·63	3·03	2·88	2·56	2·74	2·55	2·47	2·60	2·33	2·79
Contents of stomachs	9·32	8·88	9·75	8·55	9·88	5·96	6·58	7·79	7·57	7 29
Caul-fat	2·94	4·75	4·34	5·42	4·88	6·93	4·98	5·20	4·82	6·12
Small intestines and contents	1·84	1·85	1·81	1·65	1·52	2·17	1·46	1·77	1·45	1·89
Large intestines and contents	3·45	2·75	3·34	2·60	2·78	2·13	1·55	3·26	2·38	2·30
Intestinal fat	1·75	2·44	1·77	1·63	1·57	2·22	1·78	2·39	2·20	1·53
Heart and aorta	0·40	0·32	0·33	0·40	0·39	0·43	0·32	0·37	0·41	0·40
Heart-fat	0·28	0·36	0·27	0·46	0·30	0·38	0·39	0·37	0 37	0·45
Lungs and windpipe	0·89	0·80	0·81	0 86	1·65	0·90	0·87	0·82	0·79	0·99
Blood	4·45	4·00	3·75	3·92	4·00	3·97	3·97	4·04	3·79	3·60
Liver	1·28	1·39	1·31	1·32	1·57	1·28	1·10	1·40	1·37	1·30
Gall-bladder and contents	0·05	0·06	0·03	0·05	0 05	0·08	0 10	0·14	0·09	0·09
Pancreas ("sweetbread")	0·10	0·12	0·13	0·12	0·05	0·13	0·10	0·15	0·12	0·15
Milt or spleen		0·13	0·10	0·13	0·13	0·13	0·13	0·16	0·14	0·11
Head	3·23	2·82	3·17	3·28	3·13	3·31	3·22	3·30	3·13	3·42
Skin and wool (with feet, &c.)	9·30	10·10	11·54	9·60	8·97	8·04	9·50	8·63	9·37	9·45
Total "offal" parts †	41·91	43·80	45·33	42·55	43·61	40·61	38·52	42·59	40·33	41·88
Carcass	58·09	56·21	54·67	57·45	56·39	59·39	61·48	57·41	59 67	58·12
Loss by evaporation, error in weighing, &c.	0·00	−0·01	0·00	0·00	0·00	0·00	0·00	0·00	0·00	0·00
	100·00	100·00	100·00	100·00	100·00	100·00	100 00	100·00	100·00	100·00

Separate parts of the "offal."

* For particulars of the *feeding* experiment, refer, under the head of "Experiments with Sheep—Series 2,"
† In the case of these animals the Bladder was not weighed.

Organs, and other separated Parts, in the Fasted Live-weight, of SHEEP.

Food *.   *Moderately* Fattened.   Bred, fed, and killed at Rothamsted.   Period of Feeding Killed October 17, 1848.

	Lot 3.—Food:— Barley—in fixed quantity. Clover Chaff—*ad libitum*.				Lot 4.—Food:— Malt—in fixed quantity. Clover Chaff—*ad libitum*.					Means of—				
No. 11.	No. 12.	No. 13.	No. 14.	No. 15.	No. 16.	No. 17.	No. 18.	No. 19.	No. 20.	Lot 1.	Lot 2.	Lot 3.	Lot 4.	The 20 Sheep.
2·94	2·94	3·06	3·01	3·42	2·34	2·56	2·45	2·57	2·90	2·77	2·55	3·07	2·56	2·74
9·35	7·39	10·91	10·02	10·43	8·90	8·23	5·62	7·65	8·90	9·28	7·04	9·62	7·86	8·45
4·26	3·62	4·92	3·79	4·30	3·33	3·34	3·96	3·79	5·60	4·47	5·61	4·18	4·01	4·56
1·49	1·16	1·28	1·34	1·27	1·59	1·51	1·34	1·45	1·34	1·73	1·75	1·31	1·45	1·56
2·59	2·71	3·06	1·96	2·74	2·34	2·47	2·21	2·51	2·68	2·98	2·33	2·61	2·44	2·59
1·62	1·69	1·66	1·70	1·23	2·02	1·97	2·07	1·83	2·07	1·83	2·02	1·58	1·99	1·86
0·31	0·43	0·38	0·38	0·42	0·35	0·41	0·38	0·37	0·39	0·37	0·39	0·38	0·38	0·38
0·19	0·43	0·31	0·42	0·31	0·35	0·39	0·46	0·42	0·39	0·33	0·39	0·33	0·40	0·36
1·12	0·63	0·89	0·78	0·88	0·84	0·96	0·84	0·94	0·91	1·00	0·87	0·86	0·90	0·91
4·21	4·73	3·94	3·75	4·16	4·03	4·12	4·23	4·45	4·28	4·02	3·87	4·16	4·22	4·07
1·27	1·30	1·15	1·27	1·32	1·22	1·28	1·34	1·22	1·56	1·37	1·29	1·26	1·33	1·31
0·04	0·08	0·06	0·13	0·07	0·06	0·05	0·07	0·06	0·08	0·05	0·10	0·08	0·06	0·07
0·12	0·12	0·13	0·12	0·10	0·08	0·12	0·13	0·13	0·15	0·10	0·13	0·12	0·12	0·12
0·16	0·15	0·15	0·11	0·14	0·15	0·13	0·16	0·13	0·14	0·12	0·13	0·14	0·14	0·13
3·20	3·16	3·28	3·35	3·68	3·14	3·52	3·46	3·32	3·29	3·12	3·28	3·33	3 35	3 27
9·21	9·22	9·49	10·58	9·42	8·72	11·12	11·72	10·91	8·08	9·90	9·04	9·59	10·11	9·66
42·08	39·76	44·67	42·71	43·89	39·46	42·18	40·44	41·75	42·76	43·44	40·79	42·62	41·32	42·04
57·92	60·24	56·03	57·29	56·11	60·54	57·82	59·56	58·25	56·54	56·56	59·21	57·52	58·54	57·96
0·00	0·00	−0·70	0·00	0·00	0·00	0·00	0·00	0·00	0·70	0·00	0·00	−0·14	0·14	0·00
100·00	100·00	100·00	100·00	100·00	100·00	100·00	100·00	100·00	100·00	100·00	100 00	100 00	100 00	100·00

Article—"Sheep Feeding and Manure," Journal of the Royal Agricultural Society of England, vol. x. part 1.

APPENDIX.—TABLE LVI. Showing the *Percentage Proportion* of the individual

CLASS XVI.—25 Sheep of *Hampshire Down Breed*, divided into 6 Lots, each with different Food*.

Killed

Designation of Parts.	Lot 1.—Food:—Barley (ground)—in fixed quantity. Mangolds—*ad libitum.*				Lot 2.—Food:—Malt (ground), and Malt-dust—in fixed quantity. Mangolds—*ad libitum.*				Lot 3.—Food:—Barley (ground and *steeped*)—in fixed quantity. Mangolds—*ad libitum.*			
	No. 1.	No. 2.	No. 3.	No. 4.	No. 5.	No. 6.	No. 7.	No. 8.	No. 9.	No. 10.	No. 11.	No. 12.
Stomachs	2·49	2·80	2·69	2·64	2·83	2·77	2·34	2·61	2·65	2·55	2·55	2·55
Contents of stomachs	3·31	3·32	4·36	3·84	4·21	5·10	4·78	3·40	5·66	4·45	4·47	3·21
Caul-fat	5·24	3·95	4·43	4·90	4·36	5·30	4·84	5·47	3·12	3·89	5·52	5·53
Small intestines and contents	1·73	1·38	1·71	1·88	1·46	1·89	1·04	1·40	1·81	1·28	1·38	1·81
Large intestines and contents	1·64	2·43	2·54	2·12	1·99	2·41	1·76	1·94	2·07	1·54	1·83	1·80
Intestinal fat	2·29	3·32	2 93	2·73	1·94	2·02	2·89	2·41	2·26	1·74	1·83	2·45
Heart and aorta	0·40	0·48	0·55	0·38	0·51	0·43	0·41	0·38	0·43	0·45	0·41	0·44
Heart-fat	0·38	0·35	0·45	0·39	0·61	0·36	0·60	0·60	0·43	0·83	0·43	0·61
Lungs and windpipe	1·09	1·00	1·36	0·98	0·98	1·11	1·02	1·17	1·08	0·98	0·96	1·19
Blood	3·91	3·80	4·11	4·34	4·18	3·96	3·89	3·56	4·63	4·19	3·71	4·34
Liver	1·46	1·50	1·35	1·53	1·52	1·35	1·38	1·24	1·62	1·34	1·30	1·44
Gall-bladder and contents	0·06	0·03	0·03	0·03	0·06	0·05	0·02	0·08	0·07	0·07	0·04	0·05
Pancreas ("sweetbread")	0·17	0·20	0·19	0·18	0·18	0·20	0·14	0·19	0·16	0·14	0·21	0·12
Milt or spleen	0·16	0·13	0·20	0·18	0·18	0·17	0·14	0·11	0·24	0·18	0·20	0·18
Head	3·38	3·19	3·28	3·11	3·40	3·43	2·90	2·97	3·14	3·14	3·16	3·17
Skin (with feet, &c.)	7·02	7·63	8·10	7·29	6·36	7·65	7·00	6·84	7·28	7·40	6·90	7·44
Wool previously shorn	4·80	5·27	4·05	5·37	3·89	5·01	7·29	6·87	5·46	4·52	5·43	5·27
Total "offal" parts†	39·48	40·78	42·55	41·89	38·66	43·21	42·44	41·24	42·11	38·69	40·33	41·69
Carcass	59·68	59·43	56·73	57·24	60·51	54·69	55·35	57·65	57·21	59·50	57·21	57·82
Loss by evaporation, error in weighing, &c.	0·84	−0·21	0·72	0·87	0·83	2·10	2·21	1·11	0·68	1·81	2·46	0·58
	100·00	100·00	100·00	100·00	100·00	100·00	100·00	100·00	100·00	100·00	100·00	100·00

(The rows from "Heart and aorta" through "Milt or spleen" are bracketed together under "Separate parts of the 'offal'.")

* For particulars of the *feeding* experiment, refer, under the head of "Experiments with Sheep—Series 4," to Article—"Sheep Feeding and Manure," Journal of t

† In the case of these animals the Bladder was not weighed.

Organs, and other separated Parts, in the Fasted Live-weight, of SHEEP.

Moderately Fattened.   Bred, fed, and killed at Rothamsted.   Period of Feeding Experiment 70 days.

June 13, 1849.

Lot 4.—Food:— Malt (ground and *steeped*), and Malt-dust—in fixed quantity. Mangolds—*ad libitum*.				Lot 5.—Food:— Malt (ground), and Malt-dust—in fixed quantity. Mangolds—*ad libitum*.					Lot 6.—Food:— Oilcake—in fixed quantity. Mangolds—*ad libitum*.				Means of—						
No. 13.	No. 14.	No. 15.	No. 16.	No. 17.	No. 18.	No. 19.	No. 20.	No. 21.	No. 22.	No. 23.	No. 24.	No. 25.	Lot 1.	Lot 2.	Lot 3.	Lot 4.	Lot 5.	Lot 6.	The 25 Sheep.
2·65	2·23	2·67	2·40	2·57	2·51	3·35	2·53	2·93	2·41	2·92	3·62	2·82	2·70	2·64	2·57	2·54	2·78	2·67	2·66
5·74	3·26	4·80	4·85	4·93	6·54	5·48	8·18	7·40	4·31	4·43	4·75	4·88	3·71	4·37	4·45	4·66	6·51	4·59	4·79
4·17	4·81	6·05	4·43	3·88	3·68	4·63	5·26	3·18	5·05	5·02	4·25	4·82	4·63	4·99	4·51	4·87	4·14	4·79	4·63
1·56	0·94	1·29	1·70	1·29	1·67	1·69	2·80	1·67	0·99	1·38	1·06	1·52	1·66	1·45	1·57	1·37	1·82	1·24	1 53
1·94	1·42	1·66	2·05	2·04	2·39	1·44	3·19	2·13	2·25	2·95	1·74	2·27	2·18	2·03	1·81	1·77	2·04	2·09	1·98
2·15	2·36	3·15	2·01	3·06	2·92	1·66	1·76	2·05	2·22	3·01	1·74	1·93	2·82	2·32	2·07	2·42	2·27	2·22	2·35
0·38	0·39	0·42	0·44	0·45	0·42	0·48	0·42	0·39	0·41	0·44	0·45	0·50	0·43	0·43	0·43	0·41	0·43	0·45	0·43
0·55	0·43	0·56	0·48	0·49	0·47	0·45	0·44	0·45	0·52	0·47	0·33	0·32	0·38	0·54	0·58	0·50	0·46	0·41	0·48
1·05	1·01	0·97	0·99	1·22	0·93	1·01	0·86	1·07	0·91	0·90	1·06	1·02	1·11	1·07	1·05	1·90	1·02	0·97	1·01
3·89	3·69	3·92	4·17	3·52	3·68	4·31	4·01	4·18	3·79	3·69	3·95	4·31	4·04	3·90	4·22	3·92	3·92	3·91	3·98
1·32	1·12	1·59	1·30	1·85	1·19	1·42	1·24	1·47	1·44	1·71	1·48	1·74	1·46	1·37	1·12	1·33	1·43	1·50	1·44
0·07	0·08	0·11	0·03	0·07	0·09	0·10	0·10	0·09	0·08	0·10	0·07	......	0·04	0·05	0·06	0·07	0·09	0·08	0·06
0·18	0·15	0·17	0·17	0·16	0·16	0·17	0·11	0·19	0·11	0·18	0·15	0·15	0·19	0·18	0 16	0·17	0·16	0·15	0·17
0·15	0·15	0·20	0·13	0·14	0·12	0·20	0·16	0·16	0·16	0·17	0·17	0·16	0·17	0·15	0 20	0·16	0·16	0·17	0·17
3·21	3·15	3·02	3·10	3·12	3·25	3·17	2·90	3·43	3·09	2·90	3·17	3·41	3·24	3·18	3·15	3·42	3·17	3·14	3·17
7·71	6·65	6·47	7·20	7·21	6·35	6·26	7·51	7·86	7·44	7·02	7·63	8·50	7·51	6·96	7·26	7·01	7·44	7·66	7·31
5·61	5·92	3·84	4·64	7·39	5·76	5·87	4·82	3·69	4·31	5·80	5·55	4·81	4·87	5·76	5·17	5·05	5·55	4·67	5·22
42·53	37·76	40·89	40·29	43·59	42·03	43·61	45·31	42·36	39·49	42·09	38·07	43·22	41·18	41·39	40·68	40·37	43·39	40·99	41·41
55·98	61·80	58·10	58·66	54·64	58·45	55·68	54·77	55·78	58·73	56·78	59·76	55·22	58·27	57·05	57·94	58·63	55·88	57·61	57·50
1·49	0·44	1·01	1·05	1·77	-0·58	0·71	-0·08	1·84	1·78	1·13	1·95	1·56	0·55	1·56	1·38	1·00	0·73	1·40	1·09
100·00	100·00	100·00	100·00	100·00	100·00	100·00	100·00	100·00	100·00	100·00	100·00	100·00	100·00	100·00	100·00	100·00	100·00	100·00	100·00

Royal Agricultural Society of England, vol. x. part 1.   See also, the fuller note at the foot of the Table of the "*Actual Weights*" to which the *Percentages* in this Table refer (Appendix-Table XXXI).

APPENDIX.—TABLE LVII. Showing the *Percentage Proportion* of the individual

CLASS XVII.—14 Sheep of *Hampshire Down Breed*, divided into 3 Lots—Fed respectively, for 63 days, and Mangolds, and Lot 3 with Oilcake and Mangolds. Total period of Feeding Experiment 96 days;

Designation of Parts.		Lot 1.—Food:— Clover Chaff—in fixed quantity. Swedish Turnips, highly manured, or Mangolds—*ad libitum*.				
		No. 1.	No. 2.	No. 3.	No. 4.	No. 5.
Separate parts of the "offal."	Stomachs	3·07	2·26	2·22	2·64	2·86
	Contents of stomachs	6·66	5·75	4·49	5·11	6·69
	Caul-fat	4·70	3·92	4·78	4·53	4·20
	Small intestines and contents	2·35	1·47	1·98	1·81	1·86
	Large intestines and contents	2·58	2·13	2·10	1·98	2·80
	Intestinal fat	1·92	1·94	2·47	2·00	2·19
	Heart and aorta	0·47	0·39	0·37	0·38	0·40
	Heart-fat	0·41	0·46	0·49	0·45	0·48
	Lungs and windpipe	1·24	0·86	0·90	1·03	0·99
	Blood	2·63	3·90	4·10	3·87	4·24
	Liver	1·45	1·34	1·60	1·36	1·46
	Gall-bladder and contents	0·03			0·04	0·03
	Pancreas ("sweetbread")	0·15	0·16	0·16	0·18	0·17
	Milt or spleen	0·19	0·16	0·16	0·15	0·16
	Head	3·37	3·36	3·01	3·29	3·26
	Skin (with feet, &c.)	7·45	7·20	7·12	6·82	7·04
	Wool previously shorn *	5·04	3·45	5·15	5·63	5·55
Total "offal" parts †		43·71	38·75	41·10	41·27	44·40
Carcass		54·31	59·31	56·65	57·04	53·17
Loss by evaporation, error in weighing, &c.		1·98	1·94	2·25	1·69	2·43
		100·00	100·00	100·00	100·00	100·00

* Wool shorn May 29.

† In the case of these animals the bladder was not weighed.

Organs, and other separated Parts, in the Fasted Live-weight, of SHEEP.

with Clover Chaff, and Turnips, differently manured; then, for 33 days, Lots 1 and 2 with Clover Chaff namely, from March 7 to June 11. Bred, fed, and killed at Rothamsted. Killed June 12, 1849.

| Lot 2.—Food:—Clover Chaff—in fixed quantity. Swedish Turnips, manured with Superphosphate of Lime alone, or Mangolds—*ad libitum*. | | | | Lot 3.—Food:—Clover Chaff—in fixed quantity. Swedish Turnips, unmanured—*ad libitum*. or Oilcake—in fixed quantity. Mangolds—*ad libitum*. | | | | | Means of— | | | |
No. 6.	No. 7.	No. 8.	No. 9.	No. 10.	No. 11.	No. 12.	No. 13.	No. 14.	Lot 1.	Lot 2.	Lot 3.	The 14 Sheep.
2·85	2·52	3·21	2·76	2·35	2·26	2·62	2·53	2·71	2·61	2·83	2·49	2·63
6·34	5·66	5·53	5·60	5·29	5·59	4·95	4·05	7·49	5·74	5·78	5·47	5·66
3·49	6·64	3·94	3·27	5·31	4·31	4·71	7·59	3·12	4·43	4·53	5·01	4·61
1·70	1·78	1·95	2·08	1·41	2·11	1·98	1·68	2·38	1·89	1·88	1·91	1·89
2·68	2·21	1·90	2·24	1·27	2·13	2·19	1·79	2·05	2·32	2·26	1·86	2·14
1·84	1·82	1·94	2·93	3·04	1·97	1·81	3·70	2·37	2·10	2·13	2·58	2·28
0·51	0·34	0·39	0·47	0·37	0·45	0·44	0·42	0·46	0·40	0·43	0·43	0·42
0·36	0·38	0·27	0·37	0·48	0·43	0·49	0·25	0·30	0·46	0·34	0·39	0·40
1·21	0·94	1·02	1·16	0·81	1·20	1·04	1·11	1·13	1·00	1·08	1·05	1·04
3·71	3·95	4·67	4·20	3·47	4·46	3·87	4·00	4·21	3·75	4·13	4·00	3·95
1·47	1·30	1·37	1·42	1·46	1·58	1·57	1·57	1·56	1·44	1·39	1·55	1·46
0·09	0·08	0·09		0·04	0·10	0·09	......	0·04	0·03	0·08	0·07	0·06
0·13	0·19	0·15	0·15	0·17	0·15	0·14	0·11	0·23	0·16	0·16	0·16	0·16
0·18	0·19	0·18	0·17	0·17	0·13	0·15	0·18	0·17	0·16	0·18	0·16	0·17
3·35	3·13	2·96	3·46	2·60	3·12	3·38	3·38	3·68	3·26	3·22	3·23	3·24
7·25	6·99	7·41	7·57	7·46	9·65	8·04	6·53	7·03	7·13	7·31	7·74	7·40
5·86	4·69	4·89	5·65	3·78	3·86	6·92	4·83	4·96	4·96	5·27	4·87	5·02
43·02	42·79	41·87	43·50	39·48	43·50	44·39	43·72	43·89	41·84	42·80	43·00	42·53
54·94	56·25	58·27	54·23	59·55	57·37	54·37	55·22	54·41	56·10	55·92	56·18	56·08
2·04	0·96	−0·14	2·27	0·97	−0·87	1·24	1·06	1·70	2·06	1·28	0·82	1·39
100·00	100·00	100·00	100·00	100·00	100·00	100·00	100·00	100·00	100·00	100·00	100·00	100·00

APPENDIX.—TABLE LVIII. Showing the *Percentage Proportion* of the individual

CLASS XVIII.—21 Sheep of various Breeds and Modes of

Designation of Parts.	Hampshire Down Breed. Killed December 18, 1851.				Sussex Down Breed.					
	No. 1.	No. 2.	No. 3.	No. 4.	No. 5.	No. 6.	No. 7.	No. 8.	No. 9.	No. 10.
Separate parts of the "offal": Stomachs	1·93	2·19	1·08	1·97	2·15	2·32	2·26	1·98	1·76	2·18
Contents of stomachs	1·33	5·11	4·22	2·62	3·30	3·03	2·75	2·58	3·21	3·15
Caul-fat	7·05	5·52	5·85	6·56	5·29	4·92	7·69	7·49	5·25	5·65
Small intestines and contents	0·86	1·02	1·24	1·07	1·40	1·61	1·13	1·24	0·97	1·18
Large intestines and contents	1·18	1·69	1·30	1·25	1·59	1·50	1·52	1·38	1·89	1·45
Intestinal fat	3·11	1·99	2·05	3·16	2·68	3·66	3·00	3·84	2·42	2·93
Heart and aorta	0·36	0·36	0·39	0·36	0·37	0·55	0·35	0·42	0·53	0·39
Heart-fat	0·21	0·23	0·36	0·60	0·25	0·35	0·37	0·32	0·18	0·41
Lungs and windpipe	0·98	0·93	0·84	0·70	0·78	1·04	0·74	0·84	1·14	0·70
Blood	3·42	3·74	3·68	3·41	3·67	4·12	3·36	3·84	4·13	4·40
Liver	1·47	1·21	1·39	1·01	1·40	1·48	1·23	1·38	1·06	1·36
Gall-bladder and contents	0·07	0·08	0·01	0·05	0·04	0·03	0·08	0·04	0·03	0·06
Pancreas ("sweetbread")	0·13	0·10	0·12	0·12	0·11	0·17	0·12	0·08	0·21	0·14
Milt or spleen	0·13	0·16	0·17	0·16	0·21	0·20	0·18	0·16	0·29	0·21
Bladder	0·03	0·02	0·04	0·03	0·02	0·02	0·03	0·03	0·02	0·03
Head	2·59	2·75	2·71	2·65	2·89	2·70	2·43	2·76	3·38	2·83
Skin and wool* (with feet, &c.)	9·48	11·22	8·87	7·51	10·90	11·66	8·75	9·92	12·66	10·45
Miscellaneous trimmings	......	......	......	......	......	......	......	......	......	......
Total "offal" parts	34·33	38·32	35·22	33·24	37·05	39·36	35·99	38·30	39·15	37·52
Carcass	65·16	60·88	64·78	66·76	62·95	60·64	64·01	61·70	60·85	62·48
Loss by evaporation, error in weighing, &c.	0·51	0·80	0·00†	0·00†	0·00†	0·00†	0·00†	0·00†	0·00†	0·00†
	100·00	100·00	100·00	100·00	100·00	100·00	100·00	100·00	100·00	100·00

* In the case of these animals killed in December, the wool shorn in the previous Spring is not included

† In these cases the sum of the weights taken for the separated parts exceeded the Fasted Live-weight,

Organs, and other separated Parts, in the Fasted Live-weight, of SHEEP.

Feeding, about 1¼ year old; of more than Average Fatness.

Killed December 18. 1851.				Leicesters and Cross-breds. Killed December 21, 1853.							Means of—			
				Cross-bred Ewe.	Cross-bred Wether.	Leicester Wethers.					The 4 Hants Downs.	The 10 Sussex Downs.	The 7 Leicesters and Cross-breds.	The 21 Sheep.
No. 11.	No. 12.	No. 13.	No. 14.	No. 15.	No. 16.	No. 17.	No. 18.	No. 19.	No. 20.	No. 21.				
1·99	2·15	2·04	2·12	2·38	2·44	2·45	2·58	2·61	2·84	2·38	1·79	2·09	2·60	2·19
3·23	......	4·01	2·67	5·17	4·79	4·93	4·59	3·76	6·63	5·85	3·32	3·10	5·10	3·83
6·92	6·13	5·48	6·16	3·69	3·91	3·63	2·78	3·18	2·74	2·79	6·24	6·10	3·25	5·18
1·01	1·23	1·05	1·15	1·42	1·49	1·83	1·66	1·61	2·37	1·93	1·05	1·20	1·76	1·36
1·72	2·15	1·73	1·69	1·92	2·46	1·92	2·19	1·99	2·65	2·52	1·35	1·66	2·24	1·80
3·43	2·39	2·82	3·03	2·23	1·14	1·63	1·58	1·73	1·22	1·53	2·80	3·02	1·58	2·50
0·36	0·40	0·44	0·47	0·36	0·42	0·36	0·48	0·44	0·42	0·40	0·37	0·43	0·41	0·41
0·41	0·38	0·61	0·32	0·50	0·50	0·61	0·59	0·48	0·64	0·49	0·35	0·36	0·54	0·42
0·74	0·80	0·80	0·79	0·82	0·79	1·43	1·07	1·04	1·21	1·28	0·86	0·84	1·09	0·93
3·55	4·18	3·82	4·12	3·45	4·12	3·74	4·04	3·66	4·17	4·32	3·56	3·92	3·93	3·86
1·30	1·39	1·32	1·31	1·33	1·26	1·51	1·49	1·51	1·85	1·57	1·27	1·32	1·50	1·37
0·03	0·04	0·08	0·06	0·02	0·02	0·02	0·06	0·07	0·06	0·06	0·03	0·05	0·04	0·05
0·12	0·14	0·12	0·15	0·10	0·09	0·09	0·10	0·10	0·13	0·09	0·12	0·14	0·10	0·12
0·17	0·20	0·20	0·23	0·12	0·14	0·14	0·15	0·14	0·14	0·16	0·15	0·20	0·14	0·17
0·02	0·03	0·02	0·02	0·04	0·03	0·05	0·03	0·04	0·05	0·05	0·03	0·02	0·04	0·03
2·51	2·83	2·62	2·61	2·77	2·85	2·36	2·95	2·74	3·15	3·06	2·68	2·78	2·84	2·78
10·03	10·51	9·45	10·52	11·83	12·11	11·58	14·16	12·58	13·07	13·55	9·27	10·49	12·74	11·01
......	......	......	......	......	0·04	......	......	......	0·14	......	......	......	0·09	0·09
37·54	34·95	36·61	37·62	38·15	38·60	38·28	40·50	37·68	43·48	42·63	35·27	37·72	39·99	38·12
62·38	61·42	63·13	62·38	62·29	62·21	61·28	59·77	60·85	56·34	57·96	64·40	62·19	60·10	61·91
0·08	3·63	0·26	0·00†	−0·44	−0·81	0·44	−0·27	1·47	0·18	−0·79	0·33	0·09	−0·09	−0·03
100·00	100·00	100·00	100·00	100·00	100·00	100·00	100·00	100·00	100·00	100·00	100·00	100·00	100·00	100·00

in the calculations. For the *actual weights* of the shorn wool, see Appendix-Table XXXIII.

and this *sum* has been taken as the standard, in calculating the Percentages.

APPENDIX.—Table LIX. Showing the *Percentage Proportion* of the individual
CLASS I.—9 Pigs, divided into 3 Lots, each with rather different Food*.

Designation of Parts.	Lot 1.—Food:—Bean and Lentil meal—in fixed quantity. Bran—*ad libitum.*		
	No. 1.	No. 2.	No. 3.
Stomach and contents	2·19	1·48	1·30
Caul-fat	0·34	0·43	0·39
Small intestines and contents	4·56	1·91	3·36
Large intestines and contents	7·53	3·60	5·00
Intestinal fat, "mudgeon," &c.	0·92	0·76	0·66
Heart and aorta	0·33	0·35	0·30
Lungs and windpipe	0·78	1·04	0·98
Blood	4·41	4·64	3·18
Liver	1·75	1·39	1·72
Gall-bladder and contents	0·05	0·12	0·06
Pancreas ("sweetbread")	0·14	0·24	0·16
Milt or spleen	0·16	0·20	0·25
Bladder	0·14	0·05	0·05
Penis (or uterus)	0·25	0·29	0·18
Tongue	0·58	0·69	0·48
Toes	0·12	0·11	0·11
Miscellaneous trimmings	0·41	0·22	0·11
Total "offal" parts	24·66	17·52	18·29
Carcass (including head and feet)	73·94	81·86	79·59
Loss by evaporation, error in weighing, &c.	1·40	0·62	2·12
	100·00	100·00	100·00

Separate parts of the "offal." (side label)

* For particulars of the *feeding* experiment, refer to Pens 9, 10, and 11, under the head of " Experiments with

Organs, and other separated Parts, in the Fasted Live-weight, of PIGS.

Somewhat *under* Fattened—the Food containing a considerable portion of Bran.

Lot 2.—Food:— Indian meal—in fixed quantity. Bran—*ad libitum.*			Lot 3.—Food:— Bean and Lentil meal, and Indian meal—in fixed quantity. Bran—*ad libitum.*			Means of—			
No. 4.	No. 5.	No. 6.	No. 7.	No. 8.	No. 9.	Lot 1. 3 Pigs.	Lot 2. 3 Pigs.	Lot 3. 3 Pigs.	The 9 Pigs.
1·37	1·90	1·66	1·91	1·55	1·34	1·66	1·71	1·60	1·66
0·74	0·62	0·48	0·67	0·54	0·45	0·39	0·61	0·55	0·52
2·11	3·72	3·00	2·77	3·16	2·86	3·27	2·95	2·93	3·05
3·04	5·62	4·72	4·59	5·08	5·01	5·38	4·46	4·90	4·91
1·39	0·96	0·80	1·03	0·98	0·69	0·78	1·05	0·90	0·91
0·32	0·18	0·32	0·29	0·27	0·26	0·33	0·27	0·28	0·29
0·84	0·72	0·86	0·09	0·83	0·90	0·93	0·81	0·91	0·88
4·32	4·00	3·43	3·83	3·69	4·20	4·08	3·92	3·91	3·97
1·30	1·61	1·50	1·53	1·39	1·74	1·62	1·47	1·55	1·55
0·07	0·05	0·06	0·09	0·04	0·06	0·08	0·06	0·06	0·07
0·23	0·18	0·16	0·21	0·14	0·14	0·18	0·19	0·16	0·18
0·16	0·12	0·14	0·16	0·13	0·16	0·20	0·14	0·15	0·16
0·10	0·07	0·05	0·10	0·06	0·06	0·08	0·07	0·07	0·07
	......	0·22	......	......	0·25	0·24	0·22	0·25	0·24
0·63	0·49	0·48	0·48	0·60	0·43	0·58	0·53	0·51	0·54
0·10	0·05	0·08	0·08	0·09	0·11	0·11	0·08	0·09	0·09
0·06	0·32	0·11	0·05	0·10	0·19	0·25	0·16	0·12	0·18
16·78	20·61	18·27	18·78	18·65	18·87	20·16	18·70	18·94	19·27
83·58	78·04	81·41	80·26	82·01	81·27	78·46	81·01	81·18	80·22
−0·36	1·35	0·32	0·96	−0·66	−0·14	1·38	0·29	−0·12	0·51
100·00	100·00	100·00	100·00	100·00	100·00	100·00	100·00	100·00	100·00

Pigs—Series I," Article—"Pig Feeding," Journal of the Royal Agricultural Society of England, vol. xiv. part 2.

APPENDIX.—TABLE LX. Showing the *Percentage Proportion* of the individual

CLASS II.—12 Pigs, divided into 4 Lots, each with rather different Food*.   *Moderately*

Designation of Parts.	Lot 1.—Food:—Bean and Lentil meal—*ad libitum.*			Lot 2.—Food:—Indian meal—in fixed quantity. Bean and Lentil meal—*ad libitum.*		
	No. 1.	No. 2.	No. 3.	No. 4.	No. 5.	No. 6.
Stomach and contents	1·49	1·01	1·43	0·75	1 11	0·70
Caul-fat..	0·46	0·70	0·37	0·59	0·40	0·49
Small intestines and contents..................	1·77	2·09	2·17	1·73	2·11	2·01
Large intestines and contents	3·61	3·75	5·16	3·47	4·01	2·76
Intestinal fat, "mudgeon," &c.	1·74	1·69	1·40	2·16	1·27	1·39
Heart and aorta	0·25	0·25	0·30	0·24	0·26	0·32
Lungs and windpipe	0·69	0·67	0·72	0 67	0·61	0 65
Blood..	3·71	3·84	4·27	3·66	4·02	4·46
Liver	1·85	1·95	1·71	1·61	1·42	1·79
Gall-bladder and contents	0·08	0·06	0·05	0·05	0·05	0·06
Pancreas ("sweetbread")	0·10	0·21	0·25	0·31	0 22	0·26
Milt or spleen	0·15	0·14	0·16	0·12	0·17	0·14
Bladder.............	0·06	0·06	0·11	0·09	0·07	0 05
Penis (or uterus)...............................	0·30	......	......	0·18	......	0·16
Tongue	0·45	0·45	0·53	0·40	0·44	0·41
Toes	0 08	0·10	0·08	0 06	0·09	0·08
Miscellaneous trimmings......................	0·31	0·32	0·31	0·19	0·30	0·19
Total "offal" parts	17·10	17·31	19·02	16·28	16·55	15·94
Carcass (including head and feet)	83·83	82·48	79·40	82·52	82·50	84·04
Loss by evaporation, error in weighing, &c.	−0·93	0·21	1·58	1·20	0·95	0·02
	100·00	100·00	100·00	100·00	100·00	100·00

* For particulars of the *feeding* experiment, refer to Pens 1, 2, 3, and 4, under the head of "Experiments with

Organs, and other separated Parts, in the Fasted Live-weight, of PIGS.

Fattened—the Food containing a considerable proportion of Bean and Lentil meal.

Lot 3.—Food:— Bran—in fixed quantity. Bean and Lentil meal—ad libitum.			Lot 4.—Food:— Indian meal and Bran—in fixed quantity. Bean and Lentil meal—ad libitum.			Means of—				
No. 7.	No. 8.	No. 9.	No. 10.	No. 11.	No. 12.	Lot 1. 3 Pigs.	Lot 2. 3 Pigs.	Lot 3. 3 Pigs.	Lot 4. 3 Pigs.	The 12 Pigs.
1·21	1·75	1·45	1·16	1·50	1·69	1·31	0·96	1·47	1·45	1·27
0·60	0·55	0·35	0·46	0·62	0·33	0·51	0·49	0·50	0·47	0·49
2·84	2·57	2·30	2·33	2·09	2·21	2·01	1·95	2·57	2·21	2·19
4·31	4·62	4·62	4·35	4·50	4·60	4·17	3·41	4·55	4·49	4·16
1·03	0·58	1·26	1·16	1·54	0·91	1·61	1·61	0·95	1·20	1·35
0·16	0·33	0·25	0·32	0·27	0·34	0·27	0·27	0·24	0·31	0·27
0·72	0·87	0·63	0·71	1·00	0·84	0·69	0·64	0·74	0·85	0·73
3·70	4·19	4·03	2·99	4·63	5·30	3·94	4·05	3·97	4·38	4·08
1·79	1·52	1·53	1·82	1·96	1·53	1·84	1·61	1·61	1·77	1·71
0·08	0·05	0·03	0·04	0·08	0·04	0·06	0·06	0·05	0·05	0·05
0·24	0·22	0·22	0·20	0·24	0·21	0·19	0·26	0·23	0·22	0·22
0·13	0·16	0·13	0·14	0·17	0·18	0·15	0·14	0·14	0·16	0·15
0·07	0·11	0·10	0·08	0·10	0·12	0·08	0·07	0·09	0·10	0·09
......	......		0·13		......	0·30	0·17	......	0·13	0·19
0·52	0·54	0·41	0 36	0·46	0·47	0·48	0·42	0·49	0·43	0·46
0·09	0·11	0·10	0·09	0·11	0·11	0·09	0·08	0·10	0·10	0·09
0·63	0·47	0·37	0·20	......	0·32	0·31	0·23	0·49	0·26	0·33
16·12	18·64	17·78	16·54	19·47	19·20	16·01	16·32	18·19	18·58	17·63
80·84	81·61	81·12	83·64	82·71	80·20	81·90	83·02	81·19	82·18	82·07
1·04	−0·25	1·10	−0·18	−2·18	0·60	0·09	0·66	0·62	−0·76	0·10
100·00	100·00	100·00	100 00	100·00	100·00	100·00	100·00	100·00	100·00	100·00

Pigs—Series 1," Article—" Pig Feeding," Journal of the Royal Agricultural Society of England, vol. xiv. part 2.

APPENDIX.—TABLE LXI. Showing the *Percentage Proportion* of the individual

CLASS III.—15 Pigs, divided into 5 Lots, each with rather different Food*.

Designation of Parts.	Lot 1.—Food:— Indian meal—*ad libitum.*			Lot 2.—Food:— Bean and Lentil meal—in fixed quantity. Indian meal—*ad libitum.*			Lot 3.—Food:— Bran—in fixed quantity. Indian meal—*ad libitum.*		
	No. 1.	No. 2.	No. 3.	No. 4.	No. 5.	No. 6.	No. 7.	No. 8.	No. 9.
Separate parts of the "offal." Stomach and contents	1·16	1·67	1·02	0·76	0·98	0·86	1·06	1·02	1·00
Caul-fat	0·64	0·49	0·52	0·55	0·41	0·73	0·53	0·64	0·45
Small intestines and contents	1·82	1·67	1·97	1·34	1·71	1·56	1·28	1·64	1·75
Large intestines and contents	2·77	3·15	2·56	3·46	2·91	2·95	4·51	3·95	2·75
Intestinal fat, "mudgeon," &c.	1·84	1·39	0·83	1·78	1·14	2·24	1·08	1·68	1·43
Heart and aorta	0·27	0·32	0·32	0·26	0·29	0·25	0·27	0·31	0·29
Lungs and windpipe	0·72	0·72	0·81	0·62	0·65	0·76	0·54	0·69	0·61
Blood	3·58	3·61	3·76	3·68	2·91	3·58	3·04	3·62	2·73
Liver	1·34	1·45	1·42	1·48	1·36	1·31	1·77	1·58	1·41
Gall-bladder and contents	0·04	0·02	0·07	0·06	0·05	0·06	0·04	0·03	0·05
Pancreas ("sweetbread")	0·22	0·18	0·27	0·18	0·13	0·25	0·16	0·17	0·26
Milt or spleen	0·10	0·15	0·13	0·11	0·15	0·14	0·10	0·16	0·12
Bladder	0·04	0·07	0·05	0·08	0·09	0·06	0·06	0·09	0·10
Penis (or uterus)	0·21	......	0·25	0·45	......		0·24	......	
Tongue	0·43	0·45	0·47	0·39	0·41	0·46	0·46	0·58	0·43
Toes	0·08	0·11	0·08	0·07	0·08	0·09	0·06	0·08	0·08
Miscellaneous trimmings	0·28	0·31	0·03	0·20	0·60	0·30	0·56	0·13	0·24
Total "offal" parts	15·54	15·76	14·58	15·47	13·87	15·60	15·76	16·37	14·10
Carcass (including head and feet)	85·75	86·04	84·48	83·77	85·61	83·91	83·89	82·91	84·26
Loss by evaporation, error in weighing, &c.	−1·29	−1·80	0·94	0·76	0·52	0·49	0·35	0·72	1·64
	100·00	100·00	100·00	100·00	100·00	100·00	100·00	100·00	100·00

* For particulars of the *feeding* experiment, refer to Pens 5, 6, 7, 8, and 12, under the head of "Experiments with

Organs, and other separated Parts, in the Fasted Live-weight, of PIGS.

Well Fattened—the Food containing a considerable proportion of Indian-corn Meal.

Lot 4.—Food:— Bean and Lentil meal, and Bran—in fixed quantity. Indian meal—ad libitum.			Lot 5.—Food:— Bean and Lentil meal, Indian meal, and Bran—each ad libitum.			Means of—					
						Lot 1. 3 Pigs.	Lot 2. 3 Pigs.	Lot 3. 3 Pigs.	Lot 4. 3 Pigs.	Lot 5. 3 Pigs.	The 15 Pigs.
No. 10.	No. 11.	No. 12.	No. 13.	No. 14.	No. 15.						
0·95	1·29	1·20	1·68	1·82	1·16	1·29	0·87	1·02	1·15	1·55	1·18
0·60	0·53	0·64	0·49	0 97	0 38	0·55	0 56	0·54	0·59	0·61	0·57
1·80	1·71	2·22	1·45	2 04	1·32	1·82	1·54	1·56	1·91	1·60	1·69
3·39	4·34	3·19	3·00	3·41	2·78	2·84	3·11	3·73	3·64	3·06	3·28
1·80	1·05	0·74	0·96	1·76	0 87	1·36	1·72	1·40	1·20	1·20	1·37
0·23	0 27	0·25	0·28	0·28	0·24	0·30	0·26	0·29	0·27	0·27	0·27
0·57	0 72	0·68	0·68	0·78	0·30	0·75	0·67	0·68	0·66	0·65	0·68
3 12	3·82	3·63	3·23	3·56	3·42	3·65	3·39	3·20	3·52	3·40	3·43
1·45	1·34	1·39	1·26	1·53	1·38	1·40	1·38	1·59	1·39	1·39	1·43
0·04	0·04	0·10	0·04	0 02	0·04	0·04	0·06	0·04	0 06	0 03	0·05
0·28	0·19	0·18	0·12	0·19	0 19	0·22	0·19	0 20	0 22	0·17	0·20
0·11	0·14	0·13	0·12	0·11	0·12	0·13	0·13	0·13	0·13	0·12	0·13
0·08	0·07	0 05	0·06	0·05	0·11	0·05	0·08	0·08	0 07	0·07	0·07
......	0·22	0·23	0·14	0·21	......	0·23	0·45	0·24	0·22	0·17	0·24
0·39	0·41	0·44	0·56	0·47	0·40	0·45	0·42	0·49	0·41	0·48	0·45
0·07	0·08	0 07	0 08	0·11	0·08	0 09	0 08	0·07	0 07	0 09	0·08
0·42	0·14	0 25	0·28	0·34	0·25	0·21	0·37	0·31	0 27	0·29	0·29
15·36	16·36	15·39	14·43	17·64	13·24	15·38	15·28	15·57	15·78	15·15	15·41
83·87	82·80	83·84	84·94	80·78	85·89	85·42	84·43	83·69	83·50	83·87	84·18
0·77	0·84	0·77	0·63	1·58	0·87	−0·80	0·29	0·74	0·72	0·98	0·41
100·00	100·00	100·00	100·00	100·00	100·00	100·00	100·00	100·00	100·00	100·00	100·00

Pigs—Series 1," Article—"Pig Feeding," Journal of the Royal Agricultural Society of England, vol. xiv. part 2.

APPENDIX.—TABLE LXII. Showing the *Percentage Proportion* of the individual

CLASS IV.—12 Pigs, divided into 4 Lots, according to the Food*.   *Moderately* Fattened.

Designation of Parts.	Lot 1.—Food:— Lentils, and Bran—in fixed quantity. Sugar—*ad libitum.*			Lot 2.—Food:— Lentils, and Bran—in fixed quantity. Starch—*ad libitum.*		
	No. 1.	No. 2.	No. 3.	No. 4.	No. 5.	No. 6.
Stomach and contents	0·87	1·08	1·27	1·44	0·93	0·92
Caul-fat..................................	0·61	0·71	0·51	0·64	0·54	0·40
Small intestines and contents	1·81	2·19	1·82	2·27	1·96	2·04
Large intestines and contents	4·70	4·79	4·14	5·86	5·08	6·78
Intestinal fat, "mudgeon," &c.	0·57	0·65	0·57	0·62	0·44	0·59
Heart and aorta	0·32	0·35	0·31	0·28	0·30	0·37
Lungs and windpipe	0·69	0·84	0·91	0·78	0·87	1·06
Blood	3·12	3·53	3·61	3·83	3·72	4·52
Liver	1·45	2·01	1·61	1·74	1·51	1·78
Gall-bladder and contents	0·06	0·09	0·03	0·12	0·11	0·12
Pancreas ("sweetbread")	0·14	0·23	0·14	0·19	0·18	0·19
Milt or spleen	0·13	0·15	0·16	0·12	0·13	0·16
Bladder......................................	0·12	0·06	0·05	0·12	0·05	0·08
Penis (or uterus)	......	0·17	......	0·19	0·16	0·18
Tongue	0·67	0·63	0·66	0·62	0·46	0·53
Toes	......	......	0·09	0·08	0·08	0·08
Miscellaneous trimmings	......	......	......	0·10	0·08	0·08
Total "offal" parts	15·27	17·48	15·88	19·00	16·60	19·07
Carcass (including head and feet)	83·78	81·17	84·24	78·35	82·50	79·55
Loss by evaporation, error in weighing, &c......	0·95	1·35	−0·12	2·65	0·90	0·48
	100·00	100·00	100·00	100·00	100·00	100·00

(Separate parts of the "offal")

* For particulars of the *feeding* experiment, see Article " On the Equivalency of Starch and

Organs, and other separated Parts, in the Fasted Live-weight, of PIGS.

The Food consisted, in considerable proportion, of either Starch or Sugar.

Lot 3.—Food:—Lentils, and Bran—in fixed quantity. Sugar, and Starch—*ad libitum.*			Lot 4.—Food:—Lentils, Bran, Sugar, and Starch—each *ad libitum.*			Means of—				
No. 7.	No. 8.	No. 9.	No. 10.	No. 11.	No. 12.	Lot 1. 3 Pigs.	Lot 2. 3 Pigs.	Lot 3. 3 Pigs.	Lot 4. 3 Pigs.	The 12 Pigs.
1·27	1·19	1·17	0·82	1·39	1·56	1·07	1·10	1·21	1·26	1·16
0·60	0·55	0·53	0·66	0·54	0·67	0·61	0·56	0·59	0·62	0·59
1·82	2·07	2·46	2·01	2·66	2·64	1·94	2·09	2·12	2·45	2·15
4·50	5·44	4·37	4·63	4·40	5·91	4·54	5·91	4·77	4·98	5·05
0·82	0·54	0·73	0·69	0·75	0 51	0·60	0·55	0·70	0·65	0·63
0·32	0·33	0·32	0·29	0·29	0·31	0 33	0·31	0 32	0·29	0·31
0 74	0·72	0 73	0·69	0·78	0·69	0·81	0·90	0·73	0·72	0·79
3·35	3·72	3·06	3·61	3·17	3·74	3·42	4·02	3·38	3·51	3·59
1·62	1·49	1·52	1·65	2 09	1·89	1·69	1·68	1·55	1·88	1·70
0 07	0·09	0·06	0·09	0·10	0·07	0·06	0·12	0·07	0·09	0 08
0·19	0·16	0·14	0·18	0·16	0 21	0·17	0·19	0·16	0·19	0·18
0·15	0 13	0·11	0·12	0·11	0·12	0·15	0·14	0·13	0·12	0·14
0·07	0·10	0·07	0·08	0·08	0·09	0·08	0·08	0·08	0·08	0·08
......			0·16	0·28	......	0·17	0·18	......	0·23	0·19
0·54	0·54	0·48	0·46	0·44	0·44	0·65	0·53	0·52	0·44	0·53
0·07	0·08	0·10	......	0·08	0·09	0·09	0·08	0·08	0·08	0·08
0·14	0 13	0·16	0·15	0·19	0·04	......	0·09	0·14	0·12	0·12
16·27	17·38	16·01	16·34	17·51	16·98	16 38	18·53	16·55	17·71	17·37
81·77	81·35	82·08	82·24	80·78	79·51	83·06	80·13	81·74	80·84	81·44
1·96	1·27	1·91	1·42	1·71	1·51	0·56	1·84	1·71	1·45	1·19
100·00	100·00	100·00	100·00	100·00	100·00	100·00	100·00	100·00	100·00	100·00

Sugar in Food "—Report of the British Association for the Advancement of Science for 1854.

APPENDIX.—TABLE LXIII. Showing the *Percentage Proportion* of the individual Organs, and other separated Parts, in the Fasted Live-weight, of PIGS.

CLASS V.—6 Pigs, divided into 2 Lots, each with rather different Food *. Well Fattened. Food comprised a portion of dried Cod-fish.

Designation of Parts.	Lot 1.—Food:— Dried Cod-fish—in fixed quantity. Bran and Indian meal, equal parts—*ad libitum.*			Lot 2.—Food:— Dried Cod-fish—in fixed quantity. Indian meal—*ad libitum.*			Means of—		
	No. 1.	No. 2.	No. 3.	No. 4.	No. 5.	No. 6.	Lot 1. 3 Pigs.	Lot 2. 3 Pigs.	The 6 Pigs.
Stomach and contents	0·99	1·74	0·97	1·03	1·16	1·11	1·23	1·10	1·17
Caul-fat	0·55	0·44	0·37	0·60	0·63	0·47	0·45	0·57	0·51
Small intestines and contents	1·61	2·38	1·87	1·43	1·44	1·19	1·96	1·35	1·66
Large intestines and contents	3·99	3·15	2·60	2·37	2·22	2·22	3·26	2·27	2·76
Intestinal fat, "mudgeon," &c.	1·19	0·83	1·06	1·04	1·13	0·95	1·02	1·04	1·03
Heart and aorta	0·24	0·41	0·26	0·19	0·17	0·26	0·30	0·21	0·25
Lungs and windpipe	0·44	0·55	0·46	0·50	0·98	0·51	0·48	0·66	0·57
Blood	3·53	3·47	3·12	2·93	2·95	2·65	3·38	2·94	3·11
Liver	1·34	1·47	1·50	0·99	1·20	1·02	1·44	1·07	1·26
Gall-bladder and contents	0·08	0·06	0·04	0·06	0·06	0·09	0·06	0·07	0·06
Pancreas ("sweetbread")	0·18	0·22	0·17	0·19	0·17	0·17	0·19	0·18	0·19
Milt or spleen	0·12	0·13	0·11	0·12	0·12	0·13	0·13	0·12	0·12
Bladder	0·07	0·06	0·06	0·05	0·07	0 06	0·06	0·06	0·06
Penis (or uterus)	0·22	0·21	…	0·19	…	…	0·21	0·19	0·20
Tongue	0·47	0·51	0·46	0·48	0·37	0·38	0·48	0·39	0·43
Toes	0·06	0·07	0·07	0·08	0·07	0·06	0·07	0·07	0·07
Miscellaneous trimming	0·24	0·14	0·39	0·15	0·23	0·19	0·26	0·16	0·21
Total "offal" parts	15·32	15·86	13·51	12·30	12·97	11·40	14·97	12·35	13·66
Carcase (including head and feet)	84·55	83·70	85·63	87·76	86·67	87·52	84·63	87·32	85·98
Loss by evaporation, error in weighing, &c.	0·13	0·44	0·86	−0·06	0·36	1·08	0·40	0·33	0·36
	100·00	100·00	100·00	100·00	100·00	100·00	100·00	100·00	100·00

(Separate parts of the "offal.")

* For particulars of the *feeding* experiment, refer to Pens 1 and 2, under the head of "Experiments with Pigs—Series 3," Article—"Pig Feeding," Journal of the Royal Agricultural Society of England, vol. xiv. part 2.

APPENDIX.—TABLE LXIV. Showing the *Percentage Proportion* of the individual Organs, and other separated Parts, in the Fasted Live-weight, of PIGS.

5 Pigs, divided into 2 Lots, according to condition of Maturity when put to Fatten.

CLASS VI.—Put to Fatten when in Store condition, and fed till only Half-fattened.

CLASS VII.—Put to Fatten when Half-fat, and fed till Moderately Fattened.

Designation of Parts	Class 6. Put to Fatten when in Store condition, and fed till only Half-fattened.		Class 7. Put to Fatten when Half-fat, and fed till Moderately fattened.			Means of		
	No. 1.	No. 2.	No. 3.	No. 4.	No. 5.	Class 6.	Class 7.	The 5 Pigs.
Stomach and contents	2·70	0·92	0·85	1·04	1·07	1·81	0·99	1·32
Caul-fat	0·52	0·43	0·51	0·53	0·52	0·47	0·52	0·50
Small intestines and contents	5·00	2·96	2·17	2·97	1·96	3·98	2·36	3·01
Large intestines and contents	4·44	4·24	2·70	4·21	3·17	4·34	3·38	3·75
Intestinal fat, "inudgeon," &c.	0·63	0·72	1·29	0·65	0·68	0·67	0·87	0·79
Heart and aorta	0·30	0·25	0·26	0·30	0·32	0·28	0·29	0·29
Lungs and windpipe	1·04	0·65	0·83	1·44	0·91	0·85	1·06	0·98
Blood	2·86	3·21	3·21	3·56	3·34	3·04	3·37	3·24
Liver	2·22	1·52	1·50	1·64	1·35	1·87	1·56	1·69
Gall-bladder and contents	0·04	0·07	0·06	0·11	0·09	0·05	0·09	0·07
Pancreas ("sweetbread")	0·14	0·19	0·20	0·18	0·18	0·17	0·18	0·18
Milk or spleen	0·21	0·14	0·11	0·12	0·22	0·17	0·15	0·16
Bladder	0·07	0·06	0·07	0·12	0·10	0·06	0·10	0·08
Penis (or uterus)	0·17	0·20	0·19	0·29	0·26	0·18	0·24	0·22
Tongue	0·54	0·43	0·31	0·59	0·42	0·49	0·51	0·50
Miscellaneous trimmings	0·36	0·33	0·60	0·45	0·15	0·35	0·40	0·38
Total "offal" parts	21·24	16·32	15·08	18·40	14·74	18·78	16·07	17·16
Carcass (including head and feet)	76·25	82·26	84·00	81·66	84·51	79·26	83·39	81·74
Loss by evaporation, error in weighing, &c.	2·51	1·42	0·92	—0·06	0·75	1·96	0·54	1·10
	100·00	100·00	100·00	100·00	100·00	100·00	100·00	100·00

Separate parts of the "offal."

MEMORANDA, ERRATA, ETC.

[NOTE.—The numerical errors in the Tables, which are noticed in the following list, are the most important that have been detected; but, though it seemed desirable to correct them for purposes of reference, none of them affect the conclusions given in the text. It will be seen, that the larger number of the required corrections are due to but a few original errors in the statement of actual quantities; the results of which, however, ramify into the lines of *Totals*, into the columns of *Means*, into the corresponding *Percentages*, and generally also into more than one Table. A few others, of still less importance, have been observed, to which it is thought unnecessary to call special attention. They occur chiefly in one or two of the Tables of *Percentage Proportion* of Organs or Parts, and in amount are within the range of the second decimal place.]

Page 538, line 4: *for*—"than that of the more moderately fattened animal." *read*—than that of the more moderately fattened animal, or than that of either Oxen or Sheep.

Page 556, last sentence of second paragraph: *for*—"Of these, Tables XVII., XVIII., XIX., XX., XXI., and XXII.," &c., *read*—Of these, Tables XVII., XVIII., XIX., XX., XXI., XXII., and XXIII., &c.

Table XVII. p. 558:—
Column 1. *For*—"6 0·5" in line of Contents of stomachs, *read*—4 12·1; and accordingly, *for*—"85 4·9" in line of Total Offal parts, *read*—84 0·5. *For*—"156 10·9" in line of Carcass, *read*—158 3·5. And in accordance with these alterations, *for*—"8 12·3" in line of Loss by evaporation, error in weighing, &c., *read*—8 8·0. [Note—The same amended numbers as here given, should be carried in (in the corresponding lines of course), in the last Column but three, of Appendix-Table XV. p. 595.]
Column 3. *For*—"97 4·7" in line of Contents of stomachs, *read*—95 15·2; *for*—"17 1·3" in line of Small Intestines and contents, *read*—18 1·7; and *for*—"13 4·6" in line of Large Intestines and contents, *read*—13 10·0. [Note—The same amended numbers as here given, should be carried in, in the last Column but one, of Appendix-Table XV. p. 595.]
Column 4. *For*—"93 15·8" in line of Contents of stomachs, *read*—92 12·8; *for*—"16 13·6" in line of Small Intestines and contents, *read*—17 12·0; and *for*—"13 2·3" in line of Large Intestines and contents, *read*—13 7·0. [Note—The same amended numbers as here given, should be carried in, in Column 1, of Table XXIII. p. 564; and in the last Column of Appendix-Table XV. p. 595.]
Column 6. *For*—"1 7·0" in line of Miscellaneous trimmings (=Heart trimmings only, see also Appendix-Table II. p. 581), *read*—3 6·2, as in Appendix-Table XV. p. 595, Column of Bullock No. 13. And accordingly, *for*—"423 10·3" in line of Total Offal parts, *read*—425 9·5; and *for*—"10 10·7" in line of Loss by evaporation, error in weighing, &c., *read*—8 11·5.
Column 7. *For*—"33 12·5" in line of Caul Fat, *read*—29 13·0. The difference, 3 15·5 (Heart trimmings, see Appendix-Table III. p. 582)+5 1·0 (trimmings from the neck)=9 0·5; which amount, *insert* in line of Miscellaneous trimmings, as in Appendix-Table XV. p. 595, Column of Bullock No. 12. And accordingly, *for*—"460 13·3" in line of Total Offal parts, *read*—465 14·3; and, *for*—"18 12·7" in line of Loss by evaporation, error in weighing, &c., *read*—13 11·7.

Table XVIII. p. 559:—
Column 2. *For*—"152 5·8" in line of Final weight unfasted, *read*—156 0·8. *For*—"0 2·1" in line of Miscellaneous trimmings, *read*—0 3·1; and in accordance with this, *for*—"58 13·2" in line of Total Offal parts, *read*—58 14·2; and *for*—"0 13·0" in line of Loss by evaporation, error in weighing, &c., *read*—0 12·0.
Column 3. *For*—"124 11·4" in line of Original weight, *read*—99 1·8.
Column 4. *For*—"115 1" in line of Original weight, *read*—124 7·2. *For*—"144 13·1" in line of Final weight unfasted, *read*—148 0·1.
Column 5. *Omit* figures—"96 11·4" in line of Original weight. *For*—"6 2·7" in line of Contents of stomachs, *read*—6 7·7; *for*—"4 12·2." in line of Head, *read*—4 11·4; and in accordance with these

alterations, *for*—" 64 6·4 " in line of Total Offal parts, *read*—64 10·6 ; and *for*—" 0 0·1 " in line of Loss by evaporation, error in weighing, &c., *read*, —0 4·1. [Note—The same corrections as here given, should be carried in, in the last column, of Appendix-Table XXXIII. p. 625.]

Column 6. *For*—" 109 13·5 " in line of Original weight, *read*—107 7·2. *For*—" 160 4·9 " in line of Final weight unfasted, *read*—162 15·4.

Column 9. *For*—" 0 8·5 " in line of Gall-bladder and contents, *read*—0 0·8 ; and in accordance with this, *for*—" 47 3·6 " in line of Total Offal parts, *read*—46 11·9 ; and *for*—" 1 9·3 " in line of Loss by evaporation, error in weighing, &c., *read*—2 1·0.

Table XIX. p. 560 :—

Column 3. *For*—" 245 10·7 " in line of Final weight unfasted, *read*—235 10·7.

Column 8. *For*—" 222 9·8 " in line of Final weight unfasted, *read*—220 1·1.

Table XX. p. 561 :—

Column 1. *For*—" 2·39 " in line of Contents of stomachs, *read*—1·89 ; and accordingly, *for*—" 34·04 " in line of Total Offal parts, *read*—33·54. *For*—" 62·53 " in line of Carcass, *read*—63·13." And in accordance with these alterations, *for*—" 3·43 " in line of Loss by evaporation, error in weighing, &c., *read* —3·33. [Note—The same amended numbers as here given, should be carried in, in the last Column but three, of Appendix-Table XL. p. 637.]

Column 3. *For*—" 8·44 " in line of Contents of stomachs, *read*—8·33 ; *for*—" 1·49 " in line of Small Intestines and contents, *read*—1·57 ; and, *for*—" 1·18 " in line of Large Intestines and contents, *read*—1·21. [Note—The same amended numbers as here given, should be carried in, in the last Column but one, of Appendix-Table XL. p. 637.]

Column 4. *For*—" 8·44 " in line of Contents of stomachs, *read*—9·34 ; *for*—" 1·52 " in line of Small Intestines and contents, *read*—1·60 ; and *for*—" 1·22 " in line of Large Intestines and contents, *read*—1·24. [Note—The same amended numbers as here given, should be carried in, in Column 4, of Table XXIII. p. 564 ; and also in the last Column of Appendix-Table XL. p. 637.]

Last Column. *For*—" 2·38 " in line of Caul Fat, *read*—2·10 ; and in line of Miscellaneous trimmings, *insert*—0·64. And in accordance with these alterations, *for*—" 32·48 " in line of Total Offal parts, *read*— 32·84 ; and *for*—" 1·32 " in line of Loss by evaporation, error in weighing, &c., *read*—0·96.

Table XXI. p. 562 :—

Column 5. *For*—" 3·62 " in line of Contents of stomachs, *read*—3·85 ; *for*—" 5·31 " in line of Caul Fat, *read*—5·18 ; *for*—" 10·84 " in line of Skin and Wool, *read*—11·01 ; and in accordance with these alterations, *for*—" 37·71 " in line of Total Offal parts, *read*—37·98. *For*—" 62·28 " in line of Carcass, *read*—61·91 ; and *for*—" 0·01 " in line of Loss by evaporation, &c., *read*—0·11.

Column 9 (Half-fat Sheep). *For*—" 0·506 " in line of Gall-bladder and contents, *read*—0·051 ; and in accordance with this, *for*—" 44·948 " in line of Total Offal parts, *read*—44·493 ; and *for*—" 1·506 " in line of Loss by evaporation, error in weighing, &c., *read*—1·961.

Page 571, last line of first paragraph : *before* the word—" Carcass " *insert* the words—here reckoned.

Appendix-Table XV. pp. 594—595 :—

Mem. : in line of " Bladder, with penis, or womb," the amounts set down to Bullocks Nos. 9, 12, 13 and 14, include both Bladder and Penis ; those set down to the other Bullocks refer to Bladder only. In the same line, in the last column but one, *for*—" 0 16·7," *read* 1 0·7 ; which amount is the *sum* of the mean of the Bladder, and of that of the Penis, each taken separately. In the same line, in the last column, the amount represents Bladder only ; the Penis, or Womb, being included with the " Loss by evaporation, error in weighing, &c."

Column 2. *For*—" 8 3·0 " in line of Contents of stomachs, *read*—5 10·2 ; and in accordance with this, *for*—" 87 12·7 " in line of Total Offal parts, *read*—85 3·9. *For*—" 157 7·5 " in line of Carcass, *read*

—100 0·0. And in accordance with these alterations, *for*—" 18 7·8 " in line of Loss by evaporation, error in weighing, &c., *read*—12 15·1.

Column of Bullock No. 12.   *For*—" 84 4·0 " in line of Contents of stomachs, *read*—77 3·8 ; *for*—" 8 11·7 " in line of Small Intestines and contents, *read*—14 10·5 ; and *for*—" 5 2·5 " in line of Large Intestines and contents, *read*—6 4·0.

Column of Bullock No. 13.   *For*—" 100 1·0 " in line of Contents of stomachs, *read*—88 0·0 ; *for*—" 8 5·0 " in line of Small Intestines and contents, *read*—16 13·0 ; and *for*—" 6 0 0 " in line of Large Intestines and contents, *read*—9 9·0.

Appendix-Table XVIII. pp. 600—601 :—

  Column 6. *For*—" 1 7 " in line of Loss by evaporation, &c., *read*—0 1·7.

  Column 10. *For*—" 132 4 " in line of Live-weight after fasting, *read*—132 14.

  Column 14 : in line of Bladder, the amount represents both Bladder and Womb, that one Sheep being an Ewe.

Appendix-Table XXI. p. 606. Mem. : in Columns 2 and 3, respectively, the amount set down for Bladder includes one Testicle.

Appendix-Table XXVI. p. 613. Column 8. *For*—" 0 1·2 " in line of Heart-fat, *read*—1 2·0.

Appendix-Table XXX. p. 616. Column 1. *For* " 142 2·6 " in lines of Final weight, after fasting, and of Live-weight after fasting, *read*—141 2·6. *For*—" 83 0 " in line of Carcass, *read*—82 0.

Appendix-Table XXXIII. pp 624—625 :—

  Column 15. *For*—" 57 5·6 " in line of Total Offal parts, *read*—57 3·6 ; and in accordance with this, *for*—" -0 12·6 " in line of Loss by evaporation, error in weighing, &c., *read*, —0 10·6.

  Last column but two. *For*—" 4 10·6 " in line of Contents of stomachs, *read*—5 2·9 ; and in accordance with this, *for*—" 61 14·7 " in line of Total Offal parts, *read*—62 7·0 ; and *for*—" 0 0·7 " in line of Loss by evaporation, error in weighing, &c., *read*, —0 7·6.

Appendix-Table XXXVI. pp. 630—631. Column 17. *For*—" 144 5·3 " in line of Original weight, *read* —148 5·3.

Appendix-Table XL. pp. 636—637 :—

  Column of Designation of Parts. Omit the words—" Live-weight after fasting " in the bottom line.

  Column 2. *For*—" 3·17 " in line of Contents of stomachs, *read*—2·18 ; and in accordance with this, *for*—" 33·93 " in line of Total Offal parts, *read*—32·97. *For*—" 60·86 " in line of Carcass, *read*—62·05. And in accordance with these alterations, *for*—" 5·21 " in line of Loss by evaporation, error in weighing, &c., *read*—4·98.

  Column of Bullock No. 4. *For*—" 0·11 " in line of Bladder, &c., *read*—0·04 ; and in accordance with this, *for*—" 41·11 " in line of Total Offal parts, *read*—41·04 ; and *for*—" 2·08 " in line of Loss by evaporation, error in weighing, &c., *read*—2·15.

  Column of Bullock No. 9. Mem. . the amount " 0·07 " in line of Bladder, &c., includes both Bladder and Penis.

  Column of Bullock No. 12. *For*—" 5·92 " in line of Contents of stomachs, *read*—5·44 ; *for*—" 0·62 " in line of Small Intestines and contents, *read*—1·08 ; *for*—" 0·36 " in line of Large Intestines and contents, *read*—0·44 ; *for*—" 0·72 " in line of Heart-fat, *read*—0·44 ; and *for*—" 0·36 " in line of Miscellaneous trimmings, *read*—0 64.

  Column of Bullock No. 13. *For*—" 8·12 " in line of Contents of stomachs, *read*—7·14 ; *for*—" 0·67 " in line of Small Intestines and contents, *read*—1·36 ; and *for*—" 0·49 " in line of Large Intestines and contents, *read*—0·78. *For*—" 0·31 " in line of Heart-fat, *read*—0·20 ; and in accordance with this, *for*—" 34·54 " in line of Total Offal parts, *read*—34·43 ; and *for*—" 0·71 " in line of Loss by evaporation, error in weighing, &c., *read*—0 82.

www.ingramcontent.com/pod-product-compliance
Lightning Source LLC
Chambersburg PA
CBHW031059280326
41928CB00049B/1167